"THE FIRST DAYS & "THE LAST DAYS

A VERSE-BY-VERSE COMMENTARY
ON THE BOOK OF MOSES AND JS—MATTHEW
IN LIGHT OF THE TEMPLE

J. James Tissot, 1836-1902: *The Prophecy of the Destruction of the Temple*, 1886-1894

THE FIRST DAYS & THE LAST DAYS

A VERSE-BY-VERSE COMMENTARY ON THE BOOK OF MOSES AND JS—MATTHEW IN LIGHT OF THE TEMPLE

JEFFREY M. BRADSHAW

TempleThemes.net

The Interpreter Foundation
InterpreterFoundation.org

Eborn Books
EbornBooks.com

2021

Published by the Interpreter Foundation, Orem, Utah, InterpreterFoundation.org, in cooperation with Eborn Books, Salt Lake City, EbornBooks.com.

Editing: Julie Newman. Typesetting: Jeffrey M. Bradshaw. Cover design: Bjorn W. Pendleton of Pendleton Creative

Cover art: James C. Christensen (1942–2017): *The Enoch Altarpiece*, 2004
With permission

Jeffrey M. Bradshaw (1956–)
The First Days and the Last Days: A Verse-by-Verse Commentary on the Book of Moses and JS–Matthew in Light of the Temple

ISBN: 979-8-772-31214-8 (Softbound)
ISBN: 978-1-890-71897-8 (Hardcover)

The Interpreter Foundation supports The Church of Jesus Christ of Latter-day Saints through scholarship in the following ways:

- *Promotion: We provide tools to encourage and facilitate personal learning by study and faith, and we disseminate accurate information to the public about the Church.*
- *Explanation: We make the results of relevant scholarship more accessible to nonspecialists.*
- *Defense: We respond to misunderstandings and criticisms of Church beliefs, policies, and practices.*
- *Faithfulness: Our leadership, staff, and associates strive to follow Jesus Christ and be true to the teachings of his Church.*
- *Scholarship: Our leadership, staff, and associates incorporate standards of scholarship appropriate to their academic disciplines.*

The Interpreter Foundation is an independent 501(c)(3) organization that supports but is not owned, controlled by, or affiliated with The Church of Jesus Christ of Latter-day Saints. The material published by the Interpreter Foundation is the sole responsibility of the respective authors of each chapter and should not be interpreted as representing the views of the Interpreter Foundation or of The Church of Jesus Christ of Latter-day Saints.

Contents

CONTENTS

Moses 6: Enoch, the Seer and Preacher   121

CONTENTS

JOSEPH SMITH—MATTHEW

BIBLIOGRAPHY

James C. Christensen (1942–2017): *The Enoch Altarpiece (Left Wing, Right Wing)*, 2004

"For over a year, artist James C. Christensen painted under the guise of an obscure, 15th century Flemish painter, best known for, and named after, a multi-paneled masterpiece called 'The Enoch Altarpiece.' Also known as 'Jehovah Teaches Enoch the Plan of Salvation,' what remains of 'The Enoch Altarpiece' are the two sides that once flanked the (missing) center panel."[1]

"The central panel showed Jehovah teaching Enoch as they walked near the City of Enoch. The angels on the wings of the altarpiece bless the scene, and the symbols at their feet describe the divine plan. At the feet of the angel in the left panel we see fruit with a serpent, a clear representation of the Garden of Eden and the Fall of man. On the right, the symbol at the angel's feet is a skull with an Easter lily growing out of it, symbolizing the triumph of Christ over death and the Fall of man. The City of Enoch in the altarpiece was described as 'a city of surpassing beauty radiating the light of truth and righteousness, the fruit of souls who were at one with God's plan.'"[2] The idea of the missing center panel is a play on the fact that Enoch along with his entire city were taken from the earth to be preserved in God's own bosom until they come back in a future day of righteousness. "No one is certain what happened to the missing center panel of 'The Enoch Altarpiece,' but the hope is," says Christensen, with a smile, "it will one day return."[3]

---

1   James C. Christensen, "James C. Christensen on 'The Enoch Altarpiece.'" https://www.youtube.com/watch?v=N6wV_kD5SfE.

2   James C. Christensen, *Passage by Faith: Exploring the Inspirational Art of James C. Christensen.* Salt Lake City, UT: Deseret Book, 2012, 100.

3   Christensen, "Enoch Altarpiece."

PREFACE

Like a perfectly formed pair of bookends, the Book of Moses and Joseph Smith's inspired translation of Matthew 24 (JS—Matthew) bracket within their pages the essential survival guide for our times. In the "first days," Adam and Eve looked forward to Christ's coming; in the "last days," we look backward to Christ's mortal life and forward to His return in glory. In the beginning, Enoch learned the ordinances and covenants that would allow his people to dwell in the presence of God; to the end, we will treasure the same ordinances and covenants. Through faith in Jesus Christ and faithfulness to these covenants we hope to stand someday in the holy place with perfect assurance.

This comprehensive phrase-by-phrase commentary on the Book of Moses and JS—Matthew is the result of decades of loving study of their wonderful words. In its pages you will find both everyday guidance and the answers to life's most important questions. Importantly, this book is a witness that the doctrines and ordinances of the temple are deeply woven into the fabric of these supernal works of scripture, containing persuasive evidence of their authenticity and antiquity. Carefully selected images, coupled with detailed explanations, enrich the commentary. Rather than simply illustrating the text, they seek to enter into dialogue with it.

Since my childhood, I have loved the book of Genesis. In 2010, with the kind encouragement of John W. Welch and other friends, I felt impressed to write and publish a commentary on Moses 1–6:12, entitled *Creation, Fall, and the Story of Adam and Eve*. In 2014, with the appearance of a companion volume *Enoch, Noah, and the Tower of Babel*, this commentary became a two-part series entitled *In God's Image and Likeness (IGIL1; IGIL2)*. These large books, totaling almost 1,700 pages, were intended to be somewhat encyclopedic in scope, pulling together many scattered sources from the ancient world, modern scholarship, and Latter-day Saint thought. The insights on priesthood and temple doctrines provided in these and related studies begged for a separate, simpler, and more discursive approach. Two related volumes were the result: *Temple Themes in the Book of Moses* and *Temple Themes in the Oath and Covenant of the Priesthood*. Additional temple themes in scripture continued to emerge through collaboration with colleagues who participated in Stephen D. Ricks' series of *Temple on Mount Zion* conferences, held in honor of our friend Matthew B. Brown, whose writings continue to inspire.

The present work tries to squeeze the essential content of *IGIL1* and *IGIL2* into a book that is a fraction of their size, while also including many fascinating updates from continuing research over the last decade. I hope this effort will appeal to some who found the *IGIL* volumes to be too long, too digressive, too physically cumbersome, or too expensive. In the wake of a joint study of the Pearl of Great Price undertaken at the invitation of my friend Stephen O. Smoot, the idea of combining commentary on the Book of Moses and Joseph Smith—Matthew into a single book eventually came into my mind.

PREFACE

Much of the new research on the Book of Moses that has been included here, and in its companion volume *Enoch and the Gathering of Israel*, has resulted from four concurrent developments:

- *Book of Moses Essays.* The invitation from Book of Mormon Central for content to complement the Stephen O. Smoot's Book of Abraham Insights on their Pearl of Great Price Central website resulted over the course of nearly two years in a series of seventy online essays on the Book of Moses. Thanks to Alan Sikes, the essays were also posted on the Interpreter Foundation website. These essays benefitted from collaboration, comments, and feedback provided by Matthew L. Bowen, Ryan Dahle, Mark J. Johnson, Jared W. Ludlow, Kerry Muhlestein, and Stephen T. Whitlock. Spencer Kraus, Kirk Magleby, Ruth Schmidt, and John W. Welch also provided support and encouragement.

- *Responses to Book of Moses Textual Issues.* Allen Wyatt and Jeff Lindsay, the editors of *Interpreter: A Journal of Latter-day Saint Faith and Scripture,* kindly offered to have a series of essays and blog posts on selected Book of Moses textual issues reviewed and, eventually published. These essays were co-authored by colleagues Matthew L. Bowen and Ryan Dahle. Because they were written in response to issues raised by Colby Townsend, Charles R. Harrell, and Thomas A. Wayment, we are grateful for the friendly dialogue with these three scholars that ensued, despite some differences of opinion, throughout the writing process. The authors learned much not only from their scholarship but also from their examples of how dialogue on differences need not jeopardize mutual respect and collegiality.

- *Tracing Ancient Threads in the Book of Moses.* Through the support of the Interpreter Foundation, Brigham Young University Department of Religious Education, Book of Mormon Central, and FAIR Latter-day Saints, groundbreaking conferences exploring evidence of antiquity within the Book of Moses were held in 2020 and 2021. Research results from these conferences added immeasurably to the new insights reported in the present commentary. The proceedings from these conferences, co-edited with David Rolph Seely, John W. Welch, and Scott A. Gordon, included the following contributors: Elder Bruce C. and Sister Marie K. Hafen, Richard L. Bushman, Jackson Abhau, Matthew L. Bowen, Jeffrey M. Bradshaw, S. Kent Brown, David Calabro, Stanford A. Carmack, Ryan Dahle, Kristine Frederickson, Terryl L. Givens, Matthew J. Grow, Kent P. Jackson, David J. Larsen, Jeff Lindsay, Jared W. Ludlow, Kerry Muhlestein, Daniel C. Peterson, Jasmin Gimenez Rappleye, Noel B. Reynolds, Jonathon Riley, David Rolph and Jo Ann H. Seely, Avram R. Shannon, Stephen O. Smoot, John W. Welch, and Stephen T. Whitlock. In addition, Samuel H. Bradshaw, Trevor Holyoak, Kirk Magleby, Zander Sturgill, and Robert D. Starling offered technical and other tangible support.

- *ScripturePlus Book of Moses Minutes.* At the invitation of Taylor Halverson, acting on behalf of Book of Mormon Central ScripturePlus app team, I prepared a commentary on the Book of Moses and Genesis. Many of the helpful suggestions of Taylor and his expert editors—Sarah W. Johnson and Morgan Tanner—have made their way into this commentary.

The prodigious writings of Hugh W. Nibley on Moses, Enoch, and the temple were constantly at my elbow as I wrote. The recent volume entitled *Hugh Nibley Observed*, co-edited with Shirley S. Ricks and Stephen T. Whitlock and published as a collaboration between The Interpreter Foundation, Book of Mormon Central, and FAIR Latter-day Saints, with the kind cooperation of the Nibley family, is a tribute to Nibley's research and discipleship. The declaration of James, "I will shew thee my faith by my works" (James 2:18), is nowhere better demonstrated in modern times than by an examination of the Complete Bibliography of Hugh Nibley (CBHN), now online at the Interpreter website, thanks to the efforts of Gary P. Gillum, Shirley S. Ricks, Alan Sikes, Stephen T. Whitlock, and others.

I am grateful to the generous donors and friends at the Interpreter Foundation whose support has made this book possible, specifically Stephen Densley, Kristine Frederickson, Jeff Lindsay, Daniel C. Peterson, Deborah Peterson, Shirley S. Ricks, Alan Sikes, and Allen Wyatt. Editor Julie Newman continually delighted me with her uniquely perceptive observations and suggestions that have significantly improved this book. Since many changes and additions were made in the post-editing stage, the errors that remain are my own. I am also grateful for the cover design by Bjorn W. Pendleton of Pendleton Creative—a beautiful marriage of form and function.

Special mention should be made of those who have reviewed or directly co-authored research relating to this commentary over the years or who have provided significant help of other kinds, including Gary N. Anderson, Danel W. Bachman, Margaret Barker, Matthew L. Bowen, Robert Boylan, Matthew B. Brown, S. Kent Brown, David Calabro, Josh Coates, Ryan Dahle, Bret and Cindy Eborn, Brenden Fullmer, Nick Galieti, Elder Bruce C. and Sister Marie K. Hafen, Ronan J. Head, Kent P. Jackson, Mark J. Johnson, David J. Larsen, Michael B. James, Jared W. Ludlow, Chris Miasnik, Kerry Muhlestein, Donald W. Parry, Maurine and Scott Proctor, Neal and Jasmin Gimenez Rappleye, Jacob Rennaker, Noel B. Reynolds, Shirley S. and Stephen D. Ricks, Jared Riddick, Hanna Seariac, David Rolph Seely, John W. Welch, Stephen T. Whitlock, and Samuel Zinner.

This volume is written in grateful memory of my parents, Mark J. and Elma Singleton Bradshaw, who "died in faith, not having received the promises, but ... were persuaded of them, and embraced them" (Hebrews 11:13). I am also grateful for the love and faith of my sisters and brothers and their families: Judi Morrell, Bonnie B. Robinson, Jonathan D. and An Bradshaw, and Scott B. and Linn Bradshaw.

I dedicate this book to my eternal companion, Kathleen Peterson Bradshaw. We are grateful to our children and their spouses—Robert W. and Camille James Bradshaw, M. Elizabeth and Sakiusa Vakalala, Thomas M. and Lisa Paulson Bradshaw, and Samuel H. Bradshaw—for their love and support. We appreciate the daily sacrifices they make to bless the lives of our beloved grandchildren, who will witness the culminating events of the last days: Lydia, Ruby, Abe, Ian, Harmony, Meresiana, Glenn, Nasuikau, Moroni, Matthew, Asaeli, Marie, Peter, Andrew, and Esther.

We will receive them into our bosom, . . . and we will fall upon their necks, and they shall fall upon our necks, and we will kiss each other; . . . and it shall be Zion, . . . and for the space of a thousand years, the earth shall rest (Moses 7:63).

INTRODUCTION TO THE BOOK OF MOSES

In this introduction, I will explain why this commentary presents the Book of Moses "in light of the temple." This approach revealed itself to me as I considered three questions:

1. Why did God command Joseph Smith to translate the Bible?
2. What could Joseph Smith have learned from translating Genesis?
3. Why is the Book of Moses important today?

After addressing these three items, we will discuss a two additional questions:

4. How does the Book of Moses fit the temple narrative pattern?
5. How does the Book of Moses fit with Genesis and ancient texts?

1. Why Did God Command Joseph Smith to Translate the Bible?

Of course, the simple answer is that the time was right. 1830 was a pivot point. The priesthood had been restored, the Book of Mormon had been published, the Church had been formally organized and was beginning to grow. Then, suddenly, God asked Joseph Smith to translate the Bible. What made this a good time?

Here is one guess: With all the previous pieces now in place, God intended the Church to take a signficant next step. He wanted the Restoration to do something more than to produce congregations of decent, church-going folks. He was on the verge of revealing the blueprints for Zion, a society of transformed people that, from a small nucleus of gathered Saints, would eventually grow to "fill the world."[1] While building Zion included many facets, the beating heart of this great enterprise and the source of its strength would be the temple and the priesthood power with which worthy men and women would be endowed and sealed as families. God needed a people who understood and lived the fulness of the New and Everlasting Covenant.

What did a new translation of the Bible have to do with all that? The Bible is where the original story of Zion is told. While hints of temple teachings and covenants can be found throughout scripture, the foundation of those covenants was laid in the first book of the Bible: Genesis. The Israelites, the Nephites, and early Christians had all looked back to Genesis as a way ot remember the covenants God made with His children, going back to Adam and Eve. They had built little Zions by using the brick and mortar of lived covenants, adapting revealed patterns as necessary to the unique circumstances of their peoples. Because the passage

---

1   Wilford Woodruff, "Origin of Zion's Camp; Notable Prophecy by Joseph Smith; Christ to Come to the Saints in the Mountains." In *Conference Reports: Sixty-eighth Annual General Conference of the Church of Jesus Christ of Latter-day Saints*, 57–58. Salt Lake City, UT: Deseret News, 1898. Reprint, Salt Lake City, UT: Hawkes Publishing, n. d. https://archive.org/details/conferencereport1898a/page/56/mode/2up, 57.

of time had blurred and sometimes even erased the original patterns, there was a need to reveal them anew to the Latter-day Saints if they were to fulfill their calling to lay the foundations of a permanent Zion society that would, unlike all previous attempts, endure throughout the millennium and on into eternity.

2. What Could Joseph Smith Have Learned from Translating Genesis?

What seems to be the Lord's primary purpose in Joseph Smith's translation effort might be discerned by noticing the priority that Genesis took over every other book in the Bible. Of course, readers of the Joseph Smith Translation (JST) would be correct if they concluded "that the Prophet went all the way through the Bible from Genesis to Revelation."[2] However, without knowing more than this, they might also incorrectly assume that each chapter of the Bible received the same attention from the Prophet. In actuality, by looking at the known durations of periods when each part of the translation was completed, we can discover that the first twenty-four chapters of Genesis occupied nearly a quarter of the total time Joseph Smith spent on the entire Bible translation. As a proportion of page count, changes in Genesis occur four times more frequently than in the New Testament and twenty-one times more frequently than in the rest of the Old Testament. The changes in Genesis are not only more numerous but also more significant. Though we cannot know how much of Joseph Smith's daily schedule the translation occupied during each of its phases, it seems that Genesis 1–24, the first one percent of the Bible, must have received a much more generous share of the Prophet's time and attention than did the remaining ninety-nine percent.

What important things could Joseph Smith have learned from translating Genesis 1–24? To begin with, the story of Enoch and his righteous city would have had pressing relevance to the mission of the Church as the Prophet worked to help the Saints understand the law of consecration, a law whose keeping would be essential to establish Zion on a firm footing in Missouri. Thus, it is understandable that Moses 6–7 was the first extract of the JST to be published in 1832 and 1833. However, we should not allow the initial timeliness of the Enoch story to overshadow the importance of the fact that the first twenty-four JST Genesis chapters also relate the stories of other prophets and patriarchs; in particular Adam, Noah, Melchizedek, and Abraham. The stories of the first twenty-four chapters, augmented by the selective but significant attention given to other parts of the Bible in the JST and related revelations, both illustrate and provide the doctrinal foundation for the temple teachings and covenants needed to gather and prepare a Zion people.

In consideration of this and other evidence from significant early sections of the Doctrine and Covenants received during this period—notably including Joseph Smith—Matthew (see table 1)—it seems that the most important impact of the translation process may have been the early tutoring Joseph Smith received in priesthood and temple-related doctrines, especially as he revised and expanded Genesis 1–24 under inspiration. The early chapters of Genesis included in the Book of Moses are perhaps the strongest evidence that Joseph Smith's extensive knowledge of temple matters was the result of early revelations, not late inventions.[3]

---

2   R. J. Matthews, *Plainer*, 215.

3   Jeffrey M. Bradshaw. "What Did Joseph Smith Know about Modern Temple Ordinances by 1836?"

Table 1. Approximate Concurrence of Doctrine and Covenants and JST Revelations[4]

1830–31	Doctrine and Covenants Revelations	JST Revelations
March	Section 19	
April	Sections 20–23	
May		
June		Moses 1
July	Sections 24–26	Moses 2–3 (July–September)
August	Section 27	
September	Sections 28–31	Moses 4–5:43 (September–October 20)
October	Sections 32–33	Moses 5:43b–51 (approximate)
November	Section 34	Moses 5:52–6:18 (approximate)
December	Sections 35–37	Moses 6:19–8:12 (approximate)
January	Sections 38–40	
February	Sections 41–44	Moses 8:13–30; Genesis 7:11–20:18 (approximate)
March	Section 45	Genesis 21:1–24:41 (approximate)
Spring 1831		Joseph Smith—Matthew

In *The Temple: Ancient and Restored. Proceedings of the 2014 Temple on Mount Zion Symposium*, edited by Stephen D. Ricks and Donald W. Parry. Temple on Mount Zion 3, 1–144. Orem and Salt Lake City, UT: Interpreter Foundation and Eborn Books, 2016. http://www.templethemes.net/publications/01-Bradshaw-TMZ%203.pdf.

4   The table is adapted from Kerry Muhlestein, "The Doctrine and Covenants and the Book of Moses: An Outpouring of Revelations and the Beginning of Joseph Smith's "New Translation" of the Bible." In *Tracing Ancient Threads in the Book of Moses: Inspired Origins, Temple Contexts, and Literary Qualities*, edited by Jeffrey M. Bradshaw, David R. Seely, John W. Welch and Scott Gordon, 137–62. Orem, UT; Springville, UT; Redding, CA; Tooele, UT: The Interpreter Foundation, Book of Mormon Central, FAIR, and Eborn Books, 2021. https://www.youtube.com/watch?v=2S3U38h6Jk0; https://interpreterfoundation.org/conferences/2021-book-of-moses-conference/,104–5.

3. WHY IS THE BOOK OF MOSES IMPORTANT TODAY?

Elder Bruce C. Hafen has commented as follows about the importance of the Book of Moses today:[5]

> The Book of Moses is an ancient temple text[6] as well as the ideal scriptural context for a modern temple preparation course. In answering the question "Why do we care about the Book of Moses?" John Welch said, "To me, it's all about the temple," even though the Lord revealed this temple text to Joseph "well before [Joseph] had any idea about building a temple, let alone what was to be done in the temple." And yet, "much of the blueprint for the endowment is here and only here."[7]

> I have for years encouraged people preparing to receive their temple endowment to study the Book of Moses. The book gives them unique and rich doctrinal perspective for understanding the endowment—the concept of heavenly ascent, the Creation, Fall, Atonement, the purposes of mortality and its trials, ritual prayer, sacrifice, obedience, consecration, priesthood, revelation, building Zion, and preparing to meet God. And, as Welch points out, the Book of Moses also teaches the difference between secular, self-centered marriage and "God-sanctioned, interdependent, child-rearing marriage."
>
> . . .

> In the early temples of this dispensation, as a patron moved from the baptistry to each succeeding ordinance, he or she stepped up, literally, to a higher level. . . .

> This upward pattern could plausibly derive from the Book of Moses, given to Joseph twelve years before he administered the first endowments in Nauvoo. In a clear prologue to the Adam and Eve story, chapter one begins with Moses in God's presence, learning that he is God's son and that God has a work for him to do. Knowing his identity and purpose, he then falls back to the earth, where he must overcome Satan's power before beginning his upward journey of return, calling on God, hearing His voice, seeing His heavenly vision, and regaining His presence.

> The same cosmic pattern repeats in Adam and Eve's story of Creation, Fall, overcoming opposition, redemption, and growing into a return to God. Then Enoch, their descendant, experiences and extends the pattern, moving on to lead his entire city back to God's presence. Thus "the temple themes in the Book of Moses extend beyond the . . . story of Adam and Eve"[8] to their culmination in the story of Enoch.

---

5   Bruce C. Hafen and Marie K. Hafen. "Adam, Eve, the Book of Moses, and the Temple: The Story of Receiving Christ's Atonement." In *Tracing Ancient Threads in the Book of Moses: Inspired Origins, Temple Contexts, and Literary Qualities*, edited by Jeffrey M. Bradshaw, David R. Seely, John W. Welch and Scott Gordon, 1–50. Orem, UT; Springville, UT; Redding, CA; Tooele, UT: The Interpreter Foundation, Book of Mormon Central, FAIR, and Eborn Books, 2021. https://journal.interpreterfoundation.org/adam-eve-the-book-of-moses-and-the-temple-the-story-of-receiving-christs-atonement/ ; https://www.youtube.com/watch?v=VWUWMZN-5fA..

6   John W. Welch. "The Temple in the Book of Mormon: The Temples at the Cities of Nephi, Zarahemla, and Bountiful." In *Temples of the Ancient World*, edited by Donald W. Parry, 297–387. Salt Lake City: Deseret Book, 1994, 300–301.

7   John W. Welch, email message to Bruce C. Hafen, September 9, 2020.

8   Jeffrey M. Bradshaw, "The Book of Moses as a Temple Text." In *Tracing Ancient Threads in the Book of Moses: Inspired Origins, Temple Contexts, and Literary Qualities*, edited by Jeffrey M.

When discussing temple-related matters in the commentary, I will follow the example of Hugh W. Nibley, who was, according to his biographer Boyd Jay Petersen, "respectful of the covenants of secrecy safeguarding specific portions of the Latter-day Saint endowment, usually describing parallels from other cultures without talking specifically about the Mormon ceremony."[9]

4. How Does the Book of Moses Fit the Temple Narrative Pattern?

The story of Adam and Eve's departure from the Garden of Eden and their return to the presence of God parallels a common pattern in ancient Near Eastern writings: departure from home, mission abroad, and happy homecoming.[10] The pattern is at least as old as the Egyptian story of Sinuhe from 1800 BCE and can be seen again in scriptural accounts of Israel's apostasy and return as well as in the lives of biblical characters such as Jacob (Genesis 27:33). The pattern appears in modern literature and media as often as it did in those times.[11]

To the ancients, however, it was more than a mere storytelling convention, since it reflected a sequence of events common in widespread temple ritual practices for priests and kings.[12] More generally, it is the story of the plan of salvation in miniature, as seen from the personal perspective. This pattern can be found in the Savior's parables of the Prodigal Son[13] and the Good Samaritan.[14] The life of Jesus Christ Himself also followed this two-part pattern, though, unlike ordinary

Bradshaw, David R. Seely, John W. Welch and Scott Gordon, 421–68. Orem, UT; Springville, UT; Redding, CA; Tooele, UT: The Interpreter Foundation, Book of Mormon Central, FAIR, and Eborn Books, 2021. https://journal.interpreterfoundation.org/the-book-of-moses-as-a-temple-text ; http://templethemes.net/publications/210911-Bradshaw-Temple%20Text-s.pdf, 425.

9   Boyd Jay Petersen. *Hugh Nibley: A Consecrated Life.* Draper, UT: Greg Kofford Books, 2002, 354. For Nibley's views on confidentiality as it relates to temple ordinances, see, for example, Hugh W. Nibley. "On the Sacred and the Symbolic." In *Temples of the Ancient World*, edited by Donald W. Parry, 535–621. Salt Lake City: Deseret Book, 1994, 553–54, 569–72.

10   Avraham Gileadi, ed. *The Literary Message of Isaiah.* New York, NY: Hebraeus Press, 1994, 12.

11   See, for example, Northrop Frye, *The Secular Scripture: A Study of the Structure of Romance. The Charles Eliot Norton Lectures*, 1974-1975. Cambridge, MA: Harvard University Press, 1976.

12   See, for example,, Dexter E. Callender, *Adam in Myth and History: Ancient Israelite Perspectives on the Primal Human.* Winona Lake, IN: Eisenbrauns, 2000, 211-18. From a ritual perspective, these three parts correspond to van Gennep's classic stages of separation (*préliminaire*), transition (*liminaire*), and reintegration (*postliminaire*) (Arnold van Gennep, *The Rites of Passage.* Translated by Monika B. Vizedom and Gabrielle L. Caffee. Chicago, IL: The University of Chicago Press, 1960, 11).

13   Luke 15:11–32. See, for example, Robert L. Millet, *Lost and Found: Reflections on the Prodigal Son.* Salt Lake City, UT: Deseret Book, 2001; Matthew R. Linford, "The Parable of the Benevolent Father and Son." *Interpreter: A Journal of Latter-day Saint Faith and Scripture* 22 (2016): 149-78. https://www.mormoninterpreter.com/the-parable-of-the-benevolent-father-and-son/#sdfootnote12sym.

14   Luke 10:29–37. See, for example, John W. Welch, "The Good Samaritan: A Type and Shadow of the Plan of Salvation." *BYU Studies* 38, no. 2 (1999): 51-115; Welch,. "The Good Samaritan: Forgotten symbols." *Ensign* 37, February 2007, 40-47.

mortals, He was without sin: "I came forth from the Father, and am come into the world: again, I leave the world, and go to the Father" (John 16:28).

Old Testament scholar Margaret Barker described how the thinking of early Christians applied this pattern to the story of Adam and Eve, and how it may have reflected their own hopes for a return to the original faith, the authentic priesthood, and the true temple:[15]

> The Christian vision reverses the story in Genesis 1–3, and has humans restored to Eden. . . . Adam was remembered as the first high priest, and Jesus was described as the new Adam. The Christians remembered and hoped for the earlier Eden—the true temple—and saw themselves returning to the place and the priesthood from which they had been driven. This was their world view.

Consistent with the perspective offered by Barker, the narrative pattern of temple worship does not recount a simple, unbroken rise to glory. As it turns out, temple narrative generally has two main parts: ritual *descent* (part 1) followed by ritual *ascent* (part 2).

Stories of ritual descent are naturally situated at the high point of heaven, beginning at the beginning of all things with an explicit telling of the Creation. Detailed tellings of the Creation are a near universal feature of temple rites throughout the ancient Near East.[16] The fact that the modern endowment also opens with a recital of the events of Creation[17] is one of many evidences of the antiquity of Latter-day Saint temple ordinances.

Following the story of Creation, the endowment enacts a ritual descent with the story of the Fall. Then, after transitioning to part 2, the temple narrative concludes by recounting Adam and Eve's ritual ascent, a journey back to the presence of the Father enabled by their accepting the covenants and blessings of the Atonement of Jesus Christ.[18] Note that the temple approach to teaching the plan of salvation emphasizes what Elder Bruce R. McConkie called the "three pillars" of eternity—the Creation, the Fall, and the Atonement.[19] A similar teaching pattern can be

---

15   Margaret Barker, *Temple Theology*. London, England: Society for Promoting Christian Knowledge (SPCK), 2004, 4, 7. See also Margaret Barker, *The Revelation of Jesus Christ: Which God Gave to Him to Show to His Servants What Must Soon Take Place (Revelation 1.1)*. Edinburgh, Scotland: T&T Clark, 2000, 20, 327.

16   See, for example, John H. Walton, A*ncient Near Eastern Thought and the Old Testament: Introducing the Conceptual World of the Hebrew Bible*. Grand Rapids, MI: Baker Academic, 2006, 123–127; Hugh W. Nibley, "Meanings and functions of temples." In *Encyclopedia of Mormonism*, edited by Daniel H. Ludlow. 4 vols. Vol. 4, 1458-63. New York City, NY: Macmillan, 1992. http://www.lib.byu.edu/Macmillan/, 1460–61.

17   See, for example, James E. Talmage, *The House of the Lord*. Salt Lake City, UT: Deseret Book, 1971, 83.

18   Talmage, *House*, p. 83.

19   Bruce R. McConkie, "Christ and the Creation." *Ensign* 12, June 1982, 8-15.

found in the Book of Mormon and the Doctrine and Covenants.[20]

It will be obvious to endowed Latter-day Saints that the storyline of the Book of Moses follows the same teaching pattern given in ancient and modern temples. In Moses 2–4 is found the story of the "down-road," while chapters 5–8 follow the journey of Adam and Eve and the righteous branches of their posterity along the "up-road." In Moses 4:31, the "up-road" is called the "way of the tree of life"—signifying the path that leads to the presence of God and the sweet fruit held in reserve for the righteous in the day of resurrection. The down-road and the up-road of Moses 2–8 are prefigured in the prophetic experience described in Moses 1 (figure 1–1), which serves as a prologue to the Book of Moses as a whole.

5. How Does the Book of Moses Fit with Genesis and Ancient Texts?

The Book of Moses is an amalgam composed of long revealed passages with little or no parallels in the Bible, along with shorter interpretive clarifications and modernizations of terms and grammar. Like nearly all of the revelations and translations of Joseph Smith, the Book of Moses draws on the vocabulary, phrasing, and imagery of the King James Bible. There is some evidence of Hebraic literary features, especially in the long additions to Genesis.[21] Significantly, there is a focus on priestly concerns that would have been of interest to a Levite such as Moses.[22]

The book opens in chapter 1 with the doctrinally rich visions of Moses that function as a prologue to the stories of the Creation, the Fall, and the Atonement in subsequent chapters. Ancient Jewish texts such as the *Book of Jubilees* and the *Apocalypse of Abraham* similarly couch their accounts of the Creation and the Fall as follow-ons to prophetic visions. The narrative structure of *Apocalypse of Abraham*, in particular, contains significant resemblances to Moses 1 in both content and

---

20   See, for example, 2 Nephi 2:22–26; Alma 18:36, 39; 22:13; Mormon 9:12, Doctrine and Covenants 20:17–18, 20–25; Moses 6:54–59; Articles of Faith 1:1–3. This "Christ-centered" presentation of the plan of salvation, consistent with temple patterns of teaching, is a contrast to the "location-centered" diagram that is used widely in classroom settings to illustrate the sequence of events that chart the journey of individuals from premortality to the resurrection.

21   Mark J. Johnson, "The Lost Prologue: Reading Moses Chapter One as an Ancient Text." *Interpreter: A Journal of Latter-day Saint Faith and Scholarship* 36 (2020): 145-86. https://journal. interpreterfoundation.org/the-lost-prologue-reading-moses-chapter-one-as-an-ancient-text/; Jonathan Riley, "Hebraisms in the Book of Moses: Laying Groundwork and Finding a Way Forward." In *Tracing Ancient Threads in the Book of Moses: Inspired Origins, Temple Contexts, and Literary Qualities*, edited by Jeffrey M. Bradshaw, David R. Seely, John W. Welch and Scott Gordon, 703–32. Orem, UT; Springville, UT; Redding, CA; Toole, UT: The Interpreter Foundation, Book of Mormon Central, FAIR, and Eborn Books, 2021.

22   John W. Welch and Jackson Abhau. "The Priestly Interests of Moses the Levite." In *Tracing Ancient Threads in the Book of Moses: Inspired Origins, Temple Contexts, and Literary Qualities*, edited by Jeffrey M. Bradshaw, David R. Seely, John W. Welch and Scott Gordon, 163–256. Orem, UT; Springville, UT; Reading, CA; Toole, UT: The Interpreter Foundation, Book of Mormon Central, FAIR, and Eborn Books, 2021. https://interpreterfoundation.org/conferences/2020-book-of-moses-conference/papers/ ; https://www.youtube.com/watch?v=Mvgn2fC4da8.

narrative sequence from start to finish.[23] Remarkably, a series of temple-related names and titles purportedly given to Moses at various points in his life seem to prefigure the divine name given him by God Himself in Moses 1.[24]

Moses 2–5 generally follows the description of events of the corresponding Genesis account of the Creation and the Fall, though with important additions and variations. For example, the opening of chapter 4 includes a significant account of Jehovah's premortal appointment as the Savior of humankind and of Satan's rebellion as a prelude to the story of his role as a tempter in the Garden of Eden.[25]

Moses 5–8 provide stories illustrating the making and breaking of a specific sequence of temple covenants, starting with the laws of obedience and sacrifice and culminating with the law of consecration.[26] After describing explicit prophecies to Adam and Eve about the coming "sacrifice of the Only Begotten of the Father" (v. 7) with no parallel in Genesis, chapter 5 further elaborates the biblical account of the murder of Abel, explicitly highlighting the conspiracy of Cain with Satan (vv. 21–31). Importantly, themes relating to the Book of Moses stories of Satan's attempts to influence the posterity of Adam and Eve and the emphasis on the prophecies of the Atonement of Jesus Christ find significant echoes in medieval Christian traditions. Important to the idea of the Book of Moses as a temple text is that many of these traditions have significant ritual overtones.[27]

---

23 Jeffrey M. Bradshaw, David J. Larsen, and Stephen T. Whitlock. "Moses 1 and the *Apocalypse of Abraham*: Twin Sons of Different Mothers?" In *Tracing Ancient Threads in the Book of Moses: Inspired Origins, Temple Contexts, and Literary Qualities*, edited by Jeffrey M. Bradshaw, David R. Seely, John W. Welch and Scott Gordon, 789–922. Orem, UT; Springville, UT; Reading, CA; Toole, UT: The Interpreter Foundation, Book of Mormon Central, FAIR, and Eborn Books, 2021. https://journal.interpreterfoundation.org/moses-1-and-the-apocalypse-of-abraham-twin-sons-of-different-mothers/.

24 Jeffrey M. Bradshaw and Matthew L. Bowen. "'Made Stronger Than Many Waters': The Names of Moses as Keywords in the Heavenly Ascent of Moses." In *Tracing Ancient Threads in the Book of Moses: Inspired Origins, Temple Contexts, and Literary Qualities*, edited by Jeffrey M. Bradshaw, David R. Seely, John W. Welch and Scott Gordon, 943–1000. Orem, UT; Springville, UT; Redding, CA; Tooele, UT: The Interpreter Foundation, Book of Mormon Central, FAIR, and Eborn Books, 2021. Reprint, *The Temple: Past, Present, and Future. Proceedings of the Fifth Interpreter Foundation Matthew B. Brown Memorial Conference, 7 November 2020*, edited by Stephen D. Ricks and Jeffrey M. Bradshaw. *Temple on Mount Zion* 6, 239–96. Orem and Salt Lake City, UT: The Interpreter Foundation and Eborn Books, 2021. https://www.youtube.com/watch?v=hk6nB9_PC-A ; http://templethemes.net/publications/210911-Bradshaw-jb-s.pdf.

25 John W. Welch finds resonances to Jesus' parable of the willing and unwilling sons with the story in Moses 4:1–4 of Jehovah and Lucifer in the heavenly council. See his "Symbolism in the Parable of the Willing and Unwilling Two Sons in Matthew 21." In *Let Us Reason Together: Essays in Honor of the Life's Work of Robert L. Millet*, edited by J. Spencer Fluhman and Brent L. Top. Salt Lake City, UT: Deseret Book, 2016. https://rsc.byu.edu/let-us-reason-together/symbolism-parable-willing-unwilling-two-sons-matthew-21.

26 Bradshaw, "Book of Moses as a Temple Text."

27 David Calabro, "'This Thing Is a Similitude': A Typological Approach to Moses 5:1–15 and Ancient Apocryphal Literature." In *Tracing Ancient Threads in the Book of Moses: Inspired*

In Moses 6–7, we encounter the extensive revealed record of the teachings, prophecies, and grand visions of Enoch, a character mentioned in only a handful of biblical verses. Enoch texts containing Mesopotamian influences, such as the *Book of Giants*,[28] are replete with ancient affinities for the Enoch accounts in the Book of Moses, ranging from details such as analogues to specific names,[29] messianic titles,[30] and rare phrases[31] to larger themes such as the prophet's gathering of the righteous to cities of refuge.[32] In the Bible, we learn only that "Enoch walked with God: and . . . God took him" (Genesis 5:24). However, in the Book of Moses, we learn that Zion, an entire community of Saints, was taken to heaven with him.[33]

Moses 8 recounts the opening events of the biblical career of Noah, stopping just short of the Lord's instructions for the building of the ark. Its most significant addition to Genesis is the description of the wicked "children of men" who falsely proclaimed themselves to be "the sons of God" (Moses 8:20–21). The nature and identity of these so-called sons of God is a long-standing interpretive puzzle for Bible scholars that is largely resolved in the Book Moses.

Origins, Temple Contexts, and Literary Qualities, edited by Jeffrey M. Bradshaw, David R. Seely, John W. Welch and Scott Gordon, 468–504. Orem, UT; Springville, UT; Reading, CA; Toole, UT: The Interpreter Foundation, Book of Mormon Central, FAIR, and Eborn Books, 2021. https://interpreterfoundation.org/conferences/2020-book-of-moses-conference/papers/ ; https://www.youtube.com/watch?v=Mvgn2fC4da8.

28 Jeffrey M. Bradshaw, "Moses 6–7 and the *Book of Giants*: Remarkable Witnesses of Enoch's Ministry." In *Tracing Ancient Threads in the Book of Moses: Inspired Origins, Temple Contexts, and Literary Qualities*, edited by Jeffrey M. Bradshaw, David R. Seely, John W. Welch and Scott Gordon, 1041–256. Orem, UT; Springville, UT; Redding, CA; Tooele, UT: The Interpreter Foundation, Book of Mormon Central, FAIR, and Eborn Books, 2021. https://www.youtube.com/watch?v=HP6GYxbieNQ ; https://journal.interpreterfoundation.org/moses-6-7-and-the-book-of-giants ; http://templethemes.net/publications/210911-Bradshaw-jmb-s.pdf. See also Jeffrey M. Bradshaw, *Enoch and the Gathering of Zion: The Witness of Ancient Texts for Modern Scripture*. Orem, Springville, and Salt Lake City, UT: The Interpreter Foundation, Book of Mormon Central, and Eborn Books, 2021. https://interpreterfoundation.org/books/enoch-and-the-gathering-of-zion/.

29 Jeffrey M. Bradshaw, Matthew L. Bowen, and Ryan Dahle. "Where Did the Names Mahaway and Mahujah Come From? A Response to Colby Townsend's 'Returning to the Sources,' Part 2 of 2." *Interpreter: A Journal of Latter-day Saint Faith and Scholarship* 40 (2020): 181–242, https://journal.interpreterfoundation.org/where-did-the-names-mahaway-and-mahujah-come-from-a-response-to-colby-townsends-returning-to-the-sources-part-2-of-2/, 211–15.

30 S. Kent Brown and Jeffrey M. Bradshaw. "Man and Son of Man: Probing Theology and Christology in the Book of Moses and in Jewish and Christian Tradition." In *Tracing Ancient Threads in the Book of Moses: Inspired Origins, Temple Contexts, and Literary Qualities*, edited by Jeffrey M. Bradshaw, David R. Seely, John W. Welch and Scott Gordon, 1257–332. Orem, UT; Springville, UT; Redding, CA; Tooele, UT: The Interpreter Foundation, Book of Mormon Central, FAIR, and Eborn Books, 2021. http://templethemes.net/publications/210911-Brown%20Bradshaw%202021-s.pdf ; https://www.youtube.com/watch?v=axRLPR8T5Ck.

31 Bradshaw, "Moses 6–7," 1095–98, 1121–22

32 Bradshaw, "Moses 6–7," 1123–33.

33 Bradshaw, "Moses 6–7," 1143–46.

Comparison of the Book of Moses with Genesis and other ancient records has increased my appreciation of otherwise obscure details in both ancient and modern texts. I hope readers will find both their understanding of scripture and their testimony of the Prophet Joseph Smith strengthened by their study.

Note: In the commentary, references to OT1 and OT2 refer to the original manuscripts of the Joseph Smith Translation of the New Testament. See the section entitled "History of the Book of Moses" for more details.

THE BOOK OF MOSES

Visions of Moses as Revealed to Joseph the Seer in 1830

CHAPTER 1
THE HEAVENLY ASCENT OF MOSES

PROLOGUE

1 ¹ The words of God, which he spake unto Moses at a time when Moses was caught up into an exceedingly high mountain, ² and he saw God face to face, and he talked with him, and the glory of God was upon Moses; therefore Moses could endure his presence.

---

1   The visions described in Moses 1 took place after Jehovah called Moses out of the burning bush (v. 17) but before he had returned to Egypt to deliver the children of Israel (vv. 25–26). The chapter describes a "heavenly ascent, whereby Moses comes into the presence of God and speaks with Him face-to-face. Enoch, Abraham, Isaiah, Jeremiah, Ezekiel, and others described similar experiences by which they acquired membership and a mission in a divine council (SOSIAM). By way of contrast, Latter-day Saint temple ordinances symbolize a figurative journey of "ritual ascent." Hugh Nibley called heavenly ascent the "completion or fulfillment" of the "types and images" of ritual ascent (JMBIGIL1, 37).

In some ways Moses' heavenly ascent resembles the journey of ritual ascent that Latter-day Saints experience in temple worship (figure 1–1). The chapter opens with a vision of the spirit world where all of us lived before we came to earth (Moses 1:3–8). Moses then "falls" to the telestial world, the world where we now live. There Satan attempts to tempt and try him (Moses 1:9–23). Finally, he climbs upward in a step-by-step return to the celestial world in a journey that corresponds to our personal ascent back to God through covenant-keeping (Moses 1:24–32). Moses 1 provides a fitting prologue to Genesis, emphasizing, among other things, that God's purpose is "to bring about the immortality and eternal life of man" (Moses 1:39). He does this by allowing us to be tested on earth to see whether we will ultimately follow Satan or stay true to Him by making and keeping sacred covenants that will bring us back into His presence. Remarkably, the heavenly ascent chapters of the first century *Apocalypse of Abraham* (*ApAb*) resemble the account in Moses 1 from start to finish (AKRETRO). Like Moses 1, *ApAb* ends with a vision of the Creation, the Garden of Eden, and the Fall of Adam and Eve (MOSESS 33–41; JMBTWIN).

1:1–2   ***Prologue.*** Verses 1 and 2 are a prologue to Moses 1. They summarize the most important event of the chapter: Once Moses has been tried and proven, the "glory of God" will come upon him, enabling him to enter into God's presence through the heavenly veil (vv. 27–31).

1:1   ***exceedingly high mountain.*** The term "mountain" is often used figuratively to describe temples (Isaiah 2:2; Psalm 48:2). When temples have not been available, mountains have often provided the same function. See MOSESS 34.

1:2   ***he saw God face to face.*** The eyewitness quality of Moses' experience is emphasized by repeated references to its visual aspects: "saw" (Moses 1:2, 20), "look" or "looked" (vv. 4, 8, 13–14), "behold" or "beheld" (vv. 5, 7–8, 11, 22, 25, 27–29, 35, 39), "show" (v. 7), "eyes" (vv. 11, 24), and "discerned" (v. 28).

glory of God was upon Moses. The Hebrew word for glory is *kabod*, which conveys the weighty magnificence of God's presence. The sense in which this may also signal a real bodily appearance is captured in the English phrase "He was there in all his glory." "Glory" is repeated twelve times in Moses 1, highlighting the contrast between God's bright splendor and Satan's shriveled darkness.

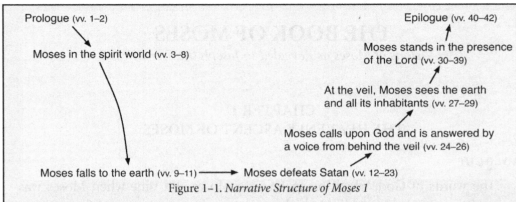

Figure 1–1. *Narrative Structure of Moses 1*

THE TWO-PART PATTERN OF HEAVENLY ASCENT IN MOSES 1

Several of the episodes in Moses 1 are well known to students of the Book of Moses—Moses' confrontation with Satan, his comprehensive vision of the earth and all its inhabitants, and God's declaration about His "work and glory." Yet how all these pieces join beautifully into a coherent whole is underappreciated. Like the Latter-day Saint temple endowment, Moses 1 starts with a "down road" and ends with an "up road":

1–2   *Prologue.* The prologue declares that Moses will be "caught up" to "an exceedingly high mountain" where he will receive the glory of God and enter into His presence (see MOSESS 34).

3–8   *Moses in the spirit world.* Moses was given a description of God's attributes and a confirmation of his foreordained calling and status as a "son" of God "in the similitude of [the] Only Begotten." He was then shown the "world upon which he was created"—the premortal spirit world—and "all the children of men which are, and which were created"—as was also seen by Enoch (see Moses 6:36), Abraham (see Abraham 3:22–26), and individuals in Jewish and Islamic tradition (see MOSESS 34).

9–11   *Moses falls to the earth.* Having left the presence of God and no longer being clothed with His glory, Moses fell to the earth—meaning literally that he collapsed in weakness and figuratively that he descended again to the relative darkness of the telestial world. In this way, his experience was similar to the journey of Adam and Eve when they left the Garden of Eden. Moses was then left to himself to be tested in a dramatic encounter with Satan (see MOSESS 35).

12–23 *Moses defeats Satan.* Satan tempted Moses—now in a physically weakened state—to worship him. After Satan's defeat, a context of priesthood ordinances is implied. For example, having banished Satan by calling upon the name of the Only Begotten (a motif that precedes baptism in some ancient Christian sources), Moses was immediately afterward "filled with the Holy Ghost" (see MOSESS 36).

24–26 *Moses calls upon God and is answered by a voice from behind the veil.* Having continued to press forward, Moses "call[ed] upon the name of God" in sacred prayer. After he "fell to the earth," Moses could no longer speak face to face with the Lord, having been "shut out from his presence" (Moses 1:9; 5:4). Following his prayer, Moses was answered by a voice from behind the heavenly veil promising blessings, including the assurance that his commands would be obeyed "as if thou wert God" (see MOSESS 37–39).

27–29 *At the veil, Moses sees the earth and all its inhabitants.* While "the [divine] voice was still speaking," Moses was permitted to pass through the heavenly veil and, from within, look downward and outward toward God's handiwork. He beheld every particle of the earth, all of its inhabitants, and "many lands; . . . each . . . called earth" (see MOSESS 40).

30–39 *Moses stands in the presence of the Lord.* Moses, having continued to inquire of the Lord, came to stand in His presence. God described His purposes for this earth and its inhabitants. Moses was then shown the events of the Creation and the Fall and the manner by which the plan of redemption was given to Adam and Eve. From Moses 1:40, it appears that Moses was commanded to record an account something like, but not identical to, what we have today as chapters 2–8 of the Book of Moses (see MOSESS 41).

40–42 *Epilogue.* The epilogue describes the loss of the story of Moses' heavenly ascent and its restoration in the last days (see MOSESS 42).

MOSES IN THE SPIRIT WORLD

³ And God spake unto Moses, saying: "Behold, I am the Lord God Almighty, and Endless is my name; for I am without beginning of days or end of years; and is not this endless? ⁴ And, behold, thou art my son; wherefore look, and I will show thee the workmanship of mine hands; but not all, for my works are without end, and also my words, for they never cease. ⁵ Wherefore, no man can behold all my works, except he behold all my glory; and no man can behold all my glory, and afterwards remain in the flesh on the earth.

⁶ "And I have a work for thee, Moses, my son; and thou art in the similitude of mine Only Begotten; and mine Only Begotten is and shall be the Savior, for he is full of grace and truth; but there is no God beside me, and all things are present with me, for I know them all.

1:3   ***God spake unto Moses.*** Although Moses 1:6 makes it seem that God the Father is speaking directly to Moses, some have understood the voice as belonging to Jehovah, the premortal Jesus Christ. This view is consistent with the teachings of Church leaders who have said that Jesus Christ or the Holy Ghost may be authorized to speak and act as if they were the Father—a concept called "divine investiture." Another idea was offered by Elder Alvin R. Dyer, who held the view that both the Father and the Son were present during Moses' vision. He thought that Moses' experience may have been "similar to that which was experienced by Joseph Smith in the Sacred Grove, wherein God the Father appeared and announced His Son" (JMBIGIL1, 45).

    I am. This phrase begins a typical "aretalogy," wherein the attributes of God are proclaimed.

    Almighty. The title recalls the demonstration of God's power over the waters as the first act of Creation. Moses will in like manner "be made stronger than many waters" (Moses 1:25).

    Endless. The endlessness of God, His works, and His words will be repeated throughout the chapter: "without end," "numberless," "without number," "innumerable," "cannot be numbered," and "no end" (Moses 1:4, 28, 33, 35, 37, 38). In medieval Jewish mysticism, the term *Ein Sof* is a way of referring to eternity, depicted visually as a set of concentric circles with their "end embedded in their beginning, and their beginning in their end" (DCMZOHAR1, xlvii). Such imagery recalls the description in Latter-day Saint scripture of God's course as "one eternal round" (1 Nephi 10:19).

1:4   ***my . . . mine.*** The Lord stresses the possessives "my" and "mine" throughout Moses 1, thus emphasizing His deep personal interest in His Creation and His creatures.

1:5   ***works.*** This is given as "work" in OT2. However, OT1 reads "works" (SHFJST, 591, 59).

    no man can behold all my glory, . . . on the earth. No one can behold all God's glory before one has received God's fulness—thus Moses' vision must now be limited to "this one thing" (v. 7).

    on the earth. The words "on the earth" were added in OT2 (SHFJST, 591).

1:6   ***thou art in the similitude of mine Only Begotten.*** Moses' work is to be patterned after God's own as he assumes the role of lawgiver, savior, and mediator to his people (Exodus 32:30ff.).

    Only Begotten. Though at first glance the words "Only Begotten" and "full of grace and truth" in Moses 1 might seem to be nothing more than obvious borrowings in language from the Gospel of John, biblical and extrabiblical texts convincingly demonstrate that these expressions are completely at home in an ancient text about Moses (MOSESS 15; JMBTWIN, 254–55).

    the Savior. This title is not present in OT1 but was added in OT2 (SHFJST, 83, 591).

    full of grace and truth. Doctrine and Covenants 93 makes it clear that receiving the "fulness" is accomplished gradually by continuing from "grace to grace."

    all things are present with me. Elder Neal A. Maxwell comments: "God does not live in the dimension of time as do we. . . . In ways that are not clear to us, He sees rather than foresees the future, because all things are at once present before him" (JMBIGIL1, 48–49; Alma 40:8).

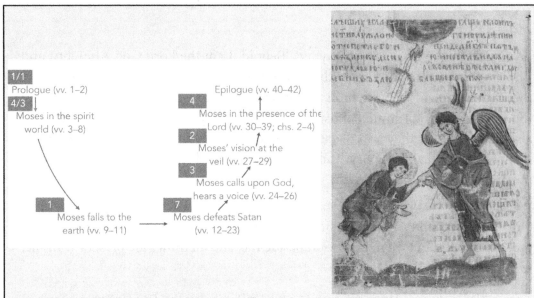

Figure 1–2. Left: *Number of resemblances with* ApAb *chapters 9–23 superimposed on the narrative structure of* Moses 1; Right: *Abraham falls to the earth and is raised by Yahoel from the* Sylvester Codex manuscript *of* ApAb

COMPARING THE *APOCALYPSE OF ABRAHAM* TO MOSES 1

Among the most remarkable evidences of ancient threads in the Book of Moses are the striking resemblances between Moses 1 and the *Apocalypse of Abraham* (*ApAb*), one of the earliest and most important Jewish texts describing heavenly ascent.

Alexander Kulik calls *ApAb* "the earliest mystical writing of Judaeo-Christian civilization" (AKRETRO, 1). It has also been described as a foundational text for Islamic scripture. For this reason, *ApAb* plays a prominent—and in some respects unique—role in its genre. Of particular relevance to Latter-day Saints is BYU professor Jared W. Ludlow's observation that *ApAb* is "the only Jewish text to discuss foreordination, Satan's rebellion, and premortal existence." Notably, the first English translation of *ApAb*, based on Bonwetsch's German version, was made by Latter-day Saint Richard T. Haag and published in the Church's *Improvement Era* magazine in 1898.

In the overview diagram at left above, thematic resemblances of the heavenly ascent chapters of *ApAb* to the narrative themes of Moses 1 have been roughly classified according to the section of the Moses 1 account in which they appear. The frequency of resemblances of *ApAb* to Moses 1 in a given section is represented by a number. The slash and second number that appear next to the first two sections refer to a few of the significant resemblances of *ApAb* to the Book of Abraham. Although more significant resemblances are found in Moses 1, the Book of Abraham affinities should not be ignored. Overall, the resemblances paint an interesting picture. It is evident that they are not confined to limited sections of Moses 1 but rather are spread throughout the chapter. They are highly varied and tend to be unique within a given section of the narrative. Importantly, the sequence of common elements of the two texts is almost identical.

Above at right, one of the remarkable thematic resemblances is illustrated. Following their initial divine encounter, both Moses and Abraham are said to have experienced a "fall to the earth" that left them vulnerable to the will of the adversary. In *ApAb*, Abraham is reported as saying, "I . . . fell down upon the earth, for there was no longer strength in me" (AKRETRO, 10:2, p. 17), closely resembling the description in Moses 1 where we are told that Moses "fell unto the earth" and lost his "natural strength" (Moses 1:9–10). While modern readers might easily skim over the description of the fall and the raising of the two prophets, thinking it of little interest, it was clearly a significant event to the ancient illustrator, who found it important enough to include it among the six passages he highlighted with visual depictions. The drawing helps us understand the meaning of the event in Moses 1. It shows Abraham being raised up out of sleep—perhaps suggesting spiritual death—by the hand of Yahoel, who, using the right hand, lifts him firmly by the wrist in what seems to be a ritual handclasp. The rays emanating from the hand of God above them symbolize the spirit of life, recalling the creation of Adam, when God "breathed . . . the breath of life" into the first man, and he became "a living soul" (Moses 3:7). For a thorough comparison of *ApAb* to Moses 1, see JMBTWIN.

[7] "And now, behold, this one thing I show unto thee, Moses, my son, for thou art in the world, and now I show it unto thee." [8] And it came to pass that Moses looked, and beheld the world upon which he was created; and Moses beheld the world and the ends thereof, and all the children of men which are, and which were created; of the same he greatly marveled and wondered.

Moses Falls to the Earth

[9] And the presence of God withdrew from Moses, that his glory was not upon Moses; and Moses was left unto himself. And as he was left unto himself, he fell unto the earth. [10] And it came to pass that it was for the space of many hours before Moses did again receive his natural strength like unto man; and he said unto himself: "Now, for this cause I know that man is nothing, which thing I never had supposed.

[11] "But now mine own eyes have beheld God; but not my natural, but my spiritual eyes, for my natural eyes could not have beheld; for I should have withered and died in his presence; but his glory was upon me; and I beheld his face, for I was transfigured before him."

Moses Defeats Satan

[12] And it came to pass that when Moses had said these words, behold, Satan came tempting him, saying: "Moses, son of man, worship me." [13] And it came to pass that

---

1:8   *the world upon which he was created.* In other words, the premortal spirit world. This is contrasted in Moses 1:40 with the mortal earth, called "this earth upon which thou standest." See MOSESS 34.

1:9   *Moses . . . fell unto the earth.* Having left the presence of God and no longer being clothed with His glory, Moses fell to the earth—literally collapsing in weakness and figuratively descending again to the relative darkness of the telestial world. In this way, his experience resembled the journey of Adam and Eve when they left the Garden of Eden. For this reason, Nibley describes this scene as "Moses, landing on earth as a natural man" (JMBIGIL1, 51). Having left the presence of God, he will be compelled to face his adversary alone. See MOSESS 35. See figure 1–2.

1:10   *for this cause I know.* OT1 and OT2 give this as "for this once I know" (SHFJST, 83, 592).

       man is nothing. James Faulconer notes: "Recognizing his own nothingness . . . is . . . coming to a full realization of his dependence upon God, of his inability to save himself and of God's merciful willingness to save him. . . . [It is a] realization of his relation to God as a child" (JMBIGIL1, 52).

1:11   *my spiritual eyes.* Joseph Smith explained that the things of God "are revealed to our spirits precisely as though we had no bodies at all" (JMBIGIL1, 52).

1:12   *Satan came.* "Notice," writes Nibley, "when the hero is at his lowest, when he is the most helpless, that is the time that Satan strikes. . . . Satan does not play fair" (HWNPGP, 216). For more details on this episode, see MOSESS 36.

       tempting. The word "tempt" corresponds to Hebrew (*nsh*) and Greek (*peirazo*)—meaning to try, test, or prove. Such tests may be instigated by God (as in Genesis 22:1), by Satan (as in Luke 4:2), or by others.

       Moses, son of man. In this verse, the words refer to a descendant of Adam—in other words, "any mortal man" (Daniel 8:17). However, it should be remembered that Moses had just been told in vv. 3, 6, 7 that he was *God's* son—in other words, the son of the "*Man* of Holiness" (Moses 7:35; emphasis added).

Figure 1–3. *The Temptation of Christ.* King Gagik I of Kars Gospels, ca. 1050

"Where Is Thy Glory, for It Is Darkness unto Me?"

In both Moses 1 and *ApAb*, the prophet recognizes Satan's attempt to disguise his identity. Lacking divine glory and heavenly inheritance, the devil is easily—and humiliatingly—exposed.

Documenting other instances of the adversary's deception, the Apostle Paul, drawing on early Jewish tradition, spoke of Satan transforming himself "into an angel of light" (2 Corinthians 11:14). With similar language, Joseph Smith also spoke of the devil having appeared deceptively in his day "as an angel of light" (Doctrine and Covenants 128:20).

Michael Stone, a scholar of ancient Adam and Eve traditions, sees a passage in the Latin *Life of Adam and Eve* as implying that "all Satan lacked to look like a heavenly angel was the glory. He lost the glory when he fell, and he could take it on temporarily in order to deceive Adam and Eve." Thus, Satan is depicted in illustrations of the temptation of Christ, as elsewhere in early Christian art, as angelic in form but differing in color—for example, appearing in "false glory" in a blue tint rather than in a bright whiteness of glory, as shown in the figure above. One might also interpret Satan's blue color as his appearing, deceptively, in a form corresponding to the blue robe of the high priest (worn in the figure by Jesus), a robe that represented being clothed in the likeness of the body—the blue-black "shadow"—of the incarnate Logos. By way of contrast, Satan is naked—his apron symbolizes counterfeit authority (see commentary on Moses 4:13).

Moses, having received a taste of the celestial heights, had already learned to distinguish God's glory from Satan's pale imitation. He challenged the adversary, saying, "Where is thy glory, for it is darkness unto me? And I can judge between thee and God" (Moses 1:14). Satan was told to depart and cease his deception. The Book of Moses records Moses as saying, "Get thee hence, Satan; deceive me not" (1:16) while *ApAb* relates similar words from Yaho'el, "Depart from [Abraham]! You cannot deceive him" (AKRETRO, 13:12–13, p. 20) In both accounts, Satan departs only after three attempts to banish him. Moses will succeed the last time only when he invokes the name of the Only Begotten (Moses 1:21).

Moses looked upon Satan and said: "Who art thou? For behold, I am a son of God, in the similitude of his Only Begotten; and where is thy glory, that I should worship thee? ¹⁴ For behold, I could not look upon God, except his glory should come upon me, and I were transfigured before him. But I can look upon thee in the natural man. Is it not so, surely?

¹⁵ "Blessed be the name of my God, for his Spirit hath not altogether withdrawn from me, or else where is thy glory, for it is darkness unto me? And I can judge between thee and God; for God said unto me: 'Worship God, for him only shalt thou serve.' ¹⁶ Get thee hence, Satan; deceive me not; for God said unto me: 'Thou art after the similitude of mine Only Begotten.' ¹⁷ And he also gave me commandments when he called unto me out of the burning bush, saying: 'Call upon God in the name of mine Only Begotten, and worship me.'" ¹⁸ And again Moses said: "I will

1:12   ***worship me.*** In a fashion that recalls Satan's encounter with Christ in the wilderness (in Matthew 4:8–9), Satan tempted Moses—now in a physically weakened state—to worship him. The title conferred by Deity on Moses, son of *God*, is explicitly challenged by Satan, who calls him a "son of *man*" (vv. 4, 12; emphasis added). The devil's repeated demands for worship recall a story in ancient sources that the premortal rebellion began when Satan refused God's request to bow down in homage to the newly created Adam (JMBIGIL1, 53).

1:13   ***I am a son of God, in the similitude of his Only Begotten.*** These words constitute what Nibley calls a "humiliating exposure of Satan"—an announcement that Moses "actually *is* what his adversary falsely *claims to be*" (HWNOPEN, 5; emphasis added).

    where is thy glory that I should worship thee? Moses taunts Satan. Satan is not worthy of worship because he has no glory. "The glory of God is intelligence, or, in other words, light and truth. Light and truth forsake that evil one" (Doctrine and Covenants 93:36–37). Satan possesses neither light nor truth.

1:14   ***transfigured before him.*** The 1843 *Times and Seasons* publishers altered the text to read "strengthened before him" (KPJMOSES, 14).

1:15   ***where is thy glory, for it is darkness unto me?*** Moses had already learned to distinguish God's glory from Satan's pale imitation. Satan no doubt appeared to Moses deceptively as an angel of "light," but fake light is darkness (2 Corinthians 11:12–15; 2 Nephi 9:9; Doctrine and Covenants 128:20; 129:4–7). Michael Stone sees a passage in the Latin *Life of Adam and Eve* as implying "that all Satan lacked to look like a heavenly angel was the glory. He lost the glory when he fell, and he could take it on temporarily in order to deceive Adam and Eve" (JMBIGIL1, 54). OT1 and OT2 read "blackness" in place of "darkness" (SHFJST, 84, 592). See figure 1–3.

    Worship God, for him only shalt thou serve. In his reply to Satan, the words of Moses fittingly parallel a saying of Jehovah, just as Christ, the embodied Jehovah, later cites the words of Moses during His temptation (Deuteronomy 6:13; Matthew 4:10).

1:16   ***Get thee hence, Satan.*** Moses will fail three times in his attempts to banish Satan (Moses 1:16, 18, 20), succeeding at last only when he invokes the name of the Only Begotten (Moses 1:21). Note that when Jesus banished Satan following his temptation in the wilderness, a single command from the Only Begotten Himself had sufficed (Matthew 4:10–11).

1:17   ***commandments.*** OT1 and OT2 read "commandment" (SHFJST, 84, 592).

1:17   ***Call upon God.*** Discoursing on 2 Peter 1:10, the Prophet urged the Saints: "I would exhort you to go on and continue to call upon God until you make your calling and election sure" (JMBIGIL1, 55). Moses' perseverance in calling upon God illustrates this pattern and eventually will be rewarded when Moses enters the Lord's presence and speaks with Him face to face.

    in the name of mine Only Begotten. Exodus 3:13–15 records that Moses learned the name of Jehovah when he saw the burning bush. Adam received the same commandment (Moses 5:8).

POETIC ARRANGEMENTS OF MOSES 1

Mark J. Johnson has suggested the following concentric (chiastic) arrangement of Moses 1, highlighting the crucial importance of the verse where Moses called on God for strength (MOSESS 45; MJJLOST):

A The word of God, which he spoke unto Moses upon an exceeding high mountain (1)
  B Endless is God's name (3)
    C God's work and his glory (4)
      D The Lord has a work for Moses
        E Moses is in the similitude of the Only Begotten (6)
          F Moses beholds the world and the ends thereof (7–8)
            G The presence of God withdraws from Moses (9)
              H Man, in his natural strength, is nothing (10)
                I Moses beheld God with his spiritual eyes (11)
                  J Satan came tempting him (12)
                    K Moses' response to Satan (13–15)
                      L Moses commands Satan to depart (16–18)
                        M Satan ranted upon the earth (19)
                          N Moses began to fear
                            O Moses called upon God
                          N' Moses received strength (20)
                        M' Satan began to tremble and the earth shook
                      L' Moses cast Satan out in the name of the Only Begotten (21)
                  K' Satan cried with weeping and wailing
                J' Satan departs from Moses (22)
              I' Moses lifted up his eyes unto heaven (23–24)
            H' Moses is made stronger than many waters
          G' Moses beheld God's glory again (25)
        F' Moses is shown the heavens and the earth (27–31)
      E' Creation by the Only Begotten (32–33)
  B' God's works and words are endless (38)
    C' God's work and his glory (39)
      D' Moses to write the words of God (40–41)
A' The Lord spoke unto Moses concerning the heaven and earth (Moses 2:1)

Johnson has also suggested the following parallel panel arrangement, which tries to account for what otherwise would seem to be an intrusive interruption by the narrator in v. 23. This arrangement highlights the importance of the theme of the loss and restoration of Moses' words (MOSESS 45; MJJLOST):

A Moses is caught up to see God (1)
B   God declares himself as the Almighty (3)
C   God is without beginning of days or end of years (3)
D   Moses beholds the world (7)
E   Moses beholds the children of men (8)
F   Moses sees the face of God (11)
G   Moses to worship the Only Begotten (17)
H'   Moses bore record of this, but due to wickedness, it shall not be had among the children of men (23)
A' Moses beholds God's glory (24–25)
B'   God declares himself [as the] Almighty (25)
C'   God to be with Moses until the end of his days (26)
D'   Moses beholds the earth (27)
E'   Moses beholds the earth's inhabitants (28)
F'   Moses sees the face of God (31)
G'   Creation through the Only Begotten (33)
H'   Moses to write the words of God, but they shall be taken away (41)

not cease to call upon God, I have other things to inquire of him: for his glory has been upon me, wherefore I can judge between him and thee. Depart hence, Satan."

[19] And now, when Moses had said these words, Satan cried with a loud voice, and ranted upon the earth, and commanded, saying: "I am the Only Begotten, worship me." [20] And it came to pass that Moses began to fear exceedingly; and as he began to fear, he saw the bitterness of hell. Nevertheless, calling upon God, he received strength, and he commanded, saying: "Depart from me, Satan, for this one God only will I worship, which is the God of glory."

[21] And now Satan began to tremble, and the earth shook; and Moses received strength, and called upon God, saying: "In the name of the Only Begotten, depart hence, Satan." [22] And it came to pass that Satan cried with a loud voice, with weeping,

1:18   *his glory has been upon me.* OT1 and OT2 add "and it is glory unto me" (KPJMOSES, 41).

1:19   *Satan cried with a loud voice.* Moses' continued resistance calls for a dramatic change in tactics. In the words of Nibley, "Satan . . . casts aside his celebrated but now useless subtlety and launches a frontal attack of satanic fury, a tremendous tantrum" (HWNOPEN, 5). The Armenian version of the *Life of Adam and Eve* records that Satan, blaming Adam for all his troubles, "wept loudly" as he railed forth in self-pity, and the Latin version has him "groaning." The Georgian version highlights the manipulative intent of the devil's theatrics, stating that he "began to cry with forced tears" (JMBIGIL1, 56).

    ranted upon the earth. The term "ranted" is a guess at the meaning of "wrent" in OT1 and OT2 (SHFJST, 84, 593). To rant is to speak in a violent, loud, extravagant, and vehement manner for maximal rhetorical effect. However, based on parallel spellings in the printer's manuscript of the Book of Mormon and the JST, Kent Jackson rightfully concludes that the original manuscript term "wrent" "is likely a regional spelling of 'rent,' the past tense of 'rend,' 'to tear'" (KPJMOSES, 50). In other words, Satan "tore upon the earth." This reading perfectly fits the character of the adversary: Satan's objective is to rend and destroy, while Christ's mission is to unite and atone.

    commanded. Satan counters Moses' stubborn obedience to God's commandment with a direct command of his own. However, in the end, it will be Satan who yields to Moses' command—a command executed in the authority and power of the priesthood after the order of the Only Begotten Son of God.

1:20   *Moses began to fear exceedingly. . . . Nevertheless, calling upon God, he received strength.* Nibley summarizes: "True to the ancient pattern, the hero is momentarily bested, overcome by the powers of darkness. . . . But with his last ounce of strength he calls upon God from the depths and is delivered" (HWNPGP, 118).

1:21   *Satan began to tremble, and the earth shook.* The thunderous shaking of the ground echoes the emotional intensity of Satan's rage with terrifying reverberations. Compare Isaiah 14:3–4, 7, 16; James 2:19.

    Moses received strength, and called upon God. In the previous verse, Moses received strength after calling upon God—here, the order of these events is reversed. The verse has a complex history of revisions (SHFJST, 84, 593; KPJMOSES, 62).

1:21   *"In the name of the Only Begotten, depart hence, Satan."* Moses had already tried twice, unsuccessfully, to banish Satan. Now, when he makes his third attempt, he invokes divine authority, relying on the power of the priesthood after the order of the Son of God (Moses 1:20–21). The dramatic turning point of this episode hinges on Satan's desperate, false claim to be the Only Begotten, countered by Moses's triumphant invocation of the name of the *true* Only Begotten.

1:22   *Satan cried with a loud voice.* In an elegant parallel to v. 19, Satan cries out a second time with a loud voice. In this instance, however, the cry is not a flourish of rhetorical melodrama but rather a despairing wail reflecting the misery and hopelessness of the damned.

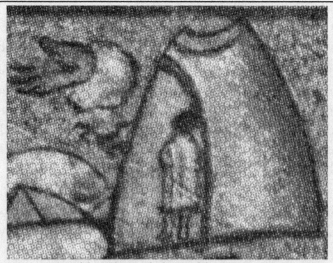
Figure 1–5. *Detail from the Torah shrine of the Dura Europos synagogue*

ENTERING THE PRESENCE OF GOD: A VEIL AND A VOICE

Moses 1:25 tells us that Moses "beheld [God's] glory." However, in an important divergence from the Book of Moses, the *Apocalypse of Abraham* (*ApAb*) has Yaho'el declare to Abraham: "the Eternal One . . . you will *not* see" (AKRETRO, 16:3, p. 22). Thus, according to Andrei Orlov, *ApAb* explicitly rejects any visualization of God and "insists on expressing the divine Presence in the form of the Deity's Voice" alone.

Importantly, however, the divine whisper or echo (Hebrew *bat ḳōl*—literally, "daughter of the voice") through which, in Jewish tradition, divine revelation continued audibly even after the open visions of the prophets had ceased, was depicted for centuries in the art of Jewish synagogues and Christian churches as a divine hand. In portrayals of ritual or heavenly ascent, this hand was often shown as emerging from behind a cloud or veil, representing the obscuring boundary that separates earth from heaven.

A relevant example is shown in this illustration from a decoration on the Torah shrine of the synagogue at Dura Europos. According to Shira Lander, it is the "earliest known depiction of the hand of God in either Jewish or Christian art." Isaac, depicted behind the scene of his near sacrifice and clad in white clothing marked with red *clavi*, is shown entering behind the veil of a tent sanctuary at the top of Mount Moriah. This reading is supported by Jewish and early Christian texts suggesting that, in the Akedah, Isaac literally died, ascended to heaven, and was resurrected. The disembodied hand, a representation of God's body and of His heavenly utterance from behind the veil (that is, the *bat ḳōl*), is shown above the scene of the arrested sacrifice and to the immediate left of the tent sanctuary.

In ancient literature, passage through the veil is frequently accompanied not only with the sorts of divine utterance just described but also with human speech. For example, instances of formal prayer and exchanges of words at the veil are variously described in Egyptian ritual texts, Jewish pseudepigrapha, and the Book of Mormon. Similarly, in *ApAb*, a recitation of a fixed set of words, often described as a "hymn," "precedes a vision of the Throne of Glory" (Alexander Kulik).

In *ApAb*, Abraham is instructed by the angel Yaho'el to recite a "hymn" in preparation for his ascent to receive a vision of the work of God. Significantly, Martha Himmelfarb observes that *ApAb*, unlike other similar accounts, "treats the [hymn] sung by the visionary as part of the means of achieving ascent." At last, "while [he] was still reciting the [hymn]" (AKRETRO, 18:1, p. 23) the veil opens and the throne of glory appears to his view.

Moses 1:25–31 describes the revelation of God as a progressive phenomenon, beginning with "a voice" and ending with a "face to face" encounter. Notably, the same sequence of divine disclosure is present in the story of the brother of Jared's intimate encounter with the Lord "at the veil." In that account, the prayer of the brother of Jared is answered first with a divine voice, then with seeing the finger of the hand of the Lord, and finally with a view of the "body of [His] spirit." See MOSESS 37, 38; JMBEZEKIEL, 11–12, 18–20.

and wailing, and gnashing of teeth; and he departed hence, even from the presence of Moses, that he beheld him not. ²³ And now of this thing Moses bore record; but because of wickedness it is not had among the children of men.

Moses Calls upon God

²⁴ And it came to pass that when Satan had departed from the presence of Moses, that Moses lifted up his eyes unto heaven, being filled with the Holy Ghost, which beareth record of the Father and the Son; ²⁵ and calling upon the name of God, he beheld his glory again, for it was upon him; and he heard a voice, saying: "Blessed art thou, Moses, for I, the Almighty, have chosen thee, and thou shalt be made stronger than many waters; for they shall obey thy

1:23   *of this thing Moses bore record.* Mark J. Johnson views this verse in company with v. 41 as a marker for a parallel panel structure comprising vv. 1–23 and 24–41. See figure 1–4; MOSESS 45; MJJLOST.

       because of wickedness it is not had among the children of men. Rodney Turner wryly comments, "No doubt Satan was not anxious to have this demeaning episode publicized" (JMBIGIL1, 59).

1:24   *Moses lifted up his eyes unto heaven.* After Satan's defeat, Moses ascended step by step to the presence of God. The steps of Moses' climb appear to symbolize ordinances and covenants. Drawing on the teachings of Joseph Smith about Jacob's vision of a ladder stretching to heaven in Genesis 28, President Marion G. Romney taught, "Jacob realized that the covenants he made with the Lord were the rungs on the ladder that he himself would have to climb in order to obtain the promised blessings—blessings that would entitle him to enter heaven and associate with the Lord" (JMBIGIL1, 351; JMBFAITH, 61–78). As one example of hints relating to ordinances in Moses 1, we read that after Moses banished Satan by calling upon the name of the Only Begotten (a motif that precedes baptism in some ancient Christian traditions [JMBIGIL, 59]), he was immediately "filled with the Holy Ghost" (Moses 1:24). Note also the explicit mention of the Father, the Son, and the Holy Ghost in close proximity, recalling the words of the baptismal prayer (Doctrine and Covenants 20:73). When Moses "lifted up his eyes unto heaven" (cf. Matthew 3:16; Mark 1:10; Luke 3:22), he was "filled with the Holy Ghost." See MOSESS 37.

1:25   *calling upon the name of God.* In his discussion of early Christian and Jewish rituals related to temple practices, John Tvedtnes discusses the prayer circle, noting that "prayer opens the veil to allow one to enjoy the presence of God" (JMBIGIL1, 59–60).

       he beheld his glory again, for it was upon him. OT1 reads "was upon him," but OT2 is significantly different: "he beheld again his glory, for it rested upon him" (SHFJST, 85, 593). Perhaps the altered wording was meant to imply that the glory now conferred on Moses was of a permanent rather than transient nature ("rested upon him" vs. "was upon him" [vv. 2, 9, 11, 14, 18])—now that he has "put on the garment of glory" (GWN1ENOCH1, 62:15–16, p. 81), even "the robe of righteousness" (2 Nephi 9:14).

       he heard a voice. Since the moment he "fell unto the earth" (v. 9), Moses could no longer speak face to face with the Lord, having been "shut out from his presence" (Moses 5:4). Now we are told that a voice speaks to Moses from beyond the heavenly veil, portending his return back into the Lord's presence (Moses 1:31). Ancient texts affirm that in preparation for entry into the holy presence, the initiate exchanged words with a divine voice at the veil, sometimes depicted visually as the welcoming hand of God that was grasped by the initiate (figure 1–5; MOSESS 37, 38).

       thou shalt be made stronger than many waters. The most obvious reference here is to the power Moses will be given to divide the Red Sea (Exodus 14:21–22; cf. Joshua 3:14–17). However, the phrase also recalls God's subduing of the waters at creation, particularly in light of the phrase that follows: "as if thou wert God." All this can be taken to mean that Moses is being promised the blessings of exaltation (See figure 3–5; MOSESS 39; JMBSTRONGER). In addition, MOSESS 43 explores how the verse also evokes the symbolism of baptism.

BOOK OF MOSES	APOCALYPSE OF ABRAHAM
1:25: "Calling upon the name of God … [God's glory] was upon him; and *he heard a voice*"	• 17:1: *"While [the angel] was still speaking*, behold, a fire was coming toward us"
• 1:27: *"as the voice was still speaking"*	• 18:1: *"While I was still reciting the song*, the edge of the fire … rose up c high"
1:30-31: "Moses called upon God … and … the glory of the Lord was upon Moses … and [he] *talked with him face to face*"	• 19:4: *"While [God] was still speaking*, the levels opened"
	• 30:1: *"While [God] was still speaking*, found myself on the earth"

Figure 1–6. *The phrase "as the voice was still speaking" in Moses 1 and similar phrases in the* Apocalypse of Abraham *seem to signal sacred speech that accompanies traversals of the veil*

AN ANCIENT WAY TO SIGNAL SACRED SPEECH AT THE VEIL?

In v. 25, Moses hears God's voice but does not yet see Him "face to face." His experience parallels that of Adam and Eve, when they also "called upon the name of the Lord" in sacred prayer. We read that "they heard the voice of the Lord from the way toward the Garden of Eden, speaking unto them, and they saw him not, for they were shut out from his presence" (5:4). The "way toward the Garden of Eden" is, of course, the path that terminates in "the way of the Tree of Life" (4:31). In the corresponding symbolism of the Garden of Eden and the temple, the Tree of Knowledge hides the Tree of Life, just as the veil hides the presence of God in His heavenly sanctuary (JMBTREE). To proceed further, the veil must be opened to the petitioner.

In both Moses 1 and the *Apocalypse of Abraham* (ApAb), multiple openings of various veils are signified explicitly, if somewhat cryptically. We observe that in Moses 1:25, a significant opening bookend begins with a description of how, after "calling upon God," the Lord's glory "was upon" Moses "and he heard a voice." In verses 30–31, the closing bookend finishes in similar fashion but states, significantly, that Moses sees God rather than just hearing Him: "Moses called upon God . . . the glory of the Lord was upon Moses so that Moses stood in the presence of God, and talked with him face to face." Sandwiched between the opening and closing bookends is a phrase that is intriguing because at first blush it seems both gratuitous and inexplicable: "as the voice was still speaking."

Surprisingly, *ApAb* repeats variants of a similar phrase (for example, "And while he [the angel] was still speaking"). Further examination of these instances revealed a commonality in each of the junctures where the phrase is used. Briefly, in each of the four instances where this phrase appears in *ApAb*—as in its single occurrence in Moses 1:27—the appearance of the phrase seems to be associated with a sacred speech at heavenly veils (AKRETRO, 17:1, p. 22; 18:1, p. 23; 19:4, p. 25; 30:1, p. 34).

In Moses 1, the phrase appears at the expected transition point in Moses' ascent. We have already argued that when he "heard a voice" in v. 25, he was still positioned outside the veil. Immediately following the phrase "as the voice was still speaking," he seems to have traversed the veil, allowing him to see every particle of the earth and its inhabitants projected on the inside of the veil. In this fashion, the veil serves in the Book of Moses as it typically does in similar accounts of heavenly ascent, namely as "a kind of 'visionary screen.'" After the vision closes, Moses stands "in the presence of God" and talks with him "face to face."

We see a similar phenomenon repeated in *ApAb*. For example, the account explicitly describes how Abraham, after his upward ascent and while the angel "was still speaking," looked down and saw a series of heavenly veils open beneath his feet, enabling his subsequent views of heavenly things (AKRETRO, 19:4, p. 25). Moreover, as Abraham traverses the heavenly veil in a downward direction as part of his return to the earth, the expression "And while he was still speaking" recurs (AKRETRO, 30:1, p. 23). Consistent with the change of glory that typically accompanies traversals of heavenly veils in such accounts, Abraham commented immediately afterward, "I found myself on the earth, and I said . . . I am no longer in the glory which I was above" (AKRETRO, 30:1, p. 23). See MOSESS 38.

command as if thou wert God. ²⁶ And lo, I am with thee, even unto the end of thy days; for thou shalt deliver my people from bondage, even Israel my chosen."

MOSES' VISION AT THE HEAVENLY VEIL

²⁷ And it came to pass, as the voice was still speaking, Moses cast his eyes and beheld the earth, yea, even all of it; and there was not a particle of it which he did not behold, discerning it by the spirit of God. ²⁸ And he beheld also the inhabitants thereof, and there was not a soul which he beheld not; and he discerned them by the Spirit of God; and their numbers were great, even numberless as the sand upon the sea shore. ²⁹ And he beheld many lands; and each land was called earth, and there were inhabitants on the face thereof.

MOSES IN GOD'S PRESENCE

³⁰ And it came to pass that Moses called upon God, saying: "Tell me, I pray thee, why these things are so, and by what thou madest them?" ³¹ And behold, the glory of the Lord was upon Moses, so that Moses stood in the presence of God, and talked with him face to face. And the Lord God said unto Moses: "For mine own

---

1:25   ***as if thou wert God.*** The current text is consistent with OT1. OT2 replaces these words with "even as my commandments" (SHFJST, 85, 593).

1:27   ***as the voice was still speaking.*** Remarkably, the *Apocalypse of Abraham* repeats variants of a similar phrase four times. In each of the four instances in *ApAb*—as in its single mention in Moses 1:27—the appearance of the phrase seems to be associated with sacred speech at the opening of a heavenly veil (figure 1-6; MOSESS 38).

   Moses cast his eyes and beheld the earth. Previously, as Moses stood on the earth, he had "lifted up his eyes unto heaven" (v. 24). Now, after ascending to heaven, he casts his eyes down to see the earth and all its inhabitants (vv. 27–28). He witnesses its entire history from beginning to end like Adam, Enoch, the brother of Jared, John the Beloved, and others. Jewish traditions about similar experiences relate that such visions allow the prophet to see a "blueprint" of eternity that has been worked out before the Creation. It is said that this blueprint can only be viewed from heaven, since it is depicted on the inner side of the heavenly veil. See MOSESS 40.

   even all of it. OT1 and OT2 read "even all the face of it" (SHFJST, 85, 593).

1:29   ***each land was called earth.*** Taken in the context of vv. 30–38, these words seem to imply that Moses saw many peopled planets, each one of which was called earth by its inhabitants. Alternatively, his view of "many lands" could be simply a part of "an account of this earth" (v. 35), to which his vision was originally to be limited.

1:30   ***Tell me . . . why . . . and by what.*** OT2 was changed to read "shew me" (SHFJST, 594), emphasizing the visual nature of Moses' experience. Consistent with the current text, OT1 reads "by what," while OT2 reads "by whom" (SHFJST, 85, 594).

1:31   ***the glory of the Lord.*** OT1 and OT2 read "the glory of God" (SHFJST, 85, 594)—perhaps implying that Moses now stands in the presence of the Father rather than the Son.

   the Lord God said unto Moses. Speaking face to face, God now replies to the questions Moses raised in v. 30. Though God says here that He will not reveal the answer to Moses' first question ("why these things are so"), later He does give a limited explanation (v. 39). His answer to Moses' second question ("by what") is summarized in v. 32 and elaborated in the account of the Creation in Moses 2–3. See MOSESS 41.

Figure 1–7. *Abraham and Yahoel see the Lord face to face*, illustrations from the *Apocalypse of Abraham*. Left: Image from the *Sylvester Codex*; Right: Image from Facsimile Edition. Photographs by Stephen T. Whitlock

SEEING THE LORD FACE TO FACE

Adding inestimably to the value of the text itself is the singular series of six beautiful color illustrations within the *Codex Sylvester*, "the oldest and the only independent manuscript containing the full text of *ApAb*" (AKRETRO, 3). The images shed light on how medieval Christians in the East understood the text. In at least one case, it is clear that these Christians interpreted these stories differently than did the first- or second-century redactor.

Contradicting the text of *ApAb* where Yahoel declared to Abraham that "the Eternal One . . . himself you will not see," the 14th-century Christian illustrator of the *Codex Sylvester* seems to have had no qualms about representing God visually. Commenting on these sorts of contradictions, Margaret Barker observed (MBCHRISTMAS, 14–15):

> To see the glory of the Lord's presence — to see beyond the veil — was the greatest blessing. The high priest used to bless Israel with the words: "The Lord bless you and keep you: The Lord make his face to shine upon you, and be gracious unto you: The Lord lift up his countenance upon you, and give you peace" (Numbers 6:24–26). . . . Seeing the glory, however, became controversial. Nobody knows why. There is one strand in the Old Testament that is absolutely opposed to any idea of seeing the divine. . . . [On the other hand,] Jesus said: "Blessed are the pure in heart, for they shall see God" (Matthew 5:8); and John saw "one seated on the throne" (Revelation 4:2). There can be no doubt where the early Christians stood on this matter.

In the illustration above Abraham and Yahoel are "traveling . . . about the air" with "no ground [beneath] to which [Abraham] could fall prostrate." The individual pictured on the throne seems to be Christ. His identity is indicated by the cruciform markings on His nimbus. Behind the enthroned Christ is a second personage, perhaps alluding to the statement in *ApAb* that "Michael is with me [that is, the Lord] in order to bless you forever" (AKRETRO, 10:17, p. 18). Beneath the throne are fiery seraphim and many-eyed "wheels" praising God. The throne is surrounded by a series of heavenly veils separating the Lord from the material world—the latter being signified by the outermost dark blue veil. The representation of the veils as multicolored may stem from an interpretation of Ezekiel 1:28, where the glory of the Lord is likened to a rainbow. In the depiction shown here, the illustrator has deliberately chosen to use the colors of red, green, and blue. See MOSESS 41; JMBTWIN, 804, 834–835.

purpose have I made these things. Here is wisdom and it remaineth in me. ³² And by the word of my power, have I created them, which is mine Only Begotten Son, who is full of grace and truth. ³³ And worlds without number have I created; and I also created them for mine own purpose; and by the Son I created them, which is mine Only Begotten. ³⁴ And the first man of all men have I called Adam, which is many. ³⁵ But only an account of this earth, and the inhabitants thereof, give I unto you. For behold, there are many worlds that have passed away by the word of my power. And there are many that now stand, and innumerable are they unto man; but all things are numbered unto me, for they are mine and I know them."

1:31   *Here is wisdom and it remaineth in me.* The Book of Moses phrase "it remaineth in me" subtly echoes scripture passages that depict God and wisdom as inseparably associated since before the creation of the earth (e.g., Proverbs 8:12, 22–30). This exclusive relationship makes the mysteries of true wisdom inaccessible to man except as made known through God Himself (Job 28; 1 Corinthians 2:7–10; Alma 12:9–11; Doctrine and Covenants 76:7, 10; 84:19; 107:18–19). The Book of Mormon uses a similar phrase to describe how God's hidden intentions—in this case, the preservation of Nephite records—are "wise purpose[s] in him"—things that can be known only by revelation (1 Nephi 9:5).

1:33   *worlds without number.* E. Douglas Clark cites a passage in the *Zohar* that tells of "'a hidden region, so transcendent that it passes all understanding, the very source whence the worlds were designed and came into being.' . . . So also, according to the Syriac *Apocalypse of Baruch*, Moses was shown 'the worlds which have not yet come'" (EDCPROLOGUE, 139). See also MOSESS 48.

    by the Son I created them. OT1 and OT2 read "by the same" (SHFJST, 85, 594). That the worlds were not only created by the Son but also redeemed by Him is made clear by the Prophet's poetic paraphrase of Doctrine and Covenants 76:23–24:

> And I heard a great voice, bearing record from heav'n,
> "He's the Savior, and only begotten of God—
> By him, of him, and through him, the worlds were all made,
> Even all that career in the heavens so broad,
>
> Whose inhabitants, too, from the first to the last,
> Are sav'd by the very same Savior of ours;
> And, of course, are begotten God's daughters and sons,
> By the very same truths, and the very same pow'rs." (JMBIGIL1, 66)

1:34   *Adam, which is many.* Draper, Brown, and Rhodes conclude that the phrase "which is many" could mean one of three things: (1) that Adam is the first man of all men among all the worlds God has created; (2) that Adam is the name given to the first man on each of the many worlds God has created; or (3) that there are many descendants of Adam on this earth (RDDPGP, 33).

    In Abraham 1:3, the word Adam is associated with the idea of Adam being a "first father." Note that Eve is similarly referred to in Moses 4:26 as the "first of all women" and that Nephi refers to Adam and Eve as our "first parents" (1 Nephi 5:11). President Brigham Young taught, "Every world has an Adam, and an Eve: named so, simply because the first man is always called Adam, and the first woman Eve." By implication, Phillip B. Munoa connects "the motif of . . . being the first" with that of being "the oldest"—hence, the use of "'Ancient of Days' as a title for Adam" (JMBIGIL1, 66–67).

1:35   *innumerable are they unto man.* OT1 and OT2 read "numberless" (SHFJST, 85, 594). President Brigham Young said: "How many earths are there? . . . You may take the particles of matter composing this earth, and if they could be enumerated they would only be a beginning to the number of the creations of God; and they are continually coming into existence, and undergoing changes and passing through the same experience that we are passing through" (JD, 14:71).

³⁶ And it came to pass that Moses spake unto the Lord, saying: "Be merciful unto thy servant, O God, and tell me concerning this earth, and the inhabitants thereof, and also the heavens, and then thy servant will be content." ³⁷ And the Lord God spake unto Moses, saying: "The heavens, they are many, and they cannot be numbered unto man; but they are numbered unto me, for they are mine. ³⁸ And as one earth shall pass away, and the heavens thereof even so shall another come; and there is no end to my works, neither to my words. ³⁹ For behold, this is my work and my glory—to bring to pass the immortality and eternal life of man."

Epilogue

⁴⁰ "And now, Moses, my son, I will speak unto thee concerning this earth upon which thou standest; and thou shalt write the things which I shall speak. ⁴¹ And in a day when the children of men shall esteem my words as naught and take many of them from the book which thou shalt write, behold, I will raise up another like

1:38 ***there is no end to my works, neither to my words.*** God's endless works and words are inseparably linked (JMBIGIL1, 67–68). Writes Matthew L. Bowen: "The Book of Moses' view of the creative 'Word' (v. 32) parallels its view of the written 'words' of God with its implicit notion of a 'canon': 'There is no end to my works, neither to my words.' There is no end to creation. There is no end to scripture or revelation—the revealed word. *The universe is an open canon.*" (MLBBY, 745; MOSESS 48).

1:39 ***this is my work and my glory—to bring to pass the immortality and eternal life of man.*** OT1 reads more briefly, "This is my work to my glory to the immortality and the eternal life of man" (SHFJST, 85). Of the significance of this verse, the most frequently cited in the Pearl of Great Price, Kathleen Flake writes: "With this reply, [Joseph] Smith rejected 1,500 years of Christian theological anthropology by making God ontologically related to creation. God is both defined as Father and glorified as God by the capacity and purpose to engender the divine life in humans. To Smith, 'Father God' is not only a metaphor for expressing divine love, but is definitive of God and indicative of human possibility, even human capacity to receive the divine nature" (JMBIGIL1, 68).

Elder Bruce R. McConkie taught: "Immortality is to live forever in the resurrected state with body and spirit inseparably connected" (JMBIGIL1, 68). This is a blessing that will be given to each of God's children (1 Corinthians 15:22). On the other hand, according to President Spencer W. Kimball, eternal life "is to gain exaltation in the highest heaven," which means, according to President Joseph Fielding Smith, having "the kind of life that God has" (JMBIGIL1, 68).

1:40 ***this earth upon which thou standest; and thou shalt write.*** As this verse makes clear, Moses authored an original version of the Creation account by specific assignment, perhaps similar to—but certainly not identical with—what we have in Moses 2. E. Douglas Clark discusses similar instructions given to Moses in the Jewish *Book of Jubilees* (EDCPROLOGUE).

As a possible witness to a textual link between Moses 1 and 2, Mark J. Johnson sees a small chiasm stretching from Moses 1:40 through Moses 2:1 pivoting around the prophecy of another one like Moses being raised up, with v. 42 being treated as parenthetical (MOSESS 45).

1:41 ***take many of them from the book which thou shalt write.*** Compare Moses 1:23; 1 Nephi 13:4, 24–28. In this connection, note that the overwhelming bulk of JST Genesis revisions consist of additions rather than omissions of material. A specific example of material presumably removed from a later chapter of Genesis is the prophecy of Joseph recorded in JST Genesis 50:24–37 (SHFJST, OT2 pp. 64–65, pp. 681, 683, 685) and 2 Nephi 3:5–22.

I will raise up another like unto thee; and they shall be had again among the children of men.

unto thee; and they shall be had again among the children of men—among as many as shall believe." ⁴² (These words were spoken unto Moses in the mount, the name of which shall not be known among the children of men. And now they are spoken unto you. Show them not unto any except them that believe. Even so. Amen.)

Compare *2 Enoch*: "And . . . another generation will arise, the last of many. . . . And I shall raise up for that generation someone who will reveal to them the books in your handwriting and those of your fathers. And he will have to point out to . . . truthful men, and those who carry out my will" (FIA2ENOCH, 35:1–2, p. 158; see also Luke 2:14). Moses uses similar words in his prophecy of the coming of the Savior (Deuteronomy 18:15). However, the current passage seems also to refer to Joseph Smith, who is specifically compared to Moses in other scriptures (2 Nephi 3:9; Doctrine and Covenants 28:2; 103:16; 107:91).

1:42   ***These words were spoken unto Moses.*** Matthew L. Bowen notes that v. 1 begins similarly ("The words of God, which he spake unto Moses"), these two bookends thus forming an *inclusio* similar to Deuteronomy 1:1. "The Lord's earlier statements that his 'words' have 'no end' and 'never cease' become the basis for his promise that 'they shall be had again' [v. 41]—that is, re-added. By implication, human efforts 'to take many of them' away from 'the book which [Moses would] write' and from future repositories of divine words (see, for example, 1 Nephi 13:26–29) or to otherwise limit them through a closed 'canon' will ultimately fail (Moses 1:41)" (MLBBY, 739; MOSESS 42).

Show them not unto any except them that believe. *Fourth Ezra* records that the Lord commanded Moses to openly reveal only part of his visions on Mt. Sinai; the rest were to be kept secret. Similarly, Ezra is reported to have been told that certain books were to be read by the "worthy and unworthy," whereas others were to be given only "to the wise" (BMM4EZRA, 14:6, 45–47, pp. 553, 555).

The current text follows OT1, except that the archaic "shew" has been changed to "show" (SHFJST, 86). In OT2, a slightly different phrase is crossed out: "And now they are also spoken unto you. Shew them not unto any except them that believe until I command you. Amen." The phrase "Even so" is omitted in OT2, so the chapter ends with the phrase "children of men" (SHFJST, 595).

CHAPTER 2
THE CREATION

PROLOGUE

2 ^{1} And it came to pass that the Lord spake unto Moses, saying: Behold, I reveal unto you concerning this heaven, and this earth; write the words which I speak. I am the Beginning and the End, the Almighty God; by mine Only Begotten I created these things;

2 While it is true that significant doctrinally related details in Genesis were clarified in the translation of Moses 2, it is perhaps more noteworthy that the effort did not result in a wholesale reshaping of the Creation story. However, to correctly understand the implications of the Creation account for the subsequent story of the Fall, it should be observed that the descriptions of the days of creation in Genesis and the Book of Moses differ from those found in the Book of Abraham and in modern temples. Specifically, in contrast to the latter two accounts, the narratives in Genesis and the Book of Moses seem to have been deliberately shaped to highlight resemblances between the creation of the universe, the layout and furnishings of Eden, and the architecture of the tabernacle (see figures 2–1; 3–2). Understanding these parallels helps explain why, for example, in seeming contradiction to scientific understanding, the description of the creation of the sun and moon appears *after*, rather than before, the creation of light and of the earth. In Genesis and the Book of Moses, conveying the spiritual truths of how heavenly realities are symbolically reflected in earthly temples takes precedence over the scientific truths of how the Creation unfolded in physical processes over long time periods (MOSESS 46). As we will see in chapters 3 and 4, an understanding of temple symbolism in Eden will also help explain the movements and actions of Adam and Eve in the story of the Fall (MOSESS 55, 61–65; JMBTREE, JMBMORM).

2:1 *I reveal unto you concerning this heaven, and this earth.* These words are meant to tell us that the creation account given to Moses is not all-encompassing in scope. Hugh Nibley notes that the KJV plural "heavens" is changed to the singular "heaven" in Moses 2:1, 8, possibly "because every earth has its heaven" (JMBIGIL1, 93).

I am the Beginning. BYU professor David Rolph Seely has aptly highlighted the importance of paying attention to what is said at the beginning and ending of scripture books, including the Book of Moses (DRSBOOK, 608–612). For example, the Gospel of John begins its exposition of the opening verses of Genesis with a bold Christ-centric assertion "In the beginning was the Word" [referring to Jesus Christ] (John 1:1), while the alternative gloss of Genesis 1:1 provided by Jewish midrash is book-centric: "By means of 'the beginning' [that is to say, the Torah] did God create." The Book of Moses adds its unique voice to the long history of interpretation of Genesis 1:1, taking the term "Beginning" to refer to the Father ("I *am* the Beginning"), who created all things by His Only Begotten, the living and personal "Word of [His] power" (SHFJST, 86).

by mine Only Begotten I created these things. In contrast to Genesis, the statement in Moses explicitly highlights the central role of the Son in Creation (Moses 1:32–33; Hebrews 1:2). The Book of Abraham goes even further to describe a *plurality* of Gods who participated in Creation (Abraham 4:1ff.). These included Michael (the premortal Adam), as well as others. President Brigham Young said that "the earth was organized by three distinct characters, namely, Elohim, [Je]hovah, and Michael, these three forming a quorum, as in all heavenly bodies, and in organizing element" (JD, 1:51).

Basing his remarks on an emendation of the Hebrew, Joseph Smith offered the following translation of the first verse of Genesis: "In the beginning, the head of the Gods called a council of the Gods; and they came together and concocted a plan to create the world and people it" (JSTPJS, 7 April 1844, 349). Two months later, he varied the wording: "'In the beginning the head of the Gods brought forth the Gods,' or as others have translated it, 'The head of the Gods called

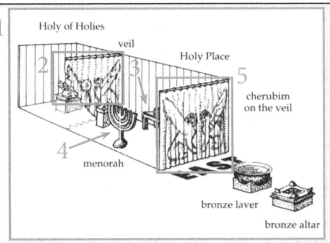

Figure 2–1. Michael P. Lyon, (1952–): *The Days of Creation and the Temple*, 1994

THE DAYS OF CREATION AND TEMPLE ARCHITECTURE

Some scholars have argued that the results of each day of Creation are symbolically reflected in temple furnishings (MOSESS 46). For example, the light of day one of Creation might be understood as the glory of God and of those who dwelled with Him in the celestial world before their mortal birth (MOSESS 47). According to this logic, the temple veil that divided the temple Holy of Holies from the Holy Place would symbolize the "firmament" that was created to separate the heavens from the earth in its original terrestrial state. According to Genesis scholar Nahum Sarna, "The verbal form [of the Hebrew term] is often used for hammering out metal or flattening out earth, which suggests a basic meaning of 'extending'" (MOSESS 46). This could well apply to the spreading out of a curtain or veil, consistent with the imagery in Moses 7:30.

The following reconstruction of ancient Jewish sources by Louis Ginzberg is consistent with this overall idea, as well as with the suggestion of several scholars that a narrative of the Creation story something like Genesis 1 may have been used within temple ceremonies in ancient Israel:

> God told the angels: [1] On the first day of creation, I shall make the heavens and stretch them out; so will Israel raise up the tabernacle as the dwelling place of my Glory. [2] On the second day I shall put a division between the terrestrial waters and the heavenly waters, so will [Moses] hang up a veil in the tabernacle to divide the Holy Place and the Most Holy. [3] On the third day I shall make the earth to put forth grass and herbs; so will he, in obedience to my commands, . . . prepare shewbread before me. [4] On the fourth day I shall make the luminaries; so he will stretch out a golden candlestick [*menorah*] before me. [5] On the fifth day I shall create the birds; so he will fashion the cherubim with outstretched wings. [6] On the sixth day I shall create man; so will Israel set aside a man from the sons of Aaron as high priest for my service. (JMBIGIL1, 148)

From this perspective, when God finished the Creation, what came of it was an earthly temple that was laid out and furnished in symbolic likeness to the heavenly temple. That earthly temple, the result of Creation, was none other than "Eden." Its Holies of Holies was the celestial top of the figurative mountain of God, and its Holy Place was a Garden of terrestrial glory located on its eastern slope (see figure 3–2).

Carrying this idea forward to a later time, Exodus 40:33 describes how Moses completed the tabernacle. The Hebrew text exactly parallels the account of how God finished the Creation. *Genesis Rabbah* comments on the significance of this parallel: "It is as if, on that day [i.e., the day the tabernacle was raised in the wilderness], I actually created the world." With this idea in mind, Hugh Nibley famously called the temple "a scale-model of the universe," a place for taking bearings on the cosmos and finding one's place within it.

The idea that Creation provides a model for earthly temple building and ritual is found throughout the ancient Near East. For example, Nibley read the Mesopotamian creation story, *Enuma Elish,* as the story of the founding of a sanctuary for the god (JMBMARI, 12; HWNPGP, 122). The language of *Enuma Elish* directly parallels Moses 3:5, thus making it clear that this much disputed verse on "spiritual creation" is meant to convey that Eden was laid out as a temple (see figure 3–2). More generally, see MOSESS 46.

Yea, in the beginning I created the heaven, and the earth upon which thou standest. ² And the earth was without form, and void; and I caused darkness to come up upon the face of the deep; and my Spirit moved upon the face of the water; for I am God.

2:1   the Gods together'" (JSTPJS, 16 June 1844, 371). Latter-day Saint scholar Kevin Barney argues that the Hebrew behind "the head [one] of the Gods" could be equated to the term "God Most High" (*El Elyon*), the God Melchizedek was said to have worshipped. Compare Hugh Nibley's translation of John 1:1: "In the ruling council was a spokesman and the spokesman was in the godhead, that is among the gods, and the spokesman was himself a god" (JMBIGIL1, 93–94).

I created the heaven, and the earth. Whereas Latter-day Saint idea of God organizing the world from preexisting matter was a part of many ancient cosmologies, later Jewish scholars articulated an alternative doctrine of *creatio ex nihilo* (i.e., creation from nothing). *Ex nihilo* Creation eventually became the prevalent interpretation in Christianity. By way of contrast, Joseph Smith stated that the word "created" should be rendered "formed, or organized." He said this is because the term "does not mean to create out of nothing; it means to organize—the same as a man would organize materials and build a ship. Hence we infer that God had materials to organize the world out of . . . chaotic matter" (JSTPJS 7 April 1844, 350–51). Kevin Barney, among others, concludes that historical and scientific evidence strongly favor "Joseph Smith's rejection of *creatio ex nihilo*" (JMBIGIL1, 94–95).

2:2   *without form, and void.* The Hebrew terms *tohu* and *bohu.* are not nouns "indicating the chaos that *precedes* the creation" but rather adjectives describing the dreary sameness that "abides *after*" creation, but before God's Spirit has begun to move upon it (MBHOW, 206). Thus, the Book of Abraham's "empty and desolate" (Abraham 4:2) is a fitting translation.

I caused darkness to come up upon the face of the deep. Genesis says that "darkness *was* upon . . . the deep" (Genesis 1:2; emphasis added). What it means for darkness to *come up* upon the deep is not obvious. One might imagine darkness as representing the cloud that cloaks the Lord when He comes down into the world (as we see frequently in Exodus). In this instance, the purpose of His coming would be to create the world. Alternatively, the coming of darkness could mean that God allowed His presence to be *withdrawn* for a time, bringing darkness (disorder, disorganization) upon the deep, as a precursor to the subsequent moving of His Spirit upon the waters and the appearance of light (order, organization). See JMBIGIL1, 96–97.

my Spirit moved upon the face of the water. The Hebrew term translated here as "moved" is used in Deuteronomy 32:11 to describe an eagle "fluttering" attentively over its young. In a context consistent with the picture in Moses 2:2, Abraham 4:2 employs the term "brooding." The imagery of "brooding" not only highlights the loving care of the Creator but may also allude to atonement symbolism. Atonement is arguably the central symbolism of Israelite temples, and it may be reflected not only in the symbolism of day one of the Creation but also in the overall schema for the unfolding of the universe. While the Creation story opens with the themes of distinction and separation, God's work in the final dispensation will culminate when He "gather[s] in one all things in Christ, both which are in heaven, and which are on earth; even in him" (Ephesians 1:10) (MOSESS 46).

my Spirit. The Hebrew term for "Spirit" (*ruach*) has the root meanings of "wind" or "breath." This recalls the role of wind as the agent by which water is separated in two other places in the Bible—at the conclusion of the Flood and at the crossing of the Red Sea. In a poetic sense, the Spirit is the light-bearing, life-giving breath of God, dispersing the darkness of the deep.

water. While OT2 and our current edition of the Book of Moses use the singular "water," Genesis, OT1, and Abraham 4:2 use the plural "waters" (SHFJST, 86, 595). The term "water" in its singular form has been equated by some commentators with unorganized matter—the unexplained unity that existed before the creation process of demarcation, distinction, separation, and naming. Summarizing the opinion of Jewish sages, Meir Zlotowitz writes: "The 'water' mentioned in this verse [Genesis 1:2] is not the water that is in the 'seas.' It is clear that there was a certain

Figure 2–2. Michelangelo Buonarroti (1475–1564): *The Creation of the Sun and the Moon*, 1511

"It Was Done as I Spake"

Distinction and separation are the central themes of the Creation account: "And I, God, said: Let there be lights in the firmament of the heaven, to *divide* the day from the night" (Moses 2:14, emphasis added). In Michelangelo's masterful depiction, God dramatically extends his arms in opposite directions, majestically assigning the golden ball of the sun to rule the day and the gray moon to rule the night. To achieve a "special otherworldly effect," the moon was "painted without paint"—in other words, it is the actual color of the bare plaster surface beneath the fresco itself (Benjamin Blech et al., MOSESS 48).

Although from a Latter-day Saint perspective it is hard to imagine a more "traditional" depiction of the Creation, Michelangelo's portrait is thoroughly unacceptable to rabbinic Judaism. For one thing, Richard S. Ellis observes, the anthropomorphic portrayal violates both the second commandment and the idea that God is "unknowable, unimaginable" and "visually unportrayable." Additionally, God is shown as effecting creation through action rather than by the sole means of "potent speech-acts that enact the creative power of language." Thus, Ellis explains, Michelangelo's God is both inexplicably busy and "un-Jewishly mute." "For the Jew," writes Susan Handelman, "God's presence is inscribed or traced within a text, not a body. Divinity is located in language, not person" (MOSESS 48; JMBIGIL1, 82).

Significantly, the term "ordered" is used in place of "spake" in the Book of Abraham—possibly to avoid the assertion that the Creation was accomplished solely by God's speech (Abraham 4:7, 9, 11). Instead, the Book of Abraham phrase could be seen as expressing the idea that all of the resultant creation was accomplished in perfect conformance to His will.

THE FIRST DAY: CREATION OF LIGHT

³ And I, God, said: "Let there be light"; and there was light. ⁴ And I, God, saw the light; and that light was good. And I, God, divided the light from the darkness. ⁵ And I, God, called the light Day; and the darkness, I called Night; and this I did by

2:2   common matter which was called 'water.' Afterwards, it was divided into three forms; a part of it became 'seas,' another part of it became 'firmament'; a third part became that which is above the 'firmament'—entirely beyond the earth. Perhaps this is why . . . water is invariably in the plural form—suggestive of this pluralistic division" (MZBEREISHIS, 1:38). Although no explicit blessing of the waters is mentioned in Moses' account, Doctrine and Covenants 61:14 records, "Behold, I, the Lord, in the beginning blessed the waters; but in the last days, by the mouth of my servant John, I cursed the waters." The mention of John's cursing may have reference to the events of Revelation 8:8–11 and Revelation 13.

2:3   *Let there be light.* God's words, heralding the coming of light, constitute His first creative act.

     there was light. The nature of the light referred to in this verse is not explained. Several possibilities have been suggested. Some understand this phrase as describing the birth of our universe as a sudden burst of light and energy of unimaginable scale. Others see it as referring to a "local" event whereby the natural light of the sun was created. It is, of course, a given that the sun was created before the fourth day, though from the vantage point of the earth, no light will appear "in the firmament" until that later time (2:14–19). Perhaps a better interpretation is to see this light as something over and above mere physical light, as described in Doctrine and Covenants 88:4–13. The idea of God Himself as the source of this special light is consistent with many ancient sources. President John Taylor wrote that God "caused light to shine upon [the earth] before the sun appeared in the firmament; for God is light, and in him there is no darkness." Some ancient sources see this light as also including the angels or premortal spirits of humankind (JMBIGIL1, 99–100). For more on the events of day one, see MOSESS 47.

2:4   *that light was good.* Light makes it possible to discern differences, and, in turn, to discern differences brings light. The books of Genesis, Moses, and Abraham describe the creation of light as an event involving perception, evaluation, and understanding, not merely passive visual examination: "that it [the light] was good" (Genesis 1:4); "that light was good" (Moses 2:4); and "they . . . comprehended the light, for it was bright" (Abraham 4:4).

     I, God, divided. The process of Creation involves the making and naming of distinctions. In the beginning, all is unorganized matter; later God divides the light from the darkness, the water above from that below the firmament, and the dry land from the sea. He then differentiates among the different species of plants and animals "after their kind" (Abraham 4:21), between humans and the animal kingdom, between man and woman, and finally between the seventh day and the other six days of Creation.

     the light from the darkness. If the light mentioned previously includes the glory and presence of God and the spirits of all people, what does it mean to say that this light was divided from the darkness? Assuming that the events of the first day of Creation took place in the spirit world, it is possible to see allusions in some ancient sources as applying to the premortal separation of the spirits who rebelled ("the darkness") and were cast out of the presence of God ("the light"). See Moses 4:3–4; JMBIGIL1, 102; MOSESS 47.

2:5   *I, God, called the light Day.* God's absolute sovereignty over His creations is shown through His naming of Day and Night, the firmament, the sea, and the earth. In similar fashion, having been granted dominion by God, humanity's sovereignty over all other creatures will be affirmed when Adam is assigned the task of naming the animals (3:19–20).

     Night. The phenomenon of darkness at nightfall is not a given everywhere in our galaxy. According to Stephen Hawking, the fact that the sky is dark at night in our part of the galaxy tells us that the beginning of the universe was recent enough that "the light from very distant stars has not had time to reach us yet. That [explains] why the sky at night isn't glowing in every direction" (JMBIGIL1, 102–3).

the word of my power, and it was done as I spake; and the evening and the morning were the first day.

THE SECOND DAY: CREATION OF THE FIRMAMENT

⁶ And again, I, God, said: "Let there be a firmament in the midst of the water," and it was so, even as I spake; and I said: "Let it divide the waters from the waters"; and it was done; ⁷ and I, God, made the firmament and divided the waters, yea, the great waters under the firmament from the waters which were above the firmament, and it was so even as I spake. ⁸ And I, God, called the firmament Heaven; and the evening and the morning were the second day.

THE THIRD DAY: CREATION OF DRY LAND AND VEGETATION

⁹ And I, God, said: "Let the waters under the heaven be gathered together unto one place," and it was so; and I, God, said: "Let there be dry land"; and it was so. ¹⁰ And I, God, called the dry land Earth; and the gathering together of the waters, called I

2:5   ***this I did by the word of my power.*** See MOSESS 48. A clue to interpreting this passage can be found in JST John 1:1–19, which invokes the language of Genesis to affirm that the Son, by whom "all things were made," is "the true light, which lighteth every man who cometh into the world" (compare Doctrine and Covenants 88:12–13). Moses 1:32 equates "the word of my power" with "mine Only Begotten Son," a reading strengthened by the fact that "Word" is capitalized in OT1 (SHFJST, 86).

   evening and the morning were the first day. A first notion of "time" appears only after the primeval unity was first divided. Note that evening and morning signify, respectively, not the earth's daily sunset and sunrise, but rather the suspension and resumption of distinct "times" of divine creativity, corresponding to groups of works performed. Thus, as recent Church leaders have affirmed, we are not limited to supposing that the Creation was accomplished in six solar days or six thousand years but rather can view the "week" of Creation as part of seemingly overlapping periods of potentially long and varying length. Note that the Hebrew term for day, *yom*, can also be used for a period of indeterminate length, as in expressions like "the day of the Lord" (Isaiah 2:12) (JMBIGIL1, 103).

2:6   ***Let there be a firmament.*** From the point of view of the Creation, this verse, according to Elder Bruce R. McConkie, describes how the waters were "'divided' between the surface of the earth and the atmospheric heavens that surround it" (JMBIGIL1, 104). Figuratively, however, it alludes to the veil that divided off the Holy of Holies in the temple.

2:9   ***Let there be dry land.*** Creation in ancient cultures begin with the appearance of a "primeval hill"—the first landmass rising out of the receding waters. In ancient Israel, the holiest spot on earth was the Foundation Stone in front of the ark of the covenant within the temple at Jerusalem. According to John M. Lundquist, Jewish tradition affirmed that the stone "was the first solid material to emerge from the waters of Creation (Psalm 104:7–9), and it was upon this stone that the Deity effected Creation." This why temples in many ancient cultures are built on a high elevation, consistent with the idea that the temple—like Eden—is a sacred mountain (JMBIGIL1, 105).

2:10   ***I, God, saw that all things which I had made were good.*** In Abraham 4, God's evaluative appraisals of the goodness of His work in Genesis are replaced by repeated variations of a phrase that describes the unbroken thread of perfect obedience running through the entire process of Creation: "And the Gods saw that they were obeyed," a theme that is paralleled in Jewish midrash (vv. 10, 12). This theme appears in the account of the creation of the earth and the waters, the plants, the lights in the heavens, and the animals. With respect to the rule of obedience that governs the universe, people are the sole, sad exception (Helaman 12:4–26; Jeremiah 5:22–24).

the Sea; and I, God, saw that all things which I had made were good.

¹¹ And I, God, said: "Let the earth bring forth grass, the herb yielding seed, the fruit tree yielding fruit, after his kind, and the tree yielding fruit, whose seed should be in itself upon the earth," and it was so even as I spake. ¹² And the earth brought forth grass, every herb yielding seed after his kind, and the tree yielding fruit, whose seed should be in itself, after his kind; and I, God, saw that all things which I had made were good; ¹³ and the evening and the morning were the third day.

THE FOURTH DAY: CREATION OF THE SUN AND MOON

¹⁴ And I, God, said: "Let there be lights in the firmament of the heaven, to divide the day from the night, and let them be for signs, and for seasons, and for days, and for

2:11   *Let the earth bring forth grass.* In Jewish tradition, the grass corresponds to the temple symbolism of the shewbread. Nibley notes that the corresponding phrase in Abraham—"Let us prepare the earth to bring forth grass" (Abraham 4:11)—makes it clear that "what they ordered was not the completed product, but the process to bring it about, providing a scheme under which life might expand. . . . Note the future tense: the [earth is] so treated that [it] will have the capacity. The Gods did not make [grass] on the spot but arranged it so that in time they might appear. They created the potential" (HWNBEFADAM, 70).

     after his kind. President Boyd K. Packer wrote: "No lesson is more manifest in nature than that all living things do as the Lord commanded in the Creation. They reproduce 'after their own kind.' They follow the pattern of their parentage" (JMBIGIL1, 107) The Prophet Joseph Smith said that it is a "fixed and unalterable . . . decree of the Lord that every tree, fruit, or herb bearing seed should bring forth after its kind, and cannot come forth after any other law or principle." (JSWORDS, 20 March 1842, 107).

     While the laws of genetics assure the usual, orderly pattern of parentage, the same laws also allow for adaptation over time. Although the official position of the Church on man's origin is not definitive in all respects, the first formal class in evolution was instituted at Brigham Young University in the fall of 1971 with the First Presidency's approval, and it is currently a required part of the core curriculum for all BYU students in the biological sciences. According to Latter-day Saint scholar Michael R. Ash, evolutionary biology has become "one of the largest and most successful graduate programs at BYU," with professors publishing in major evolutionary conferences and journals. Neither the idea of "Creationism" nor the theory of "Intelligent Design" is taught at BYU. For Church statements on evolution, see DHBCOSMOS, 445–484.

2:14   *Let there be lights in the firmament of the heaven.* Unlike the Genesis and Moses accounts, which describe the appearance of plant life before the sun and moon lighted the earth (consistent with Israelite temple symbolism—see figure 2–1), the Creation sequence presented in the temple endowment follows a different ordering and division of events. Joseph Smith's teachings support the fact that these heavenly lights were created *before* the earth: "The starry hosts were worlds and suns and universes, some of which had being millions of ages before this earth had physical form." Hence, it is clear that vv. 14–15 do not describe the creation of the sun, moon, and stars, but rather the appearance of the sun after the dust and debris had been moved from the atmosphere (JMBIGIL1, 107).

2:14   *to divide the day from the night.* Nibley explains, "Such a division had already taken place at the beginning, but this was a new time-system for this earth" (HWNBEFADAM, 74).

     let them be for signs, and for seasons, and for days, and for years. "A 'sign' is a symbol, a mark, an arbitrary indicator, a means of measuring. It is only a sign relative to a particular observer. These lights were not originally created as markers of time, but [now that they were visible to the earth] they could be used as such, they could be 'organized for' such" (HWNBEFADAM, 74). The word "seasons" is probably meant to include the functions of the sun and moon within the calendar of religious festivals.

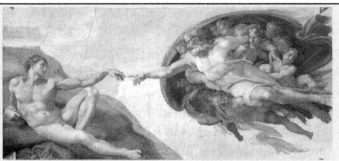

Figure 2–3a. Michelangelo Buonarroti (1475–1564): *The Creation of Adam*, 1510

SYMBOLISM IN MICHELANGELO'S CREATION OF ADAM

Of Michelangelo's immortal depiction, Pierluigi De Vecchi and Gianluigi Colalucci eloquently write:

> Perhaps the best-known of the scenes in the Sistine Chapel, *The Creation of Adam* must also have aroused particular admiration among the artist's contemporaries, who discerned in it the materialization of one of the highest ideals of Renaissance culture: the "dignity" of man, created by God "in his own image." . . . [The] exaltation of the spiritual faculties of man was never separated from that of the beauty of the human body, 'the mirror of God' and the culmination of the Creation. . . .
>
> [Giorgio] Vasari describes Adam as "a figure whose beauty, pose, and contours are of such a quality that he seems newly created by his Supreme and First Creator rather [than] by the brush and design of a mere mortal." Seen against an indistinct natural background that is only just hinted at, as if it were the dawn of the world, the youthful, athletic figure reclining on a grassy slope, almost on the edge of an abyss, seems as if he is about to rise from the ground. He holds out his arm toward that of the Lord, who, borne aloft amidst a flight of angels, stands out brightly against the shell of shadow of his huge purple mantle. The remarkable invention of the outstretched arm and the forefingers about to meet becomes a metaphor for the vital energy that passes from the Creator to the creature fashioned in his image, awakening his heroic vigor. . . . [Adam's] adolescent face, seen in profile, still lacking a definite expression, contrasts with the mature, intensely energetic one of the Lord, with his gray hair and long beard streaming in the air. (MOSESS 49)

Although Adam and the Father are the central figures of this panel, much attention has been given to the beautiful and enigmatic female figure who is intently regarding the creation of the first man while wrapped in the loving embrace of God's left arm. Her identity has variously been given as the immortal Sophia (the personification of wisdom) or as the premortal Eve. Drawing on art historian Leo Steinberg's analysis of the structure of the three Sistine Chapel Adam and Eve panels, Gary A. Anderson observes:

> Just to the right of Eve sits an infant who is also held by God the Father, though this time with just the thumb and index finger. The extension of his fingers corresponds exactly to the way a priest would grasp the Eucharistic wafer. In other words, this child is Mary's boy, the Christ child. Strikingly, he is the only figure on the entire ceiling who looks directly down into the gaze of the viewer. And so our question as we ponder the women in these three panels: Are they Eve, the first woman and spouse of Adam, or Mary, the Mother of Jesus and symbol of the Church? Or perhaps more accurately, are these women in truth both Eve and Mary? (GAAGENESIS, 4)

Anderson concludes that just as Christ is portrayed in scripture as the second Adam, Mary is depicted here as the second Eve.

Marko Ivan Rupnik reports that the cardinals supervising Michelangelo's work were initially unhappy with the result:

> Michelangelo had drawn the panel of the creation of man with the fingers of God and Adam touching each other. The cardinals . . . required not only that the fingers be separated, but also that the finger of God would be fully extended, while the last joint of the finger of Adam would bend back.
>
> A simple detail but with a surprising meaning: God is always there, but it is man who must decide to search for him. . . . Thus, the last joint of Adam's contracted finger represents free will. (MOSESS 49)

Figure 2–3b. *The Fingers of God and Adam*

years; ^{15} and let them be for lights in the firmament of the heaven to give light upon the earth"; and it was so. ^{16} And I, God, made two great lights; the greater light to rule the day, and the lesser light to rule the night, and the greater light was the sun, and the lesser light was the moon; and the stars also were made even according to my word. ^{17} And I, God, set them in the firmament of the heaven to give light upon the earth, ^{18} and the sun to rule over the day, and the moon to rule over the night, and to divide the light from the darkness; and I, God, saw that all things which I had made were good; ^{19} and the evening and the morning were the fourth day.

THE FIFTH DAY: CREATION OF THE FISH AND FOWL

^{20} And I, God, said: "Let the waters bring forth abundantly the moving creature that hath life, and fowl which may fly above the earth in the open firmament of heaven." ^{21} And I, God, created great whales, and every living creature that moveth, which the waters brought forth abundantly, after their kind, and every winged fowl after his kind; and I, God, saw that all things which I had created were good. ^{22} And I, God, blessed them, saying: "Be fruitful, and multiply, and fill the waters in the sea;

2:15   **to give light upon the earth.** It is the earth, not the heavens, that requires the illumination provided by God's light. Likewise, modern temples are made to brilliantly shine so as to light up their nighttime surroundings, while at the same time being furnished with opaque windows that restrict outside illumination (compare 1 Kings 6:4). Thus, the temple's function is symbolically portrayed as giving light, not receiving it from elsewhere, consistent with the symbolism of Doctrine and Covenants 43:15. According to Zev Vilnay, "The ancients said: 'Whoever builds windows in his house, makes them wide outside and narrow inside, that they should bring in the light. Not so in the Temple; because there the light was within, and shone forth onto the whole world.' 'As oil gives light—so the Temple gives light to the world'" (JMBIGIL1, 108).

Elder John A. Widtsoe wrote: "Spiritual power is generated within temple walls, and sent out to bless the world. Light from the house of the Lord illumines every home within the Church fitted for its reception by participation in temple privileges. The path from the temple to the home of man is divinely brilliant. Every home penetrated by the temple spirit enlightens, cheers, and comforts every member of the household. The peace we covet is found in such homes. Indeed, when temples are on earth, the whole world shares measurably in the issuing light; when absent, the hearts of men become heavy, as if they said, with the people of Enoch's day, 'Zion is fled'" (JMBIGIL1, 108–9).

2:20   **Let the waters bring forth abundantly the moving creature that hath life, and fowl.** Sea animals and birds are made on the fifth day, while animals who live on land appear on the sixth.

that hath life. The Hebrew "animate life" is used to distinguish between animals and plants. The recurrence of the special Hebrew creation term *bara* in v. 21 suggests to John H. Sailhamer "the beginning of a new stage in the Creation, namely, the creation of 'living beings'" (JHSGENESIS, 35).

2:21   **great whales.** The Hebrew term *tannin*, which appears in Canaanite myths to describe an opponent to Baal, refers to a kind of giant sea creature, later associated in the Bible with the monsters Rahab (Isaiah 51:9) and Leviathan (Isaiah 27:1).

every winged fowl. Consistent with the temple symbolism of Creation, Jewish traditions associated the creation of birds with the creation of the winged cherubim woven into the outer curtain of the temple.

2:22   **I . . . blessed them.** Following God's inspection and approval comes His benediction. God blesses the fish and fowl to "be fruitful, and multiply." Neither the plants nor the land animals

Figure 2–4. Michelangelo Buonarroti (1475–1564): *The Creation of Eve*, 1510

SYMBOLISM IN MICHELANGELO'S CREATION OF EVE

"And I, the Lord God, caused a deep sleep to fall upon Adam. . . . And the rib which I, the Lord God, had taken from man, made I a woman." Giorgio Vasari describes the scene above by contrasting the poses of Adam and Eve: "One [is] almost dead from being imprisoned by sleep, while the other comes alive completely reawakened by the benediction of God. The brush of this most ingenious artisan reveals the true difference between sleep and awakening, as well as how stable and firm His Divine Majesty may appear when speaking in human terms."

Upon closer examination, it becomes apparent that the symbolism of the painting extends beyond the Creation and looks forward to the crucifixion of Jesus Christ and the birth of the Church that would carry out the divine commission to carry the Gospel to the world. In his analysis of the painting, Genesis scholar Gary A. Anderson notes some details that are "highly unusual" (GAAGENESIS, 6–7):

> Adam lies slumped around a dead tree, an odd sight for a luxuriant garden where death was, as of yet, unknown. The only way to understand this tired figure is to see him as a prefiguration of Christ, the "second Adam," who was destined to hang on a barren piece of wood. "The sleep of [Adam]," the fourth-century theologian St. Augustine observed, "clearly stood for the death of Christ." . . . If this is how we are to read this image of Adam, perhaps a similar interpretation holds for Eve.

> To get our bearings on this we must bear in mind two facts. First, Mary as the "second Eve" is she who gives birth to Christ. Second, Mary as the "symbol of the church" is she who emerges from the rib of Christ on the Cross[, symbolized by the blood and water that issued from His side]. In this central panel of the Sistine ceiling, we see both the first and second Eve emerging from the ribs of Adam. . . .

> Further support for this comes from the history of the chapel itself. It was built on the model of Solomon's Temple and was dedicated on August 15, 1483, the feast day of the Assumption and Coronation of the Virgin Mary in Heaven. A favored image of Mary in Christian devotional practice was Mary as the ark or tabernacle of God. Like the Ark of the Covenant in the Old Testament, the throne upon which God almighty took his seat, Mary was the seat in which God took human form. Like the Temple itself, she housed the *verum corpus* or the "true body" of God." Significantly, this image is the center point of the entire chapel ceiling. (See MOSESS 50).

and let fowl multiply in the earth"; [23] and the evening and the morning were the fifth day.

THE SIXTH DAY: CREATION OF ANIMALS AND HUMANKIND

[24] And I, God, said: "Let the earth bring forth the living creature after his kind, cattle, and creeping things, and beasts of the earth after their kind," and it was so; [25] and I, God, made the beasts of the earth after their kind, and cattle after their kind, and everything which creepeth upon the earth after his kind; and I, God, saw that all these things were good.

[26] And I, God, said unto mine Only Begotten, which was with me from the beginning: "Let us make man in our image, after our likeness"; and it was so. And

---

2:25   receive a comparable blessing—the plants because they are not "living creatures" (Moses 2:24) and the land animals because of the serpent "which was destined to be cursed," according to Rashi, the great medieval Jewish commentator. Victor Hamilton observes that "the divine blessing is reserved for the three most critical junctures in the narrative: the introductory statement (v. 1); the creation of organic life (v. 20); and the creation of human life (v. 26)" (VPSGENESIS, 132).

2:26   ***Let us make.*** See MOSESS 49. Notably, both other instances of the use of the plural divine subject in Genesis involve important decisions about the fate of humanity: the expulsion of Adam and Eve from Eden (Genesis 3:22) and the dispersal of humanity after the destruction of Babel (Genesis 11:7; JST Genesis 11:5).

Despite the fact that Seixas' *Hebrew Grammar*, which Joseph Smith studied in Kirtland, describes the Hebrew term *Elohim* as singular ("God"), the Prophet came to interpret the term as plural ("gods"). The plural form of this expression has long been an interpretive problem for commentators that look at the Old Testament through the lens of strict monotheism. However, the view of many scholars, consistent with Latter-day Saint scripture (e.g., Doctrine and Covenants 121:32; Abraham 4:26) is that the setting for the verse is God addressing a heavenly council.

Describing this scene, the Prophet stated, "The head God called together the Gods and sat in grand council to bring forth the world" (JSTPJS, 7 April 1844, 348). Non–Latter-day Saint scholar Richard E. Friedman likewise wrote, "In pagan myth, the chief god, when formally speaking for the council of the gods, speaks in the plural." Since for most Christian and Jewish commentators the idea of a plurality of gods is unacceptable, a court of angels is often imagined in place of a council of the gods—though one is forced to admit that the concept of many gods is hinted at elsewhere in the Old Testament. The ancient religion of Israel, before alterations by reforming Deuteronomists, clearly distinguished (as does the Book of Mormon) between the "Most High God" and several sons of God, the chief of which was Yahweh, or Jehovah (JMBIGIL1, 111–12).

man. Consistent with the temple symbolism of Creation, Jewish traditions thought of Adam as a high priest, like Aaron. Note that "man" (Hebrew *'adam*), as used in this verse, is gender neutral. It is used in only a few cases as a proper name, "Adam." President Spencer W. Kimball further explained that "man," as used here, was not meant to describe "a separate man, but a complete man, which is husband and wife." The use of the Hebrew term *'ish* to mean "man" in the everyday sense appears only after the woman (*'ishah*) is created (JMBIGIL1, 112).

in our image, after our likeness. Unlike the earlier creatures who were each made "after his kind," man and woman were made in God's image and likeness. Moses 6:9 is more specific than 2:26, saying that man was created "in the image of his [God's] own body." Joseph Smith spoke plainly about what this means: "God Himself who sits enthroned in yonder heavens is a Man like unto one of yourselves—that is the great secret! If the veil were rent today[,] . . . you would see Him in all the person, image, fashion, and very form of a man, like yourselves. For Adam was a man formed in his likeness and created in the very fashion and image of God" (JMBIGIL1, 113).

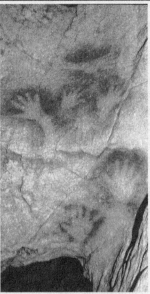

Figure 2–5. Left: Noël Pisano: *Negative of Hand and Red Dots*;
Right: *Seven Hands*. Cavern of Pech-Merle, Cabrerets, France

THOSE WHO LIVED BEFORE ADAM AND EVE

The beautiful copper engraving at left by Noël Pisano was made from meticulous observation of one of the many prehistoric paintings in the caves of Pech-Merle, in the heart of the Massif Central of southern France. Although the cave walls and ceilings contain many images of greater sophistication, this simple tracing of a single hand is singularly arresting. Its original is solidly dated to 25,000 years ago, yet while one is standing to examine it in close quarters, the gap of time between oneself and the skilled artist is suddenly erased, and one is brought to admire the beauty and subtlety of his or her technique. To create this work, the artist had to crawl into the cavern by candlelight. After contemplating his or her design and choosing the ideal place for its execution, the artist placed a hand on the wall to serve as a stencil. To create the colored outline, the artist projected pigment onto the rock by blowing, perhaps with the help of a sprayer held tight in his or her lips. This well-honed technique allowed a negative of the hand, surrounded by symbols whose meaning is now is lost to us, to be preserved tens of thousands of years later as an ancient snapshot, the sole remaining memory of the life of this individual. In another chamber, we find what is undoubtedly a family portrait. Fourteen hands of adults and children are found together here, in a deep, submerged section of the cavern now accessible only during periods of drought.

Hugh Nibley, with his deep love of God's creations, had great sympathy for these ancient individuals and pondered long and hard about how their stories fit in with those of Adam and Eve. For a thoughtful perspective on this issue, we can do no better than to cite him directly:

> The philosopher Arthur Schopenhauer, in his "Essay on the Christian System," said that the two fatal flaws of Christianity were (1) denying spirit and mind to any other creatures but ourselves and (2) allowing life on no other world but our own. . . . This . . . should be no concern [for us]. . . .

> Do not begrudge existence to creatures that looked like men long, long ago, nor deny them a place in God's affection or even a right to exaltation—for our scriptures allow them such. Nor am I overly concerned as to just when they might have lived, for their world is not our world. They have all gone away long before our people ever appeared. God assigned them their proper times and functions, as He has given me mine—a full-time job that admonishes me to remember His words to the overly eager Moses: "For mine own purpose have I made these things. Here is wisdom and it remaineth in me" (Moses 1:31).

> It is Adam as my own parent who concerns me. When he walks onto the stage, then and only then the play begins. He opens a book and starts calling out names. They are the sons of Adam, who also qualify as the sons of God, Adam himself being a son of God. This is the book of remembrance from which many have been blotted out (HWNBEFADAM, 50, 51, 82–83; see also MOSESS 51).

I, God, said: "Let them have dominion over the fishes of the sea, and over the fowl of the air, and over the cattle, and over all the earth, and over every creeping thing that creepeth upon the earth."

> ²⁷ And I, God, created man in mine own image,
>
> in the image of mine Only Begotten created I him;
>
> male and female created I them.

2:26   Joseph Smith made it clear that this phrase applied not only to the physical appearance of Adam and Eve but also to their spiritual nature, which was, in the beginning, "innocent, harmless, and spotless, bearing the same image as the Gods. And when man fell he did not lose His image, but [only] His character, still retaining the image of his Maker. . . . And through the atonement of Christ, and the resurrection and obedience in the Gospel, we shall again be conformed to the [full] image of . . . Jesus Christ [see Romans 8:29], then we shall have attained to the [full] image, glory, and character of God" (JSWORDS, 9 July 1843, 231).

Building on an idea similar to that expressed by Joseph Smith, Nahum Sarna comments: "The words used here [in Genesis 1:26] to convey these ideas can be better understood in the light of a phenomenon registered in both Mesopotamia and Egypt where the ruling monarch is described as 'the image' or 'the likeness' of a god. . . . Without doubt, the terminology employed in Genesis 1:26 is derived from regal vocabulary, which serves to elevate the king above the ordinary run of men. In the Bible this idea has become democratized. All human beings are created 'in the image of God'; each person bears the stamp of royalty" (NMSGENESIS, 12).

Let them have dominion. Hugh Nibley writes that the word "dominion" comes from the Latin *dominus* ("lord"), "specifically 'the lord of the household,' in his capacity of generous host, . . . [responsible as] master for the comfort and well-being of his dependents and guests" (HWNMANS, 7). According to Nahum Sarna, the word expresses "the coercive power of the monarch, consonant with the explanation just given for 'the image of God.' This power, however, cannot include the license to exploit nature banefully, for the following reasons: the human race is not inherently sovereign, but enjoys its dominion solely by the grace of God. . . . Thus, despite the power given him, man still requires special divine sanction to partake of the earth's vegetation, and although he 'rules' the animal world, he is not here permitted to eat flesh" (NMSGENESIS, 12–13).

To have "dominion" in the priesthood sense means to have responsibility, specifically as God's representative on the earth. As Nibley succinctly puts it, "Man's dominion is a call to service, not a license to exterminate" (HWNMANS, 18).

2:27   *created I him . . . created I them.* In verse 27, we encounter two phrases that successively juxtapose the oneness and plurality of man and woman: "created I him" and "created I them." In light of the interplay between "him" and "them" in this verse, one strand of rabbinic tradition proposes that "man was originally created male and female in one." Thus, in the creation of woman, this tradition suggests that "God . . . separated the one (female) side" (MOSESS 50). However, it would be more straightforward to conclude that the three lines of this stately poetic diction in the Book of Moses are structured to successively draw attention to three things:

1. to the creation of man in the image of the divine ("in our image, after our likeness" [v. 26]);
2. to the fact that this resemblance exactly parallels the one that exists between the Father and the Son ("in mine own image," "in the image of mine Only Begotten" [v. 27]); and
3. to the essential distinction of gender ("male and female" [v. 27]).

With respect to the oneness of man and woman in Latter-day Saint teachings, Elder Erastus Snow expressed that "there can be no God except he is composed of the man and woman united, and there is not in all the eternities that exist, nor ever will be, a God in any other way. There never was a God, and there never will be in all eternities, except they are made of these two component parts: a man and a woman, the male and the female" (JD, 19:270). This statement parallels a

²⁸ And I, God, blessed them, and said unto them: "Be fruitful, and multiply, and replenish the earth, and subdue it, and have dominion over the fish of the sea, and over the fowl of the air, and over every living thing that moveth upon the earth."

²⁹ And I, God, said unto man: "Behold, I have given you every herb bearing seed, which is upon the face of all the earth, and every tree in the which shall be the fruit of a tree yielding seed; to you it shall be for meat. ³⁰ And to every beast of the earth, and to every fowl of the air, and to everything that creepeth upon the earth, wherein I grant life, there shall be given every clean herb for meat"; and it was so, even as I spake. ³¹ And I, God, saw everything that I had made, and, behold, all things which I made were very good; and the evening and the morning were the sixth day.

2:27   statement in the Jewish Talmud commenting that "a man without a wife is not a man, for it is said, 'male and female He created them . . . and called their name Man' [i.e., only together, as man and wife, is he called 'Man']" (MOSESS 50).

male and female. Both men and women are created in the divine image and likeness, which even for some non–Latter-day Saint scholars has implications not only for human nature but also for the character of God. The 1909 and 1925 First Presidency statements commenting on the origin of humankind both include the assertion that "all men and women are in the similitude of the universal Father and Mother, and are literally the sons and daughters of Deity" (DHBCOSMOS, 449, 453).

Though masculine verbs and adjectives are used with God's name (also masculine), evidence exists that the Ugaritic goddess Asherah was sometimes worshipped as a female consort to Jehovah in preexilic times. Allusions to a female deity are also seen by some in biblical references to Wisdom and in the texts of mystic Judaism referring to the Shekhinah. Although Jeremiah spoke out against the worship of the "queen of heaven," Daniel C. Peterson points out that prophetic opposition to the idea does not seem to appear before the eighth century BCE. From his study of this verse, the eminent Bible scholar David Noel Freedman concludes: "Just as the male God is the model and image for the first man, so some divine or heavenly female figure serves as the model and likeness for the human female, the first woman" (MOSESS 50).

Is gender a primordial attribute of every person? The Church's proclamation on the family affirms that gender is an eternal aspect of the spiritual identity of each individual. This is consistent with Elder James E. Talmage's statement: "Children of God have comprised male and female from the beginning. Man is man and woman is woman, fundamentally, unchangeably, eternally" (MOSESS 50).

Nahum Sarna further notes: "No . . . sexual differentiation is noted in regard to animals. . . . The next verse shows [human sexuality] to be a blessed gift of God woven into the fabric of life. As such, it cannot of itself be other than wholesome. By the same token, its abuse is treated in the Bible with particular severity. Its proper regulation is subsumed under the category of the holy, whereas sexual perversion is viewed with abhorrence as an affront to human dignity and as a desecration of the divine image of man" (NMSGENESIS, 13).

2:28   *be fruitful, and multiply.* The Hebrew phrase for "be fruitful, and multiply" (*peru urebu*) may be a deliberate play on the "without form, and void" (*tohu vabohu*) of v. 2. Bill T. Arnold explains: "In this case, the living creatures of God's Creation are hereby empowered to perpetuate God's life-giving creativity by bringing still more life into the world, by filling up and inhabiting that which was previously empty and uninhabitable" (MOSESS 50). Nahum Sarna adds: "The difference between the formulation here and God's blessing to the fish and fowl in verse 22 is subtle and meaningful. Here God directly addresses man and woman" (NMSGENESIS, 13). While the commandment to Adam and Eve resembles the blessing given to the fish and fowl in verse 22, the other creatures are not instructed to subdue the earth or to have dominion over every other living thing. The responsibility of stewardship over the earth is uniquely conferred upon the man and the woman.

replenish the earth. The word "replenish" can be misleading to modern English speakers. The corresponding Hebrew term, *male*, does not mean to "refill" but simply to "fill" or "make full." Thus, Nahum Sarna renders the command in this verse as "Be fertile and increase, fill the earth" (NMSGENESIS, 13). Importantly, Roger R. Keller notes that the commandment anticipates the departure of Adam and Eve from Eden, since they "were commanded to multiply and replenish the earth, not the Garden" (MOSESS 50).

subdue it. The commandment to "subdue" the earth conveys the idea of settlement and agriculture. In light of later events in Genesis, Laurence Turner concludes: "Although humans increasingly dominate the animal creation and eventually rule despotically (an intensification of the original command), there is an ironic sense in which animals, through the serpent, exercise an ongoing dominion over the humans (a reversal of the original command). . . . Also, the earth becomes increasingly difficult to dominate. It overwhelms most of humanity in the Flood, and all of humanity in death" (MOSESS 50).

2:29   **herb bearing seed . . . fruit of a tree.** In the Garden of Eden, humans are to eat fruits from the trees and grain sown by seed, whereas the wild green grasses of the field are given for the food of animals.

to you it shall be for meat. For modern English speakers, the term "meat" would be better translated as "food." Vegetarianism is given as the rule in the Garden of Eden; humanity's use of animals for food will not be explicitly sanctioned until after the Flood (JST Genesis 9:10–11). Isaiah's vision of the Millennium appears to foresee all creatures again becoming herbivorous (Isaiah 11:7; 65:25).

Joseph Smith taught, "Men must become harmless before the brute creation, and when men lose their vicious dispositions and cease to destroy the animal race, the lion and the lamb can dwell together, and the sucking child can play with the serpent in safety" (JSTPJS, 26 May 1834, 71). *Second Enoch* asserts that "the Lord will not judge a single animal soul for the sake of man but human souls he will judge for the sake of the souls of their animals" and that at the time of the "great judgment . . . every kind of animal soul will accuse the human beings who have fed them badly" (FIA2ENOCH, 58:4, 6, p. 184).

2:30   **clean herb.** In Genesis and Abraham, the term "green herb" is used. The term "clean" in the Old Testament sense meant what was allowed or permitted by God's law (e.g., Genesis 7:2). Thus, the change of wording in the Book of Moses might be seen as signaling to Adam and Eve that the diet of humans and animals is not simply a matter of creaturely preference but rather is an important subject of divine interest, regulated by commandment. In this way, the mention of "clean herb" anticipates the restriction that will forbid the man and the woman from partaking of the Tree of Knowledge.

2:31   **very good.** Unlike with other living things, God did not pronounce humankind "good" at the time of its creation. Now that man and woman are both created and blessed, God can pronounce the entirety of His Creation *very* good—meaning beautiful, appropriate, and complete. Humankind is not yet in itself good in the moral sense—Adam and Eve still have to prove themselves. "Always keep in view," said Brigham Young, "that the animal, vegetable, and mineral kingdoms—the earth and its fulness—will all, except the children of man, abide their creation—the law by which they were made, and will receive their exaltation" (JD, 8:191).

By way of summary for this magnificent chapter as a whole, we have seen that the effects of the inception of light and its division from darkness "in the beginning" cascaded through the remaining days of Creation as each episode recounted the successive generation of new and finer-grained distinctions that define created elements through the principle of separation. Indeed, we see that the process of division and separation began even before the Creation, when those who kept their first estate were separated from those who did not. Moreover, the theme continues after the ending of the Creation account, as the focus of the narrative moves from the actions of God to those of Adam and Eve. Exercising the agency that has been granted them, they partake of the

2:31   forbidden fruit, and are cast out of the Garden, experiencing an immediate separation from the presence of God and, eventually, a separation of body and spirit at death.

However, making it clear that the principles of division and separation that drive the dynamics of Creation are not meant to govern the relationship of husband and wife, God declared "that it was not good that man should be alone." Indeed, as Catherine Thomas observes, a primary objective of mortality seems to have been precisely "to foster the conditions in which the man and the woman may achieve interdependence," thus affording each individual an opportunity to rise to "the challenge of not only perfecting ourselves individually but also perfecting ourselves in relationships. . . . Relationships were given to us to develop us in love" (MOSESS 50).

CHAPTER 3
THE GARDEN OF EDEN

THE SEVENTH DAY

3 ¹ Thus the heaven and the earth were finished, and all the host of them. ² And on the seventh day I, God, ended my work, and all things which I had made; and I rested on the seventh day from all my work, and all things which I had made were finished, and I, God, saw that they were good; ³ And I, God, blessed

---

3   Moses 3 begins a second Creation narrative that differs from Moses 2 in vocabulary, style, and use of the divine name (i.e., "God" vs. "Lord God"). Repetitions and seeming contradictions with elements of the previous recital of Creation events are also apparent. Such observations suggest that multiple sources were used in composing Genesis. This idea, called the "Documentary Hypothesis," is a broad scholarly consensus whose most-able current popular expositor has been Richard Friedman. However, even those who find the documentary hypothesis compelling have good reason to admire the resulting literary product on its own terms. For example, in the case of the two Creation chapters, Friedman himself writes that in the scriptural version of Genesis we have a text "that is greater than the sum of its parts. . . . The combination of the from-the-sky-down and the from-the-earth-up accounts produces a much richer and much more whole conception of Creation than we would have if there were only one account" (MOSESS 53).

3:1   ***heaven.*** Note the change from the King James Version (KJV) plural "heavens" here and in v. 4.
    finished, and all the host of them. The purpose of the verse is to express that the whole of creation is now organized and poised for action—all the actors and props are now ready for what will follow. In modern English, the phrase "all the host" is sometimes translated as "all their array." This reading preserves the sense of orderly, disciplined, and regimented arrangement conveyed by the underlying Hebrew. Unfortunately, however, replacing "host" with "array" obscures the military connotations—the idea of the hosts being "God's divine army"—associated with the use of the phrase usually found elsewhere in the Old Testament.
    Meir Zlotowitz explains that the common Old Testament phrase "host of the heavens . . . occasionally refers to the angels" (MZBEREISHIS, 1:80). The Jewish sage Ramban, with others, goes further to specifically include "the souls of humanity" as part of the host of heaven. President Joseph Fielding Smith similarly saw the mustering of the heavenly host as including the organization and foreordination of spirits in premortal life (see Moses 6:44; JMBIGIL1, 151).

3:2   ***on the seventh day I, God, ended my work.*** Nahum Sarna notes that this phrase does not necessarily imply any divine action on the seventh day; thus, the phrase could alternatively be given as "on the seventh day I, God, declared my work ended" (NMSGENESIS, 15). God's "rest" prefigures not only the institution of the Sabbath but also the future "rest" of the righteous after the Resurrection.
    Doctrine and Covenants 77:12 seems to imply that it was God's work thus far, rather than the seventh day itself, that was sanctified. Additionally, the verse can be taken as saying that the creation of man's physical body took place at the beginning of the seventh day rather than the end of the sixth: "as God made the world in six days, and on the seventh day he finished his work, and sanctified it, and also formed man out of the dust of the earth" (Doctrine and Covenants 77:12). Because the verse seems to contradict the common interpretation of Moses 2:26–27 as being an account of the physical creation of humankind, some have concluded that there is either a semantic or "grammatical ambiguity" in the revelation, or perhaps some error of transcription (JMBIGIL1, 152).
    I rested. Rather than speaking and working on the Sabbath, God blesses and sanctifies. Moreover, John Sailhamer observes: "Unlike the other days of Creation, . . . the seventh day stands apart

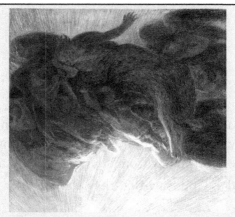

Figure 3–1. Gaetano Previati, 1852–1920: *The Creation of Light*, 1913

WHAT IS SPIRITUAL CREATION?

This magnificent painting by Gaetano Previati shows the heavenly hosts as part of the light on day one of the Creation. Wesley Williams explains: "The *pneumatikos* or spiritual first Adam, born on the first day, is associated [with] the light of Genesis 1:3. The latter reading is based on a pun on the Greek word *phōs*, used in the [Septuagint] translation of Genesis 1:3 meaning both 'light' and 'man.' Thus, the product of God's command, 'Let there be light (*phōs*),' was a divine Light-Man, an *anthropos* enveloped within and consisting of light. This interpretation is Jewish and can be found as early as the second century BCE" (JMBIGIL1, 136).

The "spiritual creation" of Eden. There is no scriptural basis for the notion that allusions to "spiritual creation" in Moses 3:5 describe a separate creation of entities made of "spirit" corresponding to each created thing. Instead, this verse describes the premortal creation of "all things" in their spiritual *state*, including the physical creation of Eden and everything in it. This is consistent with the view of Elder Bruce R. McConkie, who said that the word *spiritually* in Moses 3:5 has "a dual meaning and applies to both the premortal life and the paradisiacal creation." The "more pointed and important meaning" in this verse is that of a "paradisiacal creation" (JMBIGIL1, 135, 200). The paradisiacal creation resulted in a world of terrestrial glory, the same glory to which the earth will be restored during the Millennium.

Some readers see the planning process for the formation of the heavens and the earth as resulting in a "blueprint" that can be taken as constituting a sort of spiritual creation. Though advance planning doubtless took place, such a process is never referred to in scripture as "spiritual creation."

Note that the period of time mentioned in Doctrine and Covenants 77:6 refers to "the seven thousand years" of the earth's "temporal existence" rather than to the period of its existence in a spiritual state. Thus, this seven-thousand-year period does not include the time frame of the physical creation of the earth in its spiritual state, nor the time that led up to the Fall of Adam and Eve. Therefore, this rough description of time periods does not rule out a creation process that began billions of years ago.

Origin of the spirits of humankind. Joseph Smith taught that there is some aspect of the spirit's existence that was *not* created, although the exact nature of this eternal part of people has not been authoritatively settled. In the Book of Moses, the fact that all humankind existed as spirits in "heaven" before they came to earth is stated in simple terms (Moses 3:5). The Book of Abraham relates that when God breathed the "breath of life" into man, it meant that He took Adam's spirit and placed it into his body (Abraham 5:7).

More detail is given about social organization and preparatory events that took place in the premortal life. The Prophet summarized: "The organization of the spiritual and heavenly worlds, and of spiritual and heavenly beings, was agreeable to the most perfect order and harmony: their limits and bounds were fixed irrevocably, and voluntarily subscribed to in their heavenly estate by themselves, and were by our first parents subscribed to upon the earth" (JSTPJS, 9 October 1843, 325). Thus, "Father Adam, the Ancient of Days and father of all, and our glorious Mother Eve," among the "noble and great ones" who excelled in intelligence in their premortal lives, were foreordained to their mortal roles (Doctrine and Covenants 138:38–39; Abraham 3:22–23). Having received perfect physical bodies of a terrestrial glory, Adam and Eve were placed in a specially prepared proving ground where, until the time of their transgression, they would live in the spiritual state that prevails in terrestrial worlds (2 Nephi 2:22–23). See JMBIGIL1, 134–45, 540–45, MOSESS 54.

the seventh day, and sanctified it; because that in it I had rested from all my work which I, God, had created and made.

ALL THINGS FIRST CREATED SPIRITUALLY

4 And now, behold, I say unto you, that these are the generations of the heaven and of the earth, when they were created, in the day that I, the Lord God, made

3:3   from the other six days in not having an account of its conclusion. It is this feature of the narrative that has suggested a picture of an eternal, divine 'Sabbath.' . . . Consequently, immediately after the narrative of the Fall, . . . the verb *asah* points to an interruption of God's 'Sabbath' when, as a final act of Creation, He made coats of skin for Adam and Eve" (JHSGENESIS, 138–39).

   Current biblical scholarship does not see Creation as the sudden appearance of material elements out of nowhere followed by a simple cessation of activity. Rather, Creation is the organization of a preexisting elements so that the world would be fit for the purposes God had previously ordained for His creatures. In this way, the process of creating the universe is analogous to the building and fashioning of a temple out of materials already at hand. When the initial work of Creation is finished and God takes His place in its midst by ascending to His throne, a temple made with divine hands comes into full existence as a functional sanctuary—a "control room of the cosmos," as Bible scholar John Walton terms it (MOSESS 52).

   From this perspective we can regard the seventh day of Creation as the enthronement of God and the culmination of all prior Creation events. True rest is finally achieved only when God rules supreme over Creation from His heavenly temple and His righteous and duly-appointed regents (in this case, Adam and Eve) rule within an earthly equivalent. Happily, God's "rest" and Creation, since broken off by humanity's wickedness, will be permanently restored at the last day, when Christ "shall have delivered up the kingdom to . . . the Father" and shall have "put all things under his feet" (1 Corinthians 15:24–25). See MOSESS 52.

   blessed the seventh day. Unlike the specific blessings to the animals and people given in Moses 2:22, 28, the blessing of the Sabbath day "is undefined and pertains to time itself. . . . God, through His creativity, has already established His sovereignty over space; the idea here is that He is sovereign over time as well" (NMSGENESIS, 15).

   sanctified it. To "sanctify" something is not just to declare it good (as was done for the products of the six days of creation) but rather to make it holy. Truman G. Madsen comments: "Far from [it] being a day of strict injunctions, which are joyless duties imposed on duties of the prior day, the Sabbath is the reward for, the outcome of, indeed the climax of all other preparatory creations. It is not an imposed stoppage. It is what all the preparation was designed for" (JMBIGIL1, 153).

   rested from all my work. The term translated as "rested" means "cessation," and, according to Bill T. Arnold, implies "the celebration and completion of an accomplishment" (JMBIGIL1, 153).

3:4   **these are the generations of the heaven and of the earth.** As in its other occurrences, this formula is meant to introduce the story that follows, not to summarize the preceding account (NMSGENESIS, 48–49). Note also that the phrase "And the Gods came down" in Abraham 5:4 seems to signal the beginning of a new narrative unit rather than the end of the former one. Thus, we might alternately punctuate this passage from Moses 3:4 as follows: "these are the generations of the heaven and the earth, when they were created: At the time that I, the Lord God, made the heaven and the earth . . ."

   generations. Richard Elliott Friedman suggests that the term "generations," which recurs ten additional times in Genesis as part of the phrase "these are the generations," is better translated as "records": "The word is used both to introduce records of births and to introduce stories of events within a family. . . . It thus means historical records, and usually family records" (JMBIGIL1, 154).

   in the day. This expression should not be taken as implying that everything was created in one day, but rather in the sense of "at the time that He made" (UCCOMMENTARY, 73).

the heaven and the earth, ⁵ And every plant of the field before it was in the earth, and every herb of the field before it grew. For I, the Lord God, created all things, of which I have spoken, spiritually, before they were naturally upon the face of the earth. For I, the Lord God, had not caused it to rain upon the face of the earth. And I, the Lord God, had created all the children of men; and not yet a man to till the ground; for in heaven created I them; and there was not yet flesh upon the earth, neither in the water, neither in the air;

3:4   **Lord God.** Most scholars believe that the use of the divine name "Lord God" (as opposed to "God" in Moses 2) signals a different source for the following text. However, this does not explain why a compound form of the name is used so frequently in this part of Moses/Genesis when all other portions associated with the same source simply use "Lord." Other explanations have also been proposed. Note that in the dialogue of Eve and the serpent, the serpent exceptionally uses the name "God," not "Lord God" (JMBIGIL1, 154).

3:5   **every plant of the field before it was in the earth, and every herb of the field before it grew.** Drawing on the general word pattern of the Mesopotamian Creation story (*Enuma Elish*) the following paraphrase may provide a plainer reading of the verse: "Before there were any troublesome weeds, before the cultivated grain was grown, before God caused the rain to fall, before man was commanded to till the ground, the Lord God made all things in the spiritual state of a terrestrial world [that is, a temple-like Eden, see figures 2–1 and 3–2]. The Lord God had created all people in heaven, but no flesh was yet on earth." This explanation provides the beginning bookend to the account that ends in Moses 4:29 with the expulsion of Adam and Eve from the garden. The emphasis on how easy their life was *before* that time highlights the fact that neither the troublesome weeds (that depend on rain) nor the life-sustaining grains (that depend on human cultivation) would make their appearance until *after* the Fall. Likewise, the statement that no flesh was yet on the earth refers to mortality, another condition that will not hold until after the Fall. See commentary on Moses 3:7 "first flesh" below.

       created all things . . . spiritually, before they were naturally upon the face of the earth. This statement affirms that a spiritual creation preceded the natural (physical) creation. Spiritual creation refers to the premortal creation of all things in what may called a spiritual, a paradisiacal, or a terrestrial state, specifically the creation of the Garden of Eden and everything in its confines.

       had not caused it to rain upon the face of the earth. Water in the garden was to be provided by natural irrigation and not by rain (v. 6). After the Fall, rain was provided to water the grain.

       and not yet a man to till the ground. Although active labor will be required of Adam and Eve to care for the Garden of Eden, they won't be required to till the ground until after the Fall.

       in heaven created I them. Though some readers have seen Moses 2:26–27 as a reference to the creation of the spirits of humankind, President Joseph Fielding Smith commented: "There is no account of the creation of man or other forms of life when they were created as spirits. There is just the simple statement that they were so created before the physical creation. The statements in Moses 3:5 and Genesis 2:4 are interpolations thrown into the account of the physical creation, explaining that all things were first created in the spirit existence in heaven before they were placed upon this earth" (JMBIGIL1, 156).

       Going further, Hugh Nibley explained the seeming discontinuity between the two Creation accounts as a *purposive* shift, seeing the interlude that separates the stories in verses 3–7 as stage directions composed to accompany a drama that was part of ancient temple ritual. As the curtain closes on the drama's prologue outlining the seven days of Creation, a narrator might be seen as pausing to explain that all things were created spiritually prior to their natural appearance on the earth (Moses 3:4–5; Genesis 2:4–5). Following this interlude, the curtain might have reopened for a change of scene in the second part of the creation drama; we are now viewing the details of the story of the creation of humankind not from the vantage point of heaven but instead as it is seen from the Garden (MOSESS 53).

THE CREATION OF ADAM

⁶ But I, the Lord God, spake, and there went up a mist from the earth, and watered the whole face of the ground. ⁷ And I, the Lord God, formed man from the dust of the ground, and breathed into his nostrils the breath of life; and man became a living soul, the first flesh upon the earth, the first man also; nevertheless, all things were before created; but spiritually were they created and made according to my word.

3:6   **t*here went up a mist from the earth.*** The English term "mist" seems out of place here; however, evidence exists for a connection between the obscure Hebrew *'ed* and the Akkadian *edu*, "flood, waves, swell." Thus one might translate this phrase alternately as "a flow [or 'spring'] would well up from the ground and water the whole surface of the earth" (NMSGENESIS, 17). This is consistent with the later statement that "I, the Lord God, caused a river to go out of Eden to water the garden" (v. 10). Unlike the uncertain flows of desert wadis that would swell when God provided rain and dry up when rain was withheld, the continuous flow of water from the "deep" assured the garden of unfailing fertility. Moreover, in connection with the account of man's creation in v. 7, some commentators conclude that the resulting mixture of soil and water figuratively provided "the raw material with the proper consistency for being molded into man" (NMSGENESIS, 17).

3:7   ***the Lord God, formed man.*** The imagery is that of shaping, as one might do with clay. However, the important point is that God provided a body made of earthly elements for the premortal spirits of Adam and Eve. The process by which this was done is left obscure. As President Boyd K. Packer wrote, "We are told that [the account of the Creation] is figurative insofar as the man and the woman are concerned" (JMBIGIL1, 157).

The wording implies that God was involved in the forming of Adam and Eve in a personal way. Accordingly, scriptures and statements of Church leaders have sometimes been quoted to argue that their bodies were born of divine parentage in a very literal sense. However, the scriptures are not consistent on this point. For example, in 1830 the Prophet translated Moses 6:22, which referred to a "genealogy of the sons of Adam, who was the son of God." However, a little over a year later Joseph modified a similar KJV New Testament genealogical account ("Adam, which was the son of God") to read "Adam, who was formed of God" (JST Luke 3:45). Consistent with this interpretation, it should be observed that Moses 6:8 and 6:68 could be taken as support of the view that Moses 6:22 is meant to describe a covenant relationship rather than only a physical descent. Regarding the manner in which the bodies of Adam and Eve were created, President Spencer W. Kimball said, "We don't know exactly how their coming into this world happened, and when we're able to understand it the Lord will tell us." As Richard D. Draper concludes, "Genesis, Moses, and Abraham preserve the 'official' account of humankind's entrance into the world as revealed by God. He has not seen fit to reveal more" (JMBIGIL1, 157; see DHBCOSMOS, especially pp. 446–84).

3:7   ***from the dust of the ground.*** Note the wordplay here in the sequence of three Hebrew words: "mist/flow" (*'ed*), "man" (*'adam*), and "ground" (*'adamah*). The term "dust" reappears in Moses 4:20 ("dust shalt thou eat") and 25 ("dust thou wast, and unto dust shalt thou return"), connoting in all cases weakness and mortality. However, as Victor Hamilton observes, several passages in the Old Testament describe an "exaltation from the dust, with the dust representing either pre-royal status, poverty, or death" (VPHGENESIS, 158).

breathed into his nostrils the breath of life. Biblical and Egyptian sources associate the receiving of divine breath not merely with an infusion of life but also with royal status (e.g., Lamentations 4:20). It is interesting that the Book of Moses adds a similar phrase to describe the creation of animals (v. 19).

living soul. Doctrine and Covenants 88:15 explains that "the spirit and the body are the soul of man." The Book of Moses explains that humans, the trees (v. 9), and the animals (v. 19) in the

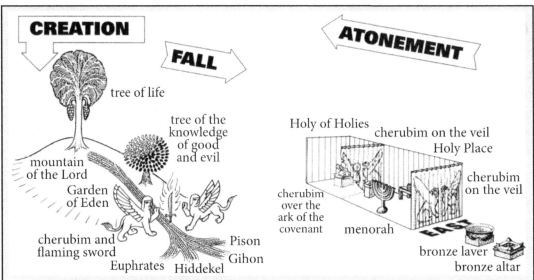

Figure 3–2. Adapted from Michael P. Lyon, b. 1952: *Sacred Topography of Eden and the Temple*, 1994

THE TWO-PART TEMPLE PATTERN OF RITUAL DESCENT AND ASCENT

The Latter-day Saint temple endowment opens its story with a recital of the events of the Creation. Notably, the pattern of beginning at the beginning—an explicit telling of the Creation—is a near-universal feature of temple rites throughout the ancient Near East. After a recital of the Creation, part 1 of the endowment continues with an account of the Fall of Adam and Eve and then, in part 2, concludes with the story of their upward journey back to the Father. This approach to teaching the plan of salvation emphasizes what Elder Bruce R. McConkie called the "three pillars" of eternity—the Creation, the Fall, and the Atonement of Jesus Christ. The approach is found in the temple and in modern scripture (e.g., 2 Nephi 2:22–26; Alma 18:36, 39; 22:13; Mormon 9:12; Doctrine and Covenants 20:17–18, 20–25; Moses 6:54–59; Articles of Faith 1:1–3).

Building on the "three pillars" outline of the plan of salvation, Donald W. Parry has shown that the *outbound* journey of the Creation and the Fall is mirrored in the *inbound* journey of the temple. The Garden of Eden can be seen as a natural "temple," where Adam and Eve lived in God's presence for a time. Significantly, each major feature of Eden (that is, the river, the cherubim, the tree of knowledge, the tree of life) corresponds to a similar symbol in the Israelite temple (that is, the bronze laver, the cherubim, the veil, the *menorah*).

The course taken by the Israelite high priest through the temple symbolizes the journey of the Fall of Adam and Eve in reverse. Just as the route of Adam and Eve's departure from Eden led them *eastward* past the cherubim with the flaming swords and out of the sacred garden into the mortal world, so in ancient times the high priest would return *westward* from the mortal world, past the consuming fire, the cleansing water, the woven images of cherubim on the temple veils, and, finally, back into the presence of God. "Thus," according to Parry, the high priest returns "to the original point of creation, where he pours out the atoning blood of the sacrifice, reestablishing the covenant relationship with God."

About the journey made within the temple, Hugh Nibley explained:

> Properly speaking, one did not go "through" the temple—in one door and out another—for one enters and leaves by the same door, but by moving in opposite directions. . . . The Two Ways of Light and Darkness are but one way after all, as the wise Heraclitus said: "The up-road and the down-road are one"; which one depends on the way we are facing.

In remarkable consistency with this pattern, the Book of Moses, like the modern temple endowment, traces the footsteps of Adam and Eve—initially, as they are sent away from Eden, and later, in their subsequent journey of return and reunion. Chapters 2–4 of the Book of Moses tell the story of the Creation and the "down-road" of the Fall, while chapters 5–8 follow the journey of Adam and Eve and the righteous branches of their posterity along the "up-road" enabled by the Atonement. In the Book of Moses, the "up-road" enabled by covenant-keeping is called the "way of the tree of life"—the path that leads to the presence of God and the sweet fruit held in reserve for the righteous in the day of resurrection (Moses 4:31; MOSESS 32).

THE PLANTING OF THE GARDEN OF EDEN

8 And I, the Lord God, planted a garden eastward in Eden, and there I put the

3:7   garden became "living souls" once the result of their prior spiritual creation was combined with natural elements. However, the fact that the trees of the garden became "living souls" does not necessarily imply that each tree possessed an individual spirit in the same sense that humans and animals do (see Doctrine and Covenants 77:2).

first flesh upon the earth. This verse has long been an interpretive problem for Latter-day Saint readers, since at face value the phrase seems to be saying that humans' appearance on earth preceded that of the animals—and thus implying that the human body was formed through "special creation." Draper, Brown, and Rhodes take a more reasonable view, commenting, "'Flesh' here, of course, refers to mortality—Adam was the first mortal human being on the earth" (RDDPGP, 223). This interpretation is consistent with most scripture references to the term "flesh." President Joseph Fielding Smith agreed, arguing that the phrase should not be interpreted to mean that animal life was absent on earth before Adam's arrival (JMBIGIL1, 159).

first man also. The First Presidency stated in 1909: "Adam, our progenitor, 'the first man,' was, like Christ, a preexistent spirit, and like Christ he took upon him an appropriate body, the body of a man, and so became a 'living soul.' . . . The word of the Lord declares that Adam was the 'first man of all men' (Moses 1:34), and we are therefore in duty bound to regard him as the primal parent of our race. It was shown to the brother of Jared that all men were created in the beginning after the image of God (Ether 3:15); and whether we take this to mean the spirit or the body, or both, it commits us to the same conclusion: Man began life as a human being, in the likeness of our heavenly Father" (JMBIGIL1, 159; see DHBCOSMOS, 446–84).

3:8   *planted a garden.* This verse should not be read as a second version of the account of the creation of plants found in Moses 2. It specifically concerns the planting of the garden from which Adam and Eve will eat.

garden. Eden is a prototype for the temple and appears to be patterned after the heavenly temple (see figure 3–2). Thus, scriptural references to "the garden of the Lord" (Genesis 13:10; Isaiah 51:3) and "the garden of God" (Ezekiel 28:13; 31:9) usually apply equally well to both Eden and to its heavenly counterpart. As to the Garden of Eden, Victor Hamilton correctly concludes that "[God] is its planter, but not its occupant" (VPHGENESIS, 161). It was created specifically for Adam and Eve.

eastward. To an ancient reader in the Mesopotamian milieu, the phrase "eastward in Eden" could be taken as meaning that the garden sits at the dawn horizon—the meeting place of heaven and earth. By its very nature, the horizon is not a final end point but rather a portal, a place of two-way transition between the heavens and the earth. Nibley writes: "'Egyptians . . . never . . . speak of [the land beyond the grave] as an earthly paradise; it is only to be reached by the dead.' . . . [It] is neither heaven nor earth but lies between them. . . . In a Hebrew Enoch apocryphon, the Lord, in visiting the earth, rests in the Garden of Eden and, moving in the reverse direction, passes through 'the Garden to the firmament.' . . . Every transition must be provided with such a setting, not only from here to heaven, but in the reverse direction in the beginning" (HWNMESSAGE, 294–95). "The passage from world to world and from horizon to horizon is dramatized in the ordinances of the temple, which itself is called the horizon" (HWNPGP, 199).

Situating this concept with respect to the story of Adam and Eve, the *Book of the Bee* says that the garden "was placed between heaven and earth, below the firmament [that is, below the celestial world] and above the earth [that is, above the telestial world], and that God placed it there . . . so that, if [Adam] kept [God's] commands He might lift him up to heaven, but if he transgressed them, He might cast him down to this earth" (JMBIGIL1, 160; see also pp. 139–44, 161).

Eden. "The name [Eden] has been derived from the Sumerian *edinu,* 'a plain,' but an Aramaic-Akkadian bilingual inscription suggests that the real meaning is 'luxuriance,'" or "abundance," more specifically an abundance of life-enriching water. . . . The idea is that man's food was ever ready at hand. The attractive, nutritious, and delectable qualities of the fruit are stressed with the

Figure 3–3. *Royal Investiture Panel at "Court of the Palms."* Mari (Tell Hariri), Syria, ca. 1800 BCE

KINGSHIP AND TEMPLE THEMES IN THE PALACE OF MARI IN OLD BABYLON

Scholars see resemblances in the layout of the Garden of Eden and that of Israelite temples (see figure 3–2). Elsewhere in the ancient Near East, temple and garden themes were also combined, as illustrated in this famous mural from Old Babylon, created in the Abrahamic era. The two sides of the panel are mirror images. Progress through the ceremonial rooms of the palace used in the annual renewal of the king's right to rule is represented as movement from the outer edges of the drawing toward the sacred center. The progression of the ceremony seems to have followed a fixed order involving stories and scenes of creation, a garden, sacrifice, the acquisition of a sequence of sacred names, and passing through a partiton ("screen") where the king would receive a final washing and be admitted to the presence of gods and divinized ancestors. Near the end of the ritual, the king would touch or grasp the hand of the god of the palace in what was called the "hand ceremony."

J. R. Porter writes of how the scene depicted in the mural "strikingly recall[s] details of the Genesis description of the Garden of Eden" (JMBMARI, 5). In particular, the mural depicts two types of tree. The drawing of the date palm on the left and right edges of the mural corresponds to a real date palm that grew in the exact center (= "midst" [Moses 3:9]) of the palace courtyard, recalling placement of the tree of life in the garden. The drawing of the second tree corresponds to treelike wooden posts that flanked a "screen" (presumably functioning as something like the veil in Israelite temples) made of "ornamented woven material" (Yasin M. Al-Khalesi, JMBMARI, 23). In Mari, this "veil" shielded the equivalent of the Israeilte "Holy of Holies" from public view, as the tree of knowledge hid the most sacred area of Eden (see figures 3–2, 4–2). Priests acting in the role of cherubim, shown here next to the treelike posts of the veil, were responsible for "the introduction of worshippers to the presence of the god" (al-Khalesi, JMBMARI, 20). Within the innermost sacred chamber, the king raises his right hand, perhaps in an oath-related gesture. At the same time, his left hand receives the rod and coil that signify his worthiness for the prerogatives of his office. These two items of regalia are measurement tools used in construction, corresponding in their general function to the later symbols of the square and compass. They served as symbols of divinely authorized power.

John Walton observed that "the ideology of the temple is not noticeably different in Israel than it is in the ancient Near East. The difference is in the God, not in the way the temple functions in relation to the God" (JMBMARI, 12–13). Of course, resemblances between authentic, revealed religion in Old Testament times and the religious beliefs and practices of other peoples do not necessarily imply that the Israelites got their religion from their neighbors. Rather, to believing Latter-day Saints, such resemblances provide "a kind of confirmation and vindication" that the gospel was preached in the beginning and that ancient evidence of distorted fragments of truth found outside biblical tradition may be the result of subsequent degeneration and apostasy (Truman G. Madsen, JMBMARI, 41). See JMBMARI, MOSESS 55.

man whom I had formed. ⁹ And out of the ground made I, the Lord God, to grow every tree, naturally, that is pleasant to the sight of man; and man could behold it. And it became also a living soul. For it was spiritual in the day that I created it; for it remaineth in the sphere in which I, God, created it, yea, even all things which

3:8   next episode in mind. The human couple will not be able to plead deprivation as the excuse for eating the forbidden fruit" (NMSGENESIS, 18).

    The ideas of luxuriance and plenty bring to mind the prominent place name "Bountiful" in the Book of Mormon (e.g., 1 Nephi 17:5; Alma 22:29–31)—in fact, an ancient site not far from the likely spot of the Old World Bountiful was reputed to be a place of such great abundance that its inhabitants were denounced by Islamic "Hud" traditions for their "attempt to create an earthly replica of paradise" (William J. Hamblin, JMBIGIL1, 161). The description also evokes the conceptually related name Joseph Smith gave to "Nauvoo" (נָאווּ = they-are-beautiful). The Sephardic transliteration of the verb in third-person plural form appeared in the Hebrew textbook he studied in Kirtland (p. 111) and is used in Psalm 93:5, Isaiah 52:7, and Song of Solomon 1:10.

    I put the man. The phrase implies that Adam's physical creation had taken place somewhere other than the Garden of Eden itself. Scholars often mention the temple as a possibility. The *Pirkei de-Rabbi Eliezer* explains the symbolism behind this idea: "The Holy One, blessed be He, showed to the first man a surfeit of love by creating him at a pure place—the location of the Temple—and in introducing him into His palace [that is, the Garden of Eden]" (JMBIGIL1, 162). Temples were usually located on the top of a mountain, while palaces were typically situated on a slightly lower slope.

3:9   *made . . . to grow every tree, naturally.* The sense of the additions made by Joseph Smith might be paraphrased as follows: "All the beautiful trees were made to grow naturally so that man could see them and enjoy their fruit. Because they were spiritual at the time they were created and remained in that 'sphere,' they also became 'living souls.' Similarly, everything else that had been prepared for man's use originally was spiritual" (JMBIGIL1, 162). The word "spiritual" seems to correspond to a state of "paradisiacal" or "terrestrial" glory. See commentary on Moses 3:5.

    pleasant to the sight of man; and . . . good for food. These words anticipate the later temptation of Eve.

    it became also a living soul. OT1 reads "they became also a living soul," while OT2 reads "it" (SHFJST, 89, 598).

    it remaineth in the sphere in which I, God, created it. Lehi explained in similar words that had it not been for the Fall, "all things which were created must have remained in the state in which they were after they were created; and they must have remained forever, and had no end" (2 Nephi 2:22). However, in the Book of Moses, the use of the term "sphere" introduces an additional nuance of meaning to this idea. If we infer the meaning from Joseph Smith's usage elsewhere (see JMBIGIL1, 139–40), the term refers either to an orbit of a heavenly body or to an area of activity, power, or influence—connotations that are near synonyms in the cosmology of Abraham 3:9, 16.

    But this interpretation immediately raises questions. For one thing, a view that the earth was physically transported from a "higher" to a "lower" sphere after the Fall through physical movement in space is impossible to harmonize with current planetary science. Moreover, the ideas that there was no death in the Garden of Eden or that the earth once existed in a mixed condition—partly spiritual and partly natural—are inconsistent with the scientific view of the earth's biology and geology.

    While the Lord has not revealed any solution to the problem of reconciling science and scripture on specifics of the Garden of Eden, Latter-day scholars have thought deeply about this problem. One suggestion is that the bodies of Adam and Eve could somehow have been prepared beforehand on the earth. Then, afterward, the couple could have been temporarily placed in a terrestrial place or state to experience the events of the Garden of Eden. Consistent with this idea,

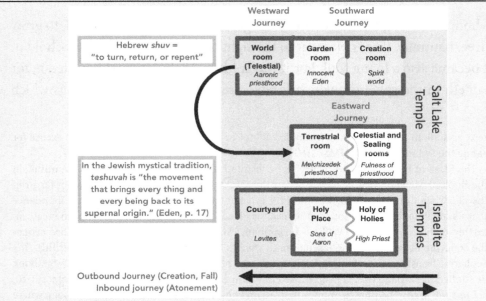

Figure 3–4. *Israelite Temples and the Salt Lake Temple.* Adapted from Nathan Richardson.

COMPARING LAYOUTS OF ISRAELITE TEMPLES AND MODERN TEMPLES

Since Latter-day Saints believe that the ordinances go back to the beginning of time, they might wonder how the covenant path was envisioned anciently. What clues we possess indicate that in other times the covenant path would not have been seen as something like a modern drive on a highway *to* the temple, but rather as an ancient walking journey *through* the various rooms of the temple.

In this image, we have vertically aligned the rooms of the Salt Lake Temple with the corresponding areas in the Israelite temple. There are three main areas associated with Israelite temples: the Courtyard, the Holy Place, and the Holy of Holies. In Latter-day Saint belief, these rooms symbolize the glories of the telestial, terrestrial, and celestial worlds. The requirement to support a two-way journey through the Salt Lake Temple—first, outbound—in the story of the Creation and the Fall—and second, inbound—in the story of the Atonement (see figure 3–2)—is met by doubling its celestial and terrestrial rooms. In other words, instead of having *one* "terrestrial room" that is traversed in both directions as in Israelite temples, the Salt Lake Temple provides *two* "terrestrial rooms"—the first representing the outbound area of the Garden of Eden where the Fall takes place and the other representing the inbound area that leads to the veil. Similarly, the Salt Lake Temple features two "celestial rooms"—one representing the outbound area of the Creation prior to the Fall and the other representing the final destination of the righteous after their return to God's presence. Note that in some modern temples, the Creation, Garden, and World rooms are combined, allowing a single space to successively represent different rooms at different points in time.

The process of repentance and return to God is beautifully reflected in the change in physical orientation of movement as the endowment progresses. As we leave the telestial glory of the World room and enter the Terrestrial room of the Salt Lake Temple, we make a U-turn from west to east. After making the turn, we are no longer moving away from God, but instead drawing near to Him again.

The rich significance of this symbolic reversal is captured by the rich Hebrew term *shuv*—meaning "to turn, return, or repent." Remember the scriptural description of the fate of mankind spelled out in Genesis 3:19: "dust thou art and unto dust shalt thou return" [*shuv*]. Consider also the way Psalm 90:3 (translated here following André Chouraqui, in the spirit of Rashi's commmentary) changes this pessimistic prediction into a harbinger of hope through God's tender of repentance: "Thou [God] turnest [*shuv*] man back to dust [figuratively, that is, through mortal suffering], but [then] Thou sayest, 'Return/Repent [*shuv*], O children of men'" (ACHBIBLE, 1187). The 180-degree U-turn movement that reverses the course of the temple journey recalls the Jewish mystical tradition in which the term *teshuvah* is used to refer to "the moment that brings every thing and every being back to its supernal origin" (compare Moses 4:31; 6:52; 7:2). In 2018, President Russell M. Nelson discussed the complete change of our minds, our knowledge, our spirit, and even our breathing as we repent and move forward incrementally in the right direction. See JMBFREE.

I prepared for the use of man; and man saw that it was good for food. And I, the Lord God, planted the tree of life also in the midst of the garden, and also the tree of knowledge of good and evil.

3:9   Moses 3:8 seems to imply that the bodies of Adam and Eve were created elsewhere and only later placed in the Garden ("There I *put* the man whom I had formed"; emphasis added). An important consequence of this view is that the subsequent Fall would not have required the movement of an entire planet from one place to another, as some have surmised, but only the removal of Adam and Eve from the state or place of Eden to the telestial earth (a form of "reverse translation")— an earth where natural conditions (including death and "time") had already prevailed from the beginning of its creation. A strength of this proposal is that it allows for an earth consistent with scientific findings of a long and continuous biological, geographical, and planetary history. The proposal is also in harmony with suggestions in some ancient religious traditions.

Of course, Latter-day Saints are also aware of the fact that scriptural descriptions of the Garden of Eden include figurative elements. The realization that the description of the Garden of Eden are at least in part figurative, combined with suggestions such as the one above, allow believers to accept the historicity of Adam and Eve, the reality of the Fall, and the tangible nature of the sacred space of Eden.

planted. OT1 reads "placed" (SHFJST, 89), a closer parallel to the term used to describe how Adam came into the garden (3:8).

tree of life. Elder Bruce R. McConkie wrote that the tree of life "figuratively refers to eternal life"—to the degree, of course, those who partake are qualified to receive it (see Doctrine and Covenants 88:28–32). Nephi referred to the tree of life as a manifestation of the "love of God" (1 Nephi 11:22–23).

It should be emphasized that the tree of life does not represent eternal life merely in an abstract sense but rather as a symbol of embodied deity. Thus, Jehovah, the premortal Jesus Christ, was represented to Moses in the burning bush as one who dwells in the midst of the glory of the tree of life (JMBIGIL1, 163). Going further, there is a sense that such trees can represent not only Deity but also humans who have, through temple rites of investiture, become royalty. The symbolism of the tree of life has also been connected specifically to the divine mother of a king, consistent with the associations of Mary, the mother of Jesus, with the tree of life in Nephi's vision (1 Nephi 11:15–23).

Ancient commentators often identify the tree of life with the olive tree. Its extremely long life makes it a fitting symbol for eternal life, and the everyday use of the oil as a source of both nourishment for people and fuel for light evokes natural associations when used in conjunction with the ritual anointing of priests and kings and the blessing of the sick. However, the date palm provides a more fitting symbol for the tree of life in some ancient cultures and in the Book of Mormon. For example, note that Lehi contrasts the fruit of the tree of life with the forbidden fruit: "the one being sweet and the other bitter" (2 Nephi 2:15). The date palm's fruit—often described as "white" in its most desirable varieties, well known to Lehi's family, and likely available in the valley of Lemuel where the family was camped at the time of Nephi's vision of the tree of life— would have provided a more fitting analogue than the olive to the love of God, which was "sweet above all that is sweet" (Alma 32:42). For a suggestion that reconciles the competing conceptions of the date palm and the olive tree, see JMBMOSES, 67. See JMBIGIL1, 163–67; MOSESS 58.

in the midst of the garden. The Hebrew of the phrase "in the midst" literally means "in the center." The phrase serves to emphasize the prominent position of the tree—there would have been no need to add the phrase if it were meant to be read "in the garden generally," as with all the other trees (UCCOMMENTARY, 110).

tree of knowledge of good and evil. The Hebrew expression "knowledge of good and evil" can mean knowledge of what is good and bad or of happiness and misery—or else knowledge of "everything" if "good and evil" is taken as a compound term. Perhaps the most relevant hint on the meaning of the phrase comes from Deuteronomy 1:39, which speaks of little children "who . . . had no knowledge of good and evil," suggesting that they were not accountable for their actions. In this sense, the term aptly refers to knowledge acquired by experience—a kind

¹⁰ And I, the Lord God, caused a river to go out of Eden to water the garden; and from thence it was parted, and became into four heads. ¹¹ And I, the Lord God, called the name of the first Pison, and it compasseth the whole land of Havilah, where I, the Lord God, created much gold; ¹² And the gold of that land was good, and there was bdellium and the onyx stone. ¹³ And the name of the second river was called Gihon; the same that compasseth the whole land of Ethiopia. ¹⁴ And the name of the third river was Hiddekel; that which goeth toward the east of Assyria. And the fourth river was the Euphrates.

3:9   of knowledge that Adam and Eve lacked before the Fall. Thus, Solomon fittingly prayed for the ability "to discern between good and bad" so that he would be able to function in his royal role (1 Kings 3:9).

   Jewish and Christian traditions often identify the tree of knowledge of good and evil as a fig tree, thus heightening the irony later on when Adam and Eve attempt to cover themselves with its leaves. The fruit of the fig tree is known for its abundance of seeds; thus an apron of green fig leaves is an appropriate symbol for Adam and Eve's ability to "be fruitful, and multiply" (Moses 2:28) after the Fall. See JMBIGIL1, 168–70; MOSESS 58.

3:10   *caused a river to go out of Eden.* The main point of vv. 10–14 is to declare that the life-giving waters of all the earth have their origin in the river of Eden. Anciently, it was thought to spring up from the ground opposite the throne of glory, and then flow down the mountain of God. Similarly, in Nephi's dream he saw the "fountain of living waters" originating at the "tree of life"—both the tree and the waters being a "representation of the love of God" (1 Nephi 11:25). Outside the garden, the river separates into four branches to water the four quarters of the world.

   Verses 10–14 have long been suspected of having come from a different source than the rest of the chapter. Perhaps this explains why vv. 11–14 are omitted from the Book of Abraham.

3:11   *Pison . . . Havilah.* The name Pison, with a possible meaning of something like "Gusher," appears nowhere else in the Old Testament. Havilah, perhaps signifying "sandy land," is mentioned elsewhere as a personal name and as a region apparently in Arabia (JMBIGIL1, 171).

3:12   *gold . . . bdellium . . . onyx.* The mention of gold and precious stones recalls scriptural descriptions of the temple (e.g., Haggai 2:7–8; Revelation 21:18; 2 Nephi 5:15–16).

3:13   *Gihon.* Gihon may be connected with a Hebrew verb that means "to break loose." In a valley at the foot of the Mount of Olives just outside of Jerusalem is a sacred spring by this name. The mention of the "land of Ethiopia" (or Cush) makes identification of the river difficult because there are several candidates for its location.

3:14   *Hiddekel.* Called the Tigris in Greek and the Dijlah in Arabic.

   Euphrates. The river was so well known that no further topographical description was required. In many places in the Bible it is called simply "the River." For example, in Psalms, it is prophesied that Solomon would "have dominion . . . from the river unto the ends of the earth" (Psalm 72:8). The passage in Psalms could be seen as a prophecy alluding to the eventual Davidic reign over the whole world, starting at the place where the world began—namely, at the source of the river of Eden (or alternatively "rivers," as seen from a vantage point outside of the garden)—and extending from thence to the four corners of the earth.

3:15   *took the man.* In Hebrew, this implies that the man is now called and given something to do.

   t*o dress it, and to keep it.* The Hebrew terms for "to dress" (*abad*) and "to keep" (*shamar*) connote, respectively, to "work, serve, till" and to "keep, watch (guard), preserve." Significantly, these are the very words that are used to describe the later tabernacle duties of the Levites (JMBIGIL1, 173). The temple parallel to this act of Creation is clear: Now that Adam has been called as a "temple worker" of sorts, the temple of the Garden of Eden can begin to function. See MOSESS 57, 70.

3:17   *thou shalt not eat of it.* Whereas the Hebrew text uses the singular "thou," implying that the commandment was given to Adam alone, the Greek Septuagint uses the plural "you." The idea

ADAM IS PLACED IN THE GARDEN; ONE TREE IS FORBIDDEN

[15] And I, the Lord God, took the man, and put him into the Garden of Eden, to dress it, and to keep it. [16] And I, the Lord God, commanded the man, saying: "Of every tree of the garden thou mayest freely eat, [17] But of the tree of the knowledge of good and evil, thou shalt not eat of it, nevertheless, thou mayest choose for thyself, for it is given unto thee; but, remember that I forbid it, for in the day thou eatest thereof thou shalt surely die."

ADAM NAMES THE ANIMALS

[18] And I, the Lord God, said unto mine Only Begotten, that it was not good that the man should be alone; wherefore, I will make an help meet for him. [19] And out

that both Adam and Eve were both present to hear this command from God was not unknown in Jewish and early Christian tradition (see figure 4–8).

In the version of this verse published in the 1835 edition of *Lectures on Faith* 2:10, the words "neither shall you touch it" follow this phrase (KPJMOSES, 75).

thou mayest choose for thyself. This added phrase to the Book of Moses makes it clear that Adam and Eve are to be placed in a situation where they must exercise their freedom to choose. President Joseph Fielding Smith offered the following paraphrase of the command: "The Lord said to Adam, here is the tree of the knowledge of good and evil. If you want to stay here then you cannot eat of that fruit. If you want to stay here, then I forbid you to eat it. But you may act for yourself and you may eat of it if you want to. And if you eat of it you will die." Elsewhere, President Smith explained: "In no other commandment the Lord ever gave to man, did he say: 'But of the tree of the knowledge of good and evil, thou shalt not eat of it, nevertheless, thou mayest choose for thyself.'" (JMBIGIL1, 174).

The Prophet Joseph Smith emphasized that "Adam did not commit sin in eating the fruits, for God had decreed that he should eat and fall. But in compliance with the decree he should die. Only he should die was the saying of the Lord; therefore the Lord appointed us to fall and also redeemed us" (JSWORDS, 9 February 1841, 63).

in the day thou eatest thereof thou shalt surely die. *Spiritual* death after the eating of the fruit would be swift, since transgression would require Adam and Eve to be separated from God's presence. *Physical* death would be just as sure but not so immediate—as seen later, the lives of Adam and Eve will be mercifully "prolonged" so that they can experience a "state of probation" (2 Nephi 2:21).

Since the tree of life is not specifically included in the prohibition here, readers have wondered whether Adam and Eve may have eaten from it to prolong their lives while they remained in the garden. But careful analysis of the Hebrew makes this possibility unlikely (see commentary on Moses 4:28). In addition, Elder Bruce R. McConkie maintained that the chief idea represented by worthily partaking of the fruit of the tree of life was not immortality but rather eternal life. Therefore, Adam and Eve's only approach to the tree of life will be by way of first taking the fruit of the tree of knowledge, then leaving the garden to pass into mortality, and returning at last to take the sweet fruit only if and when they are fully qualified—and authoritatively invited—to do so. See JMBIGIL1, 175–76.

3:18   **it was not good that the man should be alone.** This was the first declaration by God that some aspect of creation was not good. Recall that in Moses 2:27, 31 God did not declare His handiwork "very good" until after He had created woman.

an help meet for him. The Hebrew means "a helper or strength corresponding to him"—or, in other words, a completing counterpart. "This term cannot be taken as demeaning because Hebrew ʿezer, employed here to describe the intended role of the woman, is often used of God in His relation to man" (NMSGENESIS, 21). President Howard W. Hunter said, "The Lord intended

Figure 3–5. Arnold Friberg (1913–2010): *Eight Faces of Moses, 1953.* The series shows portraits of Moses at different stages in his life.

Names as Signposts along the Covenant Pathway

Temple symbolism among the members of The Church of Jesus Christ of Latter-day Saints reflects the idea that the nature of progress on the covenant pathway is incremental. It employs an invariable succession of names, relationships, roles, virtues, ordinances, priesthoods, and types of clothing as signposts corresponding to different stages of existence and their associated glories. Symbolism of this sort is not modern in origin but was once employed in a range of religious settings throughout the ancient world and in early Christianity.

With specific respect to names, we see this pattern reflected in the second-century account of the early Christian theologian, Clement of Alexandria (ca. 150–215 CE). His account is drawn from a group of "initiates" (= Greek *mystai*) who described the three successive names that they understood to have been given to Moses at different junctures of his life: "'Joachim,' given him by his mother at circumcision; 'Moses,' given him by Pharaoh's daughter; and 'Melchi,' a name he had in heaven which was given him, apparently by God, after his ascension." Though interpretations of the name "Melchi" vary, the eminent scholar of Second Temple Judaism, Erwin Goodenough, saw this third name as representing the "eternal priesthood of Melchizedek," reported in Genesis as being a "king" and "the priest of the Most High God" (Genesis 14:18. See also JST Genesis 14:25-40). Going beyond these three names reported in Clement's account, Moses 1:25 can be seen as the bestowal of a final, fourth name, implied in the divine declaration that Moses is to be "made stronger than many waters, . . . as if thou wert God." Moses' experience might be compared with the that of Marduk within *Enuma Elish*, a Babylonian ritual text. The story culminates with the conferral upon Marduk of fifty sacred titles, including the higher god Ea's own name, accompanied with the declaration: "He is indeed even as I."

The idea of names as "keywords" is very old. In a temple context, the meaning of the term "keyword" can be taken quite literally: the use of the appropriate keyword or keywords by a qualified worshipper "unlocks" each one of a successive series of gates, thus providing access to specific, secured areas of the sacred space. From his study of the matter, BYU professor John Gee concludes: "The presence of gatekeepers, stronger in some texts than others, indicates a temple initiation in the Egyptian texts and therefore suggests an initiation in the Jewish and Christian texts."

In temples throughout the ancient Near East, including Jerusalem, "different temple gates had names indicating the blessing received when entering: 'the gate of grace,' 'the gate of salvation,' 'the gate of life,' and so on," as well as signifying "the fitness, through due preparation, which entrants should have in order to pass through [each one of] the gates." In Jerusalem, the final "gate of the Lord, into which the righteous shall enter," very likely referred to "the innermost temple gate" where those seeking the face of the God of Jacob would find the fulfillment of their temple pilgrimage—the place in Nephi's conception where if one "asks" and "knocks," one is "brought into the light" (2 Nephi 32:4). One might compare this to the symbolism of modern temple worship, where those who "endure to the end" of the covenant pathway that leads through the temple symbolically receive, in an anticipatory way, the ultimate gift of "eternal life" (2 Nephi 31:20). See MOSESS 39; JMBSTRONGER.

of the ground I, the Lord God, formed every beast of the field, and every fowl of the air; and commanded that they should come unto Adam, to see what he would call them; and they were also living souls; for I, God, breathed into them the breath of life, and commanded that whatsoever Adam called every living creature, that should be the name thereof. ²⁰ And Adam gave names to all cattle, and to the fowl of the air, and to every beast of the field; but as for Adam, there was not found an help meet for him.

3:18 that the wife be . . . a companion equal and necessary in full partnership." Thus, in Moses 2 both man and woman are created in the image of God, and in Moses 3 they are described as corresponding strengths (JMBIGIL1, 176).

 Note that the Book of Abraham, unlike the Book of Moses, places the creation of woman *before* the naming of the animals (Abraham 5:16, 20–21; compare 2 Nephi 2:15).

3:19 ***out of the ground, I . . . formed every beast of the field.*** A beast of the field is a wild animal. The Hebrew admits a translation of the term behind "formed" as "*had* formed." This would allow for a creation sequence consistent with Moses 2, where the animals appeared before man's creation.

 commanded that they should come unto Adam. Nahum Sarna comments, "In Genesis 1, God bestows names only on the cosmic phenomena connected with time and space. Here He assigns to man the role of naming terrestrial animates, which . . . is another way of expressing the bestowal of authority and dominion over them, the idea contained in v. 28" (NMSGENESIS, 22).

 In Islamic tradition, a different event appears in place of the episode of the naming of animals, namely, the reciting of sacred names to angels. Like temple initiates in other cultures, Adam—before the Fall and after having been given instruction by God—is said in these sources to have been directed to recite a series of secret names to the angels in order prove that he was worthy of the elevated status of priest and king that had been conferred upon him (MOSESS 56; figures 3–5 and 4–6).

 Is it possible that Adam himself was made aware of his name as part of this episode? The fact that the first reference to Adam as a proper name in the Hebrew text is given in v. 20 seems to lend support to such a conjecture. It also seems significant that the final instance of naming in the story of the garden and the Fall—when Adam identifies the permanent proper name of Eve—occurs in immediate proximity to the account of God's making coats of skin for the couple (Moses 4:26–27).

 While Genesis 2:19 reads "and brought them," OT1 reads "and commanded that they should be brought" (SHFJST, 90), OT2 was the source of the phrase currently canonized in this verse. In this reading, unlike Eve, the animals are not brought personally by God to Adam. This contrast has the effect of highlighting the special nature of the introduction of the man and the woman in v. 22 (JMBIGIL1,177–80).

3:20 ***Adam.*** This is the first reference in Hebrew to Adam as a proper name. "The narrative now speaks of the man as a personality rather than an archetypal human" (NMSGENESIS, 22).

 there was not found an help meet for him. Through naming the animals, Adam observes the universal pairing of male and female in the animal world and becomes aware of his exceptional solitary state. Now not only God but also Adam recognized fully that it was not good to be alone. Now Adam is ready "to appreciate and cherish the gift that the Lord God was to give him" (UCCOMMENTARY, 128).

3:21 ***deep sleep.*** The Hebrew word for such a deep, divinely induced slumber connotes a transition from a former state into a new one—a "sleep and a forgetting," as William Wordsworth expressed it (JMBIGIL1, 180). Without remembrance of all that came before, Adam "was simple as a new-born child" (UCCOMMENTARY, 113).

 When the sleeping Adam lost the memory of his past, he also became ignorant of other things. The *Apocalypse of Adam* records Adam as saying to his children that "the first knowledge that breathed within us" disappeared and that "the eternal knowledge of the God of truth withdrew

	22-23 January 1832 (Doctrine & Covenants 84:33-48)	19 January 1841 (Doctrine and Covenants 124:28, 39)	4 May 1842 (1845 entry of WR; cf. DHC 5:2)
Initiatory	"sanctified by the Spirit unto the renewing of their bodies"	"your anointings and your washings"*	"washings, anointings"
Endowment**	"the sons of Moses and of Aaron"	"your memorials for your sacrifices by the sons of Levi, and for your oracles in your most holy places wherein you receive conversations, and your statues and judgments"	"endowments, and the communication of keys pertaining to the Aaronic Priesthood, and so on to the highest order of the Melchizedek Priesthood, setting forth the order pertaining to the Ancient of Days," i.e., Adam
Marriage Sealing	"the seed of Abraham"		
Fulness of the Priesthood	"the church and kingdom"	"the fulness of the priesthood"	i.e., "the highest order of the Melchizedek Priesthood"
Election Made Sure; More Sure Word of Prophecy	"the elect of God"		"secure the fulness of those blessings which have been prepared for the Church of the Firstborn"
Second Comforter	"the Father teacheth him"		(a blessing of "the Church of the Firstborn" — Doctrine and Covenants 88:3-5)
Receive the Kingdom	"all that my Father hath shall be given unto him"		"abide in the presence of the Elohim in the eternal worlds"

* "and your baptisms for the dead, and your solemn assemblies" immediately follows these words.
** As used in modern Latter-day Saint terminology. By way of contrast, Joseph Smith seems to have used the word "endowment" to refer to the entire sequence of ordinances and blessings.

Figure 3–6. *Sequence of Ordinances and Blessings*

THE ORDER OF THE ORDINANCES

In connection with the idea that the succession of ordinances is invariable (see figure 3–5), the following definitive statement from Joseph Smith can be cited: "The order of the house of God has been, and ever will be, the same, even after Christ comes; and after the termination of the thousand years it will be the same" (JSTPJS, 12 November 1835, 91. Compare JSTPJS, 22 January 1834, 59–61). Note that this statement was made 1835, as the Saints prepared to receive the ordinances that would be available to them in the Kirtland Temple. Since the Nauvoo Temple ordinances differed greatly from those given in Kirtland, it is apparent that the Prophet cannot have been asserting that his work to restore ancient temple ordinances was finished by 1835.

What is important, however, is to realize that although *additional* ordinances were given in Nauvoo, the "*order* of the house of God" did not change. Indeed, based on a careful comparison of the Kirtland and Nauvoo temple ordinances, Andrew F. Ehat observes "that the Nauvoo Temple ordinances perfectly fit within the essential framework of ordinances revealed during the Kirtland period. . . . Although they do represent a significant amplification of the Kirtland ordinances, the Nauvoo ordinances do not, however, change the order of the ordinances first administered in Kirtland" (JMBFREE).

Lists of these ordinances and blessings were provided in 1832, 1841, and 1845, as shown above. The later descriptions from the 1840s in the two rightmost columns should be compared with the much earlier description in the leftmost column. This leftmost description was taken from Doctrine and Covenants 84, a revelation given in January 1832 a full decade before the Nauvoo endowment was first administered and more than four years before the Kirtland Temple was dedicated. Thus, it seems, a complete list in the correct sequence for these ordinances and blessings were given very early in the ministry of Joseph Smith, corroborating the idea that he received extensive tutoring on priesthood and temple matters during the period he was engaged in Bible translation (JMBWHAT, 7–8; JMBFREE. For a more complete discussion of temple themes in Doctrine and Covenants 84, see JMBOATH).

Elder Boyd K. Packer provided a thorough discussion of the cluster of terms associated with the word "order," which can only be summarized briefly here. The word "ordinance" derives from the Latin term behind the word "order," which means "a rank, a row, a series." Many examples of the use of the word "order" are given in the scriptures: "established the order of the Church" (Alma 8:1); "all things should be restored to their proper order" (Alma 41:2); "all things may be done in order" (Doctrine and Covenants 20:68); "Mine house is a house of order" (Doctrine and Covenants 132:8); "order of the priesthood" (Doctrine and Covenants 94:6). Moroni defined depravity as being "without order" (Moroni 9:18). "From all this dictionary work," concluded Elder Packer, "there comes the impression that an ordinance, to be valid, must be done in the proper order" (JMBFREE).

The Creation of Eve

²¹ And I, the Lord God, caused a deep sleep to fall upon Adam; and he slept, and I took one of his ribs and closed up the flesh in the stead thereof; ²² And the rib which I, the Lord God, had taken from man, made I a woman, and brought her unto the man. ²³ And Adam said:

> "This I know now is bone of my bones,
>   and flesh of my flesh;
> She shall be called Woman,
>   because she was taken out of man.

²⁴ "Therefore shall a man leave his father and his mother, and shall cleave unto his wife; and they shall be one flesh."

3:21   from me and your mother Eve." The awakening of Adam represents the beginning of his recovery from his state of ignorance and mortality. In the *Apocalypse of Adam*, Adam is awakened by "three men" of surpassing "glory." Although Adam is at first "unable to recognize" them, they reveal knowledge to him about his Creator (JMBIGIL1, 180–81; figure 5–9).

3:22   *the rib.* President Spencer W. Kimball taught that "the story of the rib, of course, is figurative" (JMBIGIL1, 181). As Sarna describes, "The mystery of the intimacy between husband and wife and the indispensable role that the woman ideally plays in the life of man are symbolically described in terms of her creation out of his body. The rib taken from man's side thus connotes physical union and signifies that she is his companion and partner, ever at his side" (NMSGENESIS, 22).

   brought her unto the man. "As noted in a midrash, the image may well be that of God playing the role of the attendant who leads the bride to the groom. Without doubt, the verse conveys the idea that the institution of marriage is established by God Himself" (NMSGENESIS, 23). See MOSESS 57.

3:23   *Adam said.* "Man's first recorded speech is a cry of ecstatic elation at seeing the woman" (NMSGENESIS, 23). At last, he had found his own likeness, a companion whose strength corresponded to his own (see commentary on Moses 3:18).

   bone of my bones, and flesh of my flesh. In the Bible, this phrase not only has the obvious meaning but also is used to signify that two people belong to each other (Genesis 29:14; Judges 9:2; 2 Samuel 5:1; 19:12–13; 1 Chronicles 11:1). Victor Hamilton sees this as not merely a statement of relationship but, in addition, a pledge of covenantal loyalty, serving "as the biblical counterpart to the modern marriage ceremony, 'in weakness [that is, flesh] and in strength [that is, bone].' . . . Both the man and the woman share the entire spectrum of human characteristics, from strong to weak" (VPHGENESIS, 180).

   Woman . . . man. Hebrew *'ishah* and *'ish*, "though actually derived from distinct and unrelated stems, are here associated through folk etymology by virtue of assonance" (NMSGENESIS, 23).

3:24   *cleave unto his wife.* "The underlying meaning of the [idea of two distinct entities becoming attached to one another while preserving their separate identities] becomes clear, if it is noted that the verb *d-v-k* ["cleave"] is often used to describe human yearning for and devotion to God. Sexual relations between husband and wife do not rise above the level of animality unless they be informed by and imbued with spiritual, emotional, and mental affinity" (NMSGENESIS, 23; JMBIGIL1, 185).

Figure 3–7. *The Expulsion of Adam and Eve*, 1646.

ADAM AND EVE'S GARMENT OF LIGHT

"And they were both naked, the man and his wife, and were not ashamed" (Moses 3:25). Though figuratively "naked," because their knowledge of their premortal state had been taken away by a "veil of forgetfulness," Adam and Eve had come to Eden nonetheless "trailing clouds of glory." While the couple, as yet, were free from transgression, they could stand "naked" in God's presence without shame, being "clothed with purity" in what early commentators called "garments of light" or "garments of contentment." In one source, Eve describes her appearance by saying: "I was decked out like a bride, and I reclined in a wedding-chamber of light."

Having forgotten the traditions of Adam and Eve's garment of light, Western art typically portrays Adam and Eve as naked in the Garden of Eden, and dressed in "coats of skin" after the Fall. However, because the Eastern Orthodox tradition remembers the accounts that portray Adam as a King and Priest in Eden, they naturally show him—and Eve—in regal robes. Moreover, Orthodox readers interpret the "skins" that the couple wore after their expulsion from the Garden as being their own now-fully human flesh. Gary Anderson interprets this symbolism to mean that "Adam has exchanged an angelic constitution for a mortal one"—in Latter-day Saint parlance, they have lost their terrestrial glory and are now in a telestial state.

The top panel of the figure above shows God seated in the heavenly council surrounded by angels and the four beasts of the book of Revelation. The second panel depicts, from left to right: Adam and Eve clothed in heavenly robes following their creation; then stripped of their glorious garments and "clothed" only in mortal skin after eating the forbidden fruit; and finally, both clad in fig leaf aprons as Eve converses with God. The third panel shows Adam conversing with God, the couple's expulsion from the walled Garden through a door showing images of cherubim, and their subsequent hardship in the fallen world. Orthodox tradition generally leaves Adam and Eve in their aprons after the Fall and expulsion, seeing them as already having received their "coats of skin" when they were clothed in mortal flesh.

Explaining the significance of rituals and ordinances based on the story of Adam and Eve, Nibley wrote:

> The garment [of light] represents the preexistent glory of the candidate. . . . When he leaves on his earthly mission, it is laid up for him in heaven to await his return. It thus serves as security and lends urgency and weight to the need for following righteous ways on earth. For if one fails here, one loses not only one's glorious future in the eternities to come, but also the whole accumulation of past deeds and accomplishments in the long ages of preexistence (HWNMESSAGE, 489; JMBIGIL1, 236).

See MOSESS 68; figure 4–7.

²⁵ And they were both naked, the man and his wife, and were not ashamed.

3:25   ***they were both naked.*** In the garden, Adam and Eve were no longer "clothed" with the memory and glory of their earlier state. The verse attests to the couple's innocence, their lack of awareness of the change that had come over them—and of the greater change that was yet to come.

Note that the verse is meant to prepare us for Moses 4:13. It "forms the transition to the next episode by means of a word play on 'naked' (Hebrew *'arom*, plural *'arummim*) and 'shrewd' (Hebrew *'arum*). It also conveys an anticipatory hint at" how the two concepts are going to be related. Approximating the Hebrew wordplay in English, we might say (with Gordon Wenham) that the couple aspired to be shrewd (like the serpent), and they ended up nude (GJWGENESIS, 72)

were not ashamed. While the couple were as yet free from transgression they could stand "naked" in God's presence without shame (see Doctrine and Covenants 121:45), being "clothed with purity" (2 Nephi 9:14) in what early commentators called "garments of light" (JMBIGIL1, 186). These garments correspond symbolically to the equally significant but less glorious "coats of skin" that God made for Adam and Eve after the Fall.

CHAPTER 4

THE FALL

THE REBELLION OF SATAN IN THE PREMORTAL COUNCIL

4 ¹ And I, the Lord God, spake unto Moses, saying: That Satan, whom thou hast commanded in the name of mine Only Begotten, is the same which was from the beginning, and he came before me, saying—"Behold, here am

4   After a rapid sweep across the vast panorama of the Creation and the Garden of Eden in Moses 2–3, the scope narrows and the narrative slows to a more measured pace in Moses 4—and with good reason, for it is at this point that the *purpose* of creation begins to unfold. The Roman Catholic Cardinal John Henry Newman summed up a lesson that seems pertinent to the combined accounts of the Creation and the Fall: "It were better for sun and moon to drop from heaven, for the earth to fail, and for all the many millions who are upon it to die of starvation in extremest agony, so far as temporal affliction goes, than that one soul . . . should commit one single venial sin, should tell one wilful untruth, though it harmed no one, or steal one poor farthing without excuse" (MOSESS 60). From this perspective, the gravity of the innocent choice made in Eden—and of moral choices we make on a daily basis—outweigh in the eyes of God the entire amoral universe. Of course, reflecting on the lessons of the Fall is not meant to drag us down into guilt, but rather to encourage us to use the gift of moral agency wisely. As President Russell M. Nelson has said, "Nothing is more liberating, more ennobling, or more crucial to our individual progression than is a regular, daily focus on repentance" (MOSESS 60).

    For some Christians, the Fall has been seen as a tragedy that brought original sin upon Adam and Eve and all their posterity. However, for Latter-day Saints the events that brought opposition into the world (see 2 Nephi 2:11) came through the exercise of choice and were, in fact, a "necessary evil." The second article of faith teaches that sin is an individual responsibility, not the result of evil forces beyond our control. According to scripture, the purpose of earth life is to "prove" all people "to see if they will do all things whatsoever the Lord their God shall command them" (Abraham 3:25). Through the enabling grace and power of the Atonement of Jesus Christ, the means to overcome sin and death were provided and the way was opened for human salvation and exaltation (see 2 Nephi 25:23). The test given by our temporary earthly probation requires a fallen world, one that the devil himself helped institute through his temptation in the Garden of Eden. In this chapter we will see how Satan, in his efforts to thwart Adam and Eve's progression, unknowingly advanced God's own plan.

4:1   ***That Satan, whom thou hast commanded.*** In verses 1–4, the Lord digresses from the story of the Fall to describe the roles of Satan and the Savior. "Satan" is a word of Hebrew origin meaning an accuser or adversary. The qualifier ("whom thou hast commanded") refers to Moses 1:21, when Moses had commanded Satan "in the name of the Only Begotten" to depart.

    here am I, send me. Draper et al. note that this statement carries the intrinsic claim "that the speaker is in the right path, ready to do the Lord's bidding" (RDDPGP, 38): "Here am I awaiting thy command." Also significant is that *Midrash Rabbah* associates this phrase with the promised blessings of the fulness of the priesthood: "'Here am I'— ready for priesthood, ready for kingship" (MOSESS 60). However, when Satan said "Here am I, send me," his intentions were clearly in direct opposition to God's. His insincerity falsifies his claim of moral readiness, substantiating the scriptural assertion that the devil is "a liar from the beginning" (Doctrine and Covenants 93:25).

    Moreover, since Jesus Christ was already known by all to be God's "Beloved and Chosen from the beginning" (Moses 4:2), the very fact that Satan sought to answer the call was in itself a direct challenge to the Father. BYU professor Brent Top correctly concludes that "the Father's question 'Whom shall I send?' was . . . a call for our commitment and common consent rather than a request for résumés" (JMBIGIL1, 243).

Figure 4–1. William Blake, 1757–1827: *Satan in His Original Glory*, ca. 1805

BLAKE'S DEPICTION OF SATAN WITH PERVERTED SYMBOLS OF KINGSHIP

"Thou wast perfect in thy ways from the day that thou was created, till iniquity was found in thee" (Ezekiel 28:15). The fall of the king of Tyre in Ezekiel's lamentation is usually thought to have been typed on the rebellion of Satan. Blake's illustration above is derived from a reading of v. 14 of the Latin version of Ezekiel's prophecy that describes Lucifer as the "cherub with extensive wingspan." His pose is one of feigned kingship. The orb and scepter in his hands symbolize the power and authority from God given before his fall from heaven. He stands on the heavenly mountain, surrounded by "tiny, joyous figures embody[ing] the precious stones and beautifully crafted musical instruments mentioned in the Biblical text."

According to Endre Tóth, the garments and emblems of European royalty resembled those of the Israelite high priest until the fashion of military dress eventually became the style. To highlight Lucifer's perversity, Blake has conspicuously reversed the hands in which the emblems of European monarchy are normally held: what should be grasped by the right hand is portrayed in his left hand, and vice versa. For example, Satan is holding a scepter (the symbolic equivalent of a sword) in his left hand. However, in British coronation ceremonies, the sword is to be held in the *right* hand. It is meant to be used "to stop the growth of iniquity, protect the Holy Church of God and defend widows and orphans." Brannon M. Wheeler notes that "the association of swords with royal symbolism is found in many different cultural traditions. Swords are used in various cultures as symbols of investiture. The sword and the rod, for which it is a substitute, is also used as a mark of religious authority."

The orb is meant to be held in the left hand in British coronation ceremonies to signify "the domination of Christ over the whole world" (Beverley Nichols). Though monarchs are often pictured with such an orb in their cupped hand, Tóth has concluded that "no such ensign as an orb existed until the 11th century," previous depictions having been entirely "symbolic"—that is, the priestly symbol was represented by an empty hand (JMBIGIL1, 304–305). In another part of the coronation ceremony, the new British monarch holds the scepter with the cross in the right hand as an "ensign of power and justice" and the rod with the dove in the left as a "symbol of equity and mercy" (Nichols).

Note also that prior to the coronation ceremonies, the British monarch is "divested of . . . [royal] robes," clothed in simple white linen, and "screened from the general view" in order to be "imbued with grace" through the archbishop's anointing with holy oil "on hand, breast and forehead" (Nichols; JMBIGIL1, 224, 304–5). See MOSESS 59.

I, send me, I will be thy son, and I will redeem all mankind, that one soul shall not be lost, and surely I will do it; wherefore give me thine honor." ² But, behold, my Beloved Son, which was my Beloved and Chosen from the beginning, said unto me—"Father, thy will be done, and the glory be thine forever."

³ Wherefore, because that Satan rebelled against me, and sought to destroy the agency of man, which I, the Lord God, had given him, and also, that I should give

4:1   Note also that Satan's self-centeredness is fittingly reflected in the wording of his proposal. With passionate rapid-fire delivery, he narcissistically repeats the terms "I" and "me" six times in the short span of half a verse. OT1 and OT2 reinforce the stylistic egoism of the phrase "Behold, here am I" with their briefer reading: "Behold I" (SHFJST, 90, 599)—more likely the way the phrase would have been worded by an ancient speaker. See MOSESS 60.

    I will be thy son. Compare Moses 1:19, where, in a rage, Satan claimed the role he was here denied.

    I will redeem all mankind, that one soul shall not be lost. This frequently misunderstood statement was clarified by Joseph Smith in one of his discourses. In the published version of William Clayton's rough notes the following statement was recorded, "The contention in Heaven was—Jesus said there would be certain souls that would not be saved; and the Devil said he could save them all" (JSTPJS, 7 April 1844, 357). In comparing William Clayton's notes with the notes of others who heard Joseph Smith's discourse, additional details make it clear that the "contention in Heaven" was *not* about whether ordinary souls could make it to heaven if they were forced to be obedient in all things, as Latter-day Saints sometimes mistakenly teach. Rather, the contention in heaven had to do with Satan falsely claiming that he could save *even those who would commit the unpardonable sin* (MOSESS 62).

    Contradicting Satan's boast, Wilford Woodruff recorded the Prophet saying that Jesus Christ's intention was to "save all [in one of the three kingdoms of glory] *except the sons of perdition*" (JSWORDS, 7 April 1844, 347). Likewise, Brigham Young affirmed, "None are condemned except those who have the privilege of receiving the words of eternal life and refuse to receive them" (JD, 8:294). Compare Doctrine and Covenants 76:25–39.

    Ironically, Satan, the one who proposed a plan whereby no soul would be lost, became *himself* a soul whom Jesus could not save. To him was given the name "perdition"—"lost one" (JMBIGIL1, 244). See MOSESS 62.

    I will redeem. Whatever Satan exactly meant by his proposal to become the "redeemer" of all humankind, it was doubtless very different from what the Savior offered. Elder Spencer J. Condie commented, "Because [the devil's] plan . . . required no Atonement for sin, . . . he could save his own satanic skin from any suffering" (JMBIGIL1, 243).

    surely I will do it. Satan seems to be claiming not merely that he will surely redeem all humankind but also that he alone *can* do it and—even more arrogantly—that he can do it *alone.*

4:2   *my Beloved.* The phrase "my Beloved" is repeated twice in the verse, emphasizing the deep and personal regard of the Father for His Son. Contrast this with the distancing third-person reference that introduces the adversary in verse 1: "That Satan."

    Father, thy will be done. Abraham 3:27 makes it clear that it was actually Jesus Christ who was the first to answer the Father's request. In stark contrast to Satan's speech, the Savior never once mentions the words "I" or "me," being wholly focused on the will and the glory of the Father.

    glory be thine forever. Jesus later contrasted His position with the one adopted by Satan: "He that speaketh of himself seeketh his own glory: but he that seeketh his glory that sent him, the same is true, and no unrighteousness is in him" (John 7:18).

4:3   *Satan rebelled against me, and sought to destroy the agency of man.* Doctrine and Covenants 29:36 underscores the irony of Satan's efforts to destroy people's agency by pointing out that it was "*because* of their agency" that many of the "hosts of heaven" were permitted to follow him in rebellion (emphasis added).

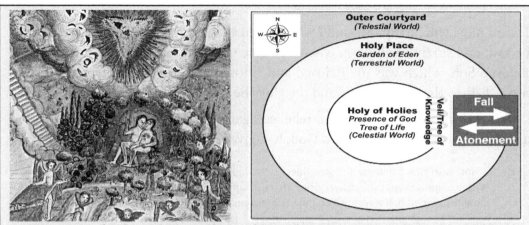

Figure 4–2. Left: Adam and Eve near the top of the newly created mountain of Eden. Frontispiece, *Treatise on the Six Days of Creation;* Right: *The Garden of Eden from a Top-Down Perspective*

Top-Down View of the Symbolic Geography of Eden

The illustration at left depicts Adam and Eve as living at first in the presence of God near the top of a paradisiacal mountain (see figure 3–2). The figure at right reflects ancient traditions that speak of a "wall" surrounding the garden and of an inner "hedge" or "veil" that separated the garden from the tree of life. In a caption to a similar figure, Genesis scholar Gary A. Anderson notes: "According to Ephrem, Adam and Eve have access to most of Eden. The animals live just outside the sacred confines, and Adam and Eve have to go to the edge of Eden to tend them. It is here, at Eden's border, that Eve converses with the snake. The tree of knowledge guards the entry point to the inner sanctum, the Holy of Holies, wherein the tree of life is found [compare figure 3–3]. Adam and Eve were not sufficiently holy at creation to enter this room. . . . Since they tried to enter prematurely, they were driven out of Eden altogether" (GAAGENESIS, 80).

Whereas figure 3–2 provides a linear illustration of how the layout of the Garden of Eden and the temple relate to the Fall and the Atonement, the figure above at right provides a top-down, circular perspective. To see how these two perspectives can share the same symbolic geography, consider how Israelite temples and some modern temples feature a linear progression toward a celestial room at one end of the building (either east or west), whereas in others the movement is in an increasingly *inward* direction. For example, the Provo Utah Temple is an example of inward progression, where "six ordinance rooms [are] surrounded by an exterior hallway" with the "celestial room . . . in the building's center" (MOSESS 61).

The "eastward" location of the Garden of Eden may thus be explained by its position relative to the Creator, who is "in the midst," meaning literally in Hebrew "in the center" (Moses 3:8–9). Note that the initial separation of Adam and Eve from God occurred when they were removed from His presence to be placed in the garden "eastward in Eden" (Moses 3:8)—that is, east of the peak of the "mountain" where, in some representations of the symbolic geography of Paradise, He is said to dwell. This interpretation also seems to be borne out in later events, as eastward movement is repeatedly associated with increasing distance from God. After God's voice of judgment visited Adam and Eve from the west (Moses 4:14), they experienced an additional degree of separation when, after the Fall, they left the garden through its eastern gate (Moses 4:31). Cain was "shut out from the presence of the Lord" as he went eastward to dwell "in the land of Nod" (Moses 5:41). The journey of Cain's posterity continued in the same direction—"from the east" to the "land of Shinar"—the place where the Tower of Babel was constructed (Genesis 11:2). Finally, Lot traveled east toward Sodom and Gomorrah when he separated himself from Abraham (Genesis 13:11).

On the other hand, westward movement is often used to symbolize return and restoration of blessings—that is, atonement. For instance, according to the *Book of Giants*, Enoch gathered his people to the west. Abraham's "return from the east is [a] return to the Promised Land and . . . the city of 'Salem'" (Genesis 14:17–20), being "directed toward blessing." The Magi of the Nativity likewise came "from the east," westward to Bethlehem, their journey symbolically enacting a restoration of temple and priesthood blessings that had been lost from the earth (Matthew 2:1; JMBIGIL1, 161, 673–74; figure 5–3). Additionally, the glorious return of Jesus Christ when He "shall suddenly come to his temple" (Malachi 3:1) is likewise represented as an east-to-west movement: "For as the light of the morning cometh out of the east, and shineth even unto the west, and covereth the whole earth, so shall also the coming of the Son of man be" (Joseph Smith—Matthew 1:26). See JMBTREE, MOSESS 61, JMBGIANTS, 1124–34.

unto him mine own power; by the power of mine Only Begotten, I caused that he should be cast down; [4] And he became Satan, yea, even the devil, the father of all lies, to deceive and to blind men, and to lead them captive at his will, even as many as would not hearken unto my voice.

4:3 Although the exercise of agency was surely a condition of the premortal existence, Moses 7:32 seems to imply, erroneously, that it did not exist until Adam and Eve came into the garden: "I gave unto [people] their knowledge, in the day I created them; and in the Garden of Eden, gave I unto man his agency." OT2, however, renders this verse differently: "I gave unto them their *intelligence* and in the Garden of Eden man *had* agency" (SHFJST, 618; emphasis added). This emendation makes it clear both that (1) agency existed before Adam and Eve were placed in the garden, and (2) that they had only "intelligence," not "knowledge." Adam and Eve began to obtain the "knowledge" of experience only after their transgression.

  The means by which Satan planned to "destroy the agency of man" have not been authoritatively explained. However, a common Latter-day Saint assumption is that, as part of the Devil's premortal proposal, he planned to compel obedience. Yet, such a plan seems impossible. As James McLachlan said: "There is a strong sense in Latter-day Saint doctrine that Satan's coercive plan is a lie from the beginning" (MOSESS 62). But is there a more plausible alternative than forced obedience by which Satan might have sought to destroy agency and thus "save" all God's children "in unrighteousness and corruption" (see Brigham Young, JD, 13:282)?

  Our best clues to another option might be found in the story of Adam and Eve itself. To begin with, we might presume that Satan's deception of Adam and Eve in the Garden was an attempt to continue on earth, insofar as possible, the same strategy he had proposed in heaven. For example, might we see Satan's efforts in heaven to destroy the agency of humankind and to "save" us in our sins as something he would have liked to have put into motion on earth through his efforts to get Adam and Eve to eat the fruit of the tree of life immediately after eating the fruit of the tree of knowledge? Alma gives us a hint of the danger of this possibility when he explains: "For behold, if Adam had put forth his hand immediately, and partaken of the tree of life, he would have lived forever, according to the word of God, having no space for repentance; yea, and also the word of God would have been void, and the great plan of salvation would have been frustrated" (Alma 42:5; compare Alma 12:26). Had this action been allowed, there would have been no "probationary time" (Alma 42:4)—hence no opportunity to exercise agency—before the spirits of Adam and Eve were forever united with an immortal body (see Alma 12:21–27; Doctrine and Covenants 132:19). In short, if Adam and Eve had taken the fruit of the tree of life immediately after having eaten from the tree of knowledge, they would have been "forever miserable," having become immortal in their fallen state (Alma 12:26). Satan's objectives to "save" Adam and Eve "in their sins" and to "destroy their agency" would have been achieved. See figure 4–8; Moses 4:28.

  that I should give unto him mine own power. Doctrine and Covenants 29:36 specifically equates the "power" mentioned here with the "honor" craved by Satan in Moses 4:1.

  by the power of mine Only Begotten. Moses had seen the power of the Only Begotten used in a similar way when, in His name, he commanded Satan to depart (Moses 1:21).

  I caused that he should be cast down. Lehi records that an "angel of God . . . had fallen from heaven; wherefore, he became a devil, having sought that which was evil before God" (2 Nephi 2:17). Although Moses 4:6 and Abraham 3:28 say only that "many" followed Satan, Doctrine and Covenants 29:35, like Revelation 12:4, is more specific: the Lord said that Satan persuaded "a third part of the hosts of heaven." However, the phrase "a third part" in scripture is probably meant to describe a rough qualitative division between three different groups rather than a precise, mathematically calculated total. It would be happy news if the fraction was not anything near 33.3 percent of all God's children.

4:4 ***father of all lies, to deceive and to blind men, and to lead them captive at his will, even as many as would not hearken unto my voice.*** This is an "announcement of plot" for what will follow. Satan will lie to Eve to *deceive* her; her eyes will not suddenly be opened with the wisdom he promised, but rather she will become (temporarily) *blind* to her true situation, and she and Adam will be

Figure 4–3. Clockwise from upper left: *A. Masjid al-Haram in Mecca at night*; *B.* Gali Tibbon (1973–): *Catholic clergy circle the edicule*, 2009; *C.* Gustave Doré (1832–1883): *L'Empyrée*; *D. The Empyrean*.

HIEROCENTRIC SPACES AND THE SACRED CENTER

The formal adjective used by scholars to describe the layout of the Garden of Eden and the temple as shown in figure 4–2 is "hierocentric" (= Greek "sacred-centered"). Hugh Nibley, following Eric Burrows, defined "the term 'hierocentric' as that which best describes those cults, states, and philosophies that were oriented about a point believed to be the exact center and pivot of the universe" (HWNHIERO, 104).

Sacred centers, described in different cultures, often coincide, as in Eden, with the location of a "mountain or artificial mound and a lake or spring from which four streams flowed out to bring the life-giving waters to the four regions of the earth. The place was a green paradise, a carefully kept garden, a refuge from drought and heat" (HWNHIERO, 110).

The temple, described by Isaiah as "the mountain of the Lord's house" (Isaiah 2:2), is a symbol of the sacred center. In ancient Israel, the holiest spot on earth was believed to be the Foundation Stone in front of the Ark within the Holy of Holies of the temple at Jerusalem. To the Jews, "it was the first solid material to emerge from the waters of creation (Psalm 104:7–9). . . . It was upon this stone that the Deity effected creation" (MOSESS 61).

In the symbolism of the sacred center, the circle is typically used to represent heaven, while the square signifies earth. Among other things, the intersection of the circle and square can be seen as depicting the coming together of heaven and earth in both the sacred geometry of the temple and the soul of the seeker of Wisdom. For example, photograph *A* above shows the sacred mosque of Mecca during the peak period of *hajj*. As part of the ritual of *tawaf*, *hajj* pilgrims enact the symbolism of the circle and the square as they form concentric rings around the rectangular Ka'bah. Islamic tradition says that near this location Adam had been shown the place of prayer for angels, which was directly above the Ka'bah in heaven. We see the same symbolism at work in photograph *B*, which shows Catholic clergy with lighted candles moving in a circle around the rectangular edicule within the Church of the Holy Sepulchre in Jerusalem. In ancient processions, tree branches and a citrus fruit (representing the tree of life's branches and fruit) were carried and waved.

In *C* is shown an illustration of the "empyrean" (Greek *empyros*, "in fire"), representing heaven as a realm lighted by the pure flame of God's glory in the midst of "circling flames of fire" (Doctrine and Covenants 137:2). Since the sacred center of the empyrean is located in heaven rather than earth, it is shown as a circle rather than a square. The heavenly throne is, in the words of Lehi, "surrounded with numberless concourses of angels in the attitude of singing and praising their God" (1 Nephi 1:8). Nibley points out: "A concourse is a circle. Of course [numberless] concourses means circles within circles" (HWNTPGP, 211). As shown in *D*, the sacred center does not ultimately represent some abstract epitome of goodness, nor merely a ceremonial altar, but rather "the blazing throne of God, whereon [is] seated the Father and the Son" Themselves (Doctrine and Covenants 137:3). See MOSESS 61.

TRANSGRESSION

⁵ And now the serpent was more subtle than any beast of the field which I, the Lord God, had made. ⁶ And Satan put it into the heart of the serpent, (for he had drawn away many after him,) and he sought also to beguile Eve, for he knew not the mind of God, wherefore he sought to destroy the world.

4:4   figuratively *led captive* in a vain effort to hide their transgression—all this because they did not *hearken* to (= obey) the voice of the Lord.

4:5   **serpent.** Nephi and John both identify Satan with the creature by referring to him figuratively as "that old serpent" (2 Nephi 2:18; Revelation 12:9). Note that the description here of the serpent as a "beast of the field" rather than as one of the "creeping things" (Moses 2:24) is consistent with ancient imagery that shows the serpent figuratively as a legged animal before the Fall (HWNMESSAGE, 315–18).

    subtle. The Hebrew term behind "subtle" depicts the serpent as shrewd, cunning, and crafty, but not wise. "Subtle" has to do with the ability to make something appear one way when it is actually another. For example, the serpent is a symbol of Christ and His life-giving power (Numbers 21:8–9; John 3:14–15; 2 Nephi 25:20; Alma 33:19). However, in the Garden of Eden, Satan speaks as a serpent, deceptively bringing death, not life. Explaining further, Draper, Brown, and Rhodes conclude that Satan "has effectively come as the Messiah, offering a promise that only the Messiah can offer, for it is the Messiah who will control the powers of life and death and can promise life, not Satan" (RDDPGP, 43). Not only has the devil come in guise of the Holy One, he seems to have deliberately appeared, without authorization, in a very sacred place (see figure 4–2). Specifically, since some Jewish and early Christian traditions see the tree of knowledge as a symbol of "the veil for the sanctuary" (JMBIGIL1, 248), it appears that Satan has positioned himself, in an extreme of sacrilegious effrontery, as the very "keeper of the gate" (2 Nephi 9:41). Thus, in the apt words of M. Catherine Thomas, Eve was induced to take the fruit "from the wrong hand, having listened to the wrong voice" (MOSESS 63).

    What was the nature of the forbidden fruit? In an answer to this question, Nibley mentions an Egyptian version of the story, where the hero takes "the book of Knowledge, which was guarded by the endless serpent." With that story in mind, he comments that, since the forbidden tree was called the tree of knowledge, "knowledge is certainly more logical" as the object of temptation than would have been a piece of actual fruit (HWNMESSAGE, 311). He further explained: "Satan disobeyed orders when he revealed certain secrets to Adam and Eve, not because they were not known and done in other worlds, but because he was not authorized in that time and place to convey them" (JMBIGIL1, 249). Though he had "given the fruit to Adam and Eve, it was not his prerogative to do so—regardless of what had been done in other worlds. (When the time comes for such fruit, it will be given us legitimately.)" (JMBIGIL1, 249). See MOSESS 63, figure 4–9.

4:6   **he had drawn away many after him.** Unlike Genesis, the Book of Moses emphasizes that the serpent is not to be identified literally with Satan himself but rather should be seen as a later recruit. This idea also appears in ancient traditions. The phrase in v. 7 "And he [Satan] spake by the mouth of the serpent" reinforces the same conclusion. Such an interpretation, however, should be considered in light of what is presented in the Latter-day Saint temple endowment.

    he sought also to beguile Eve. Nibley explains: "The perfect and beautiful union of Adam and Eve excited the envy and jealousy of the Evil One, who made it his prime objective to break it up. . . . His first step (or wedge) [was] to get one of them to make an important decision without consulting the other. He approached Adam in the absence of Eve with a proposition to make him wise, and being turned down he sought out the woman to find her alone and thus undermine her resistance more easily. It is important that he was able to find them both alone" (HWNPATR, 88).

    knew not the mind of God. Similarly, Satan lacks the power to directly discern the mind of man (Doctrine and Covenants 6:16). Nibley calls Moses 4:6 "the most encouraging verse in all the scriptures. Satan seems to be getting the upper hand all the time, but he doesn't know the mind of God. There are a lot of things he doesn't know" (HWNPGP, 208). See figure 4–9.

    sought to destroy the world. OT1 reads, "He *thought* to destroy" (SHFJST, 90; emphasis added).

Figure 4–4. Intertwined Trees of Eden. From Lutwin: *How the Devil Deceived Eve*, early 14th century

The Tree in the Sacred Center of the Garden of Eden

"We may eat of the fruit of the trees of the garden; but of the fruit of the tree which thou beholdest in the midst of the garden, God hath said—Ye shall not eat of it, neither shall ye touch it, lest ye die" (Moses 4:9). One thing that has always perplexed readers of Genesis is the location of the two special trees within the Garden of Eden. Although scripture initially applies the phrase "in the midst" only to the tree of life (Genesis 2:9), the tree of knowledge is later said by Eve to be located there too (see Genesis 3:3). In the context of these verses, the Hebrew phrase corresponding to "in the midst" literally means "in the center." How can both trees be in the center? Elaborate explanations have been attempted to describe how both the tree of life and the tree of knowledge could share the center of the Garden of Eden. For example, it has been suggested that these two trees were in reality different aspects of a single tree, that they shared a common trunk, or that they were somehow intertwined, as shown above.

Jewish commentary provides additional intriguing hints toward an answer. After describing how the Tree of Life was planted "*precisely* in the middle of the garden," the Zohar goes on to assert that the tree of knowledge of good and evil was "*not* precisely in the middle" (DCMZOHAR1, Be-Reshit 1:35a, 220 and 220n921).

Clarifying what this might mean, an interesting Jewish tradition about the placement of the two trees is the idea that the foliage of the tree of knowledge hid the tree of life from direct view and that "God did not specifically prohibit eating from the tree of life because the tree of knowledge formed a hedge around it; only after one had partaken of the latter and cleared a path for himself could one come close to the Tree of Life" (MZBEREISHIS, 1:101). In other words, although both trees were located, relatively speaking, in the central portion of Eden, one had to "pass through" the tree of knowledge that was "not precisely in the middle" (that is, a little lower down the slope) before one could see and gain access to the tree of life that was "precisely in the middle of the garden." The tree of knowledge, concluded Ephrem the Syrian, a fourth-century Christian, "acts as a sanctuary curtain [that is, a veil] hiding the Holy of Holies, which is the tree of life higher up" (MOSESS 61).

Consistent with this idea for the layout of the Garden of Eden, Margaret Barker sees evidence that in Solomon's temple a tree of life was originally symbolized within the Holy of Holies. For those who took the tree of life to be a representation of God's presence within the Holy of Holies, it was natural to see the tree of life as the locus of the divine throne. Barker concludes that the tree-like *menorah* was both removed from the temple and diminished in stature in later Jewish literature as the result of a "very ancient feud" concerning its significance (MBOLDER, 221).

Ephrem suggested that, by way of analogy to the sacred and restricted nature of the Holy of Holies anciently, the tree of life was in an inner place so holy that Adam and Eve would court mortal danger if they entered unprepared. From the perspective of Doctrine and Covenants 76:86–88, we might likewise conclude that although God could minister to them in the Garden, they could not now safely enter His world. Highlighting the merciful nature of God's prohibition against eating the fruit of the Tree of Life prematurely, Elder Bruce C. Hafen wrote that the cherubim and a flaming sword were placed to "guard the way of the tree of life" until Adam and Eve completed their probation on earth and learned by experience to distinguish good from evil" (BCHBROKEN, 30). See MOSESS 61, 63.

⁷ And he said unto the woman: "Yea, hath God said—Ye shall not eat of every tree of the garden?" (And he spake by the mouth of the serpent.) ⁸ And the woman said unto the serpent: "We may eat of the fruit of the trees of the garden; ⁹ but of the fruit of the tree which thou beholdest in the midst of the garden, God hath said—Ye shall not eat of it, neither shall ye touch it, lest ye die." ¹⁰ And the serpent said unto the woman: "Ye shall not surely die; ¹¹ for God doth know that in the day

4:7   *hath God said.* Victor Hamilton paraphrases this difficult Hebrew phrase as a "feigned expression of surprise" and indignation: "Indeed! To think that God said you are not to eat of any tree of the Garden!" (VPHGENESIS, 186). Thus, the serpent "grossly exaggerates God's prohibition" and attempts to move Eve's perception of God "from beneficent provider to cruel oppressor" (VPHGENESIS, 188–89). According to André LaCocque, "The serpent's obvious inaccuracy in his rendition of God's prohibition sounds like . . . lack of subtlety" but is actually a "well-known trick of the con-man to appear stupid to put others in a position of sham superiority" (ALTRIAL, 145). Moreover, in Nahum Sarna's words, the "serpent subtly softens the severity of the prohibition by using [the word 'said'] in place of the original 'command.' Then it deliberately misquotes God so that the woman cannot give a one-word reply but is drawn into conversation that forces her to focus upon the forbidden tree that he had not mentioned" (JMBIGIL1, 251).

    spake by the mouth of the serpent. Though the serpent consistently uses plural verbs in his dialogue with Eve (more noticeable in Hebrew than in English), it seems more likely that Eve was alone and that Satan's speech was meant to include Adam only indirectly. Note, however, a tradition preserved in a twelfth-century Christian source that has the scene beginning "with an unsuccessful attempt to lead Adam astray" before Satan approaches Eve (JMBIGIL1, 251).

4:8   *And the woman . . . garden.* This entire verse was inadvertently omitted in OT1.

4:9   *tree . . . in the midst of the garden.* The vague reference to "the tree" paves the way for more confusion. Whereas the previous narrative explicitly disclosed to the reader only that the tree of life was in the "midst" (= Hebrew "center") of the garden (Moses 3:9), Eve's statement reveals that the tree of knowledge must have been located in the same general direction (see figure 4–4). Going further, Satan's description of the results of eating the fruit will falsely make the two trees seem identical: "the tree of the knowledge of good and evil would open her eyes, and she would be like God, knowing both good and evil. Almost the same was true of the tree of life, for Wisdom opened the eyes of those who ate her fruit, and as they became wise, they became divine" (MBWISDOM, 2).

    While the devil—and the scripture reader—know that there are two special trees "in the midst" of the Garden, only one of them—the tree of knowledge—seems now to be visible to Eve. Ancient traditions and modern scholarship suggest that this is because the tree of knowledge hides (that is, veils) her view of the tree of life. Satan will exploit this confusion to his advantage: making the tree of knowledge appear to Eve as if it were the tree of life instead (see Moses 4:9–11).

4:10   *Ye shall not surely die.* A tone of sarcasm and derision can be discerned in the serpent's contradiction of God's words, intended to make Eve appear foolish and naive in her credulity. A similar tone can be heard in the words of Nehor, who told "the people that . . . they need *not* fear nor tremble" (Alma 1:4, emphasis added).

    The Hebrew version of this difficult phrase has been misunderstood by some readers to mean that Satan was telling the truth, with the mistaken idea that the phrase means something like "You won't *really* die!"—that the consequences of death would be only temporary. However, the repetition of the verb in the Hebrew text underlying the English translation (literally, "dying, ye shall not die") is always used as a way of making the negation ("not") even stronger. In other words, it changes the meaning "you shall not die" to something like "you shall *surely* not die" or "you *absolutely* shall not die." With this correct understanding of the Hebrew, we can see that Satan's statement is deceptively false.

Figure 4–5. Brian Kershisnik, b. 1962: *Holy Woman*, 2001

WAS EVE BEGUILED?

In light of the Latter-day Saint understanding that the Fall was a necessary prerequisite for humankind's further progression and our rejection of the generally negative portrayals of Eve in historical Christianity, Church literature typically emphasizes her perceptiveness and interpret her role as ultimately constructive. However, some have taken this view to an untenable extreme: in addition to rightfully exonerating the pure and innocent Eve from full accountability for her transgression and honoring her lifelong faithfulness, they also argue that, for various reasons, she was not actually "beguiled" by Satan in her decision to eat the forbidden fruit. Julie M. Smith calls this sincere but misguided view the "Wise Choice Theory," a perspective fraught with many obstacles (JMSPARADOX. See also MOSESS 67).

With respect to the mistaken idea that Eve was *not* beguiled, the commentary for Moses 4:10–11 argues that Satan mixed truth with falsehood in his statements to her. On the one hand, Satan told a part-truth in his assertion that Adam and Eve's eyes would "be opened, and [they would] be as gods, knowing good and evil" (Moses 4:11). On the other hand, his claim that they would "not surely die" as the result of eating the fruit was an utter falsehood (Moses 4:10). All this is consistent with Brigham Young's conclusion that Satan told Eve "many truths and some lies," or as Hyrum Andrus more specifically expressed it, "a big lie and . . . a half-truth." The Book of Mormon more than once prefaces discussions of Adam and Eve's transgression by the statement that the devil is "the father of all lies" —implying that Eve was innocently misled by a lie. Perhaps the most telling of these passages is 2 Nephi 2:18. Here the word "wherefore" logically connects the first clause (which describes who Satan is) and the second clause (which tells what he said): "The devil, who is the father of all lies, *wherefore* [or, "for this reason"] he said: Partake of the forbidden fruit, and ye shall not die, but shall be as God, knowing good and evil.".

In a different but equally mistaken interpretation, some readers admit that Satan "*sought . . . to beguile* Eve" (Moses 4:6; emphasis added) but go on to say the adversary did not actually succeed in deceiving her. They incorrectly conclude that the Hebrew term for "beguiled" does not mean that she was deceived. Unfortunately, the reasons given for this conclusion do not stand under close scrutiny. Barry Bandstra's detailed study of the Hebrew text of Genesis translates the relevant term in the context of the verse as "deceived," and even modern translations that don't translate the term as "beguiled" or "deceived" retain the basic idea in Eve's statement that the serpent successfully misled her in her innocence (for example "the serpent tricked me" or "duped me"). Indeed, the actions of Adam and Eve in making the fig leaf aprons and hiding from God witness their doubtful state of mind immediately following the transgression. However, as Elder James E. Talmage taught, this in no way implies that Eve chose evil—because, being innocent, "she knew it not."

Of course, none of this means that Eve did not have some degree of prior insight into the positive consequences of her choice, nor does it assert that her understanding was not relatively complete after she had eaten and was able to identify Satan for whom he was. Elder Talmage rightfully portrayed Adam and Eve as having played their parts perfectly in accordance with the Father's original plan. But, in light of the evidence, there is no reason that Latter-day Saints should not accept Eve's own straightforward explanation of what happened. In the admirable candor and simplicity of her confession, she both admitted the deception and rightfully laid blame on Satan—the only one who deserved it: "The serpent beguiled me, and I did eat" (Moses 4:19). See MOSESS 67; JMSPARADOX.

ye eat thereof, then your eyes shall be opened, and ye shall be as gods, knowing good and evil."

4:11   *your eyes shall be opened.* This biblical expression is used to describe a sudden vision of something that was previously hidden. Satan seems to suggest that Eve will immediately perceive divine things that lie beyond the veil. But the serpent's statement contains only a sliver of truth. What will she know after she eats the fruit? At first, only that she and Adam are naked.

    ye shall be as gods. Brigham Young said that Satan told Eve "many truths and some lies" (JM-BIGIL1, 253; figure 4–5). The truths include Satan's statement that through the fruit Adam and Eve would begin to acquire an attribute of discernment possessed by God Himself. In other words, they would begin to experience and distinguish good from evil—the "opposition in all things" described in 2 Nephi 2:11—thus "placing themselves in a state to act" (Alma 12:31). But the devil's claim also misleads because it implies that the couple will attain godhood through the mere act of eating. Elder Bruce C. Hafen argued otherwise, "Partaking of the forbidden fruit is only the beginning of [the learning] process" (BCHBROKEN, 30). Ultimately, "deification comes through obedience to God, not through disobedience" (Jack Norman Sparks, JMBIGIL1, 253).

    In an Armenian text, the serpent implies that God obtained the knowledge that made Him divine by the same means being proffered to Eve: "God was a man like you, when He ate of this fruit He became God of all. Because of this matter He said, 'Do not eat!' Lest you become god." According to this account, the serpent intended to shake Eve's confidence in God's generosity and goodness by making Him out to be a selfish rival (JMBIGIL1, 253–54).

    as gods. The serpent's statement presupposes the possibility of many gods, an idea that was not foreign to ancient Judaism. Sarna argues that an understanding of the underlying Hebrew removes "any possible ambiguity inherent" in the expression (NMSGENESIS, 25).

    knowing good and evil. In the Christian *Discourse on Abbatôn*, Satan says, "Ye shall know the good and the evil, and ye shall [be able] to separate the sweet from the bitter" (JMBIGIL1, 254). Doctrine and Covenants 29:39 affirms that "if [the children of men] never should have bitter they could not know the sweet," implying that the "forbidden tree offers an experience that is both pleasant and painful; it awakens those who partake of it to the higher knowledge and to the pain that both come with moral choice" (Adele Berlin and Marc Zvi Brettler, JMBIGIL1, 254).

    Nahum Sarna paraphrases the serpent's deceptive promise as follows: "You will be endowed with new mental powers, with the capacity for reflection that allows one to make decisions independently of God" (NMSGENESIS, 25). In other words, he is attempting to persuade Eve to take the fruit because it will enable her to achieve moral autonomy, to walk solely in the light of her own limited reason and experience without reference to divine direction (Doctrine and Covenants 1:16). Kenneth Dauber calls this futile pursuit of human independence a "substitution of [pretended] knowledge for relationship"—what André LaCocque describes as a "perverted knowledge that ponders the pro and con, the positive and the negative, the advantage and the disadvantage, outside of and as a shield against commitment, . . . [thus] objectifying partnership and partner alike" (ALTRIAL, 143).

    The proper retort to Satan's arguments that moral decisions should be based a utilitarian calculus—the "What's in it for me?" question—is "What will my choice say about my love for God?" For any sincere believer, the question of loyalty to God is prior to the question of whether a given choice will increase personal happiness. Indeed, such such loyalty has sustained many throughout history who have been compelled to embrace truth at the cost of great personal sacrifice. As C. S. Lewis puts it: "Christianity claims to give an account of facts—to tell you what the real universe is like. . . . If Christianity is untrue, then no honest man will want to believe it, however helpful it might be: if it is true, every honest man will want to believe it, even if it gives him no help at all" (JMBIGIL1, 717).

    The serpent had now successfully executed a threefold attack of temptation, subtly mixing truth with lies. First, he sought to eliminate Eve's fears through emphatically contradicting the words God had spoken in Moses 3:17. Next, the serpent attempted to undermine God's credibility by ascribing self-serving motives to Him. Finally, he appealed to "an attractive standard of utility" in promising that eating of the fruit would bring knowledge (NMSGENESIS, 25).

¹² And when the woman saw that the tree was good for food, and that it became pleasant to the eyes, and a tree to be desired to make her wise, she took of the fruit thereof, and did eat, and also gave unto her husband with her, and he did eat.

4:12   ***the woman saw that the tree was good for food.*** While Eve makes no reply, the narrator makes it clear that the tree has become the exclusive object in her imagination's view. Note the "undertone of irony in the formulation that she 'saw that it was good,' for it echoes God's recurring judgment about His creation in Genesis 1. Now, however, 'good' has become debased in the woman's mind. Its definition is no longer God's verdict but is rooted in the appeal to the senses and in utilitarian value" (NMSGENESIS, 25).

it became pleasant to the eyes. The corresponding Hebrew expresses a strong intensity of desire fueled by appetite—which Robert Alter renders in his translation as "lust to the eyes" (RABIBLE, 1:16n6). Significantly, while the King James Bible says that "it *was* pleasant" (Genesis 3:6; emphasis added), the Book of Moses says that "it *became* pleasant" (emphasis added). It seems that the more Eve looked, the more attractive the fruit appeared.

she . . . did eat. Victor Hamilton notes that the Hebrew contains six instances of doubled consonants, the "extremely difficult pronunciation . . . [forcing] a merciless concentration on each word" that amounts to a chewing of the phrase (VPSGENESIS, 190). Thus, we might say that the difficulties of diction simulate the excruciation of transgression (JMBIGIL1, 256).

gave unto her husband with her, and he did eat. BYU professor Shon Hopkin noted "the serpent's success in getting Eve to partake of the fruit while alone, separate from Adam." Of course, Hopkin also observed that Eve "is not the only culpable party in her aloneness; this reading of the story also implies that Adam was alone elsewhere in the Garden, making him complicit in the situation" (MOSESS 67).

Though Eve was beguiled by the serpent, having innocently taken the fruit "from the wrong hand" (M. Catherine Thomas), Joseph Fielding McConkie averred that "there was no deception involved when Adam partook. . . . It appears that Adam purposely fell that he might remain with Eve, according to the commandment of the Lord" (JMBIGIL1, 256–57). That said, the scriptures speak of "Adam's transgression" (Moses 6:9; Alma 12:22; Doctrine and Covenants 29:36, 40; Articles of Faith 1:2), for his action was as much a transgression as hers, albeit Eve transgressed innocently. See MOSESS 67.

Hugh Nibley elaborates on the scene and its implications. He observes that while Eve was the one deceived, she also became the first to correctly understand what must be done as a result of her transgression:

> After Eve had eaten the fruit and Satan had won his round, the two were now drastically separated, for they were of different natures. But Eve, who in ancient lore is the one who outwits the serpent and trips him up with his own smartness, defeated this trick by a clever argument. First, she asked Adam if he intended to keep all of God's commandments. Of course he did! All of them? Naturally! And what, pray, was the first and foremost of those commandments? Was it not to multiply and replenish the earth, the universal commandment given to all God's creatures? And how could they keep that commandment if they were separated? It had undeniable priority over the commandment not to eat the fruit. So Adam could only admit that she was right and go along: "I see that it must be so," he said, but it was she who made him see it. This is much more than a smart way of winning her point, however. It is the clear declaration that man and woman were put on the earth to stay together and have a family—that is their first obligation and must supersede everything else (HWNPATR, 88–89)

Eve's perceptiveness, heightened by the experience she has gained in eating the fruit, is recognized by a diversity of traditions that associate her with Wisdom (Sophia). The wisdom she had begun to acquire was demonstrated through her insightful psalm of gratitude (Moses 5:10–11).

4:13   ***the eyes of them both were opened.*** They now know that they are naked. Jacob equates a "perfect knowledge" of "nakedness" with "guilt" and "uncleanness" while associating the perfect knowledge of the "righteous" with "enjoyment" and "being clothed with purity, yea, even with the

Aprons and Hiding

¹³ And the eyes of them both were opened, and they knew that they had been naked. And they sewed fig leaves together and made themselves aprons. ¹⁴ And they heard the voice of the Lord God, as they were walking in the garden, in the cool of the

robe of righteousness" (2 Nephi 9:14). Nibley notes that in demonstration of Eve's new capacity for discernment, she "sees through Satan's disguise of clever hypocrisy, identifies him, and exposes him for what he is" (HWNPATR, 92–93).

fig leaves . . . aprons. Matthew B. Brown explains that the derivation of the Hebrew term for *apron* (ḥagorah), sometimes translated as "girdle," confirms that this was an article of clothing intended to "enclose and cover the area of [the] lap or loins" (JMBIGIL1, 258). "The fig tree has unusually large and strong leaves. Incidentally, it is indigenous to the Land of Israel, where it was cultivated very early, but it was not known in Babylon; hence this detail reflects a West Semitic, not a Mesopotamian, cultural background" (NMSGENESIS, 26). The fruit of the fig tree is known for its abundance of seeds; thus, the aprons are an appropriate symbol for Adam and Eve's ability to "be fruitful, and multiply" after the Fall (Moses 2:28).

In Moses 4:27, God Himself will be the one to clothe Adam and Eve, whereas in v. 13 we were told that Adam and Eve "made *themselves* aprons" (emphasis added). Like their tasting of the forbidden fruit (v. 12), Nimrod's endeavor to build a tower to "reach unto heaven" (Genesis 11:1–9), Sarah's essay to realize the blessing of posterity through her handmaiden Hagar (Genesis 16:1–4), and Rebekah's disguising of Jacob to assure that he would receive the birthright blessing (Genesis 27:1–40), the action of making the aprons, John Sailhamer observes, exemplifies the "recurring theme . . . of the attempt and failure of human effort in obtaining a blessing that only God can give" (JMBIGIL1, 258).

It is perfectly in character for Satan to have planted the suggestion of making aprons, since he often appropriates false signs of power and authority for himself in order to deceive (2 Corinthians 11:12–15; 2 Nephi 9:9; Doctrine and Covenants 128:20; 129:4–8). In this sense, perhaps, there is an affinity with the medieval Jewish *Zohar* (a thirteenth-century theological and mystical text) associating Adam's and Eve's fig leaves with a knowledge of "sorcery and magic," false forms of "protection" and counterfeits of the true priesthood (DCMZOHAR1, Be-Reshit 1:36b, p. 229; 1:53b, pp. 296–97; p. 229nn990–91; p. 297n1433). Moreover, it is consistent with the plan of the Adversary to encourage sinners to flee from the presence of God rather than to reconcile with and return to Him (2 Nephi 32:8). Finally, the contrast between the false clothing made from leaves and the true clothing made from the skins of animals parallels the story of Cain and Abel, in which the former makes an unacceptable offering from the fruits of the ground while the latter follows the God-given pattern of animal sacrifice.

Ancient religious traditions support the idea that the apron takes on a positive meaning when worn as authorized by God. In both Egypt and Mesoamerica, foliated aprons were used as a sign of authority, and kings in the Near East were often described as various sorts of trees. Endowed Latter-day Saints understand that for themselves, like for Abraham, the blessings of kingship, priesthood, and posterity are inseparably connected in the eternities.

Note that this is Satan's third attempt to mislead Adam and Eve by false appearances. First, he spoke in the guise of a serpent, deceptively employing a symbol of Christ. Second, he made claims that blurred the identities of the tree of knowledge and the tree of life. Finally, in the episode of the fig-leaf aprons, he suggested a course of action to Adam and Eve that substituted a self-made emblem of power and authority for the true article. See MOSESS 64.

4:14   *as they were walking.* In contrast to the Genesis account of this incident, the OT2 revision adopted here makes it clear that it was Adam and Eve that were walking, not the Lord God.

in the cool of the day. The phrase is better translated as "in the wind, breeze, spirit, or direction" of the day—in other words, the voice is coming from the west, the place where the sun sinks (MSBEREISHIS, 1:122–23). Since the voice is coming from the west, some commentators infer

day; and Adam and his wife went to hide themselves from the presence of the Lord God amongst the trees of the garden.

CONFESSION

¹⁵ And I, the Lord God, called unto Adam, and said unto him: "Where goest thou?" ¹⁶ And he said: "I heard thy voice in the garden, and I was afraid, because I beheld that I was naked, and I hid myself." ¹⁷ And I, the Lord God, said unto Adam: "Who told thee thou wast naked? Hast thou eaten of the tree whereof I commanded thee that thou shouldst not eat, if so thou shouldst surely die?" ¹⁸ And the man said: "The woman thou gavest me, and commandedest that she should remain with me, she gave me of the fruit of the tree and I did eat." ¹⁹ And I, the Lord God, said unto the woman: "What is this thing which thou hast done?" And the woman said: "The serpent beguiled me, and I did eat."

4:14   that Adam and Eve were then located on the border of the east "courtyard"—the end of the garden farthest removed from the presence of the Lord. In other words, they seem, figuratively, to have one foot outside the garden already. The idea of Adam and Eve being in the "courtyard" of Eden is an appropriate fit to the function of the outermost of the three divisions of the Israelite temple as a place of confession—the first step of reconciliation.

        to hide themselves from the presence of the Lord God. Hearing the Lord's voice, Adam and Eve quickly return from the place of their wandering at the edge of the garden. Their flimsy covering of fig leaves, coupled with their choice of hiding place "by the tree of which [they] had eaten," trumpets the nature of their transgression (Gary A. Anderson and Michael Stone, JMBIGIL1, 260).

4:15   ***Where goest thou?*** The change from the King James "Where *art* thou?" (Genesis 3:12; emphasis added) to the Book of Moses "Where *goest* thou?" (emphasis added) stresses that the Lord is not assessing Adam's location but rather is requesting him to reflect openly on his intentions—especially since his feet had just been pointed toward the exit of the garden. God's call is not issued as an angry threat but rather as an invitation for Adam to return and report on his stewardship of the garden. To accomplish His objective, God seeks to "draw rather than drive him out of hiding" (VPHGENESIS, 193). Elder David A. Bednar comments: "There was no one-way lecture to a disobedient child, as perhaps many of us might be inclined to deliver. Rather, the Father helped Adam as a learner to act as an agent and appropriately exercise his agency" (JMBIGIL1, 262). See MOSESS 65. According to John Chrysostom, God here "demonstrate[s] his own loving kindness, and . . . invites [Adam and Eve] to make admission of their faults" (JMBIGIL1, 262).

4:16   ***I heard thy voice.*** These words can also be translated as "I hearkened to thy voice." The irony of this reading of Adam's reply, of course, is evidenced in the fact that this is precisely what Adam did *not* do previously (NMSGENESIS, 26). Instead, both he and Eve had hearkened to the voice of Satan in making fig-leaf aprons and going into hiding.

4:17   ***Who told thee thou wast naked?*** Though Adam and Eve had discovered their own nakedness after their eyes were opened, God knew that it was Satan who had drawn attention to their shame and who had incited them to make aprons and hide. See MOSESS 65.

4:18   ***commandest that she should remain with me.*** Adam's response to the Lord's question is different in the Book of Moses than in Genesis. In Genesis 3:12, he is reported as saying simply, "The woman whom thou gavest to be with me, she gave me of the tree, and I did eat." However, in Moses 4:18 Adam adds, "and commandest that she should remain with me." The phrase provides a defensible rationale for his transgression: he took the forbidden fruit in order to remain with Eve, thus breaking one commandment in order to keep a prior and more important one.

        OT1 employs the past tense of the verb, "commanded." Beginning with the 1878 edition of the

Consequences

²⁰ And I, the Lord God, said unto the serpent:

> "Because thou hast done this thou shalt be cursed
>> above all cattle, and above every beast of the field;
> upon thy belly shalt thou go,
>> and dust shalt thou eat all the days of thy life;
> ²¹ and I will put enmity between thee and the woman,

Pearl of Great Price, the verb was changed to read "commandedst." In the 1981 edition, another change was made: "commandest." Jackson observes that the "deletion of the second letter 'd' [in the 1981 edition] avoids a difficult consonant cluster, yet it changes the tense of the clause from the past to the present" (KPJMOSES, 52).

4:19   ***the serpent beguiled me, and I did eat.*** In the admirable candor and simplicity of Eve's confession, she both admitted the deception and rightfully laid blame on the very one—the only one—who deserved it: "The serpent beguiled me, and I did eat." Wordplay is evident with the juxtaposition of the Hebrew words for "serpent" (*nachash*) and "beguiled" (*nasha*). See MOSESS 67; JMBIGIL1, 263.

4:20   ***I, the Lord God, said unto the serpent.*** "Of the three parties to the transgression, the serpent alone is summarily sentenced without prior interrogation—a token of God's withering disdain for it. . . . In each [of the three cases], the judgment is of a twofold nature: it affects what is of central concern in the life of each entity, and it regulates a basic relationship" (NMSGENESIS, 24, 27). As for the serpent, it is restricted henceforth to a humiliating diet and form of locomotion, and it will be crushed by the heel of the seed of the woman. The woman will suffer in childbearing and in the challenges of a marriage relationship undertaken in the conditions of a fallen world. Finally, the man is consigned to hard labor in the fields and strict obedience to the commandments.

In the case of the man and the woman, Umberto Cassuto notes that what may seem solely punishments should be regarded instead as "measures taken for the good of the human species in its new situation" (UCCOMMENTARY, 163). Adam and Eve are exposed in nakedness, but God will clothe them (Moses 4:27); they are subject to temporal and spiritual death, but God will bless them with posterity and the eventual possibility of eternal life (Moses 4:22); they are bereft of the food of the garden, but God will provide them with the seeds of life-sustaining grains (Moses 4:25).

thou shalt be cursed above. The serpent, whose blessing seems to have been anticipatorily omitted at creation, is now cursed. However, the man and the woman, previously blessed, receive no curse.

upon thy belly shalt thou go. Anciently, serpents were sometimes shown as walking creatures. For example, a legged serpent appears in illustrated form in Joseph Smith Papyrus V. Nibley elucidates the symbolic meaning of the figurative indignity imposed on the serpent in this verse: "The loss of limbs and organs guarantees that the rebel will never rise anew in his full powers, which he will never possess again. . . . He may never more progress, being bound forever in one place" (JMBIGIL1, 265).

dust shalt thou eat all the days of thy life. This constitutes an apt punishment, since the transgression itself had involved eating.

4:21   ***I will put enmity between thee and the woman.*** The serpent appeared to Eve in the guise of friendship; now that her eyes have been opened, she will recognize him as an enemy to be regarded with revulsion. N. J. Dawood's translation of Qur'an 7:11–18 records a passionate exchange of words following Lucifer's expulsion from heaven. Here Satan unleashes a tirade of threats, followed by a summary dismissal by God: "'Because . . . [Thou hast adjudged me to be erring],' [the devil] declared, 'I will waylay Your servants as they walk on Your straight path, then spring upon them from the front and the rear, from their right and from their left. . . .' 'Begone!' [God] said" (JMBIGIL1, 265).

> between thy seed and her seed;
> and he shall bruise thy head,
> and thou shalt bruise his heel."

²² Unto the woman, I, the Lord God, said:

> "I will greatly multiply thy sorrow and thy conception.
> In sorrow thou shalt bring forth children,
> and thy desire shall be to thy husband,
> and he shall rule over thee."

4:21   Nibley elaborates on the scene in Moses 4:

> [Satan,] nettled by this rebuke and the curse, . . . flares up in his pride and announces what his program for the economic and political order of the new world is going to be. He will take the resources of the earth, and with precious metals as a medium of exchange he will buy up military and naval might, or rather those who control it, and so will govern the earth—for he is the prince of this world. He does rule: he is king. Here at the outset is the clearest possible statement of a military-industrial complex ruling the earth with violence and ruin. But as we are told, this cannot lead to anything but war, because it has been programmed to do that. It was conceived in the mind of Satan in his determination to "destroy the world" (Moses 4:6). The whole purpose of the program is to produce blood and horror on this earth (JMBIGIL1, 265–66).

thy seed. This phrase is undoubtedly meant to include a reference both to Cain—who later virtually shared an identity with Satan and became a hated fugitive (Moses 5:39)—and to all the wicked. Of all these, the Lord said grievingly: "Satan shall be their father, and misery shall be their doom" (Moses 7:37).

her seed. It is significant that the statement refers not to the couple but to Eve alone. Elder James E. Talmage explains "her seed" as a reference is to Jesus Christ, who is the "only instance of offspring from woman dissociated from mortal fatherhood" (JMBIGIL1, 266).

he shall bruise thy head, and thou shalt bruise his heel. Historically, Christians have called the prophecy concerning the "seed" of the woman in Moses 4:21 the *protoevangelium*, being the first explicit Biblical allusion to the good news of the Gospel. The change in OT2 from the King James "it" to "he" emphasizes the messianic implication of the verse. Although the serpent (Satan), in its weakened condition, may afflict and torment man, his power will ultimately be destroyed by the seed of the woman (Christ). The *Targum Yerushalmi* preserves a unique reading when it has God saying, "For them [that is, for the posterity of Adam and Eve] . . . there will be a remedy, but for you [meaning the serpent] there will be no remedy; and they are to make peace in the end, in the days of the King Messiah" (JMBIGIL1, 266).

The first occurrence of "bruise" in the phrase is better rendered as "crush," since the Savior's blow to the serpent will be fatal. Indeed, the Redeemer "shall crush the head of the serpent (Satan and his kingdom) with the very heel that was bruised (the [heel of Christ, who performed the] atoning sacrifice)" (*Old Testament Student Manual*). And just as Jesus Christ will put all enemies beneath his feet (1 Corinthians 15:25–26), so the Prophet Joseph Smith taught that all people who will be saved must also, with the Savior's help, gain the power needed to "triumph over all [their] enemies and put them under [their] feet" (JSTPJS, 14 May 1843, 297), possessing the "glory, authority, majesty, power and dominion which Jehovah possesses" (JMBIGIL1, 266). See MOSESS 65, 66.

4:22   **I will greatly multiply thy sorrow and thy conception.** Before the Fall, Adam and Eve could not bear children (Moses 5:11). Now Eve is told that as part of the repeated blessings of motherhood she must also undergo the recurrent pain incident to each childbirth. John Sailhamer reminds us, however, that these birth pangs "are not merely a reminder of the . . . Fall; they are as well a sign of impending joy" because of redemption through the "seed of the woman"—namely, Jesus Christ (JMBIGIL1, 268; see Romans 8:22–23). See MOSESS 66.

In sorrow thou shalt bring forth children. "Distress" might be a better translation than "sorrow." Note that the Hebrew term used here and in verse 23 "means pain or hurt rather than grief" (RDDPGP, 48). According to Nahum Sarna, "Intense pain in childbearing is unique to the human species and generally unknown to other female mammals" (NMSGENESIS, 28).

thy desire shall be to thy husband, and he shall rule over thee. This statement has been the subject of much misunderstanding. In a sincere effort to make sense of the troubling English translation of "rule over" in the King James Version, some scholars have mistakenly suggested that it should be read instead as "rule with." Unfortunately, the "rule with" translation does not hold up under scrutiny. Specifically, in her BYU master's thesis, RoseAnn Benson argued persuasively that the "rule with" translation should be abandoned. In every occurrence of the underlying Hebrew she examined, the phrase is best understood as "rule over," as when a king rules over his subjects (MOSESS 66).

In trying to apply this statement to modern marriage relationships, we must understand it for what it is: a sad description of the fallen conditions of mortal life. Briefly, a careful study of the Hebrew text in its scriptural context will reveal that the Lord is not telling Adam and Eve how they *should* treat each other but is rather describing a tragic tendency in mortal marriages that they must *avoid*. Specifically, the Hebrew word "desire" in "thy desire shall be to thy husband," does not refer to a physical attraction but rather to a contentious wish to "overcome or defeat another" (JHSGENESIS, 58)—an equal match of opposing wills, each one contending for domination over the other. Second, In addition, the "rule" of the husband depicted in the Hebrew version of the phrase is not benevolent but controlling. The sense of this terrible situation is well captured in a modern Bible translation: "You will want to control your husband, but he will dominate you." As further evidence for this interpretation, note that the same Hebrew terms for "desire" and "rule" that describe a relationship of competition and rancor later reappear in God's warning to Cain: "Satan desireth to have thee. . . . And thou shalt rule over him" (Moses 5:23).

Victor Hamilton sees God's words as a warning to Adam and Eve. Unless they are careful, the conditions of a fallen world may lead them "to break the relationship of equality and turn it into a relationship of servitude and domination. . . . Far from being a reign of co-equals over the remainder of God's creation, the relationship [would then become] a fierce dispute, with each party trying to rule the other. The two who once reigned as one [unrighteously would] attempt to rule each other" (VPHGENESIS, 202). This is a war that can never be won.

By way of contrast, God's intent was not for one party to dominate the other. Instead, as Nahum Sarna explains, "It is quite clear from the [original] description of woman . . . that the ideal situation, which hitherto existed, was the absolute equality of the sexes" (NMSGENESIS, 28).

Like the blessing of childbirth described earlier in v. 22, the experience of married love holds out a promise of happiness, yet its practice, in a fallen world, will be frequently mixed with sorrow "till God make men of some other mettle than earth" (William Shakespeare, "Much Ado," 2:1:59). Unfortunately, as Joseph Smith observed, "there has been no change in the constitution of man since he fell" (JSTPJS, 22 January 1834, 60). "Sad experience" has shown "that it is the nature and disposition of almost all men, as soon as they get a little authority, as they suppose, [to] immediately begin to exercise unrighteous dominion," a tendency which modern prophets have repeatedly condemned (Doctrine and Covenants 121:39).

Of the great blessings that await all generations of women who have thus suffered, Elder James E. Talmage has written:

> When the frailties and imperfections of mortality are left behind, in the glorified state of the blessed hereafter, husband and wife will administer in their respective stations, seeing and understanding alike, and cooperating to the full in the government of their family kingdom. Then shall woman be recompensed in rich measure for all the injustice that womanhood has endured in mortality. Then shall woman reign by Divine right, a queen in the resplendent realm of her glorified state, even as exalted man shall stand, priest and king unto the Most High God (JMBIGIL1, 269–70). See MOSESS 66.

Figure 4–6. Left: *Guardians part the veils, taking Muhammad by the hand to see the throne of God;* Right: *Adam and Even enthroned in Paradise,* 16th century.

NAMES IN ISLAMIC TESTS OF RECOGNITION

Islamic accounts of heavenly ascent relate the use of divinely ordained names in tests of recognition. The most well-known story of heavenly ascent concerns Muhammad himself. At the heavenly Gate of the Guard, Ishmael "asks Muhammad's name and inquires whether he is indeed a true messenger." After having given a satisfactory answer, Muhammad was permitted to gradually ascend from the depths of hell to the highest of the seven heavens on a golden ladder (*mi'raj*). At the gates of the Celestial Temple, a guardian angel again "ask[ed] who he [was]. Gabriel introduce[d] Muhammad, who [was] then allowed to enter the gardens of Paradise" (see image above at left). The events that make up the pilgrimage of Muslims to Mecca (*hajj*) recall some aspects of Muhammad's heavenly ascent. When the pilgrim successfully completes the final stage of his journey, "all veils are removed and he talks to the Lord without any veil between them."

Above all, Islamic traditions emphasize the importance of the names of *God*. Though, in Islam, human language is incapable of adequately describing or even symbolizing Allah, the names serve as a prop for meditation and prayer. For example, on a large wall within the Great Mosque of Abu Dhabi, as in several other mosques, ninety-nine names of God are depicted in beautiful Arabic calligraphy on the stylized leaves of a Tree of Life. Intriguingly, the central image of the one-hundredth leaf is blank, containing no name. Patrick Ringgenberg explains: "One tradition holds that the one-hundredth name is the true Name of God, but that it remains unknowable, as a witness of the unspeakable transcendence of the One. One scholar of the seventeenth century could thus begin a poem by writing: 'In the name of He who has no name.'" A Muslim friend related that this last name is actually not unknowable in eternity, since it will be given to each of the faithful by Allah himself when he or she enters Paradise after death.

Interestingly, Islamic teachings also associate a test of naming with the marriage of Adam and Eve. In a manner similar to temple initiates in other cultures, Adam—before the Fall and after having been given instruction by God — was said to have been directed to recite a series of secret names to the angels in order to demonstrate that he was worthy of his elevated status as priest and king (see the commentary on Moses 3:19). This test culminated in an examination to determine whether Adam could identify Eve and recite *her* name. Notice how al-Tha'labi describes the incident: "When Adam awoke from his sleep he saw [Eve] sitting at his head. The angels said to Adam, testing his knowledge: 'What is this, Adam?' He answered: 'A woman.' They asked: 'And what is her name?' he replied: 'Eve (*hawwa*).'"

The exercise in heaven where Adam identified Eve through a dialogue that included her name was later repeated as a test on earth. Al-Tha'labi explained that when Adam and Eve were rejoined after the Fall "they recognized each other by questioning on a day of questioning. So the place was named *Arafat* (meaning 'questions') and the day, *'Irfah* [meaning 'knowledge or recognition']." See JMBIGIL1, 39; JMBWHAT, 12–15; figure 3–5.

²³ And unto Adam, I, the Lord God, said: "Because thou hast hearkened unto the voice of thy wife, and hast eaten of the fruit of the tree of which I commanded thee, saying—'Thou shalt not eat of it,'

> Cursed shall be the ground for thy sake;
>> in sorrow shalt thou eat of it all the days of thy life.
> ²⁴ Thorns also, and thistles shall it bring forth to thee,
>> and thou shalt eat the herb of the field.
> ²⁵ By the sweat of thy face shalt thou eat bread,
>> until thou shalt return unto the ground
>>> —for thou shalt surely die—
>>>> for out of it wast thou taken:
> for dust thou wast,
>> and unto dust shalt thou return."

Adam Calls Out Eve's New Name; God Clothes Adam and Eve

²⁶ And Adam called his wife's name Eve, because she was the mother of all living; for thus have I, the Lord God, called the first of all women, which are many. ²⁷ Unto

4:25   ***By the sweat of thy face shalt thou eat bread.*** Unlike his life before the Fall, Adam was consigned to hard labor to obtain his food. The importance of this toil is underscored when the language about the tilling of the earth and the eating of bread by the sweat of his brow is repeated in Moses 5:1, 3. "The curse lies not in the work itself, which is decreed for man even in Eden [Moses 3:15], but in the uncooperative nature of the soil, so that henceforth the wresting of subsistence from it entails unremitting drudgery" (NMSGENESIS, 28). Despite such hardships, the subsequent news of the coming Redeemer will enable Adam to exclaim, "In this life I shall have joy" (Moses 5:10).

4:26   ***Adam called his wife's name Eve.*** Both the renaming of the woman and the reclothing of the couple "speak of a future for the individual(s) beyond the miserable present" (VPHGENESIS, 207). Significantly, the Book of Moses (unlike Genesis) reveals that not only the new clothing but also Eve's new name was given her in the beginning by God Himself. Thus, we can be certain that Adam's speech was a test of recognition, not an act of naming. In other words, Adam did not "call her name Eve"—rather he "called out her name: 'Eve!'" (consistent with André Chouraqui's reliance on a secondary sense of the Hebrew *qara* [ACHBIBLE, 23]).

Eve's previous name (*'ishah* = "woman") had been provisional, pronounced before Adam and Eve had eaten the fruit of the tree of knowledge and prior to their new situation that had enabled the possibility of childbirth. Adam now saw Eve as God saw her; and could thus name her as God had originally named her. According to René Guénon, "All ancient traditions agree that the true name of a living thing reflects precisely its nature or its very essence" (JMBWHAT, 10; see also HWNMESSAGE, 451).

Nahum Sarna notes that Eve's new name "expresses her nature and destiny positively and sympathetically" (NMSGENESIS, 29). As John Sailhamer observed, "Her first name pointed to her origin ('out of man'), whereas her second name pointed to her destiny ('the mother of all living')" (JHSGENESIS, 57).

mother of all living. The name Eve corresponds to the Hebrew *havvah*, whose vocalization suggests the possible meaning of "propagator of life." Adam rejoiced in the promise of motherhood given to Eve in Moses 4:22. Though they were now subject to death, human life would continue afterward through the fulfillment of God's command to multiply and replenish the earth. Going further, in her role as the "mother of all living," Eve not only became the physical dispenser of mortal life but also, in the words of Samson Hirsch, "the spiritual and intellectual perpetrator of mankind's higher calling" (MZBEREISHIS, 1:136), namely, to seek *eternal* life (APSBOOK, 227).

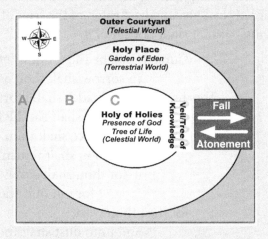

Figure 4–7. Left: William Blake, 1757–1827: *The Clothing of Adam and Eve*, 1803;
Right: *Gradients of holiness and the high priest's clothing*

THE NAKEDNESS AND CLOTHING OF ADAM AND EVE

"Unto Adam, and also unto his wife, did I, the Lord God, make coats of skins, and clothed them" (Moses 4:27).
At left above, William Blake depicts the exit scene at the gates of Eden as a tender moment of forgiveness
and farewell. In childlike submission and gratitude, Adam and Eve bow their heads and, clothed with
garments of animal skin made by the Father as a protection and a reminder of their covenants, prepare to
leave God's embrace and prove themselves by overcoming the dangers of the mortal world.

Moses 3:25 describes Adam and Eve as naked and without shame in the garden and as clothed by God in
coats of skin only later, after the Fall. However, many early depictions show a surprising reversal, portraying
Adam and Eve clothed in regal and priestly glory within Eden and naked after their expulsion. How can
this be?

Recalling the parallels between the Garden of Eden and Israelite houses of God, Gary A. Anderson points
out that "the vestments of the priest matched exactly those particular areas of the Temple to which he had
access. . . . Each time the high priest moved from one gradient of holiness to another, he had to remove one
set of clothes and put on another to mark the change" (see image at right above):

> [A] Outside the Tabernacle priests wear ordinary clothes. [B] When on duty in the Tabernacle, they
> wear four pieces of clothing whose material and quality of workmanship match that of the fabrics found
> on the outer walls of the courtyard [Exodus 28]. [C] The High Priest wears those four pieces plus four
> additional ones—these added [white] garments match the fabric of the Holy Chamber where he must
> go daily to tend the incense altar.

> In Eden a similar set of vestments is found, again each set suited to its particular space. [B] Adam and
> Eve were, at creation, vested like priests and granted access to most of Eden. [A] Had they been found
> worthy, an even more glorious set of garments would have been theirs (and according to St. Ephrem,
> they would have entered even holier ground). [C] But having [transgressed], they were stripped of their
> angelic garments and put on mortal flesh. Thus, when their feet met ordinary earth—the realm of the
> animals—their constitution had become "fleshly," or mortal (GAAGENESIS, 123).

Note that each stage in the sequence of changes in Adam and Eve's status in the Book of Moses is also
marked by a change in their appearance. The imagery of clothing is "a means of linking together in a
dynamic fashion the whole of salvation history." This imagery also makes clear the place of each individual's
priesthood ordinances "within the divine [system] as a whole" (Sebastian Brock, JMBIGIL1, 235–36; more
broadly, see 234–40). See MOSESS 68; figure 3–7.

Adam, and also unto his wife, did I, the Lord God, make coats of skins, and clothed them.

GOD SENDS ADAM AND EVE FORTH FROM EDEN

²⁸ And I, the Lord God, said unto mine Only Begotten: "Behold, the man is become as one of us to know good and evil; and now lest he put forth his hand and partake

4:27 *coats of skins.* As a replacement for their flimsy aprons of fig leaves and in partial compensation for the loss of what Jewish tradition called their "garments of light," the Lord's "garments of skin" were intended to protect Adam and Eve in their exposed and fallen state, to remind them of their covenants, and to serve as a token of the glorious celestial robes that await them through their faithfulness. Nibley commented, "A garment is a sign of protection, of dignity, of modesty; it is not just a sign of those things, it actually does impart them" (JMBIGIL1, 274).

At the time of Moses, the function of the skin garment, worn outwardly, was subsumed by the linen coat and breeches worn next to the skin by priests in the Tabernacle precincts (see Exodus 39:27–28). As Matthew B. Brown observed, "The fine linen worn by heavenly beings is described as 'clean and white' or 'pure and white' and is therefore an appropriate symbol of worthiness or righteousness (see Revelation 3:4–5; 15:6; 19:8). Since linen is not the product of an animal that is subject unto death, or 'corruption' as it is called, it is also a fitting symbol of immortality, which is also called 'incorruption'" (MOSESS 68).

Later echoes of this event in scripture and tradition leave no doubt that the account of the clothing of Adam and Eve, immediately following the mention of the naming of Eve, was meant to be understood in a ritual context. For example, Brown sees Jacob's manner of dress in receiving his birthright blessing as an "investiture with sacrificial goatskins" and mentions traditions that "on this occasion Jacob was dressed in the priestly robes of Adam" (JMBIGIL1, 274–75).

4:28 *man is become as one of us to know good and evil.* Vv. 28–31 provide God's summary about what has just happened and give a rationale for His removal of Adam and Eve from the Garden of Eden. While the serpent had painted a picture of wrathful punishment by a jealous God, the Lord's actions will instead further bless the couple by enabling them to gain knowledge through experience. He will provide a Savior for them and will make the gospel with its covenants and ordinances available so that, through their faithfulness, they might be sanctified and return to His presence.

In contrast to the Bible, which includes only the phrase "good *and* evil," the Book of Mormon and the Book of Moses contain nine instances of "good *from* evil." With experience, Adam and Eve will come to "know good *from* evil . . . with a perfect knowledge, as the daylight is from the dark night" (Moroni 7:15, emphasis added).

lest he . . . partake. Though no explicit prohibition relating to the tree of life occurs before this verse, several lines of evidence converge to suggest that Adam and Eve had not eaten its fruit while they lived in Eden. For example, a unique Samaritan commentary on Moses 3:16 excludes the tree of life from the other trees in the garden from which Adam and Eve were originally given permission to eat (JMBIGIL1, 276). In addition, the use of the term "also" (Hebrew *gam*) in verse 28 suggests that Adam and Eve had not yet partaken of its fruit at the time these words were spoken. Moreover, James Barr studied 131 cases of "lest" (Hebrew *pen*) in the Bible "and found none which means 'lest someone continue to do what they are already doing'" (JMBIGIL1, 277). Finally, the case for such a reading is strengthened conclusively if eating of the fruit of the tree of life is taken not merely as the means of ensuring immortality but as representing the gift of eternal life (see Doctrine and Covenants 14:7)—bestowed in the appropriate degree to those who partake of the fruits of Christ's Atonement. Geerhardus Vos concurs with this reading, concluding that "the tree was associated with the higher, the unchangeable, the eternal life to be secured by obedience throughout the probation" (JMBIGIL1, 277). According to this view, Adam and Eve never would have been permitted to partake of the fruit of the tree of life at their own discretion. Rather, their only approach to the tree of life will be by way of

Figure 4–8. Left: *God Creating Eve*. Right: *God Instructing Adam and Eve*. Late twelfth century.

WHY DID GOD PREVENT ACCESS TO THE TREE OF LIFE AFTER THE FALL?

"I placed at the east of the Garden of Eden, cherubim and a flaming sword, which turned every way to keep the way of the tree of life" (Moses 4:31). Herrad of Hohenbourg was a twelfth-century abbess under whose direction a copiously illustrated compendium of salvation history, called *Hortus Deliciarum* ("Garden of Delights"), was assembled. Though it was tragically destroyed during the siege of Strasbourg in 1870, portions of the text and illustrations had been previously copied, enabling the later partial reconstruction of the work. The illustration depicts the "first commandments" (Alma 12:31) wherein Adam and Eve both were commanded to multiply and replenish the earth and also prohibited from eating the fruit of the tree of knowledge (Moses 2:28, 3:16–17).

Gary A. Anderson points out an interesting divergence between the Genesis story and the drawing featured here: "Whereas Genesis 2 recounts that Adam was created first (Genesis 2:4–7), given a commandment (Genesis 2:16–17), and only then received a spouse (Genesis 2:19–24), the *Hortus Deliciarum* has it that Adam was created, then Eve was drawn from his rib, and finally both were given a commandment" (GAAGENESIS, 83) At right, God gestures toward the tree of knowledge in warning as He takes Adam by the wrist. At the same time, Eve raises her arm in what seems a gesture of consent to God's commandment.

The battle begun in the premortal councils and waged again in the Garden of Eden was a test of *obedience* for Adam and Eve. However, it should be remembered that the actual prize at stake was *knowledge*—the knowledge required for them to be saved and, ultimately, to be exalted. The Prophet Joseph Smith taught that the "principle of knowledge is the principle of salvation" (JSTPJS, 14 May 1843, 331; compare Doctrine and Covenants 130:18–19), therefore "anyone that cannot get knowledge to be saved will be damned" (JSWORDS, 14 May 1843, 200). This raises a question: Since salvation was to come through knowledge, why did Satan encourage—rather than try to prevent—the eating of the fruit of the tree of knowledge by Adam and Eve? Surprisingly, the scriptural story makes it evident that their transgression must have been as much an important part of the devil's strategy as it was a central feature of the Father's plan. In this one respect, the programs of God and Satan seem to have had something in common. However, the difference in intention between God and Satan became apparent only when it was time for Adam and Eve to take the *next* step. In this regard, the scriptures seem to suggest that the Adversary wanted Adam and Eve to eat of the fruit of the tree of life *directly after* they ate the fruit of the tree of knowledge—a danger which moved God to take immediate preventive action by the placement of the cherubim and the flaming sword (Moses 4:28–31; Alma 12:23; 42:2–3). For had Adam and Eve eaten of the fruit of the tree of life at that time, said Alma, "there would have been no death" and no "space granted unto man in which he might repent"—in other words no "probationary state" to prepare for a final judgment and resurrection (Alma 12:23–24). Thus, "the great plan of salvation would have been frustrated" (Alma 42:3–5). See also figure 4–9.

An essential part of that plan was for Adam and Eve to have children. In the middle of the drawing above, a tree of life has sprouted human faces resembling Adam and Eve, attesting to ancient traditions about individual premortal existence. This "Tree of Souls," which, in Jewish legend, represented the heavenly tree of life, was thought to produce "new souls, which ripen and then fall from the tree into the *Guf*, the Treasury of Souls in Paradise. There the soul is stored until the angel Gabriel reaches into the treasury and takes out the first soul that comes into his hand" so it can be born into mortality (Howard Schwartz; JMBIGIL1, 228–30). See MOSESS 57.

also of the tree of life, and eat and live forever, [29] therefore I, the Lord God, will send him forth from the Garden of Eden, to till the ground from whence he was taken; [30] for as I, the Lord God, liveth, even so my words cannot return void, for as they go forth out of my mouth they must be fulfilled." [31] So I drove out the man, and I placed at the east of the Garden of Eden, cherubim and a flaming sword, which

4:28   leaving the garden to pass into mortality and then returning at last to take of the sweet fruit only when they have completed their probation and are authoritatively invited to do so (Doctrine and Covenants 88:68). In this way, their lives, their knowledge, and their exercise of divine power would be wisely limited until they completed the process of sanctification.

eat and live forever. During their sojourn in the Garden of Eden, Adam and Eve had enjoyed immortality, but their partaking of the forbidden fruit now made them subject to death. As a result of their choice, "the new situation to be avoided is . . . the eating from the [tree of life] after having taken from the Tree of Knowledge" (Terje Stordalen, JMBIGIL1, 277).

Applying the lesson that was taught by the Levitical laws of rigorous purity for those who served in ancient temples to the situation of Adam and Eve, Gary A. Anderson observes: "Exile [from the garden] was not simply punishment; it was a form of protection. For to remain before God in Eden, while defiled by sin, was to court unnecessary danger, perhaps even death" (GAAGENESIS 129). To prevent such catastrophe, concludes Anderson, the Lord immediately restricted their access to the tree of life. See figure 4–8; commentary on Moses 4:3.

4:29   *to till the ground.* According to John Sailhamer, the human requirement to till the ground is "to be seen as an ironic reversal of their original purpose" to worship and to obey in the spirit of rest originally ordained for the unending paradisiacal Sabbath. A Hebrew wordplay underscores the change of situation for Adam and Eve: instead of worship (*le-obdah*), they will till the ground (*la-abod*), and their failure of obedience (*le-somrah*) has caused them to be kept (*lismor*) from the tree of life (JHSGENESIS, 45, 47–48).

4:30   *my words . . . go forth . . . must be fulfilled.* In other words, Adam and Eve were "sent forth" to fulfill the words of the Lord that had previously "gone forth." The unstated implication is that because God's words will not return "void," so in the end Adam and Eve will not return without having accomplished all that they had been commanded to do.

4:31   *I drove out the man.* This second reference to Adam and Eve's departure from the Garden of Eden, which uses the Hebrew word *geresh* ("drove out"), is harsher than the first reference in verse 29 that used the term *shillah* ("send him forth"). Significantly, the Lord uses the same two terms in the same order to describe how Pharaoh will expel Israel from Egypt (Exodus 6:1).

at the east of the Garden. The entrance to the garden—and presumably the only means of access—is on the east side, at the end farthest away from the mountain of God's presence.

cherubim. The term, which is left untranslated, may be related to the Akkadian *karibu* ("intercessor") or *karibi* ("gatekeepers"). In temple contexts, the essential function of priests who act in the role of "cherubim" is analogous to the role of cherubim in the garden: the priests are sentinels guarding the portals of the temple against unauthorized entry, governing subsequent access to secure compartments, and ultimately assisting in determining the fitness of worshippers to enter God's presence (Doctrine and Covenants 132:19).

flaming sword. Translated by Sarna as "the fiery ever-turning sword," this is a "separate, protective instrument, not said to be in the hands of the cherubim" (NMSGENESIS, 30). While the function of the cherubim is to selectively admit those authorized to enter, Nibley argues that the fire and steel combined in the sword are specifically meant to repulse the serpent, forever preventing its return to the garden (HWNMESSAGE, 319–20).

Was There a Similar Fall on Other Worlds?

In short, it seems possible that the answer is no. To understand why will take a little explaining. Of course, we are now in the realm of speculation. In trying to describe why Satan was condemned for introducing the fruit of the Tree of Knowledge to Adam and Eve, Hugh Nibley wrote: "Satan disobeyed orders when he revealed certain secrets to Adam and Eve, not because they were not known and done in other worlds, but because he was not authorized in that time and place to convey them" (JMBIGIL1, 249). Although Satan had "given the fruit to Adam and Eve, it was not his prerogative to do so—regardless of what had been done in other worlds. (When the time comes for such fruit, it will be given us legitimately)" (JMBIGIL1, 249). Nibley's statements provide helpful answers to the question of why Satan should not have done what he did, but the question remains: Why was timing an issue?

Wondering similarly, the fifteenth-century *Adamgirk* asks: "If a good secret [or mystery (p. 53n108; compare JSTPJS, 5 October 1840, 169)] was in [the evil fruit], why did [God] say not to draw near?" (ADAMGIRK, 3:2:5, p. 53). The text then answers its own question implicitly. Simply put, it says that the gift by which Adam and Eve would "become divine" (ADAMGIRK, 1:3:71, p. 101) and for which the tree of knowledge evidently constituted a part of the approach, was, as yet, "an unattainable thing that was not *in its time*" (ADAMGIRK, 1:3:27, p. 96, emphasis added). This thought evokes a statement often attributed to Joseph Smith: "That which is wrong under one circumstance, may be, and often is, right under another. . . . Everything that God gives us is lawful and right; and it is proper that we should enjoy His gifts and blessings whenever and wherever He is disposed to bestow; but if we should seize upon those same blessings and enjoyments without law, without revelation, without commandment, those blessings and enjoyments would prove cursings and vexation" (JSDHC, 11 April 1842, 5:135).

The application of these statements to the eating of the fruit from the two special trees seems clear. In both cases, those who eat become in some measure "partakers of the divine nature" (2 Peter 1:4). While the tree of knowledge is meant to help those who ingest its fruit legitimately to become "as gods, knowing good and evil" (Moses 4:11; see also 4:28), the tree of life seems to symbolize the means by which eternal life itself is granted to the faithful. But the story of the Fall teaches, that eating the fruit of the tree of knowledge in an unprepared state brings about serious consequences that can be reversed only through Christ's atonement, enabling Adam and Eve to overcome spiritual and physical death.

Going further, although Satan seems to have been aware of what had been "done in *other* worlds" (JMBIGIL1, 249), Moses 4:6 makes it clear that he "knew not the mind of God" with respect to *this* one. Indeed, we might say that it was his very ignorance of God's designs that paved the way of knowledge for Adam and Eve. The Adversary intended to thwart God's plan by inducing their transgression, but instead unknowingly served as the required catalyst for the divinely ordained exercise of human choice. In this set up for Satan, God had in some sense beat the Devil at his own game (see figure 4–8).

What could have been different about *this* world as compared to the others Satan apparently knew? Intriguingly, scripture mentions one respect in which this earth is unique: namely that it here that Jesus Christ wrought out His Atonement. Though Latter-day Saint teachings affirm that many worlds shared the same Creator and Savior (Doctrine and Covenants 76:23–24), they are also clear in asserting that the Atonement took place once and for all. Also, we are told *why* our planet was singled out: it was the only one among His creations that would be wicked enough to crucify their Redeemer (see 2 Nephi 10:3; Moses 7:36).

Figure 4–9. C. S. Lewis: *Perelandra*

With this understanding we might be led to ask whether there are some worlds, more enlightened than our own, on which the fruit of the tree of knowledge was not forbidden at the outset and on which there was no corresponding Fall. Specifically, are there children of God who undergo the entirety of their mortal probation on Eden-like terrestrial worlds—that is, people in addition to those who were translated to go there after having already lived for a time on a telestial world? We already know that Enoch and Jesus Christ Himself ministered to translated beings living on such worlds (JSWORDS, 3 October 1841, 77; JSTPJS, 5 October 1840, 170–71; JTMEDIATION, 76–78), "every kingdom . . . in its time" (Doctrine and Covenants 88:61). C. S. Lewis tried to imagine such a world—populated by intelligent, innocent creatures—in *Perelandra*, the second volume of his space trilogy. In addition, he seemed to have imagined a universe in which our own world, "the silent planet," was an exception to the general rule—a "shadowland" that, unlike other planets, was greatly influenced, if not largely controlled, by evil immortals.

In brief, Satan's shortsighted strategy seems to have been to opportunistically exploit his discovery of differences between this world and the "other worlds" he had known. God's success in co-opting the devil's strategy seems to have resulted, at least in part, from Satan's ignorance of His unique designs for *our* world.

turned every way to keep the way of the tree of life.

EPILOGUE

³² (And these are the words which I spake unto my servant Moses, and they are true even as I will; and I have spoken them unto you. See thou show them unto no man, until I command you, except to them that believe. Amen.)

4:31   ***to keep the way of the tree of life.*** The mention of a sacred path leading from the place of Adam's exile back to the garden ends the story on a note of hope. The cherubim will open the way for people once they are prepared to enter the celestial paradise and eat of the tree of life (Revelation 2:7; 22:14). A rabbinic tradition has it that the last divine word that rang in the ears of Adam and Eve as they left the Garden of Eden was *teshuv*, meaning "You shall return!" (ALTRIAL, 31. Regarding the Hebrew term *teshuv*, which has to do both with repentance and return, see figure 3–4).

CHAPTER 5
THE TWO WAYS

ADAM AND EVE KEEP THE LAW OF OBEDIENCE

5 ¹ And it came to pass that after I, the Lord God, had driven them out, that Adam began to till the earth, and to have dominion over all the beasts of the field, and to eat his bread by the sweat of his brow, as I the Lord had commanded him. And Eve, also, his wife, did labor with him.

² And Adam knew his wife, and she bare unto him sons and daughters, and they

---

5   While the importance of the account of the Creation and the Fall in Moses 1–4 cannot be overstated, the temple-themed story of the Book of Moses is not complete without the multi-episode drama that follows in chapters 5–8. John C. Reeves observes, "The story of Cain and Abel . . . represents a critical turning point in antediluvian history, and is (from the point of view of the final redactor of Genesis) the key crime which leads ineluctably to the Flood" (JMBIGIL1, 323). Happily, however, as Gary A. Anderson points out, the story of Adam and Eve and their family found in Moses 5–8 "is not an account of sin alone but the beginning of a drama about becoming a being who fully reflects God's very own image. Genesis [or Moses] is not only about the origins of sin; it is also about the foundations of human perfection. The work that God has begun in Creation He will bring to completion" (GAAGENESIS, 8). The clarity with which the fundamental doctrines, laws, and ordinances of the gospel begin to unfold in Moses 5 fully justifies Nibley calling it "the greatest of all chapters" in scripture (HWNPGP, 231). Consistent with the opposing themes of perfection and corruption throughout the remainder of the Book of Moses, chapter 5 contains a series of stories that highlight the contrast between those who would and those who would *not* hearken to the voice of God (vv. 16, 17, 23, 57). The divergent trajectories of the "two ways" of light and darkness is also reflected in Moses 6–8, through stories that illustrate the consequences of keeping and breaking temple covenants (see figure 5–5).

5:1   ***to till the earth.*** The tilling reported here was previously anticipated in Moses 3:5 and 4:29. "Tilling the earth" in similitude of Adam and Eve is also a theme in the Book of Mormon (2 Nephi 2:19; Alma 42:2) and is sometimes linked with the commandment to have children (2 Nephi 2:19–20; Ether 6:13–16).

      bread by the sweat of his brow. God rewarded the labor of Adam and Eve with a harvest of life-sustaining grain. Bread relieved them from the diet of wild plants and roots they had presumably followed immediately after their expulsion from Eden. Note that OT1 and OT2 read "by the sweat of *the* brow" (SHFJST, 92) instead of "*his* brow," perhaps highlighting the "unity and cooperation" of Adam and Eve (APSBOOK, 218).

      as I the Lord had commanded him. And Eve, also, his wife, did labor with him. The theme of the first two temple covenants, obedience and sacrifice, is highlighted in vv. 1–6 (see figure 5–5). These verses highlight the *obedience* of Adam and Eve by enumerating their faithfulness to each of the commandments they had been given so far. Adam, with his fellow laborer Eve, began to "till the earth, and to have dominion over all the beasts of the field, and to eat his bread by the sweat of his brow" (v. 1). Likewise, Eve fulfilled the commission she had received in the Garden of Eden and "bare . . . sons and daughters, and they began to multiply and to replenish the earth" (v. 2). In addition, "Adam was obedient unto the commandments of the Lord" and offered a *sacrifice* of "the firstlings of their flocks" for "many days," despite the fact that he did not yet fully understand the reason why he had been thus commanded (vv. 5–6).

5:2   ***Adam knew his wife.*** The Book of Moses expresses this event in the simple past rather than in the past perfect (i.e., "Adam had already known his wife"). An Armenian text states what is made obvious here, "When Adam and Eve left the Garden, they were still virgins" (JMBIGIL1, 354–55).

Figure 5–1. J. James Tissot, 1836-1902: *The Last Supper*, 1886-1894

THE PRAYER OF ADAM AND EVE

A Christian text, the *Acts of John*, gives an account of a prayer circle that was formed by the apostles, with Jesus at the center: "So he told us to form a circle, holding one another's hands, and himself stood in the middle." Ancient traditions purport to give details about similar forms of prayer going back to Adam and Eve. Their prayer is said to have included praying with uplifted hands, speaking in an unknown language, and repeated words.

Uplifted hands. The *Conflict of Adam and Eve with Satan*, a Christian text, recounts that as Adam was offering on the altar he began "to pray, with his hands spread unto God." This classical *orans* (Latin "praying") position was practiced by temple priests in the ancient world. It was formerly used in Latter-day Saint sacrament prayers and has been used by them in other settings. Christians have long connected the tradition with the posture of crucifixion. Even today, this gesture is widely recognized in non-religious settings as a sign of distress, a call for help, or a demonstration of peaceful intent. Significantly, the gesture is related to sacrifice "after the order of the Melchizedek Priesthood" (JSWORDS, 55n29)—not the Levitical offering of animal sacrifice but an ongoing dedication of one's own life in a spirit of consecration. Elder Neal A. Maxwell explained that "real, personal sacrifice never was placing an animal on the altar. Instead, it is a willingness to put the animal in us upon the altar and letting it be consumed!" (MOSESS 71).

Unknown language. No doubt echoing what he had learned from Joseph Smith, William Clayton wrote that the "first word Adam spoke" was "a word of supplication." Seemingly garbled words claiming to reproduce the words of Adam's prayer have long puzzled interpreters. For example, Hugh Nibley cites one text as saying that "Adam began to pray in a language which is unintelligible to us." Nibley explained that "speaking in an unknown language" is actually "the usual code introducing [such a] prayer" (MOSESS 71).

Repetition. The threefold repetition in some versions of the story may represent the idea that it was on the third day when Adam's urgent and persistent request for additional knowledge from the Lord was at last answered with instruction by an angel. In some Jewish traditions, the angel who came to instruct Adam bears a book that "teaches [those who are wise and God-fearing] how to call upon the angels and make them appear before men, and answer all their questions." Likewise, the Prophet Joseph Smith was anxious to teach the Saints the manner by which they could "pray and have [their] prayers answered." "For to him to whom these keys are given there is no difficulty in obtaining . . . knowledge" (Doctrine and Covenants 128:11). See MOSESS 61, 71.

began to multiply and to replenish the earth. ³ And from that time forth, the sons and daughters of Adam began to divide two and two in the land, and to till the land, and to tend flocks, and they also begat sons and daughters.

THE LAW OF SACRIFICE IS KEPT AND EXPLAINED

⁴ And Adam and Eve, his wife, called upon the name of the Lord, and they heard the voice of the Lord from the way toward the Garden of Eden, speaking unto them, and they saw him not; for they were shut out from his presence. ⁵ And he gave unto them commandments, that they should worship the Lord their God, and should offer the firstlings of their flocks, for an offering unto the Lord. And Adam was obedient unto the commandments of the Lord.

⁶ And after many days an angel of the Lord appeared unto Adam, saying: "Why

5:3   **sons and daughters.** In contrast to Genesis, the Book of Moses specifically mentions children of both genders who were born before Cain and Abel.

     two and two. The monogamous pairing described here can be contrasted with the later polygamous marriages of the wicked Lamech (v. 44) as well as the marriages outside the covenant and the general licentiousness of the people in the days of Noah (Moses 8:13–21, 28–29).

     till the land . . . and also begat sons and daughters. The wording of this verse parallels the description of Adam and Eve's faithfulness to to the law of obedience in vv. 1–2. By it, we are meant to understand that the sons and daughters followed their parents' pattern.

5:4   **Adam and Eve, his wife, called upon the name of the Lord.** Here, we are told that Adam and Eve "called upon the name of the Lord"—meaning Jehovah. Later, they will be instructed more explicitly to "call upon God in the name of the *Son*" (v. 8; emphasis added). Elsewhere in the Bible, the expression "calling upon the Lord" is used when seeking "help in connection with a ritual or invoking God's presence at a cultic site" (Genesis 12:8; 13:4; 21:33; 26:25; 1 Kings 18:24; Matthew 18:20). (JHWGENESIS, 42).

     they heard the voice of the Lord from the way toward the Garden of Eden. In response to their obedience and prayers, Adam and Eve heard the Lord's voice calling them back from their earthly exile. Later, He gave them additional commandments (and covenants) to set their feet back on the way toward the Garden of Eden, which is, of course, the path that terminates in "the way of the tree of life" (Moses 4:31; JMBIGIL1, 359). For related temple symbolism, see figure 3–4.

     for they were shut out from his presence. Lacking knowledge of the conditions by which they could receive the blessings of the Atonement, Adam and Eve experienced separation from God, amounting to a temporary state of spiritual death—the "first death, even that same death which is the last death" for the wicked (Doctrine and Covenants 29:41).

5:5   **he gave unto them commandments.** OT1 and OT2 have the singular term "commandment" (SHFJST, 93, 603). "What was the reward for diligence in prayer?" Draper, Brown, and Rhodes ask. "The answer is more commandments" (RDDPGP, 58; compare *Pirkei Avos* 4:2). These new instructions were among what Alma termed the "second commandments," given because Adam and Eve had transgressed the "first commandments" (Alma 12:31–37). Nibley continues: "Now he gives them commandments. He gives them the law of God. He gives them the *law of obedience.* He gives them *the law of sacrifice,* and he gives them *the law of the Gospel . . . ,* which they follow. They are starting on the way back now" (HWNPGP, 233; emphasis added). See figure 5–5.

     offer the firstlings of their flocks. Jewish and Islamic traditions recount how God taught Adam the practice of animal sacrifice. The ordinance of animal sacrifice given to Adam and Eve (vv. 5–9) corresponds in our day to the sacrament (Doctrine and Covenants 59:8–14). Thus, as Elder Bruce R. McConkie explained, three ordinances (baptism, sacrifice, and sacrament) are associated with one and the same covenant (JMBIGIL1, 359).

5:6   **after many days.** Jewish and early Christian traditions speak of a period of forty days of penance for Adam and Eve after the Fall. Terje Stordalen explains that the law of sacrifice was

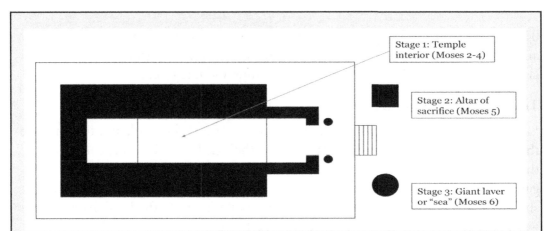

Figure 5–2. *Floor plan of Solomon's Temple, with suggested locations of the ritual described in Moses 2–6*

THE BOOK OF MOSES AS AN ANCIENT ISRAELITE TEMPLE TEXT

Building on observations about Moses' personal background as a Levite, BYU professor John W. Welch suggests "the possibility that a text such as the Book of Moses was the original underlying priestly text from which Genesis 1–6 was drawn." Noting that the discovery of two silver scrolls now on display in the Israel Museum—clearly written in minute paleo-Hebrew lettering coming from Jerusalem before 600 BCE and the Babylonian Exile but containing the High Priestly blessing in Numbers 6:24–27—shows that priestly texts existed before Ezekiel and the Exilic Period, Welch rejects the assumption that the original text of the Book of Moses had to have been composed after the Exile and, by identifying Levitical elements in the Book of Moses, strives to show that the Book of Moses is credible as a Levitical or priestly book consistent with the received fact that Moses himself was a Levite (JWWPRIESTLY).

In another essay, Welch draws on the research of Old Testament scholar Mary Douglas, who realized that the exposition of the laws contained in the Book of Leviticus could be best understood when read as if they provided a tour through the ancient Israelite temple (JWWEXPERIENC).

Writing in a similar vein, to Welch Latter-day Saint scholar David Calabro has argued, speculatively, that specific narrative features of Moses 2–6 might be linked to architectural features of the Israelite temple in ways that may reflect its relevance to temple ritual, including lamination of discourse frames; verbs of motion, repeated themes, and wordplays that relate to temple architecture; and narrative displacement. As one specific example, consider that the mention that "the Holy Ghost fell upon Adam" occurs in Moses 5:9, while the story of his baptism is "put in the mouth of Enoch, several pages later." Calabro hypothesizes that its "position in chapter 6 conforms to the setting of the ritual, near the laver, where instruction about baptism is appropriate" (DCAJSARCH, 173). Similarly, Adam and Eve are taught the law of sacrifice only after they have been driven out of the Garden, allowing those who, according to Calabro's conjecture, were participating in temple ritual to be situated near the altar of sacrifice before the presentation of that law.

Complicating the picture somewhat, Calabro has argued eloquently (primarily on the basis of New Testament ideas and language in the Book of Moses) for the intriguing suggestion that the Book of Moses, as we have it today, may be rooted in a first- or second-century Christian baptismal liturgy (DCAEARLY). Going further, however, Calabro suggests that the early Christian source for our modern Book of Moses may have been adapted from even more ancient sources that could have been used in a diferent performative context— for example, within early Israelite temples. In brief, the idea is that just as Joseph Smith restored the text in modern times, an early Christian text may also have been a restoration of an earlier temple text, although reformulated in language appropriate to its use in a later setting. Calabro's intriguing hypothesis still leaves open the possibility that the Book of Moses, in an earlier form could be conceived as a temple text for ritual use in royal investiture, analogous to temple rites restored by the Prophet Joseph Smith (JMBTWIN, 861n52).

dost thou offer sacrifices unto the Lord?" And Adam said unto him: "I know not, save the Lord commanded me." [7] And then the angel spake, saying: "This thing is a similitude of the sacrifice of the Only Begotten of the Father, which is full of grace and truth. [8] Wherefore, thou shalt do all that thou doest in the name of the Son, and thou shalt repent and call upon God in the name of the Son forevermore."

ADAM AND EVE REJOICE

[9] And in that day the Holy Ghost fell upon Adam, which beareth record of the Father and the Son, saying: "I am the Only Begotten of the Father from the beginning, henceforth and forever, that as thou hast fallen thou mayest be redeemed, and all mankind, even as many as will."

5:6   given as "a test of being faithful while not perceiving (fully) the reason behind an instruction." Here we are pointedly told that the additional light and knowledge that Adam sought did not come right away. But, wrote Nibley, "[the Lord] doesn't keep you waiting forever. Give your test sufficient time, enough to show your integrity, and you will get your answer" (HWNPGP, 234).

    an angel. Alma 12:28–35 implies that Alma was aware of the material in this chapter, either by direct revelation or through study of the brass plates. Latter-day Saint scholars Jeff Lindsay and Noel B. Reynolds have identified many other examples where the prophets of the Book of Mormon seem to have been aware of events and teachings in the Book of Moses (JDLSTRONG).

5:6   *I know not, save the Lord commanded me.* On the practical implications of Adam and Eve's example of obedience despite lack of understanding, Hugh Nibley comments, "I doubt not that when we know the reasons for some of the things we do now on faith, the practical value of the actions will be so plain that we will wonder how we could have missed it, and then we shall be heartily glad that we did what we were told to do" (JMBIGIL1, 360–61).

5:7   *This thing is a similitude of the sacrifice of the Only Begotten of the Father.* Joseph Smith taught the following about how animal sacrifice symbolized the future sacrifice of Christ: "Certainly, the shedding of the blood of a beast could be beneficial to no man, except it was done in imitation or as a type, or explanation of what was to be offered through the gift of God Himself, and this performance done with an eye looking forward in faith on the power of that great Sacrifice for a remission of sins. . . . Whenever the Lord . . . commanded [men] to offer sacrifices to Him, . . . it was done that they might look forward in faith to the time of his coming and rely upon the power of that Atonement for a remission of their sins" (JSTPJS, 22 January 1834, 58).

5:8   *do all that thou doest in the name of the Son.* Nephi also teaches: "But behold, I say unto you that ye must pray always, and not faint; that ye must not perform any thing unto the Lord save in the first place ye shall pray unto the Father in the name of Christ, that he will consecrate thy performance unto thee, that thy performance may be for the welfare of thy soul" (2 Nephi 32:9).

5:9   *in that day.* The phrase emphasizes the cause and effect relationship between what Adam has just learned and the joy he expressed in the promise of redemption.

    the Holy Ghost fell upon Adam. The explanation of the meaning of the law of sacrifice in vv. 6–8 sets the stage perfectly for a description of Adam's subsequent baptism. However, contrary to expectation, we are not told about the baptism until later, within the sermon of Enoch (Moses 6:51–64; see figure 5–2). The mention of the Father, the Son, and the Holy Ghost in this verse, a feature of the modern baptismal prayer, hints at the ordinance.

    With no human administrator available to perform Adam's baptism, it was accomplished in an exceptional manner by his being "caught away by the Spirit of the Lord, and . . . carried down into the water" (Moses 6:64). Similarly, in the Mandaean account of Adam's baptism, the ordinance was completed by divine means through the Mandaean redeemer figure. After giving the account of Adam's baptism, Enoch affirmed that Adam also received the Melchizedek Priesthood and the additional ordinances for him to become "a son of God" (Moses 6:67–68). See JMBIGIL1, 362.

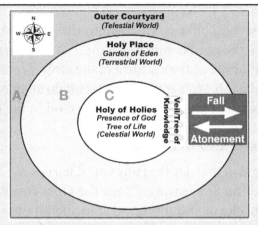

Figure 5–3. Left: *Adam and Eve Outside Paradise; Cain and Abel*, twelfth century;
Right: *Gradients of holiness and the high priest's clothing*

ADAM AND EVE'S TEMPLE: TRADITIONS ABOUT THE "CAVE OF TREASURES"

In the medieval Christian depiction above at left, we see Adam and Eve, clad only in their fig-leaf aprons, "lamenting their Fall on a brown, bare hill" (Antony Eastmond, JMBIGIL1, 670). The three vertically arranged areas of the mountain correspond symbolically to the three divisions of the temple shown above at right: the Holy of Holies (the place of the divine presence where Adam and Eve had formerly lived) [C], the Holy Place (where they prepared themselves for a return to that presence) [B], and the courtyard (the world of sin and death) [A].

Tongues of flame adorn the upper part of the hill and the entrance to the cave. The flames suggest the glory of the divine presence—a warning of potential danger for those who approach it unauthorized and unprepared. Cain and Abel offer their respective grain and animal sacrifices on the hills portrayed on either side of the central peak. God is shown consuming the sacrifice of Abel while rejecting that of Cain. At the bottom of the mountain, Cain has words with Abel, leads him out to the field, and then executes his murder.

In the heart of the mountain, an aged Adam and Eve, clad in robes of animal skins, confer within what is sometimes called the "Cave of Treasures." The treasures were gold, frankincense, and myrrh, said to have been retrieved by angels from the Garden of Eden. In Old Testament times, gold symbolized kingship and frankincense symbolized the offering of priests. The oil of myrrh—"known as the 'dew of resurrection'—had anointed the royal high priests after the order of Melchizedek and transformed them into sons of God" (MBCHRISTMAS, 120). The significance of the treasures—or "tokens," as they are sometimes described—becomes more clear with the understanding that the cave where Adam and Eve were made to dwell was a proto-temple, a divine replacement on earth for the Garden of Eden they had left behind.

Though still relatively dark and dreary when compared to their surroundings in Eden, the cave was a place of instruction, affording the couple protection from the world in their state of vulnerability and providing privacy and security for the treasures that were kept therein. But it was not meant to be their final home. Once their period of preparation was over, "the Lord took pity on them, and he sent his angel to take them out of the darkness, and he guided and brought them into this bright world" (W. Lowndes Lipscomb, JMBIGIL1, 671, 673). There, in answer to prayer, they continued to receive the additional light and knowledge they would need as they readied themselves and their children for a permanent return to God's presence. The first generations of Adam's righteous descendants are said to have lived in the upper regions of the mountain, near the cave and the garden, until they were lured down to the plain by Satan (JMBIGIL1, 669–75).

As a summary of the sudden downward pull Satan exercised on newly fallen humankind, Nibley tells the stock story of the devil's efforts to supplant God's plan of dominion with his own—a sequence of scenes that has been reenacted countless times since Adam and Eve left the Garden of Eden: "You begin by taking the treasures of the earth, and by exchanging them for the services of important people in key positions; you end up running everything your way. What if your rule is one of blood and terror? Better to rule in hell, as Milton's Satan puts it, than to be ruled in heaven!" (JMBIGIL1, 331).

¹⁰ And in that day Adam blessed God and was filled, and began to prophesy concerning all the families of the earth, saying: "Blessed be the name of God, for because of my transgression my eyes are opened, and in this life I shall have joy, and again in the flesh I shall see God." ¹¹ And Eve, his wife, heard all these things and was glad, saying: "Were it not for our transgression we never should have had seed, and never should have known good and evil, and the joy of our redemption, and the eternal life which God giveth unto all the obedient." ¹² And Adam and Eve blessed the name of God, and they made all things known unto their sons and their daughters.

5:10   ***filled.*** OT2 inserted the phrase "with the Holy Ghost," then it was crossed out (SHFJST, 603).

began to prophesy concerning all the families of the earth. Compare Doctrine and Covenants 107:56.

Blessed be the name of God, . . . in this life I shall have joy. Adam's words are phrased in elegant parallels. In vv. 10–11, Adam and Eve's individual expressions of newfound understanding and joy meld to form a harmonious dual psalm of gratitude. OT1 reads more simply: "Blessed be the name of God for my transgression for in this life I shall have joy" (SHFJST, 93).

because of my transgression my eyes are opened, . . . again in the flesh I shall see God. The second part of Adam's parallel expresses a significant insight: the crowning moment and the supernal reward of the opening of Adam's eyes (4:13) is that one day he shall see God again.

transgression. As in the second Article of Faith, the term "transgression" is deliberately used instead of the more common word "sin." Despite the fact that the two words are near synonyms in English, President Dallin H. Oaks saw an instructive parallel with "a familiar distinction in the law. Some acts, like murder, are crimes because they are inherently wrong. Other acts, like operating without a license, are crimes only because they are legally prohibited. Under these distinctions, the act that produced the Fall was not a sin—inherently wrong—but a transgression—wrong because it was formally prohibited" (JMBIGIL1, 364).

again in the flesh I shall see God. The Hebrew text of the corresponding words in Job 19:26 is notoriously corrupt. If we assume that the author of Job was deliberately citing an ancient source such as this one, the parallel phrasing of the Book of Moses would be a valuable witness of the authentic reading. A rabbinic source makes the point about resurrection "in the flesh" even more dramatically, saying that the dead will rise "in their own clothes" (JMBIGIL1, 364).

5:11   ***Eve . . . was glad, saying.*** Nibley commented, "It is [Eve] who perceives and points out to Adam that they have done the right thing after all. Sorrow, yes, but she is willing to pass through it for the sake of knowledge—knowledge of good and evil that will provide the test and the victory for working out their salvation as God intends. . . . She discovers the principle of opposites by which the world is governed and views it with high-spirited optimism: it is not wrong that there is opposition in everything, it is a constructive principle making it possible for people to be intelligently happy. It is better to know the score than not to know it" (HWNPATR, 92–93).

we never should have had seed. While absent from Adam's psalm of praise, the theme of childbearing is the focus of Eve's first expression of gratitude. Draper, Brown, and Rhodes further observe that "Eve's use of the plural [in this verse] contrasts with Adam's singular pronouns in v. 10 and divulge her broad and instinctive concern for her family members" (RDDPGP, 60).

5:12   ***made all things known unto their sons and their daughters.*** Again stressing the obedience of Adam and Eve, the text tells us that they taught "all things" to their children—no doubt now adding instruction on the *law of the gospel* to previous explanations of obedience and sacrifice.

Figure 5–4. Lutwin: *How the Devil Deceived Eve*, early fourteenth century

RITUAL TEXTS ABOUT ADAM AND EVE

The most widely known group of extracanonical accounts of Adam and Eve's experiences after they leave the Garden of Eden is the *Life of Adam and Eve* (hereafter *Life*), which probably dates from a first-century Hebrew original and exists in many later versions. A major theme of this series of stories concerns the unsuccessful attempts of Satan to deceive Adam and Eve. They become increasingly immune to his wiles through the knowledge and protective power provided by angelic visitations and the knowledge and covenants received through ordinances.

For example, the *Life* tells of how Adam, following his transgression and expulsion from Eden, spends forty days of penance standing in the Jordan River—the same river in which Christ would be baptized, and the same period of time that Catholics (including candidates for baptism) traditionally spend in prayer and fasting during Lent. Likewise, Eve is said to have agreed to spend *thirty-seven* days in the Tigris River. During Eve's penance, Satan appears as an angel of light to persuade her to leave the river prematurely. Stephen E. Robinson notes the significant warning that Adam had previously given her (MOSESS 72):

> "Take great care of thyself. Except thou seest me and all my tokens, depart not out of the water, nor trust in the words, which are said to thee, lest thou fall again into the snare." Thus, properly equipped, Eve does not succumb to Satan the second time.

In Lutwin's 14th-century Christian account, Adam is said to have prayed as follows: "'Creator, sweet God, everything that heaven and earth contain is under your command; in your mercy drive from me this evil spirit who alienates me from you. Give me the joy and the status which he lost in heaven. . . .' After these words the Devil vanished." Adam's upraised arm shown here is "a gesture of both speech and action" that could be taken as an oath-, covenant-, or prayer-related movement, a warning for Eve, and/or an attempt to repel Satan.

Given difficulties of dating, both for texts such as *Life* and for the Book of Moses, David Calabro recommends that comparisons among them be made using a careful typological approach. Importantly, he argues that "the Book of Moses and its closest comparanda share one salient feature other than similarity in contents: they are all oriented in a specific way to ritual performances. The Book of Moses, in chapters 5–6, provides a doctrinal basis for the law of sacrifice and the ordinance of baptism; the book also lays out in textual form the pattern of expulsion from paradise, repentance, and being brought back into God's presence, a pattern that the temple endowment embodies" (DCATHIS, 490). According to Calabro, this perspective "does not exclude explanations based on common ancestry or derivation. What it does, however, is permit a description of the content of these narratives in terms of how they relate to implied contexts, skirting the potential pitfalls of speculative textual histories. The Book of Moses is especially informative because the historical circumstances of the modern revelation are actually evident in contemporary sources, including original manuscripts and accounts of the translation process. Thus the study of the Book of Moses paves the way for studies of the other narratives, whose contexts are less directly evident" (DCATHIS, 491; DCAMOSES). See MOSESS 72.

SATAN PERSUADES MANY; GOD CALLS UPON ALL

[13] And Satan came among them, saying: "I am also a son of God"; and he commanded them, saying: "Believe it not"; and they believed it not, and they loved Satan more than God. And men began from that time forth to be carnal, sensual, and devilish.

[14] And the Lord God called upon men by the Holy Ghost everywhere and commanded them that they should repent; [15] and as many as believed in the Son,

5:13   ***Satan came among them.*** As soon as Adam and Eve began to teach the gospel to their children, Satan moved in to blunt their influence. The Prophet Joseph Smith said, "In relation to the kingdom of God, the Devil always sets up his kingdom at the very same time in opposition to God" (JSTPJS, 2 May 1844, 365). In contrast to the eloquent expressions of Adam and Eve, Satan's preaching is proclaimed in brash and abrupt terms. He simply said, "Believe it not," and "they believed it not" (v. 13). That so many were so easily persuaded reveals to readers how strongly predisposed the people were to do evil (JMBIGIL1, 364).

   I am also a son of God. Being a "son of God" is more than being a spirit child of God. Only those who are born again through their faithfulness to all the laws and ordinances of the gospel *become* God's "sons and his daughters" (Mosiah 5:7; Moses 6:68). Thus, Satan's statement is a lie. At one time, Lucifer had been a son of God (see Job 1:6), but no more. His title is now "Perdition."

   Nibley comments on this verse as follows: "Notice, that . . . [Satan's] appeal [is] that he is a son of God. . . . He's all for the Gospel. He is all for saving people. In the Council in Heaven he wanted them saved, too, and he wanted to do the saving. There are lots of people that way, that want to do the right thing as long as they are in charge. But if they are not in charge, all government is then just an evil. When they are in charge, they run everything. . . . When he appeared, his first step was to make a command, speak outright. He wants to be worshipped. That's what he wanted in the first place. ('Give me thine honor' [Moses 4:1].) So he commands them" (HWNPGP, 237).

5:13   ***carnal, sensual, and devilish.*** The word "carnal," from a Latin root meaning "flesh," is closely associated in scripture with the terms "natural" (Doctrine and Covenants 29:35), "temporal" (Alma 36:4), and "earthly" (James 3:15). It represents the condition of estrangement from spiritual things experienced by individuals in their fallen, mortal, and corrupt state before they are born again. The "sensual" man or woman is one who privileges the satisfaction of bodily appetites and passions. Such individuals become "devilish" when they *persist* in their "own carnal nature, and [go] on in the ways of sin and rebellion against God[; they remain] in [their] fallen state and the devil hath all power over [them]. Therefore [each becomes] . . . an enemy to God[, as] the devil [is] an enemy to God" (Mosiah 16:5; see also Mosiah 3:19). Hugh Nibley alternately the three key terms in this verse as "lecherous, pampered, and vicious" (JMBIGIL1, 365–66).

5:14   ***the Lord God called upon men by the Holy Ghost everywhere and commanded them that they should repent.*** The Holy Ghost, an invisible yet powerful opponent to Satan's preaching, provided a witness to the things that Adam and Eve taught (v. 12). But, said Nibley, "there's the rub. . . . Who wants to be told to repent? You are not going to get votes by telling people to repent, but by telling them that everything is wonderful" (HWNPGP, 237).

   Elsewhere, Nibley writes: "The test for this life is not for knowledge; it is not for intelligence, or for courage, or for anything like that. That would be a huge joke. None of us knows very much, none of us is very brave, none of us is very strong, none of us is very smart. We would flunk those tests terribly. . . . [There are] only two things we are good at: we can forgive and we can repent" (JMBIGIL1, 366). Humbly feeling his limitations in so many things after his call as an apostle, President George Albert Smith was consoled by the thought that life offers an absolutely level playing field with regard to the personal qualities that matter most: "As I have looked at other men both in the Church and out of the Church, . . . seeing many who are my superiors in education and in experience, perhaps also in intelligence and in other characteristics, I have taken satisfaction in knowing that I am the moral equal of any man alive" (JMBIGIL1, 366).

THE WAY OF LIFE	THE WAY OF DEATH
Obedience (Moses 5:1-6)	**Defiance** (Moses 5:13-14)
Sacrifice (Moses 5:4-8, 20)	**Perversion of Sacrifice** (Moses 5:18-19, 21)
The Gospel (Moses 5:58-59; 8:19)	**Works of Darkness** (Moses 5:29-31, 47-57; 8:26)
Chastity (Moses 6:1-23; 8:13)	**Licentiousness** (Moses 6:15; 8:14-21)
Consecration (Moses 7:18)	**Violence and Corruption** (Moses 5:31-33, 50; 6:15; 8:28)
Endless Life (Moses 7:23, 69; 8:27)	**Physical Death** (Moses 8:30)

Figure 5–5. *The Progressive Separation of the Two Ways in the Book of Moses*

TEMPLE COVENANTS KEPT AND BROKEN IN THE BOOK OF MOSES

Moses 5–8 is the best scriptural example of the ancient teaching of the Two Ways. The stories in these chapters not only seem to illustrate the consequences of faithfulness and unfaithfulness to each of the five temple covenants but also, remarkably, unfold in the expected sequence. In an April 2019 general conference talk, Elder David A. Bednar outlined these covenants as including "the law of obedience, the law of sacrifice, the law of the gospel, the law of chastity, and the law of consecration" (DABPREPARE, 103).

Mark J. Johnson has argued that temple covenant-making themes in former times influenced both the structure and the content of the material included in the Book of Moses. He observed that the author frequently "stops the historic portions of the story and weaves into the narrative framework ritual acts such as sacrifice, . . . ordinances such as baptism, washings, and the gift of the Holy Ghost; and oaths and covenants, such as obedience to marital obligations and oaths of property consecration" (MJJLOST, 180). For example, Johnson suggests that while the account of Enoch and his city of Zion was being read, members of the attending congregation might have been "put under oath to be a chosen, covenant people and to keep all things in common, with all their property belonging to the Lord" (MJJLOST, 181).

The pattern of structuring scripture to reflect specific temple covenants is not unprecedented. For instance, another scriptural account that seems to conform with a pattern of covenant-making was identified in John W. Welch's analysis of Matthew's Sermon on the Mount and the Book of Mormon Sermon at the Temple. Welch finds that the commandments described in these sermons "are not only the same as the main commandments always issued at the temple, but they appear largely in the same order" (MOSESS 73).

In a related vein, the eminent biblical scholar David Noel Freedman highlighted an opposite pattern of covenant *breaking* in what is called the "Primary History" of the Old Testament (Genesis 1–11). He concluded that the sequence of books in the main thread of biblical history was deliberately structured by a master editor to reveal a sequence in which nine of the Ten Commandments were broken in order, one by one. Freedman argued that the successive breaking of each of the commandments finally triggered a sort of three-strikes-and-you're-out consequence, manifested in "the downfall of the nation of Israel, the destruction of the Temple, and the banishment of survivors from the Promised Land" (MOSESS 73).

Remarkably, the Book of Moses contains stories that illustrate not only the making and breaking of temple covenants but also the ultimate consequences of these choices. In the final two chapters of the Book of Moses, Enoch and his people receive the blessing of an endless life (prefiguring *eternal* life) as they are taken up to the bosom of God (Moses 7:69) while the wicked experience untimely physical death (prefiguring *spiritual* death) in the destruction of the great Flood (Moses 8:30. See JMBBOOK, 431–41; MOSESS 73).

and repented of their sins, should be saved; and as many as believed not and repented not, should be damned; and the words went forth out of the mouth of God in a firm decree; wherefore they must be fulfilled.

ABEL KEEPS THE LAW OF SACRIFICE; CAIN PERVERTS IT

[16] And Adam and Eve, his wife, ceased not to call upon God. And Adam knew Eve his wife, and she conceived and bare Cain, and said: "I have gotten a man from the Lord; wherefore he may not reject his words." But behold, Cain hearkened not,

5:15   *And as many as believed in the Son, and repented of their sins, should be saved; and as many as believed not and repented not, should be damned.* Compare Mark 16:16. Draper, Brown, and Rhodes characterize this decree as "a legal declaration from the divine world." They note that "Jesus virtually quoted these terms as He instructed His apostles for the last time; then He gave these instructions to His New World disciples" (RDDPGP, 63; see also MLBWORD, 753–57).

5:16   *Adam and Eve, his wife, ceased not to call upon God.* There is an implied connection between the prayers of Adam and Eve and the arrival of Cain, whom Eve acknowledged as having come "from the Lord" (v. 16). Childbirth as a blessing from God in answer to prayer is also highlighted in the stories of Abraham and Sarah (Genesis 17:16) and Hannah and Elkanah (1 Samuel 1:11, 20).

    Adam knew Eve his wife. Nahum Sarna comments: "'Knowing' in the Bible is not essentially intellectual activity. . . . Rather, it is experiential, emotional, and, above all, relational. . . . For that reason, the Hebrew stem *y-d-'* can encompass a range of meanings that includes involvement, interaction, loyalty, and obligation. It can be used of the most intimate and most hallowed relationships between man and wife, and between man and God. Significantly, the verb is never employed for animal copulation" (NMSGENESIS, 31). Umberto Cassuto points out that the Hebrew term for "know/knew," found at several key points throughout Moses 5 (vv. 2, 6, 16 [twice], 21, 29, 34, 42, 51), "contains a link with the previous section, whose essential theme is centered on the Tree of Knowledge" (UCCOMMENTARY, 197).

    Cain. The Hebrew stem *k-n-h* typically means "to own or acquire" (APSBOOK, 232n11, 234n21; MLBGETTING), but there is evidence for a secondary stem meaning "to produce or create." The name is also related to the stem *k-y-n*, which means "to form, fashion, or forge," and *kayn* denotes a "smith" in Aramaic and Arabic (JMBIGIL1, 367).

    from the Lord. A better reading is given in Martin Luther's 1546 revised Bible translation, "I have gotten the man, [namely or even] the Lord." "This rendering suggests," according to Victor Hamilton, "that in the birth of Cain Eve thought, mistakenly, that the divinely promised seed of [Moses 4:21] had now come in Cain. The child, whose birth is so welcomed, could be looked on as God himself" (VPHGENESIS, 221). That Eve could have been so deceived in thinking the promised Redeemer had already come in the person of Cain is highly doubtful. However, in a wider sense, her words may be taken as foreshadowing her hope that, in contrast to her wayward progeny (Moses 4:13), Cain would "not reject [the Lord's] words" (Moses 5:16) and would become the progenitor of the righteous branch of her family through whom the promise of Moses 4:21 would eventually be fulfilled. See also APSBOOK, 232n12.

5:16   *wherefore he may not reject his words.* The theme of obedience—which formed both the hinge of the plot of Moses 4 and the central motif of the story of Adam and Eve after their expulsion in Moses 5—is once again highlighted by the hopeful words of Eve. Sadly, "Cain hearkened not" (Moses 5:16).

saying: "Who is the Lord that I should know him?" [17] And she again conceived and bare his brother Abel. And Abel hearkened unto the voice of the Lord. And Abel was a keeper of sheep, but Cain was a tiller of the ground.

[18] And Cain loved Satan more than God. And Satan commanded him, saying: "Make an offering unto the Lord." [19] And in process of time it came to pass that Cain brought of the fruit of the ground an offering unto the Lord. [20] And Abel, he

5:16 ***Who is the Lord that I should know him?*** As Draper, Brown, and Rhodes note, "Cain's arrogant question will be mirrored later by that of Pharaoh (Exodus 5:2), as well as that of King Noah" in the Book of Mormon (Mosiah 11:27). The recurrence of the word "know" (Moses 5:16) fittingly recalls the covenant relationship between Adam, Eve, and God that resulted in Cain's birth—the type of "covenant relationship that Cain refuses to enter" (RDDPGP, 65).

5:17 ***Abel.*** The announcement of a second birth cues the reader to one of the many occurrences of the Old Testament pattern of sibling rivalry, in which the younger son is the one favored by God.

For reasons that are not stated, Eve gives an explanation for Cain's name but not for Abel's. The Hebrew term for Abel's name can be translated as "breath" or "nothingness." Joseph Smith suggested that it meant "sorrow" (JMBIGIL, 369n434). Sarna comments, "The name may augur his destiny. . . . *Hevel* is often used to express the fleeting nature of life. The name may alternatively, or perhaps simultaneously, contain a reference to his vocation in that Syriac *hablâ* means a 'herdsman'" (NMSGENESIS, 32). See JMBIGIL1, 369.

Abel hearkened unto the voice of the Lord. The fundamental contrast between Abel and Cain is succinctly stated.

keeper of sheep. Victor Hamilton notes that Abel is followed by Jacob, Joseph, Moses, and David as shepherds (JMBIGIL1, 370). Nahum Sarna says, "Since, in the biblical view, mankind was vegetarian until after the Flood, the function of animal husbandry . . . was to supply milk, hides, and wool" (NMSGENESIS, 32).

Cain was a tiller of the ground. Of Cain's farming practices, Josephus reports the tradition that "Cain was not only very wicked in other respects, but was wholly intent upon getting; and he first contrived to plough the ground." Thomas W. Franxman sees Josephus' statement as a condemnation of those who dishonor God by offering him "products forced from nature by the ingenuity of grasping man," and Louis H. Feldman notes that Josephus' statement "connects Cain's name, which means 'acquisition,' . . . with this quality in his character." The overall description in Moses 5:17 recalls Doctrine and Covenants 59:18, 20, which warns that the "things which come of the earth" are "made to be used, with judgment, not to excess, neither by extortion." The term "extortion" has the sense of forcible extraction or wresting out, as when money is obtained through coercion or threats. Hugh Nibley explains, "From the wine and olive presses we get the word 'extortion,' meaning to squeeze out the last drop, another way to make a margin of profit—putting the squeeze on, wringing out the last drop." See JMBIGIL1, 370–71.

5:18 ***Make an offering unto the Lord.*** Nibley comments, "Notice [that Satan] says, 'Make an offering unto the Lord.' He doesn't say, make an offering unto me, or make an offering unto devils. . . . He claims to be running the Gospel on earth. . . . Cain is being obedient . . . but not following the law of God. . . . He's being obedient to Satan" (HWNPGP, 238–39).

5:19 ***in process of time.*** Claus Westermann notes that this phrase in Genesis "presumes that something has already happened beforehand. . . . We cannot reconstruct it" (CWGENESIS, 294). However, v. 18 in the Book of Moses appropriately supplies the mention of Cain's obedience to Satan's command as the missing prologue in Genesis to Cain's flawed and misguided sacrifice.

Cain brought of the fruit of the ground. Hyrum L. Andrus explained that Cain, at the command of Satan, "offered the fruit of the ground as a sacrifice, which was not symbolic of Christ's great act of Redemption. . . . Instead of purchasing a lamb or another animal that would serve as an appropriate sacrifice, he offered what he produced, even as Abel offered that which he produced." Speaking of the reason Cain's sacrifice was rejected, the Prophet Joseph Smith explained that

also brought of the firstlings of his flock, and of the fat thereof. And the Lord had respect unto Abel, and to his offering; ²¹ but unto Cain, and to his offering, he had not respect. Now Satan knew this, and it pleased him. And Cain was very wroth, and his countenance fell.

CAIN REJECTS THE LORD

²² And the Lord said unto Cain:

"ordinances must be kept in the very way God has appointed," in this case by "the shedding of blood . . . [as] a type, by which man was to discern the great Sacrifice which God had prepared" (JSTPJS, 5 October 1840, 169; 22 January 1834, 58). Not only must the form of the ordinance comply with the heavenly pattern, but also the heart must be filled with the spirit of sincere repentance, since, according to Joseph Smith, "the shedding of the blood of a beast could be beneficial to no man, except it was . . . done with an eye looking forward in faith on the power of that great Sacrifice for a remission of sins" (JSTPJS, 22 January 1834, 58). See JMBIGIL1, 345.

Some interpreters have argued that Cain's offering of "the fruit of the ground" should have been perfectly acceptable according to subsequent Old Testament practice. However, with reference to the idea of a cereal offering in Mosaic worship, Andrus notes: "Israel was later commanded to bring the first fruits of the field to the priests as an offering to the Lord. But these offerings were, in the main, to be given to the poor, the widows, and the fatherless (see Deuteronomy 26). In some instances they were also used in conjunction with the sacrifice of lambs, but not as a substitute for the shedding of blood (see Leviticus 23:10, 17–18)" (JMBIGIL1, 372). See also APSBOOK, 235–39.

5:20   *Abel . . . brought of the firstlings of his flock, and of the fat thereof.* Paul Ellingworth observes that in the book of Hebrews, "Abel's (pre-levitical) sacrifice [is not] contrasted with that of Christ. In this respect, there is an implied analogy between Abel . . . and Melchizedek" in the righteous nature of their actions. We are also meant to notice a difference from Cain in the care with which Abel selected his offering. About the offering of Abel, Umberto Cassuto comments, "This twofold emphasis—on the firstlings, which are the best of the flock, and on the fat portions, which are their best parts[,] . . . underlines . . . Abel's desire to gratify his Creator, and to honor him to the best of his ability" (UCCOMMENTARY, 206). See also APSBOOK, 236n26.

5:21   *Satan knew this.* What knowledge the devil has, he uses manipulatively. In this case, Satan not only knew of Cain's anger after the rejection of his sacrifice but also certainly knew beforehand that a sacrifice of the sort he commanded Cain to make would be rejected.

Cain was very wroth. The Hebrew term translated as "wroth," often used in the Bible as a "prelude to homicidal acts," can express either anger or grief (GJWGENESIS, 106). Cain's brooding carefully nursed his self-pity and resentment which, turned outward, soon sparked flames of violent passion, igniting an explosion of murderous aggression. Of Cain's ugly transformation, President Spencer W. Kimball wrote: "It is doubtful if Cain had murder in his heart when his first jealous thought crossed his mind, when the first hate began to develop; but ounce by ounce, moment by moment, the little parasite developed to rob him of his strength, his balance, and his peace. The evil took over, and Cain . . . changed his appearance, his attitudes, his life, and became a world wanderer, vicious and desolate" (JMBIGIL1, 372).

his countenance fell. The Hebrew phrase roughly corresponds to the idea of being "crestfallen" or "downcast" (JMBIGIL1, 373), the opposite of the joy a worthy priest should experience as he makes a proper offering (APSBOOK, 240n36).

5:22   *the Lord said unto Cain.* The Lord lovingly tried to persuade Cain to turn to Him, lest the outcome be unto him, as John Sailhamer puts it, "according to [Satan's] desire" (JMBIGIL1, 373). Sadly, despite the Lord's entreaties to Cain (and his spiritually defective successors) "that they should love one another, and that they should choose me, their Father; . . . they [were] without affection, and they hate[d] their own blood" (Moses 7:33).

> "Why art thou wroth?
> Why is thy countenance fallen?
> ²³ If thou doest well, thou shalt be accepted.
> And if thou doest not well, sin lieth at the door,
> and Satan desireth to have thee;
> and except thou shalt hearken unto my commandments,
> I will deliver thee up,
> and it shall be unto thee according to his desire.
> And thou shalt rule over him;

5:23 ***If thou doest well, thou shalt be accepted.*** Victor Hamilton tells us that the Hebrew text of this verse in Genesis is so riddled with difficulties for the interpreter that "every attempt to extract a meaning from the verse is more or less of a *tour de force*" (VPHGENESIS, 225). The Book of Moses agrees with the traditional rendering of the first part of the verse, but then it extends the text to clarify that it is not the abstract concept of "sin" but rather the very person of Satan who has made Cain the object of his desire. Note that it is also Satan himself, who will in the end be ruled over by Cain (JMBIGIL1, 373). Cain, in turn, will be mastered by sin.

thou shalt be accepted. The phrase in literal Hebrew refers to a "lifting up," perhaps a sort of contrast with the "crouching down" (= "lieth") in the phrase that follows. The OT1 wording of this phrase is identical to Genesis 4:7: "shalt thou not be accepted" (SHFJST, 94).

sin lieth at the door. "Sin" makes its first appearance in the Bible here. Victor Hamilton explains the meaning with this paraphrase: "Because [Cain's] offering has been rejected by God he is seething with anger. In such an emotional state he is easy prey for sin which crouches lion-like and waits to jump on him" (JMBIGIL1, 374).

Satan desireth to have thee . . . And thou shalt rule over him. The words for "desireth" and "rule" in the Hebrew text parallel the terms used in Moses 4:22 to describe the tendency for marriage relationships in a fallen world to deteriorate into a state of competition and rancor. Unwilling to escape the bands of wickedness, Satan and Cain will be eternally locked together in the utterly destructive embrace of unrighteous dominion (see Doctrine and Covenants 121:39; 2 Nephi 4:18; Alma 5:7, 10). Going further, Umberto Cassuto notes that the Hebrew term used for the verb in "bruise his heel" (Moses 4:21) comes from a stem that is cognate with "desire" as it is used here (UCCOMMENTARY, 161), thus evoking the mortal danger Cain is courting in giving in to Satan's craving to wound him, and perhaps also suggesting that he must quickly act to crush his opponent (JMBIGIL1, 374).

I will deliver thee up. If Cain persists in wickedness, God's protective power will be withdrawn.

thou shalt rule over him. God is telling Cain that unless he repents, he will become more of a devil than the devil himself. Sadly, as predicted, Satan's own ignominious titles, "Perdition" and "the father of lies," will ultimately be conferred on Cain in v. 24.

President Joseph Fielding Smith made the following comment relating to Cain's subsequent "ascendancy" ("descendancy"?) over Satan: "Now as to whether or not those who in mortal life rebel and become sons of perdition will be able to exercise greater dominion than those who followed Lucifer, who became the Devil and arch-enemy of Jesus Christ, might be a moot question. However, the Lord has made it definitely clear that Cain will hold that ascendancy in the realm of wickedness. . . . As far as Cain is concerned, the information given is definite that he became Perdition, and that Lucifer who is Satan, became subject to him. It appears that the reason Satan desired to have him was due to the fact that Cain had obtained a body of flesh and bones and therefore had superior power, and Satan was willing to accept and be obedient to him because of that condition. The natural conclusion is, therefore, that a devil with a body of flesh and bones has some power greater than one who was denied the physical body" (JMBIGIL1, 374). Note that Cain's ultimate ascendancy over Satan is foreshadowed in v. 30, when Satan takes an oath to "do according to [Cain's] commands."

²⁴ for from this time forth thou shalt be the father of his lies;
thou shalt be called Perdition;
for thou wast also before the world.
²⁵ And it shall be said in time to come—
That these abominations were had from Cain;
for he rejected the greater counsel
which was had from God.
And this is a cursing which I will put upon thee,
except thou repent."

²⁶ And Cain was wroth, and listened not any more to the voice of the Lord, neither to Abel, his brother, who walked in holiness before the Lord. ²⁷ And Adam and his wife mourned before the Lord, because of Cain and his brethren. ²⁸ And it came to pass that Cain took one of his brothers' daughters to wife, and they loved Satan more than God.

5:24   **Perdition.** Emphasizing Cain's accountability, President Joseph Fielding Smith writes, "Cain sinned with his eyes open, so he became Perdition." The title "Perdition"—from a Latin root meaning "to destroy, to ruin"—is an ironic reversal of one of the derivations of the name Cain: "to produce, to create." Importantly, Hyrum L. Andrus observes that "to become Perdition, Cain would have to commit the unpardonable sin." Tragically, Cain's willfull rebellion revealed his determination to put himself beyond the reach of the Atonement. See JMBIGIL1, 375.

    thou wast also before the world. Nibley comments: "This refers back to the time in the Council in Heaven, in glory. Satan is not going to say, you brought me into this world and put me in this terrible jam, and I had nothing to say about it. Oh no, you were in the preexistence, too. You were high up there because you are Perdition now. 'For thou wast also before the world.' You had your preexistence and your chance" (HWNPGP, 240).

5:25   ***except thou repent.*** God tenders a loving plea to Cain as this sad son of Adam nears the final crossroads. Nibley observes: "It's still not too late. This is the gospel of repentance. As long as you are in this earth, you can still repent. As long as we are in this earth, there is no one who doesn't need to repent. . . . The door is open to everyone here. . . . As Ezekiel [18:26–27] says[,] . . . however wicked the bad guys have been all their days, they can still repent and become righteous. And however righteous the good guys have been all their days, they can still fall and become the wicked" (HWNPGP, 241).

5:26   ***Cain was wroth.*** Cain demurs from answering the Lord, choosing instead to fan his inwardly smoldering resentment into a flame of murderous passion.

    listened not any more. Nibley writes, "The . . . door of repentance is held open right to the last moment, when it is Cain himself who breaks off the conversation and angrily stamps out, refusing to listen 'any more to the voice of the Lord' or to his brother's remonstrances" (HWNENOCH, 175–76). Bill T. Arnold observes: "Eve had been talked into her sin. Cain could not be talked out of his, even by God himself" (JMBIGIL1, 376).

5:27   ***mourned before the Lord.*** This expression may indicate the practice of bringing one's concern for loved ones to the altar as the subject of special prayer (RDDPGP, 67).

5:28   ***Cain took one of his brothers' daughters to wife, and they loved Satan more than God.*** The mention of Cain's brothers in v. 27, coupled with the statement that they loved Satan more than God (v. 13), makes it reasonable to suppose that Cain's wife was the daughter of one of the unbelieving sons of Adam. Note the later Old Testament custom "for men to marry a niece, as did Nahor, brother of Abraham" (RDDPGP, 67).

Figure 5–6. Pieter Bruegel the Elder, ca. 1525-1569: *The Triumph of Death*, 1562

"Swear to Me by Thy Throat"

In the performance of sacred covenants in ancient times, writes Claus Westermann, "words and actions are part of the oath. There can be the raising of the hand or some other action(s)" (CWGENESIS, 225). For example, A medieval Ethiopian Christian text portrays Adam as enacting covenantal gestures as part of his exaltation by God before the angels in the Garden of Eden:

> Then God said unto his angels, "This is My image. I have given unto him everything which is lower than Myself [in rank]. Thus saying I have appointed him to be governor [thereof]. Take four sheep which are in the Garden (i.e., Paradise), and slay them, and smear thy hand with the blood, and thy right ear, and the fingers of thy right hand, and [the toes of] the right foot. And this shall be a memorial for thy children, and thou shalt become associated with the Surafel (i.e., the Seraphim) in the mysteries." [Afterward, God clothed Adam.]

Hugh Nibley has written about the symbolism of similar gestures involving the use of blood within public and private rituals described in the Old Testament. Sometimes ancient ritual gestures represented what scholars call "self-cursing." For instance, Nahum Sarna cites an example in the Aramaic Sefire Treaty from northern Syria: "As this calf is cut up, thus [the one making the oath] . . . shall be cut up" (NMSGENESIS, 114–15; compare Alma 46:20-21). Draper, Brown, and Rhodes observed: "The throat is one of the most vulnerable parts of the body to an ancient weapon such as a knife or a spear. Hence, it is vital to the continuation of life. In addition, cutting the throat of an sacrificial animal began the process of a sacred offering. It seems plain that Satan's oaths gain credibility not through his name but only through repeating the divine name ["swear… by the living God"] and, possibly, mimicking genuinely sacred covenants made in God's name" (RDDPGP, 67–68).

As a parallel to the passage describing the oath Cain made to Satan in seeming imitation of genuine ancient religious practices, Nibley cites a Greek fragment of *1 Enoch* describing the events surrounding the marriage of the Sons of Heaven and the Daughters of Men, where their leader Semiazus [a Satan-like figure] says: "'I am afraid you will not be willing to go through with this thing. . . . And they answered him all saying, We will all swear with an oath, and bind each other by a mortal curse [literally, anathemize each other], that we will not go back on this agreement [*gnome*] until we have carried it out; . . . Then they all swore together and pronounced the doom of death on each other" (compare GWN1ENOCH1, 6:3–5, p. 174). In the same spirit, the oath between Cain and Satan is appropriately described in the Doctrine and Covenants as a "conspiracy" (Doctrine and Covenants 84:16). See MOSESS 9, JMBIGIL1, 309, 314, 377–78.

CAIN MAKES A PACT WITH SATAN AND SLAYS ABEL

[29] And Satan said unto Cain: "Swear unto me by thy throat, and if thou tell it thou shalt die; and swear thy brethren by their heads, and by the living God, that they tell it not; for if they tell it, they shall surely die; and this that thy father may not know it; and this day I will deliver thy brother Abel into thine hands." [30] And Satan sware unto Cain that he would do according to his commands. And all these things were done in secret. [31] And Cain said: "Truly I am Mahan, the master of this great secret, that I may murder and get gain." Wherefore Cain was called Master Mahan, and he gloried in his wickedness.

5:28   According to Jewish, Christian, and Islamic sources, Cain's wife had not been the first object of his desire. Accounts tell of the twin sisters of Cain and Abel and relate that Adam appointed which of the sisters each brother was to marry. Angry because the sister promised to Abel was more beautiful, Cain was said to have killed his brother "out of passion for [his] sister." President Spencer W. Kimball concurred with the plausibility of such a scenario: "If we had the record, we would probably find that Cain was promiscuous, for seldom do great crimes travel in single file" (JMBIGIL1, 376–77).

5:29   *Swear unto me by thy throat.* Anciently, discretion in the revealing of sacred religious knowledge was solemnly enjoined by the symbolic enactment of self-cursing. See figure 5–6.

     by the living God. Nibley comments, "Notice . . . , who do they swear by? By the living God. They don't swear by anybody else" (HWNPGP, 242). Similarly, we read in *1 Enoch*, "Kasbeel, the chief of the oath[,] . . . when he dwelt high above in glory[,] . . . requested [the archangel] Michael to show him the hidden name [of God], that he might enunciate it in the oath, so that those might quake before that name and oath who revealed all that was in secret to the children of men" (HWNENOCH, 182; GWN1ENOCH1, 69:13–14, p. 90).

     that thy father may not know it. Above all, Satan wants the oath to be kept secret from Adam.

5:30   *Satan sware unto Cain.* Nibley points out the illusory nature of Satan's seeming subservience: "Cain rule over Satan? Yes, that is the arrangement—the Devil serves his client, gratifies his slightest whim, pampers his appetites, and is at his beck and call throughout his earthly life, putting unlimited power and influence at his disposal through his command of the treasures of the earth, gold and silver. But in exchange the victim must keep his part of the agreement, following Satan's instructions on earth and remaining in his power thereafter. That is the classic bargain, the pact with the Devil, by which a Faust, Don Juan, Macbeth, or Jabez Stone achieve the pinnacle of earthly success and the depths of eternal damnation" (HWNENOCH, 175).

5:31   *Truly I am Mahan.* Draper et al. comment, "Cain takes a new name as an indicator of his new status, also a later characteristic of righteous persons (Abram becomes Abraham; and so on)" (RDDPGP, 68). Nibley discusses a possible etymology of the name: "The word 'secret' is *sirra* in Arabic; the eighth form of the verb, *mustirra*, means 'to hold a secret, to keep a secret.' It's the same as the Greek word *sathra* for secret. The Egyptian word is *seshet*; *mesehet* is 'to hold a secret.' *Sether* is the Hebrew word for keeping a secret (the master of the secret). So this word 'master' may not be our word 'master' at all, but 'master' means 'keeper of secret,' and 'Mahan' means 'great.' In any language, *maha* means 'great.' Words like *magnus*, mighty, might, many, *maharaja*; anything that's big is *ma*. So this could mean Master Mahan, the 'great secret keeper.' (It could be; this is just a suggestion here.)" (HWNPGP, 242). See other suggestions in APSBOOK, 234n21.

     In OT1, "Mahan" is consistently spelled "Mahon," which suggests how the Prophet might have pronounced the name while dictating the manuscript (SHFJST, 94–95).

     that I may murder and get gain. The essence of the great secret of Cain is what Hugh Nibley calls "converting life into property. Cain got the degree of Master Mahan, tried the system out on his brother, and gloried in its brilliant success, declaring that at last he could be free, as only property makes free, and that Abel had been a loser in a free competition" (JMBIGIL1, 379).

Figure 5–7. Pietro Novelli (Il Monrealese), 1603–1647, *Cain and Abel.*

CAIN SLAYS ABEL

In this unsettling scene, we see God speaking from a cloud to the fleeing Cain as he runs past the still-burning altar. Abel's lifeless body, dominating the foreground, loudly proclaims the falsity of Cain's profession of ignorance. The contrast of the skin color to the gray monochrome of the background highlights the link between the three actors. See MOSESS 72.

³² And Cain went into the field, and Cain talked with Abel, his brother. And it came to pass that while they were in the field, Cain rose up against Abel, his brother, and slew him. ³³ And Cain gloried in that which he had done, saying: "I am free; surely the flocks of my brother falleth into my hands."

CONSEQUENCES OF CAIN'S MURDER OF ABEL

³⁴ And the Lord said unto Cain: "Where is Abel, thy brother?" And he said: "I know

5:32   **Cain went.** Gordon J. Wenham observes: "The awfulness of the deed is accentuated by the stark brevity of the description. . . . The terseness conveys the feel of the story hastening to its climax" (JMBIGIL1, 380).

    into the field. Sarna notes, "Hebrew *sadeh* refers to the open, uninhabited country away from the settled areas. It was often the scene of crime" (NMSGENESIS, 33). The word "field" appears in several other stories of sibling rivalry and fratricide: the story of Jacob and Esau (Genesis 25–27), Joseph and his brothers (Genesis 37), Abimelech, who killed seventy of his brothers (Judges 9), and the war between the tribe of Benjamin and those of his brothers (Judges 20:31).

    Cain talked with Abel, his brother. Umberto Cassuto renders the phrase as "Cain appointed a place where to meet Abel his brother." Explaining his reading, Cassuto comments: "First he arranged the meeting and then he turned the meeting into an assault" (UCCOMMENTARY, 213, 215).

    Abel, his brother. The word "brother" is repeated seven times in vv. 32–36, mercilessly highlighting the grim perfidy of Cain's crime.

    slew him. The Hebrew term is *harag*, signifying intentional murder. This contrasts with the sixth commandment's *rasah*, a broader term that includes manslaughter. Nahum Sarna comments: "The transgression in the Garden was an offense against God; now it is man against his brother, which is also an offense against God. It was the 'fruit of the tree' that led to the downfall of Adam and Eve; it is the 'fruit of the soil' that leads to Cain's undoing. The first human was worried about death; now the experience of death becomes a reality" (NMSGENESIS, 31). Regarding the importance of the subsequent motif of Abel as an innocent martyr, see JMBBLOOD, 69–75.

5:33   **Cain gloried.** Cain was previously described as "very wroth" and of a fallen countenance (vv. 21–22, 26). Then, according to an Armenian text, after he "killed his brother he went away cheerfully." In a perverted counterpoint to Moses 1:39, where God gloried in the idea of *eternal life* for his children, Cain has now made the work of *death* the object of his glorying (JMBIGIL1, 381).

    I am free. Elder Bruce C. Hafen writes, "Cain was never more in bondage than when he said he was free" (BCHBELONGING,, 276). Elder Neal A. Maxwell observes: "A confused Cain, a vain Cain, not only murdered his brother while they conversed together in the field, but also gloried in the murder of Abel, when Cain said (probably shouted), 'I am free.' So often violence creates the illusion of freedom or possession. So often sin creates a momentary illusion which those involved are taken in by. . . . [It seems] that the raucousness and the shouting of sin, the Cain-like glorying in it, is also the sound of pain trying to erase itself" (JMBIGIL1, 381).

    Nibley comments: "Recently this gospel [of Cain] was proclaimed by one of the richest Americans addressing the student body of Ohio State University . . . : 'There is nothing that gives freedom,' he said, 'like bucks in the bank.' This seems to be the policy we are following today, and there is no doubt whose policy it is." "What is the market?" former French prime minister Édouard Balladur disparagingly asked. "It is the law of the jungle." This much-maligned statement was actually put to a test by Michele Piccione and Ariel Rubinstein, who found that "the notion of a jungle equilibrium"—an "anything goes" approach in the pursuit of wealth that mimics Cain's example—demonstrates "a number of standard results of competitive markets." They observed that "the virtue of the market system is that it utilizes people's natural desire to acquire wealth," while "the jungle uses people's natural willingness to exercise power and to dominate without employing central government." See JMBIGIL1, 381.

5:34   **Where is Abel, thy brother?** Sarna observes, "The question is a means of opening the,

not. Am I my brother's keeper?" [35] And the Lord said: "What hast thou done? The voice of thy brother's blood cries unto me from the ground. [36] And now thou shalt be cursed from the earth which hath opened her mouth to receive thy brother's blood from thy hand. [37] When thou tillest the ground it shall not henceforth yield unto thee her strength. A fugitive and a vagabond shalt thou be in the earth."

5:34   conversation perhaps eliciting confession and contrition." Sarna further notes that this verse "virtually reproduces" the Lord's question to the fleeing Adam in the Garden of Eden: "The divine question to the culprit in each case—'Where?'—receives an evasive reply in both chapters." The wording of the curse is similar, too—"The son, like his parents in the previous chapter, is 'banished' and settles to the east of Eden" (NMSGENESIS, 34, 31). Unlike his parents, however, Cain will not repent and begin a return to the presence of God. Like Satan and the fallen angels, Cain and those who persist in following his ways are cast out of paradise forever (Moses 5:41).

I know not. Once more the term "know" recurs in the story of Cain. His renewed effort at self-deception recalls the confession of Amulek: "I did harden my heart, for I was called many times and I would not hear; therefore I knew concerning these things, yet I would not know" (Alma 10:6).

Am I my brother's keeper? It is no coincidence that the Hebrew stem for "keeper" is the same one used in the Lord's commandment to Adam and Eve that they should "dress" and "keep" the Garden of Eden (Moses 3:15). Though the English translation we have here is more or less accurate, BYU professor Royal Skousen notes that it fails to fully convey the haughty impudence of Cain's reply: "Couldn't Abel take care of himself? Did he have to have someone look after him? The Hebrew word for 'keeper,' *shomer,* refers to a watchman, a guard, or anyone who has charge, care or oversight of something. Typically, we have keepers of sheep, baggage, wardrobes, altars, doors, houses, gates, city walls, forests, fields, and the king's women. Although *shomer* does not apply to children, the modern reader might get a better feel for Cain's answer if we paraphrased it as: 'How should I know? Am I my brother's baby-sitter?'" BYU professor Chauncey Riddle suggests an answer to Cain's question: "No, Cain, you are not expected to be your brother's keeper. But you are expected to be your brother's brother." See JMBIGIL1, 382–83.

5:35   *What hast thou done?* This would be better punctuated with an exclamation mark ("What has thou done!")—it is "not a question, but a cry of horror" (NMSGENESIS, 34).

The voice of thy brother's blood cries unto me. Draper, Brown, and Rhodes point out that "in a legal sense spilt blood stands as a witness that a crime may have been committed" (RDDPGP, 70). The Hebrew stem of "cries out" "connotes a plea for help or redress on the part of the victim of some great injustice" (NMSGENESIS, 34). For example, Victor Hamilton cites other Old Testament examples concerning the cries of "the afflicted in Sodom and Gomorrah (Genesis 18:13), the pitiable state of the enslaved Israelites in Egypt (Exodus 3:7), or the afflicted stranger, widow, or orphan" (VPHGENESIS, 231).

blood. Sarna notes that "*Mishnah Sanhedrin* 4:5, so the Targums, takes the plural [of blood used here—*damim*—]to include, apart from the blood of the victim, also that of the potential offspring now doomed never to be born: 'Whoever takes a single life destroys thereby an entire world'" (NMSGENESIS, 34).

from the ground. "The earth itself demands from God that He should execute justice on one who destroys a man" (Samson Hirsch, MZBEREISHIS, 1:152). Nibley explains: "Every creature is supposed to have its time, but the purpose of the earth is to sustain and support life. Anything that destroys life prematurely is against the purposes for which it was constructed, and the earth is offended. That negates its whole purpose" (HWNPGP, 245).

5:36   *thou shalt be cursed.* Westermann points out, "In [Moses 4] neither the man nor the woman are cursed but only the serpent. In [Moses 5], however, the man Cain is cursed" (CWGENESIS, 306).

from the earth. Leon R. Kass mentions that the "preposition here translated 'from' could also be translated 'by' or 'of' or even 'more than'; Rashi reads that Cain is now cursed more than the ground, the ground having been cursed for man's sake at the end of the Eden story"

³⁸ And Cain said unto the Lord: "Satan tempted me because of my brother's flocks. And I was wroth also; for his offering thou didst accept and not mine; my punishment is greater than I can bear. ³⁹ Behold thou hast driven me out this day from the face of the Lord, and from thy face shall I be hid; and I shall be a fugitive and a vagabond in the earth; and it shall come to pass, that he that findeth me will slay me, because of mine iniquities, for these things are not hid from the Lord." ⁴⁰ And I the Lord said unto him: "Whosoever slayeth thee, vengeance shall be taken on him sevenfold." And I the Lord set a mark upon Cain, lest any finding him should kill him.

(LRKWISDOM, 143n27). Just as the serpent who was "more subtle" than any beast of the field became more "cursed" than all cattle and beasts (Moses 4:5; 4:20), so the one who "loved Satan more than God" will be cursed more than the earth from which he wrested his living (Moses 5:18; 4:23).

5:37   *the ground . . . shall not henceforth yield unto thee her strength.* From now on, the soil will be unproductive for Cain.

    A fugitive and a vagabond. We can read these two words as a single idea, thus making Cain a "wandering fugitive." The barrenness of the ground and also the new lifestyle imposed on Cain would make it impossible for him to continue as a successful tiller of the soil. Yet more devastating is the fact that, like Ishmael and Esau, Cain "is now ousted from civilization. . . . Rootlessness is the punishment and the wilderness is the refuge of the sinner" (VPHGENESIS, 232).

5:39   *thou hast driven me out this day from the face of the Lord, and from thy face shall I be hid.* OT1 reads, "Thou hast driven me out this day from the face of the Earth" (SHFJST, 95). Hyrum L. Andrus observes that "to be shut out from the presence of the Lord means that Cain was deprived of the blessings of the priesthood. In their fall from their state of paradisiacal glory, Adam and Eve had been shut out from the presence of the Lord. But the Holy Priesthood which Adam received gave him 'the privilege of receiving the mysteries of the kingdom of heaven' (Doctrine and Covenants 107:19). Those who are ordained to that priesthood may 'have the heavens opened unto them . . . and . . . enjoy the communion and presence of God the Father, and Jesus the mediator of the new covenant' (Doctrine and Covenants 107:19)" (JMBIGIL1, 385).

    he that findeth me will slay me, because of mine iniquities. OT1 reads, "Everyone that finds me will slay me because of mine oath," presumably referring to the pact Cain had made with Satan (SHFJST, 95). Cain turned on one of his relatives and now must be on guard lest any of his relatives decide to exact blood vengeance (VPHGENESIS, 233; NMSGENESIS, 35).

5:40   *Whosoever slayeth thee.* Sarna is impressed with this phrase as a solemn legal declaration by the Lord that even a murderer such as Cain will still be under God's protection: "I promise, if anyone kills Cain . . ." (NMSGENESIS, 35). Umberto Cassuto concludes from the Lord's promise of protection for Cain that "blood-revenge is not pleasing in the sight of the Lord" (UCCOMMENTARY, 185). As Hugh Nibley notes, "In making an example of Cain, God absolutely forbade the use of Cain's own methods against him" (JMBIGIL1, 385).

    sevenfold. Umberto Cassuto argues that a penalty based on a commonsense reading of this verse would not be in accord with justice. Rather, observing that seven is the number of perfection, he argues that seven times "connotes in perfect measure, with the full stringency of the law. . . . He who slays Cain will . . . be guilty of a dual offence: the crime of shedding blood, and the sin of contemning [that is, treating with contempt] the Lord's judgment by augmenting the Divine punishment" (UCCOMMENTARY, 226).

    I the Lord set a mark upon Cain. Draper et al. note that "the mark is not the same as the curse, which carried multiple penalties" (RDDPGP, 73)—the most serious was being "shut out from the presence of the Lord" (v. 41). Indeed, in the case of Cain, the mark was a sign of divine protection and also, as Hugh Nibley observes, "a warning to all the rest of us—hands off! If Cain

Figure 5–8. Fernand-Anne Piestre (Cormon), 1845-1924: *Cain, Based on Victor Hugo's Poem,* 1880

WHAT WAS THE MARK OF CAIN?

And Cain said . . . I shall be a fugitive and a vagabond in the earth (Moses 5:38–39). Cormon's tableau depicts the furtive wanderings of the dispossessed son of Adam, as portrayed in Victor Hugo's poem:

> When Cain, dishevelled, angry, in the middle of a storm,
> Fleeing with his children wrapped in hides to keep warm,
> Was running from Jehovah, he arrived at the base
> Of a solitary mountain in the middle of a waste.

In the poem, Cain anxiously marches his family from place to place to escape the lidless gaze of the eye of his conscience "entirely open, in the depths of the sky, / which stared at him fixedly from out of the night"—a torment he could not evade, even in the final darkness of his tomb.

Though, historically, many readers have assumed that the mark of Cain was a dark skin (SRHNOAH; DMGCURSE), the text of the verse itself fails to warrant any particular conclusion about the nature of the mark. Nor is the verse explicit about whether the mark was passed on to his descendants. Of possible relevance to this question is Moses 7:22, which states that "the seed of Cain were black." Joseph Smith, the translator of this verse, along with other early Church leaders and most other Americans in the nineteenth century, believed that Black people were the descendants of Cain (JSJOURNALS2, 25 January 1842, 30). However, Alma Allred finds the staement in Moses 7:22 inconclusive, arguing that it could be a figurative expression that refers to "those who followed Cain in his wicked practices." Similarly, David M. Goldenberg has argued that, as with the four horsemen of Revelation 6:1–8, the blackness of individuals depicted in *1 Enoch* and elsewhere is used in a purely symbolic fashion to represent evil and exclusion from the covenant community (DMGCURSE, 152–54).

Consistent with this latter view is an Islamic tradition that Lamech (the son of the Sethite Methuselah—not to be confused with the Cainite Lamech of Moses 5:43-54) married Methuselcha, a descendant of Cain. Though mentioning the fact that there was "enmity that existed between the children of Seth and the children of Cain," the story implies that there was nothing in their outward appearance that would identify them as being of different lineages, since Lamech had to tell her his parentage explicitly. Described in wholly positive terms, Methuselcha was said in this tradition to have become the mother of Noah.

Ancient sources give a variety of alternative conjectures about the "distinctive mark on the body" of Cain, including a mark on the hand, arm, or brow or a horn on the forehead. Of relevance to the argument by some that the mark may have been voluntarily perpetuated after the time of Cain for purposes of tribal identification is the Book of Mormon precedent for a self-imposed "mark of red" upon the forehead adopted by a group of Nephites who aligned themselves with the Lamanites (Alma 3:4, 13).

Regardless of the exact nature of the mark imposed upon Cain, it seems reasonable to suppose that the separation between the Sethites and the Cainites paralleled the situation of the Nephites and the Lamanites, in which, even though the original distinction was lineage-based, each group eventually came to include not only actual descendants but also like-minded associates (see Jacob 1:13–14; Alma 3:13–19; 24:29; 43:13; 47:35; Helaman 11:24; 4 Nephi 1:35–38). See JMBIGIL1, 337, 386–88.

The Pursuits of Cain's Posterity

⁴¹ And Cain was shut out from the presence of the Lord, and with his wife and many of his brethren dwelt in the land of Nod, on the east of Eden. ⁴² And Cain knew his wife, and she conceived and bare Enoch, and he also begat many sons

5:40   must be punished, God does not solicit our services for the job: 'Behold, the judgments of God will overtake the wicked; and it is by the wicked that the wicked are punished' (Mormon 4:5)." See JMBIGIL1, 386.

Victor Hamilton notes that the function of the mark or sign is paralleled in "Exodus 12:13 (the blood on the doors at Passover which identifies the occupants); Genesis 1:14 (the heavenly lights which identify time periods); Numbers 2:2 (the banners in the Israelite camp which identify the various families); [and] Joshua 2:12 (the sign which identifies Rahab's house)" (VPHGENESIS, 235). As Adam and Eve are clothed with coats of skins before being driven from the garden and as God "announces the post-Flood covenant even before the Flood commences" [see JST Genesis 8:23], so "Cain is marked before he is exiled" (VPHGENESIS, 207). However, as Gordon J. Wenham observes, while Adam and Eve's clothing provide a comforting sign of God's unfailing solicitude, Cain's mark will serve "as a constant reminder of [his] banishment, his isolation from other people" (GJWGENESIS, 110). For more about the mark, see figure 5–8.

5:41   ***was shut out.*** OT1 reads "went out" (SHFJST, 95).

in the land of Nod. Victor Hamilton notes that the Hebrew term *nad* means "wanderer" and the similar term *nod* means "wandering." Thus "He who had been sentenced to be a *nad* settles in the land of *nod*. The wanderer ends up in the land of wandering" (VPHGENESIS, 235).

The Book of Moses, texts preserved by the early Christians, and older traditions of exegesis all speak of a divinely mandated separation of the Sethites from the Cainites. For example, Enoch saw a vision of the "residue of the people which were the sons of Adam" and specifically noted that "the seed of Cain . . . had not place among them" (Moses 7:22). In an Armenian text, Seth and his descendants are said to have lived "in the mountains close to the Garden [cf. Moses 7:17], while Cain with his race (dwelt) on the plain, where Cain killed Abel." Later, however, the sons of Seth and Enosh were said to have been seduced by the Cainite women. According to this tradition, they came down from the mountain and "mingled them with themselves promiscuously."

Though the covenant people have sometimes been drawn out from the world, either to reduce the risk of apostasy or to gather a number in one place sufficient to enable temple building, such separation was, of course, unnecessary in times when righteousness prevailed among all peoples (see, for example, 4 Nephi 1:17). Moreover, in our time, Church members have been specifically counseled against gathering to a central location so that the kingdom of God can be built up in every land. Because we are living in a period when the apostolic commission to "teach all nations" (Matthew 28:19) is nearing its ultimate fulfillment, President Howard W. Hunter specifically warned that there is "no room" in the gospel "for a contracted, narrow, or prejudicial view" and that our message must strike "squarely against all stifling traditions based on race, language, economic or political standing, educational rank, or cultural background" (JMBIGIL1, 388–90).

on the east of Eden. By the phrase "on the east of Eden," we are meant to understand that the place where Cain came to live was even further removed from the presence of God than was the land where Adam and Eve and their righteous descendants lived after the Fall. According to Meir Zlotowitz and Nosson Scherman, "The eastern region always forms a place of refuge for murderers, for the cities of refuge that Moses later set aside were also to the east 'the place of the sun-rise'" (MZBEREISHIS, 159–59).

5:42   ***Enoch.*** This verse does not refer to Enoch the prophet, whose story is told in Moses 6–7. A linear succession of descendants of Cain—seven firstborn sons—is given here, after which the genealogy branches. Importantly, Sarna observes: "The lineage of Cain is not mentioned again in the Bible. No details are given of his span of life, and even the fact of his death is not noted. The same is true of the list of his descendants. The entire line passes into oblivion" (NMSGENESIS, 36).

and daughters. And he builded a city, and he called the name of the city after the name of his son, Enoch. [43] And unto Enoch was born Irad, and other sons and daughters. And Irad begat Mahujael, and other sons and daughters. And Mahujael begat Methusael, and other sons and daughters. And Methusael begat Lamech. [44] And Lamech took unto himself two wives; the name of one being Adah, and the name of the other, Zillah. [45] And Adah bare Jabal; he was the father of such as dwell in tents, and they were keepers of cattle; and his brother's name was Jubal, who was the father of all such as handle the harp and organ. [46] And Zillah, she also bare Tubal Cain, an instructor of every artificer in brass and iron. And the sister of Tubal Cain was called Naamah.

5:42 *he builded a city.* Given the Lord's prophecy that Cain will become "a fugitive and a vagabond" (v. 37), we do not expect to find him building a city. Victor Hamilton suggests: "Perhaps Cain's act is one of defiance. He has had enough of the life of the nomad. He refuses any longer to abide under God's terms. The only other reference to building a city in Genesis 1–11 is the incident at Babel. . . . Here the whole city-building, tower-erecting project is one that God condemns" (VPHGENESIS, 238).

 he called the name of the city . . . Enoch. This wicked city of Enoch stands in ironic parallel to the later story of the prophet Enoch, who founded a city of righteousness and brotherly love that has become associated with his name (Moses 7:19, 69). Indeed, it is no coincidence that the descendants of the Sethites "run in seven lines with almost the same names [as the descendants of Cain]. But," asserts Nibley, "they are read differently as if you were punning on them, like twin names" (HWNPGP, 249)

5:43 *unto Enoch was born Irad.* Interestingly, there is a possible connection between Irad and the ancient world. Writes Sarna, "Curiously, in Sumerian tradition, the first city was Eridu [= Irad], now Tell abu Shahrain, in southern Mesopotamia, which excavations have revealed to be the oldest site in that part of the world" (NMSGENESIS, 36).

5:44 *Lamech took unto himself.* The wording "took unto himself" is paralleled in the description of the illicit relationships of the wicked husbands in the days of Noah (Moses 8:14, 21). Archie T. Wright observes that "there is no indication . . . that a marriage actually took place, but rather [the phrase] could be translated and understood as 'Lamech took to himself two women'" (JMBIGIL1, 392).

 two wives. According to Sarna, this mention of Lamech's wives may constitute a "tacit condemnation" of unauthorized polygamy (NMSGENESIS, 37).

5:47 *Lamech said unto his wives.* Thomas W. Franxman notes that Lamech's poetic declaration in vv. 47–48 could be taken in one of two ways: either as a declaration of his innocence ("If Cain, who killed his brother with malice, merited a sevenfold degree of protection from vengeance, I, who killed after deliberate provocation, deserve that same protection to a seventy-sevenfold extent") or as an admission of his personal guilt ("If Cain suffered seven times, I, who am guiltier, will suffer seventy-seven times"). The former interpretation clearly is a better fit to the context. See JMBIGIL1, 395.

 Thus, the purpose of Lamech's argument was to show his wives that, according to the regulations of the wicked brotherhood to which he belonged, "he had not shed innocent blood. . . . He did not 'hate his neighbor, lie in wait for him, rise up against him, and kill him' (see Deuteronomy 19:11) as Cain had done, but rather he based his appeal on a plea of self-defense"—his act of murder having been performed because he had been previously wounded and injured by the one slain. Thus, John Sailhamer's translation: "a man for wounding me, a young man for injuring me" (JHSGENESIS, 66). In this case, the "wound" inflicted by Irad would have been figurative rather than physical—the primary "injury" given to Lamech being the betrayal of the oath (see v. 50).

 Proud and cynical, Lamech's so-called sword song was not only a statement of self-justification but also a paean to his own prowess, the sort of "taunts, threats, and boastings, which are of the

WORKS OF DARKNESS SPREAD TO ALL FROM CAIN'S POSTERITY

[47] And Lamech said unto his wives, Adah and Zillah:

> "Hear my voice, ye wives of Lamech,
>> hearken unto my speech;
> for I have slain a man to my wounding,
>> and a young man to my hurt.
> [48] If Cain shall be avenged sevenfold,
>> truly Lamech shall be seventy and seven fold."

[49] For Lamech having entered into a covenant with Satan, after the manner of Cain, wherein he became Master Mahan, master of that great secret which was administered unto Cain by Satan; and Irad, the son of Enoch, having known their secret, began to reveal it unto the sons of Adam; [50] wherefore Lamech, being angry, slew him, not like unto Cain, his brother Abel, for the sake of getting gain, but he slew him for the oath's sake. [51] For, from the days of Cain, there was

kind customarily uttered in ancient times by those about to engage in combat" (NMSGENESIS, 39)—"evil words that compound ill deeds" (William Shakespeare, "Errors," 3:2:20). One is reminded of Korihor, who proudly proclaimed that "every man prospered according to his genius, and that every man conquered according to his strength; and whatsoever a man did was no crime" (Alma 30:17). Songs such as these were regularly sung in bloody contests as part of the new-year rites performed in virtually all ancient cultures. As in all such hero tales, the skilled poet exercises his craft in order to glorify actions "which, were it not for his poetry, would appear as merely violent" (Robert Sacks, cited in LRKWISDOM, 146n32).

Umberto Cassuto senses "a kind of antithetic parallelism to the statement at the beginning of the section: "Eve gloried in the fact that she had formed and given birth to a man [Moses 5:16]; here Lamech prides himself on having cut off the life of a man. The earlier vaunt was *with* the Lord; the later, *against* the Lord" (UCCOMMENTARY, 242–43).

wounding . . . hurt. Nibley explains: "If we look up these words that are used here for killing and slaying, we will find what they mean. This *patza* for 'wounding me' . . . doesn't mean wound. It means 'to place a cut or mark upon, to put a ritual mark.' The other, *khabura*, we are told, is the mark or stroke of a wound on the skin. There's a conflict in which ritual wounds are inflicted. We are told that Satan showed Cain the blows of death. . . . He taught them to him before he could have his showdown with Abel" (HWNPGP, 253). The idea of Cain's having administered the "blows of death" in the manner of Satan may lie behind the rabbinic tradition that "Cain pelted all parts of Abel's body, inflicting many blows and wounds, until he killed him by striking him on the neck" (RMZBEREISHIS, 151). Just as Cain is said to have placed gruesome ritual marks on Abel at his death, so the record has the Lord setting a mark on Cain to preserve his life—suggesting a sobering instance of "measure for measure."

5:49   *Irad . . . began to reveal it.* Apparently, Irad betrayed the oath he had made not to reveal the "great secret . . . administered unto Cain by Satan" (v. 49).

     sons of Adam. Draper, Brown, and Rhodes see this verse as describing the spread of secret combinations from the posterity of Cain to the covenant sons of Adam, who are elsewhere referred to as the "sons of God" (RDDPGP, 76; Moses 8:13–14).

5:50   *he slew him for the oath's sake.* This phrase confirms that the "wounding" and "hurt" that Lamech used to justify his act of murder were not merely the result of a chance brawl with Irad or a scheme to acquire his possessions. The fact that the victim was slain "for the oath's sake" evidences a carefully calculated assassination to protect the interests of the secret combination to which Lamech had pledged his allegiance (v. 29).

Figure 5–9. Andrei Rublev, ca. 1360–ca. 1430: *The Holy Trinity,* ca. 1408-1425

THE THREE MESSENGERS

The image above depicts both the three messengers that came to Abraham and the three members of the Godhead. "Many scholars consider Rublev's Trinity the most perfect of all Russian icons and perhaps the most perfect of all the icons ever painted." Leonid Ouspensky observes that the basic form of the icon is a circle:

> Passing through the upper part of the nimbus of the central Angel and partly cutting off the bottom of the pedestals, this circle embraces all three figures, showing very faintly. . . . [T]he gestures of the hands are directed towards the [sacramental] chalice, with the head of a sacrificial animal, which stands … as on an altar. Symbolizing the voluntary sacrifice of the Son of God, it draws together the gestures of the Angels, indicating the unity of will and action of the Holy Trinity, Who entered into a covenant with Abraham.

The Father, represented at left, is dressed differently than the other two. He wears, as Ouspensky describes it, "a pale pink cloak with brown and blue-green lights" of "sober and indefinite hue" that covers both shoulders. The Son, depicted in the middle and embodying the fulfillment of the ordinances of sacrifice performed by the Aaronic or Levitical priesthood, "has the customary colors of . . . a purple chiton [= a draped, belted tunic] and a blue cloak" draped over His left shoulder, the color of the cloak symbolizing incarnation. Behind Him grows a Tree of Life, born of His sacrificial death. The "principal color" of the Holy Spirit is green, represented in the cloak draped over His right shoulder. Here, the color green "signifies 'youth, fulness of powers.' This specifically indicates the properties of . . . renewing all things and giving them life." The symbolism recalls the promise made to those who are to be "sanctified by the Spirit unto the renewing of their bodies" through temple ordinances (Doctrine and Covenants 84:33).

Doctrine and Covenants 29:42-43 affirms that Adam and Eve received knowledge of all these things through specially appointed messengers:

> I, the Lord God, gave unto Adam and unto his seed, that they should not die . . . until I, the Lord God, should send forth angels to declare unto them repentance and redemption, through faith on the name of mine Only Begotten Son.

Jewish and Mandaean literature abounds with references to the idea that three envoys were sent to teach Adam out of the "ritual books" and to protect him from the deceptive influence of evil powers (see, for example, DCMZOHAR1, 237–38). With reference to accounts of visits of divine messengers to Adam and Eve, BYU professor Alonzo Gaskill observes that:

> Peter, James, and John, whether appearing to Adam and Eve or serving as the head of the post-resurrection Church in the meridian of time, are symbols of something much greater than themselves, namely, the Godhead . . . as [are] all subsequent First Presidencies. Whether these three brethren, or any set of tripartite messengers had physical contact with Adam and Eve (or any other Old Testament figure) makes no difference. What is of importance is what they brought and whom they represented.

See MOSESS 72, JMBIGIL1, 340, 868–70.

a secret combination, and their works were in the dark, and they knew every man his brother. ⁵² Wherefore the Lord cursed Lamech, and his house, and all them that had covenanted with Satan; for they kept not the commandments of God, and it displeased God, and he ministered not unto them, and their works were abominations, and began to spread among all the sons of men. And it was among the sons of men. ⁵³ And among the daughters of men these things were not spoken, because that Lamech had spoken the secret unto his wives, and they rebelled against him, and declared these things abroad, and had not compassion; ⁵⁴ wherefore Lamech was despised, and cast out, and came not among the sons of men, lest he should die. ⁵⁵ And thus the works of darkness began to prevail among all the sons of men.

The Law of the Gospel Preached In Response To Encroaching Evils

⁵⁶ And God cursed the earth with a sore curse, and was angry with the wicked, with all the sons of men whom he had made; ⁵⁷ for they would not hearken unto his voice, nor believe on his Only Begotten Son, even him whom he declared should come in the meridian of time, who was prepared from before the foundation of the world. ⁵⁸ And thus the Gospel began to be preached, from the beginning, being declared by holy angels sent forth from the presence of God, and by his own voice, and by the gift of the Holy Ghost.

5:51   *secret combination.* In the Book of Mormon, the oaths that were later administered to those who formed secret combinations among the Jaredites were said to have been "handed down even from Cain, who was a murderer from the beginning . . . [, and] are had among all people" (Ether 8:15, 20).

5:52   *sons of men.* In the Book of Moses, this term is always used to designate those who reject the gospel and follow Satan. In this verse, it most likely refers to the male descendants of Cain and his associates.

5:53   *Lamech had spoken the secret unto his wives.* The damaging results of Lamech's wives having "rebelled against him, and declared these things abroad" triggered an absolute clampdown among the rest of the "sons of men" on speaking to their wives (i.e., "the daughters of men") about their secret affairs (Moses 5:52–53).

5:54   *Lamech was despised, and cast out.* Lamech's associates did not immediately slay him, as the penalty of the oath allowed. Rather, he went into exile to avoid retribution.
        lest he should die. Lamech's expectation of immunity from blood vengeance, as expressed in his song, was not fulfilled.

5:58   *And thus.* In a manner with which readers of the Book of Mormon are well acquainted, this phrase signals the beginning of the solemn summary contained in the final two verses of Moses 5. The importance of the events of this chapter and the promise that the fulness of the gospel given to Adam will "be in the world, until the end thereof" is highlighted by the threefold repetition of "and thus," terminating in the concluding phrase: "and thus it was. Amen" (Moses 5:59).
        the Gospel began to be preached, from the beginning. Phrases similar to this one appear all throughout scripture—for example, John 8:56; Hebrews 1:1–2; 11:13; Jacob 4:4–5; 7:10–11; and Doctrine and Covenants 29:41–42. However, it is significant that the term "Gospel" is mentioned in only two places in the Book of Moses: first, here, immediately preceding the implicit nod to the *law of chastity* in the description of Adam's righteous family line in chapter 6, and second, in Moses 8:19, just before Noah's encounter with the "sons of men" who persuaded the granddaughters of Noah to marry scoffers *outside* the covenant (Moses 8:14–15). See figure 5–5.
        being declared by holy angels . . . , and by his own voice, and by the gift of the Holy Ghost. Mormon taught that the "office of [the] ministry [of angels] is to call men unto repentance,

117

Figure 5–10. *The New and Everlasting Covenant*

THE NEW AND EVERLASTING COVENANT

God's motivation in instituting laws is, as the Prophet Joseph Smith explained, "to instruct the weaker intelligences," allowing fallen humanity to gradually "advance in knowledge" so that eventually they "may be exalted with [God] himself" (JSTPJS, 7 April 1844, 354). The Syriac version of the *Testament of Adam* expresses the belief of early Christians who taught that the Savior Himself revealed the plan of salvation to Adam, bringing the eventual possibility of godhood within the reach of fallen humankind:

> And on this account [God] taught me in the midst of Paradise when I picked the fruit in which death was hiding. And he said to me, "Adam, do not fear. A god you desired to be; a god I will make you. However, not right now but after a space of [many] years. Right now I am going to drive you from paradise, and I will bring you down into the earth of thorns. Your back I will bend [and] your knees will quake from old age overtaking you. I am delivering you up to death. The maggot and worm will devour your body.

> And after a short time my mercy [will be] revealed to you: I will go down to you. . . . For your sake, Adam, I become an infant. . . . For your sake, Adam, I ascend the cross. . . . For your sake, Adam, I open the tomb."

The set of laws and ordinances that were given to Adam and Eve are known collectively as "The New and Everlasting Covenant." This comprehensive covenant includes the baptismal and temple covenants as well as covenants made at other times. Because God is everlasting, the covenant is also "everlasting": it was first given to Adam, and later to all prophets who led subsequent dispensations. Because it is given anew each time the gospel is restored, the Lord also describes it as "new." BYU professor Chauncey Riddle summarized the two basic parts of the covenant as follows:

> Part one is the covenant of baptism, being born of water and of the Spirit. The covenant of baptism is our pledge to seek after good and to eliminate all choosing and doing of evil in our lives, and it is also our receiving the power to keep that promise. Part two of the New and Everlasting Covenant is to receive the power and authority of God and to become perfect in using that power and authority to minister to other beings to bring about their happiness.

As to "part 1," sacrfice is an element of the process of repentance, being both a necessary precursor to baptism and a requirement for renewal of that covenant. The ordinance of sacrifice given to Adam and Eve corresponds in our day to the sacrament. Thus, as Elder Bruce R. McConkie has explained, three ordinances (baptism, sacrifice, sacrament) are associated with one and the same covenant.

As to "part 2," outlined in Doctrine and Covenants 84:33–48, the Prophet said that being "born again comes by the Spirit of God through ordinances" (JSTPJS, 2 July 1839, p. 162)—with the understanding that the bestowal of these ordinances and keys will continue in the next life. He linked the manner in which all the higher ordinances were given to the Saints to the figure of Adam, calling it the "order pertaining to the Ancient of Days" (Willard Richards account, in JSTPJS, 4 May 1842, p. 237). See MOSESS 72, JMBOATH.

⁵⁹ And thus all things were confirmed unto Adam, by an holy ordinance, and the Gospel preached, and a decree sent forth, that it should be in the world, until the end thereof; and thus it was. Amen.

5:58   and to fulfil and to do the work of the covenants of the Father, which he hath made unto the children of men, to prepare the way among the children of men, by declaring the word of Christ unto the chosen vessels of the Lord, that they may bear testimony of him" (Moroni 7:31).

5:59   *And thus.* The term "thus" in this verse is subordinate to its prior usage in v. 58. Here it signifies "in this manner" or "by this means," referring to the fact that it was through the medium of angels (e.g., v. 6), God's own voice (e.g., v. 4), and the gift of the Holy Ghost (e.g., v. 9) that "all things were confirmed unto Adam, by an holy ordinance" (v. 59).

all things were confirmed unto Adam, by an holy ordinance. A contrast is implied between Adam's having had all things confirmed by an holy ordinance from God and Cain and Lamech's having sworn an oath of allegiance to Satan. Details about the holy ordinance referred to are not given, though it is probably no coincidence that Moses 6 will focus on Adam's role as the "first father" in the order of the patriarchal priesthood (Abraham 1:3). OT1 does not include the phrase "unto Adam, by an holy ordinance" (SHFJST, 96).

a decree sent forth, that it should be in the world, until the end thereof; and thus it was. Amen. Just as the decree in v. 15 parallels a passage near the end of the Gospel of Mark, so this declaration is echoed by the final words of the Savior in Matthew: "And, lo, I am with you alway, even unto the end of the world. Amen" (Matthew 28:20).

CHAPTER 6
ENOCH, THE SEER AND PREACHER

ADAM AND EVE KEEP THE LAW OF CHASTITY; RAISE UP CHILDREN

6 ¹ And Adam hearkened unto the voice of God, and called upon his sons to repent. ² And Adam knew his wife again, and she bare a son, and he called his name Seth. And Adam glorified the name of God; for he said: "God hath appointed me another seed, instead of Abel, whom Cain slew." ³ And God revealed himself unto Seth, and he rebelled not, but offered an acceptable sacrifice, like

6   The first twelve verses of Moses 6 describe the final events in the life of Adam as a patriarch to the righteous branch of his posterity. The focus of the account is on the birth of the righteous Seth and the beginning of the patriarchal line of "preachers of righteousness" (6:23) that will culminate, in the seventh generation from Adam, with the call of Enoch. Mercifully postponing judgment in the face of rampant wickedness, God first launched successive waves of what Nibley calls a "crash program" to gather any that would hearken to the call of repentance—first to Adam-ondi-Ahman (see figure 6-1) and later to Enoch's city at the end of Moses 7 (HWNPGP, 262, 263). The absolute failure of the final ministry of the long-suffering Noah definitively confirmed that there were none but his immediate family who would listen. Thus, the sweeping destruction of the Flood in chapter 8 became inevitable.

The account of Enoch in the Book of Moses has been called the "most remarkable religious document published in the nineteenth century" (TLGGOD, 24). Writing the account of Enoch occupied a few days of the Prophet's time during December 1830 (SHFJST, 57). According to Elder Neal A. Maxwell, Joseph Smith's book of Enoch provides "eighteen times as many column inches about Enoch . . . than we have in the few verses on him in the Bible. Those scriptures not only contain greater quantity [than the Bible] but also . . . contain . . . [abundant] new material about Enoch on which the Bible is silent" (JMBIGIL2, 33). This material was not derived from deep study of scriptural references to Enoch or from exposure to the ancient Enoch literature, nor was it absorbed from Masonic or hermetic influences (JMBIGIL2, 93). While expressing "no judgment, one way or the other, upon the authenticity" of Latter-day Saint scripture, the eminent Yale professor and Jewish literary scholar Harold Bloom found "enormous validity" in these writings and could "only attribute to [the Prophet's] genius or [a divine mentor] his ability to "recapture . . . crucial elements in the archaic Jewish religion . . . that had ceased to be available either to normative Judaism or to Christianity, and that survived only in esoteric traditions unlikely to have touched [Joseph] Smith directly" (JMBIGIL2, 33–34).

6:2   ***Adam knew his wife again.*** Although *the law of chastity* is not mentioned explicitly in the chapter, the teaching is invoked implicitly in the way the chapter values the paradigm of orderly family lines and contrastingly highlights problems engendered by marrying outside the covenant (see JMBENOCH, 58–60). It does not seem coincidental that this emphasis immediately follows allusions to *the law of the gospel* being preached in Moses 5:58–59. Moses 6:2 is both a summing up of chapter 5 and an anticipation of the next several verses of chapter 6. This summary is consistent with Umberto Cassuto's two principles of biblical exposition: (1) that the "conclusion of a narrative should reflect the opening," and (2) "that the stories should have happy endings" (UCCOMMENTARY, 190). In both chapters, "Adam knew his wife" (Moses 5:2; 6:2), the child is named with reference to the Lord/God (Moses 5:16; 6:2), Cain and Abel are mentioned (Moses 5:16–17; 6:2), and two births are recorded (Moses 5:16–17; 6:2–3). Moreover, just as Adam and Eve "ceased not to call upon God" (Moses 5:16), Seth and Enos will "call upon the name of the Lord" (Moses 6:4). Likely, this parallel is meant to suggest that the prayers of Seth and Enos were answered with angelic visitations revealing priesthood covenants and ordinances, just as had been the prayers of Adam and Eve (5:4–11). See JMBIGIL1, 475, 477.

Figure 6–1. *Church History Sites in Western Missouri, 1831–39*

THE GREAT COUNCIL AT ADAM-ONDI-AHMAN AND ITS GEOGRAPHY

Joseph Smith revealed the name of the location where Adam gave his final blessing to be Adam-ondi-Ahman, which Hugh Nibley took to mean "Adam (or 'man') in the presence of God." In this place, Adam gathered his posterity three years before his death and "predicted whatsoever should befall his posterity unto the latest generation" (Doctrine and Covenants 107:56). An analogous event is portrayed in extracanonical Adam and Eve literature. Nibley argued that this "great assembly" was "the original model" for the widespread tradition of annual year-rites thereafter performed throughout the ancient world (JMBIGIL1, 458).

The Prophet said that the purpose of Adam's blessing was to "bring [his posterity] into the presence of God." Hyrum L. Andrus explained that "Adam . . . realized his desire to a degree, for 'the Lord appeared unto them' (Doctrine and Covenants 107:54). But even this blessing was short of the ultimate purpose of the Gospel, which was to bring all those of Adam's descendants who would obey its divine truths back into the presence of God and to endow them with celestial glory" (JMBIGIL1, 457).

Although, as Graham W. Doxey states in the *Encyclopedia of Mormonism*, "neither biblical records nor secular history and archaeological research" are likely to ever "identify the dimensions or the location of the Garden [of Eden] in terms of the present-day surface of the earth" (JMBIGIL1, 623), statements attributed to the Prophet Joseph Smith, if taken literally, might be read as implying indications of Adam and Eve's step-by-step migration *after* the Fall, paralleling the general direction of the Saints' movement in Missouri after their expulsion from Jackson County, the "center place" where the future temple complex of Zion, the New Jerusalem, will be built (Doctrine and Covenants 84:1–5; Moses 7:62; figure 7–4). North of Independence, in Caldwell County, is an area that the Saints named Far West. It was near that place, according remembrances of statements by the Prophet, that Cain killed Abel. Continuing about twelve miles farther in that same general direction is a less known location where the Prophet had proposed to build a stake and city to be named Seth, in memory of the son who consoled Adam and Eve after their loss of Abel. About thirteen miles north of Seth and seventy miles north of Independence is Adam-ondi-Ahman, where Adam gave a final blessing to his posterity. President Joseph Fielding Smith, among others, has described a gathering of righteous Saints that will take place at Adam-ondi-Ahman, "preparatory to the coming in the clouds of glory of our Savior Jesus Christ" (JMBIGIL1, 460). See JMBIGIL1, 457–60, 622–26.

unto his brother Abel. And to him also was born a son, and he called his name Enos. [4] And then began these men to call upon the name of the Lord, and the Lord blessed them.

THE BOOK OF REMEMBRANCE

[5] And a book of remembrance was kept, in the which was recorded, in the language of Adam, for it was given unto as many as called upon God to write by the spirit

6:2   Moses 6:5–23 continues the description of the ideal family order established by Adam and Eve. A celestial marriage order can also be inferred from Moses 8:13, in which Noah and his righteous sons are formally given the title of "sons of God," just as Adam was given the same title after having had "all things . . . confirmed . . . by a holy ordinance," including the fulness of the Melchizedek priesthood after the "order of the Son of God" (see Moses 5:59; 6:66–68; JST Genesis 14:27–40; Doctrine and Covenants 107:3–4). The patriarchal order of the priesthood, "which was in the beginning" and "shall be in the end of the world also" (Moses 6:7), is depicted as presiding over a worthy succession of generations beginning with Seth, who was in the image and likeness of Adam (Moses 6:10) just as Adam and Eve had been made in the image and likeness of God (Moses 6:9, 22). In contrast to the conduct of Adam and Eve's righteous posterity (Moses 6:23), all manner of "fornication . . . [was] spread by the sons of Cain" according to extracanonical tradition (JMBIGIL2, 203).

6:3   *Seth.* Nahum M. Sarna connects the name Seth "with the stem *sh-y-t*, 'to place, put, set'. . . . Since the noun *shat* means 'foundation,' as in Isaiah 19:10 and Psalm 11:3, there may lie behind the name the notion that, as *Numbers Rabbah* 14:20 has it, 'With him the world was founded [anew]'" (NMSGENESIS, 39). In this sense, there also may be an allusion to temple building and seership. In the Greek *Life of Adam and Eve*, Seth not only "continues humanity" but is the one who "hands on the primeval mysteries," a prominent role he is also given in later Gnostic texts (JMBIGIL1, 456). Consistent with this idea, the later "sons of God" arose out of Seth's posterity (Moses 6:68; 7:1).

Alternatively, Hugh Nibley, along with most other scholars, conjectures that "Seth means 'second or substitute or equal.' *Shetaa* means the same thing as two, double, [or] twin because it tells us in the scriptures that he will take the place of Abel" (HWNPGP, 260). Parallels between Abel and Seth are made explicit in Moses 6:2–3. The shedding of the blood of the righteous and innocent Abel, whose story has always been linked with the idea of proper sacrifice—seems to have given rise to a curious ordinance of sprinkling little children with blood and "washing" (or "baptizing") them that was denounced by the Lord in JST Genesis 17:4–7 (MOSESS 18; JMBBLOOD, 69–75).

Enos. Like the name Adam, Enos (or Enosh) means "man." Umberto Cassuto notes a second parallel between Adam and Enos: "This son would be the founder of the human race belonging to the line of Seth, which was destined to survive upon earth, just as [the Cainite] Enoch was the inaugurator of the branch of mankind descended from Cain, whose days were *not* prolonged" (UCCOMMENTARY, 246. See also p. 229).

6:5   *a book of remembrance was kept.* Genesis refers to "the book of the generations of Adam," and Moses to "a book of remembrance." Hugh Nibley infers from these statements that "the written records should be as old as the human race itself. . . . According to [the ancients], the king had access to that divine book which was consulted at the time of the creation of the world" (JMBIGIL1, 478). The medieval Jewish *Zohar* has a tradition of an esoteric book of Adam that was transmitted to him "after his departure from the Garden of Eden" by the angel Rezial and "three envoys" who accompanied him (DCMZOHAR1, 1:37b, 238). The same book was also said to have been given to the righteous Enoch and to the "sons of Elohim, who contemplate and know it" (DCMZOHAR1, 1:37b, 237–38) The book was intended to preserve "the primordial wisdom of paradise for Adam and his generations" and also "the genealogy of the entire human race" (DCMZOHAR1, 237n1041).

of inspiration; [6] and by them their children were taught to read and write, having a language which was pure and undefiled. [7] Now this same Priesthood, which was in the beginning, shall be in the end of the world also.

[8] Now this prophecy Adam spake, as he was moved upon by the Holy Ghost, and a genealogy was kept of the children of God. And this was the book of the generations of Adam, saying: "In the day that God created man, in the likeness of God made he him; [9] in the image of his own body, male and female, created he

6:5   Speaking of the difference between Adam's line of descendants and that of all other creatures that may have preceded him biologically, Nibley wrote: "Adam becomes Adam, a hominid becomes a man, when he starts keeping a record. What kind of record? A record of his ancestors—the family line that sets him off from all other creatures. . . . That gap between the record keeper and all the other creatures we know anything about is so unimaginably enormous and yet so neat and abrupt that we can only be dealing with another sort of being, a quantum leap from one world to another. Here is something not derivative from anything that has gone before on the local scene, even though they all share the same atoms" (HWNBEFADAM, 82–83).

in the language of Adam. See verses 46, 57. Verse 6 says the language used by Adam and his children "was pure and undefiled." Of relevance, as John S. Robertson acknowledges, is the "widely held [Latter-day Saint] belief that the founding members of the Jaredite civilization preserved the Adamic language at their immigration to the New World (see Ether 1:33–43; 3:24–28). Thus the description by the brother of Jared of his apocalyptic vision was rendered linguistically inaccessible without divine interpretive help, since 'the language which ye shall write I [God] have confounded' (Ether 3:21–28)." Robertson wisely cautioned that although the "concept of the Adamic language grew among Latter-day Saints out of statements from scripture, comments of early Church leaders, and subsequent tradition[, it] does not play a central doctrinal role, and there is no official Church position delineating its nature or status" (JMBIGIL1, 479). For a discussion of scientific and historical views of the origin of languages, see JMBIGIL2, 401–3.

to write by the spirit of inspiration. OT1 reads, "with the *finger* of inspiration" (SHFJST, 97).

6:7   *this same Priesthood.* OT1 reads, "Now this was in the beginning that shall be at the end of the world" (SHFJST, 97). In the beginning, God established a patriarchal order on the earth similar to the order that exists in heaven. Robert L. Millet and Joseph Fielding McConkie explained: "It was a perfect theocratic, patriarchal system with father Adam at the head. This system prevailed among the righteous from Adam to the time of Abraham and beyond" (JMBIGIL1, 480) In the last dispensation, God restored the higher priesthood and associated ordinances of the Abrahamic covenant that had been generally withheld from Israel (see Doctrine and Covenants 84:23–25). According to Lynn A. McKinlay, "Today dedicated husbands and wives enter this order in the temple in a covenant with God. The blessings of this priesthood [are] given only to husbands and wives together." Hyrum L. Andrus writes that this restored order is "the Melchizedek Priesthood organized according to an eternal family order, rather than according to offices, quorums, and councils that comprised the Church as an instrument to build up the divine patriarchal order." See JMBIGIL1, 480.

6:8   *Now this prophecy Adam spake.* Evidently, this refers to the statement recorded in v. 7.

by the Holy Ghost. This phrase was added in OT2 (SHFJST, 97, 608).

a genealogy was kept of the children of God. The scriptures are mainly a record of the patriarchs and their descendants—the fate of other lines remains more or less a mystery.

this was the book of the generations of Adam. Sarna comments: "This is most likely the title of an ancient genealogical work that served as the source for the data provided in the present chapter, in [Genesis] 11:10–27, and possibly in other genealogical lists as well. Hebrew *sefer*, here rendered ['book'], specifically denotes a written document, not an oral composition" (NMSGENESIS, 41). Seemingly interrupted by restored extracts from the lost book of Enoch (Moses 6:26–7:69), the

them, and blessed them, and called their name Adam, in the day when they were created and became living souls in the land upon the footstool of God."

¹⁰ And Adam lived one hundred and thirty years, and begat a son in his own likeness, after his own image, and called his name Seth. ¹¹ And the days of Adam, after he had begotten Seth, were eight hundred years, and he begat many sons and daughters; ¹² and all the days that Adam lived were nine hundred and thirty years, and he died.

account contained in the ancient work noted by Sarna is seemingly resumed again in Moses 8:1.

6:9   *called their name Adam.* Here "Adam" is used as a name for all people, men and women.

6:10   *in his own likeness, after his own image.* Richard Elliott Friedman writes: "The first man's similarity to his son is described with the same two nouns that are used to describe the first two humans' similarity to God [Moses 2:26–27]. It certainly sounds as if it means something physical here. . . . In any case, the significance of this verse is to establish that whatever it is that the first humans acquire from God, it is something that passes by heredity. It is not only the first two humans but the entire species that bears God's image" (JMBIGIL1, 482). Sarna concurs: "Each act of procreation is an imitation of God's original creation of man" (NMSGENESIS, 41). Victor Hamilton adds, "It is appropriate that the creation of man [in the book of remembrance] be prefaced to Adam's descendants through Seth rather than through Cain" (VPHGENESIS, 255).

6:11   *eight hundred years.* A change to OT1 in Oliver Cowdery's handwriting reads "870." This change was made sometime after his return from his mission to the Lamanites in August 1831 and before July 1832 (SHFJST, 97). He also made several other changes to the ages of the patriarchs in OT1, but they do not appear in OT2, which had been transcribed before Oliver's return (see also Moses 6:12, 14, 16, 18–20). It cannot be definitively established whether these changes were made under the direction of the Prophet—indeed, there is evidence of controversy between Joseph Smith and Cowdery relating to these changes (JMBIGIL2, 447–48). However, there is a parallel in one instance between the revised age of the prophet Enoch in Moses 8:1 and his age in Doctrine and Covenants 107:49, which was recorded in 1835.

About these changes, Kent P. Jackson and Charles Swift observe: "As we study the ages of the Patriarchs, we find there is always internal consistency for each man. There is never an instance in which the age has been changed for how long a Patriarch lived after the birth of his son without the same number of years being added to the Patriarch's life. . . . Although there is internal consistency for each Patriarch, there is no such consistency throughout the changes. No two men have the same number of years added to their lives. . . . Also, there is no discernible pattern among the changes." Moreover, none of these changes are reflected in the numerous variations found in ancient manuscripts of the Bible (JMBIGIL1, 483).

Although the long lives of the patriarchs are a puzzle, the careful attention given to their ages by the Prophet here, in Doctrine and Covenants 107:42–53, and in the *Lectures on Faith* argues that their ages were interpreted literally by him. Note that in view of the "exaggerated traditions current in the ancient East," Umberto Cassuto concludes that the ancient reader would find these numbers "low and modest" (UCCOMMENTARY, 264)! Richard Elliott Friedman writes: "It is clear that this author thought of a year as a normal solar year because that is how long the Flood lasts. The point to note is: life spans are pictured as growing shorter. The ten generations from Adam to Noah approach ages of 1,000. But the last one to live more than 900 years is Noah. The next ten generations start with Shem, who lives 600 years, and life spans decline after him. The last person to live more than 200 years is Terah. Abraham (175), Isaac (180), and Jacob (147) live long lives, but not as long as their ancestors. And Moses lives to be 120, which is understood to have become, at some point, the maximum for human life" (see Moses 8:17; JMBIGIL1, 483).

6:12   *nine hundred and thirty years.* A change to OT1 in Oliver Cowdery's handwriting reads

SETH

¹³ Seth lived one hundred and five years, and begat Enos, and prophesied in all his days, and taught his son Enos in the ways of God; wherefore Enos prophesied also. ¹⁴ And Seth lived, after he begat Enos, eight hundred and seven years, and begat many sons and daughters. ¹⁵ And the children of men were numerous upon all the face of the land. And in those days Satan had great dominion among men, and raged in their hearts; and from thenceforth came wars and bloodshed; and a man's hand was against his own brother, in administering death, because of secret works, seeking for power. ¹⁶ All the days of Seth were nine hundred and twelve years, and he died.

6:12   "1000" (SHFJST, 97). Edward Stevenson reported a statement by Joseph Smith that Adam "was within six months of a thousand years old, which is one day with the Lord's time, thus fulfilling the Lord's decree: 'In the day thou eatest of the fruit of that tree thou shalt surely die'—and he did, six months before the day was out." Note that figure of one thousand years for Adam's life span can also be found in Islamic traditions. See JMBIGIL1, 483.

he died. Three years before his death, Adam gathered his descendants to Adam-ondi-Ahman (see figure 6–1). The *Life of Adam and Eve* recounts God's instructions for the dressing of Adam and Eve in preparation for their burial and in anticipation of the Resurrection: "God spoke to Michael and said, 'Go to the Garden of the [third] heaven and bring [me] three linen cloths' . . . and cover Adam's body." Later, "Michael, the archangel, came and spoke to Seth and taught him how to dress [Eve] . . . and said, 'Thus shall you dress every human being who dies, until the day of the end, through the resurrection'" (JMBIGIL1, 484).

6:14   *eight hundred and seven years.* Oliver Cowdery wrote, "Eight hundred seventy-six years" (SHFJST, 97).

6:15   *children of men.* This phrase refers to "the sons of men" and "the daughters of men" (Moses 5:52–56), in contrast to "the children of God" (RDDPGP, 88n15). It also anticipates a recurrence of "sons/daughters of men" describing the wicked in Moses 8:14–15, 20–21 and "sons of God" describing the righteous in Moses 6:22, 68; 7:1; 8:13 (see figure 8–3). The wicked apply the term "sons of God" in jest to themselves in Moses 8:21.

Satan had great dominion among men. This digression, added to the Genesis account, underscores the wickedness of the generation in which Enos lived and provides the motivation for the migration of the "people of God" to a "land of promise" (Moses 6:17).

administering death, because of secret works. This fits the pattern set by Lamech's "works of darkness," wherein Lamech slew Irad because he began to reveal their secrets (Moses 5:49–55). Compare the Dead Sea Scroll Enoch text, the *Book of Giants*: "They knew the se[crets of . . .] [Sin was great in the earth [. . .] and they killed ma[ny . . .]" (MOSESS 9).

seeking for power. Compare Ether 8:23: "murderous combinations . . . to get power and gain."

6:16   *nine hundred and twelve years.* Oliver Cowdery wrote, "Nine hundred eighty one years" (SHFJST, 97).

6:17   *the people of God came out from the land.* Cain's posterity had already migrated eastward (Moses 5:41). The pseudepigraphal Adam literature contains stories of how the Cainites lured the descendants of Seth down from a sacred mountain adjoining the Garden of Eden to join them. In contrast, we are told here that the people of God are led to a "land of promise" (Moses 6:17).

Cainan. The land of Cainan, mentioned in Moses 6:17–19, 41–42, is not to be confused with the land of Canaan mentioned in Moses 7:6–8, 12, nor, does it seem, with the land occupied by the descendants of Cain (Moses 7:22). The current standardization of the spelling of these terms within the Book of Moses is based on corrections made by Elder James E. Talmage in 1902.

ENOS

¹⁷ And Enos lived ninety years, and begat Cainan. And Enos and the residue of the people of God came out from the land, which was called Shulon, and dwelt in a land of promise, which he called after his own son, whom he had named Cainan. ¹⁸ And Enos lived, after he begat Cainan, eight hundred and fifteen years, and begat many sons and daughters. And all the days of Enos were nine hundred and five years, and he died.

CAINAN

¹⁹ And Cainan lived seventy years, and begat Mahalaleel; and Cainan lived after he begat Mahalaleel eight hundred and forty years, and begat sons and daughters. And all the days of Cainan were nine hundred and ten years, and he died.

MAHALALEEL

²⁰ And Mahalaleel lived sixty-five years, and begat Jared; and Mahalaleel lived, after he begat Jared, eight hundred and thirty years, and begat sons and daughters. And all the days of Mahalaleel were eight hundred and ninety-five years, and he died.

JARED AND OTHER PREACHERS OF RIGHTEOUSNESS

²¹ And Jared lived one hundred and sixty-two years, and begat Enoch; and Jared lived, after he begat Enoch, eight hundred years, and begat sons and daughters. And Jared taught Enoch in all the ways of God.

Robert J. Matthews observed: "It is not always clear whether the problem created by confusion of the two words is a matter of spelling or of actual substitution of words. . . . Because these words occur in all three of the Old Testament manuscripts with considerable variation and because they have also been published with some variation, the matter [is] quite complex" (JMBIGIL2, 54).

6:18   *eight hundred and fifteen years.* Cowdery wrote, "Eight hundred fifty years" (SHFJST, 98).
   nine hundred and five years. Oliver Cowdery wrote, "Nine hundred forty years" (SHFJST, 98).
   he died. OT1 adds, "And thus it was, Amen" (SHFJST, 98).

6:19   *seventy years.* Oliver Cowdery wrote, "One hundred seventeen years" (SHFJST, 98).
   Mahalaleel. The name seems to have an obvious meaning, related to *hll* ("to praise") and *'l* ("god"). But it is also somewhat similar to more obscure and easily confused names elsewhere in this part of Genesis and the Book of Moses (Lamech, Mehujael, Mahijah). See JMBWHERE, 202–3, 220; UCCOMMENTARY, 232–33.
   nine hundred and ten years. Oliver Cowdery wrote, "Nine hundred fifty-seven years" (SHFJST, 98).

6:20   *sixty-five years.* Oliver Cowdery wrote, "One hundred fifteen years" (SHFJST, 98).
   eight hundred and ninety-five years. Oliver Cowdery wrote, "Nine hundred forty-five years" (SHFJST, 98).

6:21   *Jared taught Enoch in all the ways of God.* Compare Moses 6:41. See also 1 Nephi 1:1; Enos 1:1.
   Jared. Moses 6:21–25 speaks of how "preachers of righteousness"—who are seen in some

Figure 6–2. Book of Enoch P, *Chester Beatty XII, Leaf 3 (Verso)*, fourth century

DID JOSEPH SMITH PLAGIARIZE ANCIENT ENOCH TEXTS?

In brief, it's very unlikely. The most important ancient Enoch texts discovered to date are as follows:

1 Enoch. Of the extant Enoch manuscripts, the best known is *1 Enoch*, also referred to as *Ethiopic Enoch* or simply the *Book of Enoch*. *First Enoch* is one of the most important Jewish works of pseudepigrapha, highly valued in the early Christian community and explicitly (and implicitly) cited in New Testament epistles. The full form of the text was unknown to the Western world until 1773. It was first translated into English in 1821. Could Joseph Smith have read it? Eminent Latter-day Saint historian Richard L. Bushman concluded, "It is scarcely conceivable that Joseph Smith knew of Laurence's Enoch translation." Even if he had known of it, it would have been a relatively unfruitful source of ideas for Moses 6–7 compared with other ancient Enoch texts that Joseph Smith could *not* have encountered. Aside from the shared prominence of the "Son of Man" and related motifs in a section of *1 Enoch* called the *Book of Parables* (figure 6–9), very few significant parallels have been identified between the two Enoch chapters of the Book of Moses and the sizable text of *1 Enoch*. Resemblances are relatively sparse, and the storylines are mostly different.

2 Enoch. *Second Enoch*, also known as *Slavonic Enoch* or the *Book of the Secrets of Enoch*, is a pseudepigraphal text of Jewish origin that describes the heavenly ascent of Enoch and his initiation into the divine mysteries. Latter-day Saint readers of the Book of Moses will find interest in the *2 Enoch* account about Enoch's initiation into the heavenly mysteries (see also *3 Enoch*). It was first published in a Western language (Latin) in 1899.

3 Enoch. *Third Enoch*, also known as the *Hebrew Apocalypse of Enoch* or the *Book of Palaces*, is a Jewish pseudepigraphic text written later than *1 Enoch* and *2 Enoch* and not published in English until long after Joseph Smith's death. Among the unusual parallels to the Book of Moses Enoch are his title of "lad" (Moses 6:31; figure 6–3; *2 Enoch*), Enoch's transfiguration (Moses 7:3–4; *2 Enoch*; figure 7–2), God's bestowal of a divine throne (Moses 7:59), the spirits of the dead (Moses 7:38–39, 56–57) and of those yet to be born (Moses 6:36; 7:45).

Book of Giants. The *Book of Giants* (*BG*) is a collection of fragments discovered in 1948 among the Dead Sea Scrolls and in Manichaean sources. It seems to contain some of the oldest surviving Enoch material (see figure 6–4). Overall, it resembles little else in the Enoch tradition, yet we find in it the most extensive series of significant parallels between a single ancient text and Joseph Smith's account of Enoch's preaching mission (Moses 6:37–46; figures 6–8, 6–10), his encounter with Mahaway/Mahijah (Moses 6:40, 7:2; figures 6–6, 7–1), subsequent battles with his enemies (Moses 7:13; figures 6–5, 7–3), the complaining of the earth (Moses 7:48–49; figure 7–8), the gathering of his people to a city of righteousness (Moses 7:17–19; figure 7–4), and their heavenly ascent (Moses 7:69; figure 7–6).

In summary, it would have been impossible for Joseph Smith in 1830 to have been aware of the most important resemblances to ancient literature in his Enoch revelations. Other than the few unique and typically loose parallels found in *1 Enoch* (which Joseph Smith is unlikely to have studied), the texts that would have been required for a nineteenth-century author to derive significant parts of Moses 6–7 were not available to him. Even if other relevant traditions outside the Enoch literature (for example, Masonic or hermetic traditions) had been available to Joseph Smith by 1830, they would not have provided the many rare or peculiar details in *2 Enoch*, *3 Enoch*, and especially *BG*. See MOSESS 5 and figure 6–4.

²² And this is the genealogy of the sons of Adam, who was the son of God, with whom God, himself, conversed. ²³ And they were preachers of righteousness, and spake and prophesied, and called upon all men, everywhere, to repent; and faith was taught unto the children of men. ²⁴ And it came to pass that all the days of Jared were nine hundred and sixty-two years, and he died. ²⁵ And Enoch lived sixty-five years, and begat Methuselah.

ENOCH'S COMMISSION TO PREACH

²⁶ And it came to pass that Enoch journeyed in the land, among the people; and as he journeyed, the Spirit of God descended out of heaven, and abode upon him.

6:21   ancient sources as having descended (figuratively) from higher ground—initiated a missionary program aimed at teaching spiritual wanderers who had deliberately forsaken God. Among these preachers was Jared, the father of Enoch, the root of whose name probably means "to descend." Among those to whom they preached were the "giants" or *nephilim*, a name that fittingly means "fallen ones." See JMBGIANTS, 1129.

6:22   ***sons of Adam.*** OT1 seems to be a better reading: "And this is the genealogy of the sons of God which was [*sic*] the sons of Adam with whom God Himself conversed" (SHFJST, 98).

     son of God. Compare Luke 3:38: "Adam, which was the son of God." However, the Prophet later modified the verse in Luke to read, "Adam, who was formed of God" (SHFJST, NT2 p. 54, 375).

     with whom God, himself, conversed. Compare Moses 2:29–30; 3:16–17; 4:15–25. The qualification clarifies that "sons of God" here should be understood not as divine *beings*, but rather as *divinely commissioned* men.

6:23   ***preachers of righteousness.*** See Moses 6:13 for a brief summary of their ministry.

     called upon all men, everywhere. In contrast to Enoch's later ministry, these "preachers of righteousness" were apparently not prohibited from teaching the people of Canaan. See Moses 7:12.

     faith. Faith is explicitly mentioned in conjunction with Enoch and his preaching (Hebrews 11:5; Moses 7:13, 47).

6:25   ***Methuselah.*** In the book of Genesis, the genealogy continues unbroken so the entire stream of generations between the Creation and Flood can be presented in preparation for the story of Noah. However, following Moses 6:25, which corresponds to Genesis 5:21, the biblical account is interrupted so that an extended story of Enoch can be included. Because of the way the literary structure of Genesis is disturbed by this intrusion of significant material on Enoch, it seems likely that the story of Enoch was not simply left out of Genesis but instead once formed a separate record that was included here to maintain a relatively consistent chronological ordering of events and to anticipate later references to Enoch in the JST story of Noah (e.g., Moses 8:19; JST additions to Genesis 6:18 and 9:9, 11, 16). Following the story of Enoch, the biblical account picks up again in Moses 8:1 (cf. Genesis 5:23).

6:26   ***among the people.*** An expression that seems to indicate preaching (RDDPGP, 92). Compare Moses 6:37: "among the people."

     descended out of heaven. Compare John's description of events following Jesus' baptism: "I saw the Spirit descending from heaven like a dove, and it abode upon him" (John 1:32). Two more allusions to New Testament descriptions of Jesus' baptism can be found in verse 27 (compare Matthew 3:17). "Clearly, Enoch stands as someone who prefigures the coming Messiah" (RDDPGP, 92).

     It would be easy to try to explain away these parallels as being an obvious case of Joseph Smith borrowing from the New Testament. However, Samuel Zinner, a non-Latter-day Saint scholar, argued that the relevant New Testament motifs may actually have their origins in descriptions

27 And he heard a voice from heaven, saying: "Enoch, my son, prophesy unto this people, and say unto them—Repent, for thus saith the Lord: 'I am angry with this people, and my fierce anger is kindled against them; for their hearts have waxed hard, and their ears are dull of hearing, and their eyes cannot see afar off; 28 and for these many generations, ever since the day that I created them, have they gone astray, and have denied me, and have sought their own counsels in the dark;

6:26   of heavenly ascent in the Enoch literature. In light of this (and additional passages relating New Testament themes to the Son of Man), Zinner argued that the ideas behind all these passages "arose in an Enochic matrix"—that is, in literary traditions concerning the prophet Enoch. In short, if Zinner is correct, the New Testament accounts of Christ's baptism may allude to ideas from the ancient Enoch literature rather than vice versa. See MOSESS 1.

    The connection between Enoch's divine encounter and the baptism of Jesus becomes understandable when one regards the event, as do Margaret Barker and Gaetano Lettieri, as a heavenly "ascent experience" (JMBIGIL2, 56). Such an experience would be consistent with the idea of baptism as a figurative death and resurrection (Romans 6:4–6). This interpretation also sheds light on the Evangelists' description at Jesus' baptism of the opening of the heavens, the proclamation of divine sonship by the Father (see Matthew 3:16), and the presence of the dove as a symbol of the renewing of creation and the subduing of Satan.

    abode. Draper, Brown and Rhodes note four points related to the mention of "abode": "(1) The Spirit's action anticipates God's dwelling with His people (see Moses 7:16). (2) The Spirit remained with Enoch, bringing him astonishing gifts (see Moses 6:34; 7:13). (3) The Lord said He would 'abide' in Enoch as Enoch did in Him (Moses 6;34). (4) The resting of the Spirit is said in Christian tradition to be a characteristic of the days of the Messiah, including his earthly ministry" (RDDPGP, 92).

6:27   *a voice from heaven.* The mention of a voice from heaven is a second resemblance to the account of Jesus' baptism (Matthew 3:17). See also the prophecy of the voice of John the Baptist in his preaching in Mark 1:3–4 (RDDPGP, 92).

    my son. A third resemblance to the account of Jesus' baptism (Mark 1:11).

    prophesy unto this people. Compare the call of Moses (Exodus 3:1–4:17), Gideon (Judges 6:14–22), and Jeremiah (Jeremiah 1:5–19). Stephen D. Ricks noted that in each case the commissioning of the prophet is accompanied by a description of the grounds for the call, the protest of the one being called, and signs of a miraculous nature to confirm the call. See MOSESS 1.

    prophesy. Draper, Brown, and Rhodes observe that the spirit of prophecy concerns not only the revealing of future events but also the preaching of repentance (RDDPGP, 92). For example, we read in Revelation 19:10 that "the testimony of Jesus is the spirit of prophecy."

    this people. From Moses 6:28–29, we can assume that "this people" refers to the descendants of Cain and their associates (RDDPGP, 92).

    my fierce anger is kindled. "The image of fire [represents] a figure of judgment" (RDDPGP, 92).

    hearts have waxed hard, and their ears are dull of hearing, and their eyes cannot see afar off. Compare the similar wording of instructions Isaiah received when he was called to the ministry and had a similar vision of the Lord in His heavenly temple (Isaiah 6:10). The references to ears that do not hear and eyes that do not see may allude to blessings associated with different parts of the body that were received in ancient Jewish and Christian washing and anointing ceremonies (JMBIGIL1, 519–20, 661–62). These promised blessings are denied to individuals who have broken their covenants. In contrast to the spiritually blind and deaf, Enoch will be made to see (Moses 6:35–36).

6:28   *gone astray.* Verses 28–29 summarize the previously mentioned crimes of the people of Cain and set out the legal grounds justifying God's punishments (RDDPGP, 93). Drawing out similarities in the commissioning of Moses (Exodus 3:7, 9), Enoch (Moses 6:28–29), and Gideon (Judges 6:13), Stephen D. Ricks cites Norman Habel in describing the function of the

and in their own abominations have they devised murder, and have not kept the commandments, which I gave unto their father, Adam. ²⁹ Wherefore, they have foresworn themselves, and, by their oaths, they have brought upon themselves death; and a hell I have prepared for them, if they repent not'; ³⁰ and this is a decree, which I have sent forth in the beginning of the world, from my own mouth, from

"introductory word" given in this verse as "not merely to arouse the attention . . . [of the prophet] but to spell out the specific basis or grounds (*Gründ*) for the commission" (JMBIGIL2, 58).

denied me. Ignoring God's counsels is tantamount to denying Him.

sought their own counsels in the dark. Compare Moses 6:43.

devised murder. Compare Moses 5:31; 6:15.

the commandments, which I gave unto their father, Adam. See Moses 5:5.

6:29   *by their oaths, they have brought upon themselves death.* Compare the murderous oaths of Cain and Lamech (Moses 5:29, 49–50). Contrast Alma 15:17, when the people of the church established by Alma the Younger watched and prayed continually "that they might be delivered from Satan, and from death, and from destruction." Regarding the people in Moses 6, Nibley observes: "'Wherefore, they have foresworn themselves [they have the oaths], and, by their oaths . . .' In Moses 5:29 we read about the oaths they made to each other. 'And Satan said unto Cain: Swear unto me by thy throat, and if thou tell it thou shalt die.' By their oaths 'they have foresworn themselves.' They were false oaths. '[T]hey have brought upon themselves death; and a hell I have prepared for them, if they repent not'" (HWNPGP, 272).

A different reading is given in OT1: "by their oaths, they have eat unto themselves death" (SHFJST, 99). If this variant is not a scribal error, perhaps it may indicate a corrupt practice in which participation in ordinances by those who were ritually unclean was condemned (1 Corinthians 11:27–30), or perhaps even the "eating" of blood itself. Note that this language further echoes and extends the symbolism of the "eating of death" in the act that precipitated the Fall. Later, God said to Noah, "The blood of all flesh which I have given you for meat, shall be shed upon the ground, which taketh life thereof, and the blood ye shall not eat" (SHFJST, 116).

a hell I have prepared for them. Compare Moses 7:37.

if they repent not. Compare Moses 8:17, 20, 24.

6:30   *decree.* Draper et al. note that the term "carries both royal and legal overtones" (RDDPGP, 93). There are many examples of royal decrees in scripture, especially in the books of Daniel and Esther. Examples of God's decrees are also widespread.

Significantly, the term "decree" appears with surprising frequency in the later chapters of the Book of Moses. The description of decrees as being "firm" (Moses 5:15, 59; 6:30; 7:52) or "unalterable" (Daniel 6:7; Alma 29:4; Doctrine and Covenants 29:12; Moses 5:15) emphasizes that they cannot be changed and "must be fulfilled" (Moses 5:15; see also 4:30). In each case, the decree refers to aspects of the "plan of salvation" (Moses 6:62) that provide the substance of the preaching of Adam and Enoch.

In Moses 5:15 and 6:30, God's decree refers specifically to the idea that those who repent and accept the atoning sacrifice of Jesus Christ will be saved, whereas those who do not will be damned. In Moses 5:59, the decree refers to the promise that the gospel and its ordinances "should be in the world, until the end thereof." Finally, in Moses 7:52, the decree refers to the promise that the Lord made to Enoch that a Messiah should come and "that a remnant of [Enoch's] seed should always be found among all nations."

sent forth. In the Book of Moses, the phrase describes an authoritative dispensation of God's word to the world. The expression is used elsewhere—not only about His word, His kingdom, and His judgments or decrees, but also about both His divine and mortal servants who are commissioned to carry His word and extend His kingdom. On the other hand, Satan is described

Figure 6–3. Caravaggio ("Le Carvage"), 1571–1610: *David with the Head of Goliath*, 1607

ENOCH AS A "LAD"

There is an obvious thematic connection between the battles of Enoch with the "mighty men" (*gibborim*) and the story of David and Goliath. Besides the fact that both Enoch and David are each pointedly described as a "youth" or "lad" (Hebrew *na'ar*), it is possible that the prophecy in Psalm 89:19, said to be "of old" but applied to David, may actually contain an allusion to Enoch. In the translation of John H. Eaton, we read:

I have set a youth above the warrior; I have [exalted] a young man over the people.

Readers of the Book of Moses have often puzzled over Enoch's self-description as a "lad" (Moses 6:31), especially since he was at least sixty-five years old at the time (v. 25). Strikingly, this is the only instance of the term "lad" in modern scripture. Hugh Nibley was the first to recognize its significance, given the remarkable prominence of "lad" (or the equivalent English term "youth") as a name for Enoch in the pseudepigraphic books of *2 Enoch* and *3 Enoch* (FIA2ENOCH, 10:4, p. 119; PSA3ENOCH, 22, p. 357; 3:2, p. 357; 4:1, p. 258; 4:10, p. 259). The Prophet could not have known these ancient Enoch books.

In Moses 6:31, Enoch uses the term "lad" in a self-deprecating way: "Why is it that I have found favor in thy sight, and am but a lad . . . ?" The angels in *3 Enoch* similarly look on Enoch's status as a "lad" with disdain. They see Enoch's relative youth as reason to challenge the legitimacy of his heavenly ascent. Enoch is portrayed "as a sort of Johnny-come lately who despite his late arrival manages to become the greatest in their midst." This motif recalls the pre-rabbinic tradition of the initial reluctance of the angels to pay homage to Adam, who himself was seen as a young newcomer to the divine realm. Genesis scholar Gary A. Anderson himself wonders at the ancient references to Enoch as a "lad":

The acclamation of Enoch as "lad" is curious. It certainly recalls the question that began the story: "Why are you called 'lad' by [those] in the heights of heaven?" It is worth noting that of all the names given Enoch, the title "lad" is singled out as being particularly apt and fitting by the heavenly host. Evidently the seventy names were of a more general order of knowledge than the specific title "lad."

In answer to the question of *why* "the seventy nations of the world" called Enoch by his other names while God preferred to call him by the name of "lad," Enoch scholar Andrei Orlov proposes that Enoch served as a sort of mediator between the nations and God, with the reference to his seventy names corresponding to the seventy nations of the world. In short, to the nations, he was a ruler, the "Prince of the World," while to God he was a subordinate, a "lad" by comparison. Searching for the answer in another direction, the eminent Gershom Scholem, followed by other scholars, noticed that the title "lad" appears in the ancient Jewish literature in connection with the role of one who serves "before the heavenly throne and [ministers] to its needs" or of one who serves "in his own special tabernacle." A third explanation is found in the *Zohar* and related writings. There it is understood that Enoch "became a youth" permanently, no more subject to aging, when "God took him" to live forever in the heavenly world.

While none of these explanations is without merit, Anderson prefers the reason that Enoch himself gives for this title, as recorded in *3 Enoch* 4:10:

And because I was the *youngest* among them and a "lad" amongst them with respect to days, months, and years, therefore they called me "lad."

Though "most scholars have not been satisfied with the simple and somewhat naïve answer the text supplies" and have instead formulated a variety of more elaborate hypotheses for the name, Enoch's explanation for his title of "lad" in the Book of Moses seems to best fit the "simple and straightforward" explanation given in *3 Enoch*. See MOSESS 3; JMBIGIL2, 36–39, 61–62.

the foundation thereof, and by the mouths of my servants, thy fathers, have I decreed it, even as it shall be sent forth in the world, unto the ends thereof."

³¹ And when Enoch had heard these words, he bowed himself to the earth, before the Lord, and spake before the Lord, saying: "Why is it that I have found favor in thy sight, and am but a lad, and all the people hate me; for I am slow of speech; wherefore am I thy servant?" ³² And the Lord said unto Enoch: "Go forth and do

6:30   as the author of "lyings *sent forth* among the people" (3 Nephi 1:22, emphasis added; see also Revelation 16:14; Helaman 6:25).

beginning of the world. The decree that salvation would come only through faith in the Son and repentance, was announced in the beginning of the *mortal* world, after the Fall (Moses 5:15).

from mine own mouth. "At issue are both the source and credibility of the decree. In this case, the source is God Himself, a fact that underscores the credibility of the decree. Moreover, those who repeat it, 'my servants,' stand as credible sources and as further witnesses of the validity of the decree" (RDDPGP, 94).

by the mouths of my servants, thy fathers. Compare Moses 6:23. Note also the literal application of this concept in Enoch's commission to speak the word of the Lord: "Open thy mouth, and it shall be filled, and I will give thee utterance" (v. 32).

unto the ends thereof. Compare Moses 1:8: "the world and the ends thereof." Elsewhere in scripture, a similar expression is used to describe the universal scope of missionary work.

6:31   *bowed himself to the earth.* Compare Exodus 34:8: "Moses made haste, and bowed his head toward the earth, and worshipped." This is the first of three similarities to revelatory experiences of Moses in this verse. Compare also the resemblances to ancient Enoch texts: "And I had been until now on my face, prostrate and trembling. And the Lord called me with his mouth and said to me, 'Come here, Enoch, and hear my word(s). . . . I had my face bowed down" (GWN1ENOCH1, 14:24, p. 267). In the Mandaean *Book of Adam*, Enoch also bows down when he meets the angel of life: "My body . . . was bowed down before him, . . . my legs . . . bent in his presence." Such a reaction to a God or His messenger is common in scripture and pseudepigrapha (JMBIGIL2, 60).

before the Lord. The expression suggests that this scene is set at an altar (RDDPGP, 94).

Why is it that I have found favor in thy sight . . . ? Compare Exodus 3:11: "Who am I, that I should go unto Pharaoh, and that I should bring forth the children of Israel out of Egypt?"; Judges 6:15: "Oh my Lord, wherewith shall I save Israel? behold, my family is poor in Manasseh, and I am the least in my father's house"; and Jeremiah 1:6: "Ah, Lord God! behold, I cannot speak: for I am a child."

"Being called, Enoch shrank back in fear and pleaded his unfitness" (HWNENOCH, 208). Importantly, however, Elder Neal A. Maxwell taught that "feeling unworthy, unready, and uncertain about what we can contribute, when so called, is different from questioning the call itself." In Enoch's "honest questions . . . there was a sense of unpreparedness but not an unwillingness. . . . [God] needs our meekness . . . in order to part the curtains of our understanding." Thus, as Sheri L. Dew explained, before Enoch could receive his vision of eternity, he needed to receive "a new vision of himself." See JMBIGIL2, 61.

lad. In the only use of this term in Latter-day Saint scripture, the sixty-five-year-old Enoch is called a "lad" (compare Jeremiah 1:6). This is a striking parallel to the otherwise puzzling description of Enoch in pseudepigrapha (here identified with Metatron) as a "lad" (PSA3ENOCH, 4:1–10, p. 258; MOSESS 3; figure 6–3). "Enoch's rapid rise to spiritual maturity is indicated by the fact that he received the priesthood before his father and grandfather" (RDEENOCH, 458; Doctrine and Covenants 107:48).

hate me. Nibley notes the "general contempt" in which Enoch was held, reflecting the hatred that prevailed among the people (HWNENOCH, 209).

slow of speech. Compare Moses, who complained to the Lord that he was "slow of speech,

as I have commanded thee, and no man shall pierce thee. Open thy mouth, and it shall be filled, and I will give thee utterance, for all flesh is in my hands, and I will do as seemeth me good. ³³ Say unto this people: 'Choose ye this day, to serve the Lord God who made you.' ³⁴ Behold my Spirit is upon you, wherefore all thy words will I justify; and the mountains shall flee before you, and the rivers shall turn from their course; and thou shalt abide in me, and I in you; therefore walk with me."

6:31   and of a slow tongue" (Exodus 4:10). Indeed, it is not impossible that Moses was quoting Enoch.

     In Moses' case, as with Ezekiel, the problem was most likely not a physical speech impediment, but rather doubts about his fluency in the native language of his hearers—not Egyptian (his birth tongue), but Hebrew, as Richard Elliott Friedman convincingly argues. Enoch was likewise sent to preach repentance to a people he had not grown up with. In any event, some ancient Enoch sources seem to corroborate that Enoch had additional challenges in speaking, portraying Enoch as having been "deliberate in his speech" and "often silent" (John C. Reeves and Annette Yoshiko Reed). Curiously, in the cases of both Enoch and Moses, "it is the stammerer whose task it is to bring down God's word to the human world" (Everett Fox, citing Martin Buber). "Whatever the circumstances, the underlying idea is that prophetic eloquence is not a native talent but a divine endowment granted for a special purpose, the message originating with God and not with the prophet" (Nahum Sarna). Enoch will confound his enemies through God's gift, "the power of the language which God had given him" (Moses 7:13). See MOSESS 2.

     Commenting on Old Testament language that mentions the enabling of a prophet's "lips," "tongue," and "mouth," Bible scholar Carol Meyers found meaningful "parallels in the empowering 'opening the mouth' rituals in ancient Near Eastern texts, especially Egyptian ones" (MOSESS 2). Hugh Nibley recalled that "one purpose of the Egyptian Opening of the Mouth is to cause the initiate 'to remember what he had forgotten—that it is to awaken the mind to its full potential in the manner of the awakening of Adam in a new world" (HWNMESSAGE, 176). By rites of this sort, the mouth is also sanctified and becomes a conduit for the transmission of heavenly things.

6:32   ***Go forth.*** These words constitute the formal commission of Enoch. The fact that Enoch fulfilled this commission is demonstrated in Moses 6:37 ("Enoch went forth"). Intriguingly, the use of the word "go" in God's commission of Enoch parallels the commission of Mahijah/Mahaway to inquire of Enoch in *BG* (DWPDSS, 4Q530 frg. 2 col. ii l. 22, 951).

     no man shall pierce thee. See Doctrine and Covenants 122:9, and compare God's later words to Enoch: "mine eye can pierce *them*" (Moses 7:36; emphasis added). A parallel promise in the Mandaean *Book of Adam* reads as follows: "Little Enoch, fear not. You dread the dangers of this world, I am come to you to deliver you from them. Fear not the wicked, and be not afraid of the floods that fall on your head; for their efforts will be vain: it shall not be given them to do any harm to thee." Later, Enoch's enemies admit their utter failure to thwart him and his fellows: "In vain have we attempted murder and fire against them; nothing has been able to overcome them. And now they are sheltered from our blows" (MOSESS 4).

     Open thy mouth. Compare Ezekiel 3:27; Doctrine and Covenants 24:12; 28:16; 30:5, 11.

     I will give thee utterance. Compare 2 Enoch 39:5: "It is not from my own lips that I am reporting to you today, but from the lips of the Lord I have been sent to you. For you hear my words, out of my lips, a human being created exactly equal to yourselves; but I have heard from the fiery lips of the Lord" (FIA2ENOCH, p. 162).

     all flesh is in my hands, and I will do as seemeth me good. In other words, God is saying, "I will be in charge and I will take over the whole thing. Just trust me and do what you are told" (HWNPGP, 273).

6:33   ***Choose ye this day, to serve the Lord God.*** Compare Joshua 24:15; Alma 30:8.

     Lord God. Draper, Brown, and Rhodes note the exceptional use of the title "Lord God" here, which is associated elsewhere in scripture with God's role as Creator and in making covenants with humankind (RDDPGP, 95).

Enoch Made a Seer

³⁵ And the Lord spake unto Enoch, and said unto him: "Anoint thine eyes with clay, and wash them, and thou shalt see." And he did so. ³⁶ And he beheld the spirits that God had created; and he beheld also things which were not visible to the natural

who made you. An appeal to God's role as the Creator is characteristic of the record of Enoch's ministry (Moses 6:44, 51, 59, 63; 7:32–33, 36, 59, 64). Outside the chapters that describe the Creation itself, there is perhaps no more significant clustering of verses in scripture referring to the specific theme of God as the author of all things.

6:34   *my Spirit is upon you.* This unusual description of the Spirit's presence hearkens back to Moses 6:26, where it was said that the Spirit "abode upon" Enoch. When the Spirit of God came "upon" Zechariah, he spoke the word of God in first person (2 Chronicles 24:20), just as Enoch will do as he goes forth to preach.

mountains shall flee before you, and the rivers shall turn from their course. JST Genesis 14:25–32 gives a more extensive description of the power that was given to Enoch (SHFJST, 127–28). See Moses 7:13 for the fulfillment of the Lord's promise. Compare the account of rivers turning from their course in an experience of Enoch from the Mandaean *Book of Adam*: "The [Supreme] Life replied, Arise, take thy way to the source of the waters, turn it from its course. . . . At this command Tavril [the angel speaking to Enoch] indeed turned the pure water from its course." We find no account of a river's course turned by anyone in the Bible. It is thus remarkable that just such an event appears in this pseudepigraphal account and in the Book of Moses—and that in both instances the miraculous feat is found within a story about Enoch (MOSESS 4).

abide in me, and I in you. See Moses 6:66.

walk with me. Another scriptural occurrence of walking "with" God is found in a description of those who have been declared worthy of exaltation: "They shall walk with me in white: for they are worthy" (Revelation 3:4). The prime examples of this motif are, of course, Enoch and Noah, of whom it was explicitly said that they "walked with God" (Genesis 5:24; Doctrine and Covenants 107:49; Moses 6:39; 7:69; 8:27).

6:35   *Anoint thine eyes with clay, and wash them.* Draper, Brown, and Rhodes comment as follows: "This sequence of verbs points to Enoch's being in a sanctuary or temple. They are the same verbs that appear in the story of Jesus healing the man born blind (John 9:6–7). That event took place just beyond the southern end of the Jerusalem temple as indicated by Jesus' instruction to the man to wash in the pool of Siloam" (RDDPGP, 95). Craig Keener finds Creation symbolism in the incident that evokes the idea of spiritual rebirth in the story of Enoch: "Jewish tradition sometimes reports curing through spittle, though Jewish custom probably borrowed it from the more widespread ancient custom. But far more importantly, by making clay of the spittle and applying it to eyes blind from birth, Jesus may be recalling the creative act of Genesis 2:7 [compare John 20:22]" (JMBIGIL2, 64–65). Interestingly, in the Book of Moses, the first thing Enoch sees after having his eyes anointed with clay are the "spirits that God had *created.*" In contrast to the *physical* blindness healed through anointing and washing in John 9:6–7, Enoch's anointing and washing healed the prophet's *spiritual* sight, as will be seen in Moses 6:36.

Is it significant that Enoch's mouth was opened prior to his eyes? Nibley said this about Egyptian initiation rites: "The rite is called the Opening of the Mouth because that must come first, that being the organ by which one may breathe, receive nourishment, and speak. . . . So the mouth comes first; but to rise above mere vegetation, life must become conscious and aware, so that the opening of the eyes immediately follows" (HWNMESSAGE, 179). See MOSESS 2.

6:36   *he beheld the spirits that God had created.* Compare Moses 1:8; Abraham 3:22.

things which were not visible to the natural eye. Moses described his vision of God in similar terms: "But now mine own eyes have beheld God; but not my natural, but my spiritual eyes, for my natural eyes could not have beheld; for I should have withered and died in his presence; but his glory was upon me; and I beheld his face, for I was transfigured before him" (Moses 1:11).

Simplified Outline	Major Stories	Book of Moses	Book of Giants	Other Enoch
Beginnings				
	Begettings	X	X	X
	Call of Enoch	X		X
	Violence/ Oaths	X	X	X
	Antics of Twins		X	
First Visit to Enoch				
	Mahijah/ Mahaway	X	X	
	Repentance	X	X	
	Messianic Teachings	X		X

Simplified Outline	Major Themes	Book of Moses	Book of Giants	Other Enoch
	Dreams of Twins		X	
Second Visit to Enoch				
	Mahujah/ Mahaway	X	X	
	Enoch's glory	X		X
Parting of the Ways				
	Wicked Defeated	X	X	
	Repentant Gathered	X	X	
Happy Endings				
	Enoch's Vision	X		X
	People Ascend	X	X	X

Figure 6–4a. *Harmony of storylines in Moses 6–7, the* Book of Giants, *and Other Ancient Enoch Literature*

MOSES 6–7 AND THE *BOOK OF GIANTS*

The fragmentary *Book of Giants* (*BG*) has proven to be of tremendous importance to Enoch scholarship (see figure 6–2). It was very popular at Qumran, indeed more popular than *1 Enoch,* a text that is much better-known today. Significantly, *BG* appears to contain some of the oldest surviving ancient Enoch traditions (GWN1ENOCH1, p. 11).

Note that the English translation of the Hebrew term *gibborim* as "giants" in the title of *BG* is misleading. In the Bible, the term *gibborim* means "mighty hero" or "warrior" (see MOSESS 5, 6, and 12). This description fits the groups to whom Enoch preached in Moses 6–7 and *BG*. In later times, the terms *gibborim* and *nephilim* were often confused—the latter term originally referred to what seems to have been remembered as a remnant of a race of "giants." Consistent with this view, Moses 6–7 distinguishes "giants" (*nephilim*?) from from the people who seem to be Enoch's converts and adversaries (*gibborim*?). See Moses 7:14–15.

The table above summarizes the major storyline elements in the Book of Moses that can be found in *BG* and other important Enoch texts. Of course, since the ancient manuscripts are incomplete—especially *BG*, which is very fragmentary—the number of common elements may be greater than what is shown here.

In the table, three types of storyline elements are distinguished: (1) those are part of what can be called the "narrative core," shown in normal typeface; (2) those that contain material relating to sacred teachings, rituals, or heavenly encounters, shown in **bold**; and (3) those that are unique to *BG*, appearing neither in Moses 6–7 nor anywhere else in the ancient Enoch literature, shown in *italics*. The table reveals three interesting patterns:

- *Despite many specific differences, the basic storylines of both texts can be seen as sharing a similar beginning, focus, and outcome.* Saying it differently, at least one fragment of every narrative storyline element of the Book of Moses is also present within *BG* (normal typeface). As to the *beginning* of the story, the *BG* account seems to start with a brief reference to the Watchers that corresponds structurally to the genealogy of the righteous descendants of Adam in the Book of Moses. Afterward— and in sharp contrast to the *Book of Watchers* in *1 Enoch*—*BG* makes what Enoch scholar Loren T. Stuckenbruck calls a "most significant . . . shift of the spotlight from the disobedient angels" to Enoch's mighty human adversaries (the *gibborim*), who remain the *focus* from that point on. As to the most significant *outcome* of the texts, the common concern of both *BG* and the Book of Moses Enoch account is ultimately the fate of the *gibborim*—proud self-styled heroes—who either, on the one hand, choose to reject Enoch's message and are subsequently humbled by an ignominious defeat in battle or, on the other hand, choose to repent and eventually gather to a divinely prepared place from which they ultimately ascend to the divine presence.

Thematic Resemblances	Book of Moses	Book of Giants	Stuckenbruck's Outline
A. Begettings	·6:22 (See also 7:15; 8:13–14; Genesis 6:4)	·4Q 531, 1, 1–3; ·Henning, Text A, frg. i, 100; ·Sundermann 20 (M 8280), Verso/I/, 1–4	A
B. Murders	·6:28 (See also 6:15)	·1Q23, 9+14+15, 2–5; ·4Q203, 3, 2–4; ·Henning, Text A, frg. j	B
C. Oath-inspired Violence	·6:29 (See also 6:28; 6:15)	·1Q23, 17, 1–3; ·Henning, Text A, frg. i; ·1Q23, 9+14+15, 2; ·Henning, Text A, frg. j	B
D. A "Wild Man"	·6:38	·(Compare 4Q531, 22, 3–8)	(Compare K)
E. Name and Role of Mahijah/Mahaway	·6:40	·4Q530, 7, ii, 6–7; ·4Q530, frgs. 2 Col ii + 6 + 7 Col I + 8–11 + 12(?), 22–23	H
F. Reading Record of Deeds	·6:46–47	·4Q203, 7b, ii, 1–3; ·4Q203, 8, 1–4; ·Sundermann 1984, Fragment L Page 1 recto, II.1–10	I
G. Trembling and Weeping after Reading	·6:47	·4Q203, 4; ·Henning, Text E	I
H. Call to Repentance	·6:52	·4Q203, 8, 14–15; ·4Q530, 13, 1; ·Kósa 2016, MCP, fig. 2c; ·Henning, Text E	(Compare O)
I. Sexual Defilement	·6:55	·4Q203, 8:6-9	(Compare O)
J. Mahujah/Mahaway's Heavenly Journey to Enoch	·7:2 (Compare 7:2, OT1)	·4Q530, 7, ii, 3–5; ·Gulácsi 2015, MCP; ·Henning, Text A, frg. b (Mainz 317)	S
K. Enoch Clothed with Glory	·7:2–4	·4Q531, 14, 1–4	—
L. Gibborim Defeated in Battle	·7:13, 15–16	·4Q531, 22, 3-7; ·4Q531, 7, 5–6; ·Henning, Texts G; Q; A, frg. i; ·Kósa 2016, MCP, fig. 2a; ·Sund., M5900	K
M. The "Roar of Lions/Wild Beasts" Following Battle	·7:13	·4Q531, 22, 8; ·Henning, Text A, frg. c, frg. k	K
N. Repentant Gather	·7:16–18	·Henning, Texts G, S	—
O. Imprisonment of the Wicked	·7:38–39	·Henning, Text A, fragment l; ·4Q203, 8, 2; ·4Q203, 7b, i, 5; ·Henning, Texts T,P,S	N
P. Flood of Noah Anticipated in Vision/Dream	·7:42–43	·4Q530, 7, ii, 10; ·(Compare 4Q530, 2, Col. ii + 6 + 7 Col. i + 8–11 + 12(?), 10–12)	T
Q. Earth Cries Out	·7:48	·4Q203, 8, 9–11	(Compare E)
R. Ascent of People	·7:69	·MCP, Gulácsi 2015	

Figure 6–4b. *Thematic resemblances in Moses 6–7 and the* Book of Giants

- *The sacred storyline elements in the Book of Moses are left out of* BG, *even though they appear elsewhere in the ancient Enoch literature (shown in* **boldface***).* For example, the surviving fragments of *BG* omit details of Enoch's call; messianic prophecies in the preaching of Enoch; Enoch's being clothed in glory; and the sweeping contents of his grand apocalyptic vision—all found in other ancient Enoch texts.

- *The* BG-*unique elements are largely focused on the dreams, antics, and quarreling of 'Ohyah and Hahyah (shown in italics).* What is significant about these elements is that they appear nowhere else in the ancient Enoch literature. For this and other reasons, these elements look like they were invented out of whole cloth at some point in the history of the *BG* text (see JMBGIANTS, 1057–71).

The resemblances between Moses 6–7 and *BG* in the narrative core story elements are so striking that one is tempted to speculate that *BG* and the Book of Moses were rooted in some of the same ancient Enoch traditions but that somewhere along the line, the sacred stories now found only in the Book of Moses were either removed from the tradition inherited by the *BG* redactor(s) or, alternatively, were left out when *BG* was composed. For detailed discussion of thematic similarities and differences, see JMBGIANTS, 1072–78.

Selected thematic resemblances between Moses 6–7 and *BG* are given in the table above. The resemblances are listed in Book of Moses chapter-and-verse order. Detailed citations of passages in Moses 6–7 and *BG* follow in the second and third columns. The fourth column in the table requires additional explanation. By way of background, remember that a full grasp of the *BG* narrative is made difficult by the fact that the surviving *BG* manuscripts are short and fragmentary. In 2016, Stuckenbruck assigned letters of the alphabet A–V to selected, surviving *BG* fragments to indicate his current conjectures about their relative sequencing in the text. For *BG* themes with resemblances to passages in Moses 6–7, I have added letters in the fourth column of the table corresponding to his sequencing attempt. Because some events in *BG* have no correspondence with the Book of Moses, some of the letters are missing. And, likewise, because Stuckenbruck did not attempt to classify every theme and fragment in *BG* within his sequencing scheme, not every entry in the last column has a corresponding letter. Significantly, Stuckenbruck's classification of fragments corresponds with the order of most of the Book of Moses resemblances. Note also that the *BG* resemblances are not confined to a small fraction of the Moses 6–7 account, but instead range throughout the main storyline. For more detailed discussion, see JMBGIANTS, 1078–85.

BG is arguably the most powerful single witness of ancient threads in Moses 6–7. Although the combined fragments of the Qumran *BG* scarcely fill three pages in the English translation of Florentino García Martínez, the results indicate that this single text contains eighteen, fully three-fifths, of the thirty proposed thematic resemblances of the combined ancient Enoch literature to the Moses Enoch account. Further anlaysis has shown that the thematic resemblances of *BG* to Moses 6–7 are not only relatively numerous and dense, but also strong and specific. They range from general themes in the storyline to specific occurrences of rare terms or phrases in appropriate contexts (JMBGIANTS, 1147–56. See JMBGATHERING.

Figure 6–5. *Giorgio Schiavone (1436/7–1504), Samson Smiting a Philistine with the Jawbone of an Ass. In the background lies a beast he has already slain.*

"THE WILD MAN THEY CALL ME"

The term "wild man" is rare in Second Temple literature. In both *BG* and Moses it fairly pops out at the attentive reader. It is used only once elsewhere in all of scripture, as part of Jacob's prophecy about how Ishmael would live to become everyone's favorite enemy (Genesis 16:12). It translates the literal Hebrew "wild-ass man," calling to mind "the sturdy, fearless, and fleet-footed Syrian onager (Hebrew *pere'*), who inhabits the wilderness and is almost impossible to domesticate" (NMSGENESIS, 121n12). Intriguingly, in light of the presumed Mesopotamian background of both Moses 6–7 and BG, the description of Ishmael as an "onager man" matches that of Enkidu as *akkanu* ("onager") in the Gilgamesh epic. Enkidu is portrayed as an indomitable warrior whose prowess was proved in bloody battle: a "wild ass on the run, donkey of the uplands, panther of the wild" who "slaughtered the Bull of Heaven" and "killed Humbaba" (MOSESS 6).

At the beginning of the Book of Moses story, the facetious depiction of Enoch as a "wild man" by the *gibborim* was merely an instance of tasteless mockery. However, by the time we approach the end of the story, we realize that Enoch's initial self-characterization as being "but a lad" who is "slow in speech" has prepared us for the ironic turning of the tables that plays out on a larger stage in his final military victory (Moses 6:31). One of the primary lessons of the story may be that Enoch was empowered to conquer his foes through the "virtue of the word of God" (Alma 31:5) while the *gibborim*, aspiring wild men who, like Korihor, "conquered according to [their] strength" (Alma 30:17), went down in a humiliating defeat.

Consistent with the moral of such a lesson, later biblical authors pointedly taught that "Israel's future did not lie along" the "way [of] all [their] warriors [*gibborim*]" (Hosea 10:13), but rather in "turn[ing] back to the Lord with all [one's] heart" (2 Kings 23:25). Proverbs 24:25 averred that "a wise man is mightier than a strong one." Paraphrasing, we might understand this to mean that the "wise man" is more of a *geber* than the *gibbor*—in other words, the "wise man" is more of a "man" than the "he man." Similarly, the preacher of Ecclesiastes 9:16 concluded that "wisdom (*ḥokmâ*) is superior to ["manly"] heroism (*gĕbûrâ*)." Perhaps the redactors of *BG* intended to make a similar point in their story. See MOSESS 6.

The Book of Moses and *BG* are different kinds of text, published millennia apart, each with a unique past and its own story to tell. That said, whatever may be intended by the use of the term "wild man" in these two accounts, the fact that this rare and peculiar description shows up in these already closely related stories about Enoch hints that they may share shards of a common, preexisting literary tradition. So far as can be determined at present, the single occurrence of the term "wild man" in the surviving ancient Enoch literature is in *BG*, and the only instance of it in the scripture translations of Joseph Smith is in the Enoch account in the Book of Moses. And, from a literary perspective, the conjecture of a paired usage of the term in *BG* that would couple a mocking reference of "wild man" to a meek and mild adversary at the beginning of the story with a painful application of the term to the proud, defeated leader of the *gibborim* at the end of the story seems a poignant and sophisticated instance of poetic justice. From a literary perspective, the twofold occurrence of "wild man" might be explained as yet another instance of the pattern of "doublings" that Stuckenbruck noticed in *BG* (LTSGIANTS, 20). See MOSESS 6; JMBGIANTS, 1095–98.

eye; and from thenceforth came the saying abroad in the land: "A seer hath the Lord raised up unto his people."

ENOCH GOES FORTH

³⁷ And it came to pass that Enoch went forth in the land, among the people, standing upon the hills and the high places, and cried with a loud voice, testifying against their works; and all men were offended because of him. ³⁸ And they came forth to hear him, upon the high places, saying unto the tent-keepers: "Tarry ye here and keep the tents, while we go yonder to behold the seer, for he prophesieth, and there is a strange thing in the land; a wild man hath come among us." ³⁹ And it came to

6:36   Enoch's ability to see "things which were not visible to the natural eye" is consistent with the Lord's command in *2 Enoch* for Enoch to make a "record of all His creation, visible and invisible" (FIA2ENOCH, 64:5 (J), p. 190), and with his having seen God make "invisible things descend visibly" (FIA2ENOCH, 25:1 (J), p. 144). Another Jewish account tells of Enoch training himself to see divine visions of invisible things while "in his normal (i.e., bodily) state" (MOSESS 2).

     seer. In Old Testament usage, the term "seer" is used as another word for "prophet" (1 Samuel 9:9). However, in modern scripture and current Latter-day Saint usage, it is used as a title for members of both the First Presidency and the Quorum of the Twelve Apostles (who are sustained in their offices as "prophets, seers, and revelators") and also to describe specific spiritual gifts linked to, but not identical with, the gift of prophecy. In Mosiah 8:13, the gift of seership is associated with the right to look into divine "interpreters" with the object of translating ancient records. More generally, Mosiah 8:15–17 states that "a seer is greater than a prophet. . . . A seer is a revelator and a prophet also; and a gift which is greater can no man have, except he should possess the power of God, which no man can; yet a man may have great power given him from God. . . . A seer can know of things which are past, and also of things which are to come, and by them shall all things be revealed, or, rather, shall secret things be made manifest, and hidden things shall come to light, and things which are not known shall be made known by them, and also things shall be made known by them which otherwise could not be known."

6:37   *went forth.* Enoch fulfills the commission he previously received to "go forth" (Moses 6:32).

     standing upon the hills and the high places. This may indicate that he preached at sites of worship, which in the ancient world were often on hilltops (RDDPGP, 96).

     all men were offended because of him. Nibley commented: "All men are offended because he doesn't bring good news. Remember what the people say to Samuel the Lamanite, 'Tell us what's right with Zarahemla; don't tell us what's wrong with Zarahemla.' Samuel the Lamanite said: 'When a person comes and tells you how wonderful you are, you clothe him in fine apparel; you carry him on your shoulders and say he is a true prophet. If he tells you your sins, you immediately cry out, 'Kill him; he's a false prophet!' (see Helaman 13:26–28). This is the situation here. Nobody likes him at all . . . Why? Because he testified against their works" (HWNPGP, 275). Compare Matthew 13:57: "And they were offended in him."

6:38   *they came forth to hear him, upon the high places.* Similarly, in *Bet ha-Midrasch* we read: "And all the people gathered together and went up . . . to Enoch to hear this thing." *2 Enoch* 64:1–3 paints a similar picture: "And they all conferred, saying: Come, let us greet Enoch. And two thousand men assembled, and they came to the place Azouchan" (JMBIGIL2, 67).

     tent-keepers. From this verse, Draper, Brown, and Rhodes infer that Enoch was preaching among the people of Cain, who were previously described as tent dwellers (RDDPGP, 96).

     strange thing in the land. The crowds evidently had more interest in seeing some "strange thing" than in hearing their entrenched beliefs challenged. Elder Neal A. Maxwell wrote: "A fresh view is not always welcomed, being jarring to those who are intensely set in their ways. Sin enjoys its own status quo" (JMBIGIL2, 68; MOSESS 6).

     wild man. Enoch, of course, was *not* a wild man—not in any sense comparable to the "mighty

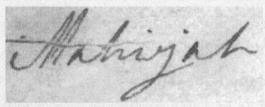

Figure 6–6. Left to Right: Gordon C. Thomasson; Matthew Black; Hugh W. Nibley;
Mahijah (Moses 6:40) as written by Emma Smith in OT1

RESEMBLANCES BETWEEN MAHIJAH/MAHUJAH AND MAHAWAY

Hugh W. Nibley was the first scholar to notice a resemblance between a prominent *Book of Giants* (*BG*) character named Mahaway (Aramaic MHWY) and the Book of Moses names "Mahijah" (likely spelled anciently as MHYY or MḤYY) and "Mahujah" (likely spelled MHWY or MḤWY). See Moses 6:40; 7:2.

Mahijah is the only nonbiblical name in the Book of Moses and the only named character in Moses 6 besides Enoch himself. Like Mahaway in *BG*, Mahijah's only role is to pose questions to the prophet.

Mahaway, like some of the other prominent names in *BG* (such as Gilgamesh), is likely of East Semitic origin. One of several possibilities for its origin is the Akkadian *maḫḫû*, denoting "a certain class of priests and seers" (UCCOMMENTARY, 232). What was the role of these seers? Among other things, the royal archives of the Old Babylonian kingdom of Mari recount the comings and goings of *maḫḫû* as intermediaries and messengers, bearing words of warning from the gods for the king, a role that can be compared to that of both Mahaway and Mahijah. *BG* scholar Jens Wilkens calls Mahaway "the messenger par excellence of the [*gibborim*]" (JWIREMARKS, 227).

Some non–Latter-day Saints have noticed the resemblance of these prominent names in the Book of Moses and the *BG*. For example, in his master's thesis at the University of Durham, Salvatore Cirillo, drawing on similar conclusions of the well-known Enoch scholar Loren T. Stuckenbruck (LTSGIANTS, 27), considers the names of the *gibborim*, notably including Mahaway, as "the most conspicuously independent content" in *BG*, being "unparalleled in other Jewish literature." Cirillo argues in strong terms that Joseph Smith must have known about *BG* as he prepared the Book of Moses account of Enoch. But he does not attempt to explain how a manuscript that was not discovered until 1948 could have influenced revelation written in 1830.

The only known attempt to explain how such influence might have taken place comes from the separate remembrances of Gordon C. Thomasson and Hugh Nibley about the well-known Aramaic scholar Matthew Black, who collaborated with Józef Milik in the first translation of the fragments of *BG* into English in 1976. Black was impressed enough with the correspondence between the names in the Book of Moses Enoch account and the prominent and unique appearance of the similar name in *BG* when Thomasson mentioned it to him that he made a previously unplanned trip to Brigham Young University to learn more. According to Thomasson, Professor Black:

> acknowledged that the name Mahujah could not have come from *1 Enoch*. He then formulated a hypothesis, consistent with his [just-delivered] lecture, that a member of one of the esoteric groups he had described [that is, secret groups who had quietly maintained a religious tradition based in the writings of Enoch that predated Genesis] . . . must have survived into the 19th century, and hearing of Joseph Smith, must have brought the group's Enoch texts to New York from Italy for the prophet to translate and publish.

Over the years, no documentary evidence has surfaced that bears out Black's unsupported hypothesis that Joseph Smith somehow obtained access to an Enoch manuscript like *BG* from a secret religious group in Europe or anywhere else. On the other hand, during this same span of time, much additional evidence has come forth linking Joseph Smith's translation of the Moses 6–7 to ancient textual traditions, including *BG*. The Mahijah/Mahujah resemblance is just one of many ancient connections for which there is no completely satisfying historical explanation. The idea that these similarities have come by coincidence or through borrowing from the Bible is unconvincing. Instead, it seems more reasonable to believe that they are due to common traditions that predate both texts, as Matthew Black apparently believed. Nibley remembered a conversation with Black that occurred near the end of the latter's 1977 visit to BYU. He asked Black if he had an explanation for the appearance of the name Mahujah in the Book of Moses and reported his answer as follows: "Well, someday we will find out the source that Joseph Smith used."

See MOSESS 7, 8; JMBWHERE; HWNPGP, 267–69; GCTBLACK, SKBENOCH.

pass when they heard him, no man laid hands on him; for fear came on all them that heard him; for he walked with God.

Enoch Explains His Mission to Mahijah

⁴⁰ And there came a man unto him, whose name was Mahijah, and said unto him: "Tell us plainly who thou art, and from whence thou comest?" ⁴¹ And he said unto them: "I came out from the land of Cainan, the land of my fathers, a land of righteousness unto this day. And my father taught me in all the ways of God. ⁴² And it came to pass, as I journeyed from the land of Cainan, by the sea east,

---

6:38   men" (*gibborim*) to whom he was preaching. They simply *called* him a wild man in mockery. However, in a striking passage from *BG*, the arrogant leader of the wicked *gibborim* army, 'Ohya, declared, "The wild man they call [me]," giving himself a title identical to the one given here to Enoch. How is this self-reference to be understood? Consistent with the dramatic irony that permeates the rest of the story, note that 'Ohya did not utter this title in a moment of victory, as one might have expected, but rather as he muttered to himself in doubt and dismay after a humiliating defeat by Enoch's forces. After the dramatic turn of events that resulted in his ignominious loss to Enoch in battle, it seems that readers are meant to understand that 'Ohya could no longer be credibly seen as a mighty "wild man" in the proud tradition of the *gibborim*. Instead, his defeat had transformed him into the beastly wild man of Mesopotamian and biblical tragedy. Joseph Angel ably compared the humbling of 'Ohya to the principal theme of Nebuchadnezzar's story. See MOSESS 6 and figure 6–5.

6:39   ***no man laid hands on him.*** This phrase recalls the story of Abinadi (Mosiah 13:2–5).

     fear came on all them that heard him. Compare Luke 7:16.

     he walked with God. Compare Genesis 5:24; Moses 6:34; 7:69; 8:27.

6:40   ***Mahijah.*** Note that in Moses 7:2, "Mahujah," a variant of the name used as a place name, is used and may be associated with the same person mentioned here. Mahijah, who bears the only nonbiblical name in the Book of Moses, plays a similar role to Mahaway in *BG*. According to Nibley, "The only thing the Mahijah in the Book of Moses is remarkable for is his putting of bold direct questions to Enoch. And this is exactly the role, and the only role, that the Aramaic Mahujah [= Mahaway] plays in the story" (HWNENOCH, 278). See figure 6–6.

     Tell us plainly who thou art. Other wicked people challenging the credentials of prophets in scripture include Pharaoh (Exodus 5:2); King Noah (Mosiah 11:27); the Ammonihahites (Alma 9:6); Cain (Moses 5:16); the scribes, Pharisees, and chief priests (for example, Luke 5:21); and Herod (Luke 9:9). To this list we might add, in ironic role reversal, Moses' questioning of Satan's credentials (Moses 1:13). In the *Bet ha-Midrasch*, we read a similar request for Enoch to identify himself, followed by his preaching to a multitude: "And Enoch went out [after his long hiding] and there came a voice saying: Who is the man who rejoices . . . in the ways of the Lord? . . . And all the people gathered together and came unto Enoch[,] . . . [who] taught all the people again to keep the ways of the Lord" (HWNENOCH, 212).

     from whence thou comest. Enoch is unknown to his hearers. This may be simply because he has come from a distant land (Moses 6:41). Or else it may be related to pseudepigraphal accounts of Enoch that emphasize his withdrawal from human society before beginning his ministry (see GWN1ENOCH1, 12:1–2, p. 233).

6:41   ***the land of Cainan, the land of my fathers.*** This answers the second part of Mahijah's question, concerning where Enoch came from. See 6:17.

     my father taught me in all the ways of God. Compare Moses 6:21. See also 1 Nephi 1:1.

6:42   ***sea east.*** In the Bible and elsewhere in the ancient Near East, eastward movement is repeatedly associated with increasing distance from God (see figure 4–2). In line with the presumed hierocentric, symbolic geography of Enoch's world, it is not a surprise to read the significant detail

Figure 6–7. *Detail of the Manichaean Cosmology Painting*

ENOCH ILLUSTRATED: THE MANICHAEAN COSMOLOGY PAINTING

In addition to many surviving *BG* text fragments, we are fortunate to have a version of the story of Enoch in pictures. The Manichaean Cosmology Painting (MCP), depicted on a hanging scroll, is shown in part above. It is one of nine recently discovered Chinese Manichaean paintings preserved in Japan and is dated to the fourteenth-fifteenth centuries.

Paul Mirecki describes Manichaeism as "one of the major world religions and the only such religion to align itself closely with late antiquity's Near Eastern Gnostic tradition. . . . The religion was founded by the Iranian prophet Mani (216-277 CE), who deliberately created a universal and propagandistic religion that incorporates Christian, Zoroastrian, and Buddhist concepts. The religion moved east toward India and west into the Roman Empire already in Mani's lifetime, reaching as far west as Algiers and southern Europe and as far east as Central Asia and southeast coastal China, where traces of the religion datable to the early seventeenth century can be identified" (JMBIGIL1, 883).

In Manichaean tradition, paintings such as MCP were often created for teaching purposes. It was only recently discovered that this painting illustrates much of the *BG* story of Enoch. It fills gaps in our overall understanding of the story and defines some of the events and characters more concretely.

With one exception, the relevant details from MCP are included in a hierocentric depiction (see figure 4–3) of the eighth and fifth layers layers of the earth. These layers, shown within the bottom third of MCP, feature a symbolic representation of the earth below a large, central treelike mountain. In Indian culture, this feature is identified as Mount Sumēru, a sacred center place. The mountain is not only to a place in the symbolic geography of the story but also to an actual mountain located in the Himalayas.

Mount Sumēru is surrounded by four continents and the great ocean. Thirty-two palaces at the top of Sumēru surround a larger palace of Deity, pictured with an attendant on each side. The four supplicants surrounding the throne may correspond to four figures who bring the judicial complaint of the earth or a plea for clemency of the repentant wicked before the heavenly judge. The four archangels mentioned in *BG*, who (in the Manichaean version) led the battles against the wicked and, with Enoch, gathered the repentant, are clothed in armor in front of a seated deity—likely Enoch—among the smaller green mountains at the foot of the sacred mountain. In other parts of the painting (not shown) wicked "demons" are imprisoned. In the upper right quadrant, two repentant figures, likely *gibborim*, kneel. In addition, a solitary figure at right—perhaps Mahujah/Mahaway—kneels while perched on a high mountaintop, seemingly evoking themes from Mahujah/Mahaway's second journey to meet Enoch. See JMBGIANTS, 1087–88.

I beheld a vision; and lo, the heavens I saw, and the Lord spake with me, and gave me commandment; wherefore, for this cause, to keep the commandment, I speak forth these words."

ENOCH PREACHES THE CREATION AND THE FALL

⁴³ And Enoch continued his speech, saying: "The Lord which spake with me, the same is the God of heaven, and he is my God, and your God, and ye are my brethren, and why counsel ye yourselves, and deny the God of heaven? ⁴⁴ The heavens he made; the earth is his footstool; and the foundation thereof is his. Behold, he laid

6:42   that his missionary journey in the Book of Moses took Enoch away from the "sacred center"—in other words, he went out "from the land of Cainan," "a land of righteousness" in the west, to preach in the land of the wicked, which was presumably near the western edge of "the sea east" (Moses 6:41–42; see figures 6–7; 7–4). Remarkably, description of Enoch's journey and vision "by the sea east" in the Book of Moses recalls the direction of the prophet's voyage in *1 Enoch* 20–36, where the text seems to imply that Enoch continued his travels even farther east—to the "ends of the earth," "from the west edge of the earth to its east edge" (GWN1ENOCH1, p. 290). Significantly, *1 Enoch* 13:7–8 also records a vision that Enoch received "by the waters of Dan," arguably a "sea east" (GWN1ENOCH1, 13:7, p. 237; MOSESS 24).

    the Lord spake with me, and gave me commandment. This statement answers the first part of Mahijah's question by providing Enoch's preaching credentials (RDDPGP, 97).

6:43   *Enoch continued his speech.* Consistent with the temple-related teaching pattern frequently found in scripture, Enoch now gets to the meat of his message: Creation, Fall, and Atonement. Providing a fitting title for this section of the story, a notation likely written by John Whitmer on the OT1 manuscript above Moses 6:52b reads "The Plan of Salvation" (SHFJST, 101). It would seem natural to apply this title to the passage beginning with Moses 6:43 and ending with Moses 7:1. In both places, the phrase "Enoch continued his speech" appears, thus bracketing the passage explicitly. A later section of the story that Joseph Smith called "Extracts from the Prophecy of Enoch" begins in Moses 7:2 (JMBIGIL2, 70).

    why counsel ye yourselves . . . ? See Moses 6:28. Compare Moses 5:25: "He rejected the greater counsel which was had from God." Counseling with God and counseling with others are essential, complementary methods for reaching wise decisions. While the divinely given pattern of "counseling with our councils" is an integral part of Church leadership, it is ineffective and may even become counter-productive if discussion is not undertaken in a manner that invites revelation, "counsel . . . from God," as part of the process. Illustrating this point, Hugh Nibley wrote: "If we form a committee; if we get our strength from each other; if we support each other and form a society (a very impressive order or group) then we think we are getting something accomplished and doing something simply by counseling among ourselves. No, you [ultimately] get your counsel directly from the Lord" (HWNPGP, 276).

    deny the God of heaven. Compare Moses 6:28.

6:44   *The heavens he made.* This verse describes God's role as Creator and constitutes God's legal claim to the right to reclaim His children (RDDPGP, 97). See Moses 6:33.

    the earth is his footstool. Compare Isaiah 66:1: "The heaven is my throne, and the earth is my footstool"; and Abraham 2:7: "I dwell in heaven; the earth is my footstool." About this imagery, Donald W. Parry et al. write: "The throne represents the Lord's role as eternal king (Doctrine and Covenants 128:33). All heaven is His throne in that it is from there that He rules. But, more particularly, the Lord dwells in the heavenly temple, which is heaven itself, and in that temple is His throne (Psalm 11:4; Revelation 4:2, 20:11). The earth as a footstool suggests a position of complete submission. The Lord rules from His throne, but He puts the earth under His feet."

it, an host of men hath he brought in upon the face thereof. ⁴⁵ And death hath come upon our fathers; nevertheless we know them, and cannot deny, and even the first of all we know, even Adam. ⁴⁶ For a book of remembrance we have written among us, according to the pattern given by the finger of God; and it is given in our own language." ⁴⁷ And as Enoch spake forth the words of God, the people trembled, and could not stand in his presence.

⁴⁸ And he said unto them: "Because that Adam fell, we are; and by his fall came death; and we are made partakers of misery and woe. ⁴⁹ Behold Satan hath come among the children of men, and tempteth them to worship him; and men have become carnal, sensual, and devilish, and are shut out from the presence of God."

6:44   Imagery of the same nature is used to describe the ark of the Israelite temple. Susan Ackerman writes: "What seems to be imagined here is a throne whereby the Deity sits invisibly above the Ark, on the outstretched wings of cherubim, with the Ark itself serving as God's footstool. This image of a cherub throne with footstool is frequently found in West Semitic art, and biblical texts explicitly refer to the Ark as a footstool [e.g., 1 Chronicles 28:2] and describe cherub wings unfolded above the Ark after it is housed in Solomon's temple (1 Kings 6:23–28; 8:6–7)." See JMBIGIL2, 71.

the foundation thereof is his. This refers to the foundation of the earth (Isaiah 48:13). Like the preceding phrases describing the heaven and the earth, this is an idea with strong temple resonances. In ancient Israel, the holiest spot on earth was believed to be the Foundation Stone in front of the ark of the covenant within the temple at Jerusalem. As John Lundquist explains, the Foundation Stone "was the first solid material to emerge from the waters of Creation [e.g., Psalm 104:5–9], and it was upon this stone that the Deity effected Creation" (JMBIGIL2, 71).

an host of men. See Moses 3:1.

6:45   *death hath come upon our fathers.* Since Adam was still alive when Enoch began his ministry, it is not clear whom this verse refers (RDDPGP, 97).

the first of all we know, even Adam. Throughout the remainder of the chapter, Enoch makes an appeal to the witness of Adam, as recorded in the book of remembrance (Moses 6:5, 46).

6:46   *book of remembrance.* Compare Moses 6:5. In addition to preserving the words of God to the people, the book records the good and bad deeds of humankind (MOSESS 10). Correspondingly, in *BG*, a book in the form of "two stone tablets" is given by Enoch to Mahujah to stand as a witness of "their fallen state and betrayal of their ancient covenants" (JCRGIANTS, 109; HWNENOCH, 214). Apparently, a similar record of the people's wickedness is also kept in heaven (JMBIGIL2, 72).

according to the pattern given by the finger of God. Nibley explains: "God didn't write it. Enoch said he wrote it 'according to the *pattern* given by the finger of God'" (HWNPGP, 269). Likewise, in *BG*, we read of Enoch's handwritten reply to Mahujah: ". . . to you, Maha[wai . . .] . . . The book [. . .] Copy of the second tablet of the l[etter . . .] written by the hand of Enoch, the celebrated scribe [. . .] and holy, to Shemiḥazah and to all his [companions . . .]" (4Q203 frg 7 col. ii l. 5; frg. 8 l. 1–5, García Martínez translation). See JMBIGIL2, 72–73.

it is given in our own language. Compare Moses 6:6: "And by them [i.e., the words of the book of remembrance] their children were taught to read and write, having a language which was pure and undefiled." In the Book of Moses, the designation of "pure" language is a straightforward reference to the "language of Adam" (Moses 6:5, 57). However, it should be observed more generally that "pure and undefiled" language is not merely a matter of literacy but also concerns the state of the individual heart (JMBIGIL2, 73).

6:47   *the people trembled.* Similarly, in *BG* we read that the leaders of the mighty warriors "bowed down and wept in front of [Enoch]" (4Q203 frg 4 l. 6, García Martínez translation). See MOSESS 11. *1 Enoch* 13:3–5 describes a similar reaction after Enoch finished his preaching (GWN1ENOCH1, pp. 234, 237).

Enoch Preaches Salvation through the Atonement of Christ

50 "But God hath made known unto our fathers that all men must repent. 51 And he called upon our father Adam by his own voice, saying: 'I am God; I made the world, and men before they were in the flesh.' 52 And he also said unto him: 'If thou wilt turn unto me, and hearken unto my voice, and believe, and repent of all thy transgressions, and be baptized, even in water, in the name of mine Only Begotten Son, who is full of grace and truth, which is Jesus Christ, the only name which shall be given under heaven, whereby salvation shall come unto the children of men, ye shall receive the gift of the Holy Ghost, asking all things in his name, and whatsoever ye shall ask, it shall be given you.'

carnal, sensual, and devilish. Compare Moses 5:13.

shut out from the presence of God. "That is the ultimate exclusion," observes Nibley (HWNPGP, 277).

6:50   *God hath made known unto our fathers that all men must repent.* See Moses 5:8.

6:51   *he called upon our father Adam.* In the remarkable direct speech of Moses 6:51–68, God Himself lays out the points of the plan of salvation one by one. This speech is laden with features of Hebrew poetry and seems to be an excerpt of God's words to Adam in his book of remembrance. Significantly, Enoch (Henoch or Hanoch, Hebrew *ḥănôk*) sounds identical to the Hebrew passive participle of the verbal root *ḥnk*, to "train up," "dedicate." Thus, for a Hebrew speaker, the name *ḥănôk*/Enoch would evoke "trained up" or "initiated"—bringing to mind not only the general role of a teacher but also the idea of someone who was familiar with the temple and was responsible for training and initiating others (MOSESS 14). See MOSESS 14–21 for detailed commentary on this passage. Here, Enoch is highlighted not as a prophet, seer, or preacher, but rather as a teacher.

I made the world. See Moses 6:33. Naturally, the theme of Creation is foundational to the story of the Fall and the Atonement that will be summarized later (vv. 51–68). In addition, Benjamin McGuire observes that this verse serves "as a 'motive clause' of the sort we might anticipate from an Old Testament text." The motive clause is meant to convey that since God "has called man and the universe into being, man owes Him obedience and is subject to His commandments," including the commandments to hearken, to believe, to repent, and to be baptized that are outlined in v. 52 (MOSESS 14).

men before they were in the flesh. The existence of our human souls before we were born is described in both the Book of Moses and *2 Enoch* (FIA2ENOCH, 23:4 (J), p. 140). The clarifying words "in the flesh" were added in OT2 (SHFJST, 612).

6:52   *If thou wilt turn unto me.* The Hebrew term *shuv* (= "turn") conveys the primary meaning of repentance: "turning from sin to righteousness" (David Noel Freedman, JMBIGIL2, 75; see figure 3–4). It usually concerns the way a person directs the feet and the will (RDDPGP, 101).

repent of all thy transgressions. In *BG*, like the Book of Moses but unlike any other ancient Enoch text, Enoch also gives hope to the wicked through repentance: "Now, then, unfasten your chains [of sin] . . . and pray" (JCRGIANTS, 4Q203 frg. 8 l. 14–15, p. 103). In addition, John C. Reeves conjectures that another difficult-to-reconstruct phrase in the *Book of Giants* might also be understood as an "allusion to a probationary period for the repentance of the Giants" (see figure6–8). Unfortunately, as we see later in the story, the initial sorrowing of the *gibborim* brought about only short-lived repentance (MOSESS 11).

the only name which shall be given under heaven, whereby salvation shall come. Compare Acts 4:12; 2 Nephi 25:20; Doctrine and Covenants 18:23. Both physical and spiritual healing come through the name or authority of Jesus Christ. The wide semantic range of the word "salvation" is captured in the term "saving health," which comes from an English translation

Figure 6–8. Demons kneeling and repenting (?) on pitch-dark clouds with their hands clutched (Detail of MCP)

ENOCH OFFERS HOPE THROUGH REPENTANCE

As Enoch spake forth the words of God, the people trembled, and could not stand in his presence (Moses 6:47). Paralleling Moses 6:47, *BG* tells how the *gibborim* sorrowed and trembled after Enoch read their wicked deeds out of the book of remembrance. Both the Book of Moses and *BG* contain a "prediction of utter destruction and the confining in prison that is to follow" (Hugh Nibley, MOSESS 13). However, in contrast to the irrevocable punishment outlined in *1 Enoch*, the Book of Moses and the *Book of Giants* both tender the possibility of repentance.

In the Book of Moses, Enoch draws attention to God's invitation of repentance that had been given to Adam:

> If thou wilt turn unto me, and hearken unto my voice, and believe, and repent of all thy transgressions, and be baptized, . . . ye shall receive the gift of the Holy Ghost . . . and whatsoever ye shall ask, it shall be given you. (Moses 6:52)

BG relates Enoch's call for repentance as follows: "Set loose what you hold captive . . . and pray" (DWPDSS, 4Q203 frg 8 l. 14–15, p. 947). It seems that at least part of the group of hearers subsequently "[prostrat]ed" themselves (DWPDSS, 4Q203 frg. 13 l. 1, p. 947) as shown above. While this repentant group was "very, very glad at seeing the apostle [referring to Enoch]" and "assembled before him," Enoch's message was not received uniformly by all: "those that were tyrants and criminals [referring to the unrepentant faction] . . . were [worried] and much afraid" (WBHGIANTS, text E, 66).

Reeves conjectures that an additional difficult-to-reconstruct phrase in *BG* might be understood as an "allusion to a probationary period for the repentance of the [*gibborim*]" (JCRGIANTS, 103). The description of a period of repentance seems to echo a specific Jewish tradition that continues to modern times. In this regard, note Geo Widengren's description of the Jewish tradition that "on New Year's Day, . . . the judgment is carried out when three kinds of tablets are presented, one for the righteous, one for sinners, and one for those occupying an intermediate position." Widengren explains that "people of an intermediate position are granted ten days of repentance between New Year's Day and Yom Kippurim" (MOSESS 11; JMBGIANTS, 1106).

What of those who do not repent in this life? Latter-day Saints frequently cite 1 Peter 3:18–20 and 4:5–6 as proof that the Gospel will be preached in the spirit world. But it is not common knowledge that Peter is making allusion to the wicked at the time of Enoch in these verses. Enoch scholar George Nickelsburg does not doubt that Peter is "alluding to the tradition about the Watchers" of *1 Enoch*," and in 1 Peter 3:19–20 "attributes to Jesus a journey to the underworld that parallels Enoch's interaction with the rebel watchers," while comparing "baptism with the purifying effects of the Flood." If Nickelsburg is correct, then Peter's writings imply the hope that God's mercy will be extended even to the wicked who rejected Enoch while they lived on earth, such that, through eventual repentance and the power of the Atonement, they might eventually "live according to God in the spirit." Similarly, Nibley concludes: "It was specifically the spirits who were disobedient in Enoch's day who were to enjoy the preaching of the Lord and the promise of deliverance in the meridian of times" (HWNENOCH, 192). See MOSESS 13 and 24.

53 "And our father Adam spake unto the Lord, and said: 'Why is it that men must repent and be baptized in water?' And the Lord said unto Adam: 'Behold I have forgiven thee thy transgression in the Garden of Eden.' 54 Hence came the saying abroad among the people, that the Son of God hath atoned for original guilt, wherein the sins of the parents cannot be answered upon the heads of the children, for they are whole from the foundation of the world.

55 "And the Lord spake unto Adam, saying: 'Inasmuch as thy children are conceived in sin, even so when they begin to grow up, sin conceiveth in their hearts, and they taste the bitter, that they may know to prize the good. 56 And it is given unto them to know good from evil; wherefore they are agents unto themselves, and I have

6:52   tradition that stretches from the Renaissance to modern times. In his moving musical setting, William Byrd (1543–1623), a student of the great Thomas Tallis (ca. 1505–85), immortalized this English version of Psalm 119:174–75: "I have longed for thy saving health, O Lord; thy law is my delight. O let my soul live, and it shall praise thee; and thy judgments shall help me." In his discussion of the comprehensive nature of Christ's power to heal affliction of all kinds, President Dallin H. Oaks enumerated a tragic litany of physical, emotional, mental, and spiritual maladies. Then he testified simply that Christ healed them all (JMBIGIL2, 75).

    ye shall receive the gift of the Holy Ghost. This phrase about receiving the Holy Ghost was added in OT2 (SHFJST, 612). Compare Moses 6:61, which expands on the blessings of this gift.

6:53   *Why is it that men must repent and be baptized in water?* Hugh Nibley answered this question as follows: "'I've forgiven the cause. Now, you have to get rid of the effect. The cause was the Fall. It made you dirty, but you have to wash off now. You have to take advantage in good faith of the sacrifice that has been made for you. Here's the chance. It's a very simple thing to do, but you have to do it.' Why is it that man must repent and be baptized? 'Not because you are damned but because I have forgiven you,' He says. . . . 'I have taken care of the transgression in the Garden of Eden.' That's . . . the primal sin. To think we are not responsible for that and, therefore, we are not to blame for our sins is ridiculous. That sin has been forgiven, so if you want to go on what you do then is wash off and get started again. He says here, 'The Son of God hath atoned for original guilt, wherein the sins of the parents cannot be answered upon the heads of the children, for they are whole from the foundation of the world' (Moses 6:54). But 'when they begin to grow up, sin conceiveth in their hearts' [Moses 6:55]" (HWNPGP, 278).

    I have forgiven thee thy transgression. This verse witnesses that the Atonement is effective long before it is actually carried out (RDDPGP, 102). OT1 uses the plural term "transgressions" (SHFJST, 101).

6:54   *the Son of God.* In OT1, the term "Christ" is used instead (SHFJST, 101).

    original guilt. I.e., Adam's transgression. See Moses 6:53.

    children . . . are whole from the foundation of the world. This is because the "blood of Christ atoneth for their sins" (Mosiah 3:16).

6:55   *thy children are conceived in sin.* This has nothing to do with "original sin" but rather is the result of the moral transgressions of Enoch's wicked hearers. As Hugh Nibley expressed it, "The wicked people of Enoch's day . . . did indeed conceive their children in sin, since they were illegitimate offspring of a totally amoral society" (JMBIGIL2, 48). The relevant passage in *BG* reads, "Let it be known to you th[at] . . . your activity and that of [your] wive[s and of your children] . . . through your fornication" (LTSGIANTS, 4Q203 frg. 8 l. 6–9, p. 90. See also JCRGIANTS, 114n9). See MOSESS 11.

    prize the good. Nibley asked: "How does sin teach you to prize the good? Does sickness teach you to prize health? Well, it certainly does" (HWNPGP, 278).

6:56   *given unto them to know good from evil.* We know evil "on sight," Nibley explained. "You have that reaction. Remember, 'I will place enmity between thee and the serpent' (Moses 4:21)—that

Figure 6–9. Gustav Kaupert, 1819–97: *Jesus Christ*, 1880

"The Son of Man, Even Jesus Christ, a Righteous Judge"

Some readers of the Book of Moses are surprised to encounter references to the name, titles, and aspects of the mission of Jesus Christ that are much more detailed and explicit than one finds in the Old Testament. Although Christians are divided on the issue of how much Old Testament peoples and prophets knew about Jesus Christ, The Church of Jesus Christ of Latter-day Saints embraces the belief that details of the life and mission of Jesus Christ were known to prophets from Adam onward.

While additional research is needed, the following examples from ancient Enoch literature are offered for consideration. In this respect, the *Book of Parables*, one of five relatively disjointed sections of *1 Enoch* and arguably not subject to Christian influences, has been a very fruitful source of messianic prophecies. Remarkably, information relating to the cluster of four interlinked titles mentioned together in the Book of Moses Enoch story (Moses 6:57) are better paralleled in the *Book of Parables* Enoch account than anywhere else:

- **Only Begotten.** Threads related to the special status and sacrificial role of the "firstborn" and "only begotten" son as applied to Old Testament figures such as Moses, to Christ Himself, and eventually to the disciples of Jesus Christ are rooted in concepts that go back significantly beyond the New Testament. The key to the meaning of this concept in Moses 6:57 is found in the immediately preceding mention of God as the "Man of Holiness" and the pronoun in the term "his Only Begotten." As Frederick Borsch has argued at length, the concept of God as "the Man" of whom Enoch eventually becomes a filial "counterpart" is at the very heart of the *Book of Parables*, as further explained in the discussion of the title "Son of Man" immediately below.

- **Son of Man.** In hearing the name-title "Son of Man," Jews in the first century CE would have thought of texts in the books of Daniel and Enoch. Significantly, the title "Son of Man," which is even more prominent in the *Book of Parables* than in Daniel, also appears in marked density throughout Enoch's grand vision in the Book of Moses. In addition, and even more remarkably, the related titles "Chosen One," "Anointed One" (that is, "Messiah") and "Righteous One" are featured in both the Book of Moses (Moses 6:57; 7:45, 47, 67; 7:39) and the *Book of Parables* (SKBMAN, 1316nn43–45). Shirley Lucass has affirmed that the Son of Man, as "a heavenly redeemer figure who stands in close relationship to the God of Israel[,] is not a corruption of Jewish monotheism by Christianity, nor an invention of a Hellenistic or 'Gentile' Paul, but is an integral feature of Second Temple Judaism."

- **Jesus Christ.** The name-title "Jesus Christ," of course, derives directly from its Greek New Testament equivalent, which might be more clearly translated for modern English speakers as "Joshua (Yeshua) the Messiah," the term "Messiah" referring to one who is anointed by God. Consistent both with the teachings of Moses 6:57 and with Nickelsburg and VanderKam's conclusions that the various titles mentioned in the *Book of Parables* refer to a single individual (GWN1ENOCH2, 119), James Waddell argues in addition that the "author(s) of the [book] understood the messiah figure to be distinct from the divine figure who is the one God."

- **Righteous Judge.** Remarkably, the single specific description of the role of the Son of Man given in Moses 6:57 as a "righteous Judge" is also highly characteristic of the *Book of Parables*, in which the primary role of the Son of Man is also that of a judge (GWN1ENOCH2, 119).

In summary, it is significant that, outside the Old Testament, the Enoch pseudepigrapha are arguably the pre-Christian documents of Jewish origin that best prefigure the range of Christological concepts and titles found in the New Testament. Thus, to readers of latter-day scripture it should not be surprising that Christological themes and concepts are also present in the Book of Moses account of Enoch. See MOSESS 15; SKBMAN.

given unto you another law and commandment. [57] Wherefore teach it unto your children, that all men, everywhere, must repent, or they can in nowise inherit the kingdom of God, for no unclean thing can dwell there, or dwell in his presence; for, in the language of Adam, Man of Holiness is his name, and the name of his Only Begotten is the Son of Man, even Jesus Christ, a righteous Judge, who shall come in the meridian of time.

[58] ""Therefore I give unto you a commandment, to teach these things freely unto your children, saying: [59] "That by reason of transgression cometh the fall, which

6:56   gut reaction when something is wrong. You know what it is. You can't excuse yourself. Therefore, men are 'without excuse' (Romans 1:20). He says: 'They know with a perfect knowledge as night from day' (Moroni 7:15); all of them do. You don't have to be a member of the Church . . . to know that" (HWNPGP, 279).

6:57   *no unclean thing can dwell there.* Nibley offered this illustration: "An unclean thing is completely out. Remember, one defect (the slightest defect) in a structure that's to last for an infinite length of time will destroy it. No matter how trifling it is, if it is to last for . . . millions of years, that will be a fatal defect. So you have to be completely cleaned up if you are going back to the presence of the Father" (HWNPGP, 279). See Moses 7:16. Compare 1 Nephi 10:21; 15:33–34; Alma 7:21; 11:37; 40:26; 3 Nephi 27:19.

 language of Adam. Compare Moses 6:5–6, 46.

 Man of Holiness is his name. See Moses 7:35. Elder Bruce R. McConkie commented:
 The whole body of revealed writ attests to the eternal verity that the Supreme God is a Holy Man. . . . Thus, when Jesus asked the ancient disciples, "Whom do men say that I the Son of man am?" (Matthew 16:13) it was as though he asked: "Who do men say that I am? I testify that I am the Son of Man of Holiness, which is to say, the Son of that Holy Man who is God, but who do men say that I am?" In this same vein, one of the early revelations given in this dispensation asks: "What is the name of God in the pure language?" The answer: "Ahman." Question: "What is the name of the Son of God?" Answer: "Son Ahman." The term "Son Ahman" is used in Doctrine and Covenants 78:20 and 95:17. Doctrine and Covenants 78:20 originally was given as "Jesus Christ," but was later modified in the handwriting of William W. Phelps to read "Son Ahman." The term also appears as part of the place-name of Adam-ondi-Ahman in Doctrine and Covenants 78:15; 107:53; 116:1; 117:8, 11. (JMBIGIL2, 78)

 the Son of Man. The term "Son of Man," frequently found in the *Book of Parables* in *1 Enoch*, is here understood to refer to Jesus Christ. After considering the debate among scholars about the single or multiple referent(s) of the titles of "Son of Man," "Chosen One," "Anointed One," and "Righteous One" in the *Book of Parables* and their relationship to other texts, Nickelsburg and VanderKam conclude that the author of the *Book of Parables,* like the Book of Moses, "saw the . . . traditional figures as having a single referent" (GWN1ENOCH2, 119). For a more extensive discussion, see figure 6–9.

 a righteous Judge. Given the single specific description of the role of the Son of Man in this verse as a "righteous Judge," it is significant that the *Book of Parables* also cites the primary role of the Son of Man as a judge. Nickelsburg and VanderKam write, "If the central message of the *Parables* is the coming of the final judgment, the Son of Man/Chosen One takes center stage as the agent of this judgment" (GWN1ENOCH2, 119).

 meridian of time. From Latin *medius* ("middle") + *dies* ("day"). Compare Moses 6:62; 7:46.

6:59   *by reason of transgression cometh the fall.* The current wording of this verse varies significantly from OT1. The OT1 version intimates clearly that the description of the new birth is meant to include not only baptism but also ordinances that in our day are administered in temples. Changes are shown in italics for emphasis: "that insamuch as *they* were born into the world *by the* fall bringeth death, and inasmuch as ye were born into the world by water, and blood, and the spirit, which I have made, and so became of dust a living soul, even so ye must be born again into the kingdom of heaven, of water, and of the Spirit, and be cleansed by blood, even the blood of mine Only Begotten; that ye might be sanctified from all sin, and enjoy the words of eternal life in this world, and eternal life in the world to come, even immortal glory; ⁶⁰ for

> by the water ye keep the commandment;
> by the Spirit ye are justified, and
> by the blood ye are sanctified.

6:59   *fall, which bringeth death*, by water, and blood, and the spirit which I have made, and so became of dust a living soul, even so ye must be born again ["into the kingdom of heaven" is omitted] of water, and the Spirit, and cleansed by blood, even the blood of mine Only Begotten, *into the mysteries of the kingdom of heaven*; that ye might be sanctified from all sin, and enjoy the words of eternal life in this world, and eternal life in the world to come, even immortal glory" (SHFJST, 102).

    I have made. See Moses 6:33.

    born again. The Prophet Joseph Smith taught that being "born again comes by the Spirit of God through ordinances" (JSTPJS, 2 July 1839, 162). Specifically, as we progress through the prescribed series of saving ordinances, we are repeatedly "reborn," our nature transformed over and over as we experience the cleansing justification of "the Spirit of Christ" (Doctrine and Covenants 20:37), the symbolism of death and resurrection through baptism in water (Romans 6:4–6), the new life granted us when we receive the gift of the Holy Ghost (2 Nephi 31:13), the spiritual and physical "renew[al]" of the initiatory ordinances (Doctrine and Covenants 84:33), and the unfolding stages of the drama of our existence in the endowment. Indeed, the endowment itself enacts our individual progress through multiple "rebirths" (JMBSTRONGER, 943)—from the spirit world to mortal life and from thence to becoming sons and daughters of Christ and ultimately of the Father Himself, receiving "all that [the] Father hath" (Doctrine and Covenants 84:38) as "joint-heirs with Christ" (Romans 8:17). According to the OT1 manuscript of Moses 6:59 discussed above, the ordinances that prepare one for these blessings constitute "the mysteries of the kingdom of heaven" (MOSESS 21).

    cleansed by blood. In Doctrine and Covenants 88:68–69, 74–75, the Lord told the Saints who were preparing for temple blessings about the blessings of the "great and last promise" that awaited them through their faithfulness: "Therefore, sanctify yourselves that your minds become single to God, and the days will come that you shall see him; for he will unveil his face unto you, and it shall be in his own time, and in his own way, and according to his own will. Remember the great and last promise which I have made unto you; . . . sanctify yourselves; yea, purify your hearts, and cleanse your hands and your feet before me, that I may make you clean; that I may testify unto your Father, and your God, and my God, that you are clean from the blood of this wicked generation; that I may fulfill this promise, this great and last promise, which I have made unto you, when I will." See MOSESS 20.

    the words of eternal life in this world, and eternal life in the world to come. A significant distinction is made here between the "*words* of eternal life" and "eternal life" itself. Although we have no authoritative interpretation of this distinction, one possible interpretation for the "words of eternal life" is that they are a reference to the sure promise of exaltation that can be received only in an anticipatory way "in this world" through the earthly and heavenly ordinances that reveal the "mysteries of the kingdom of heaven" (SHFJST, 102). Of course, "eternal life" itself can be given only "in the world to come," after the end of one's probation (MOSESS 16).

6:60   *by the water ye keep the commandment.* See MOSESS 17, 18.

    by the Spirit ye are justified. See MOSESS 19.

⁶¹ "'Therefore it is given to abide in you; the record of heaven; the Comforter; the peaceable things of immortal glory; the truth of all things; that which quickeneth all things, which maketh alive all things; that which knoweth all things, and hath all power according to wisdom, mercy, truth, justice, and judgment." ⁶² And now, behold, I say unto you: This is the plan of salvation unto all men, through the blood of mine Only Begotten, who shall come in the meridian of time. ⁶³ And behold, all things have their likeness, and all things are created and made to bear record of me, both things which are temporal, and things which are spiritual; things which are in the heavens above, and things which are on the earth, and things which are in the earth, and things which are under the earth, both above and beneath: all things bear record of me.'"

by the blood ye are sanctified. See MOSESS 20. Hugh Nibley summarizeed this as follows: The water is an easy act of obedience. . . . "By the water ye keep the commandment." "I know not, save the Lord commanded me" (Moses 5:6). That's your sacrifice. So you get baptized as an act of obedience. Then "by the Spirit ye are justified." That's the Holy Ghost. That's your state of mind. If you just go through the motions as obedience, that's the first necessary step here. The Spirit gives you the state of mind. Naturally, you enter into it—the understanding, the agreement without which any act would be utterly meaningless. You are not just being baptized as a "bag of sand" [Joseph Smith]. You've got to be baptized physically, but then it goes beyond that to the Spirit, where you understand and are aware of what's going on. The Holy Ghost does that. He brings all things to your mind and "all things to your remembrance" (John 14:26). Then the last thing is "and by the blood ye are sanctified." You can't sanctify yourself but by completely giving up life in this world, which means suffering death, which means the shedding of blood. This is the end of earthly life, and people avoid and dread that more than anything else. That is why we find substitutes and the like. That's why we find proxies for the sacrifice. . . . So the shedding of blood is your final declaration that you are willing to give up this life for the other, and it is an act of faith. (HWNPGP, 279–80)

6:61 **Therefore it is given to abide in you; the record of heaven.** Having explained the doctrine of rebirth in the previous verses, the Lord now describes how one can come to a sure knowledge of that doctrine through what is termed the "record of heaven" and be sealed up to eternal life "through the blood of mine Only Begotten" (Moses 6:61–62). The phrase that opens v. 61 expands on the promise given in v. 52: "Ye shall receive the gift of the Holy Ghost." Whereas in v. 52 the blessing of the promise mentioned specifically has to do with asking and receiving, in v. 61 other blessings are mentioned, including "the peaceable things of immortal glory" (in OT1—see SHFJST, 102) or "the keys of the kingdom of heaven" (in OT2—see SHFJST, 614). Note, however, that Doctrine and Covenants 42:61 implies that both the "peaceable things" and "the mysteries" are the results of revelation. This further strengthens the connection between the OT1 phrasing and Doctrine and Covenants 42:61: "If thou shalt ask, thou shalt receive revelation upon revelation, knowledge upon knowledge, that thou mayest know the mysteries and peaceable things— that which bringeth joy, that which bringeth life eternal."

Observe that the OT2 phrasing recalls the words of Jesus Christ to Peter in Matthew 16:19, which are associated with the sealing power: "And I will give unto thee the keys of the kingdom of heaven: and whatsoever thou shalt bind on earth shall be bound in heaven: and whatsoever thou shalt loose on earth shall be loosed in heaven." Elsewhere, Joseph Smith equates the "power which *records*" with the sealing power—or, in other words, the power that "binds on earth and binds in heaven" (Doctrine and Covenants 128:9, emphasis added; MOSESS 16).

6:63 **all things are created and made to bear record of me.** Here, the Lord builds on His declaration of the revelatory witness of the Holy Ghost to affirm that everything He has created, in heaven

Figure 6–10. E. S. Drower (1879–1972): *The Kushta*, 1956

THE BAPTISM AND HEAVENLY ASCENT OF ADAM IN MANDAISM

Not only the Book of Moses but also several Islamic, Christian, Mandaean, and Manichaean accounts speak of the baptism of Adam and Eve. For instance, Latter-day Saints will find interest in Mandaean teachings rituals that relate baptism and heavenly ascent. Indeed, Hugh Nibley saw the "whole Mandaean ritual complex with its endless washings, garments, ritual meals, embraces, grips and crownings [as being] reminiscent of the Egyptian endowment."

Mandaean scripture describes divine messengers ('*uthras*) who come to earth to help humankind. In the preeminent position is Manda d-Hiia (Knowledge of Life), followed by three "brothers . . . sometimes [paradoxically] seen as belonging in three different generations": Hibil [Abel, son of Adam], Sitil [Seth, son of Adam], and Anosh [Enoch, son of Seth]. In the beginning, these three messengers were sent down from the "Lightworld" ito instruct Adam and Eve in the ordinances and in prayer. Importantly, because the figure of Enosh is often confused with Enoch, the figure of Enosh has often been an inadvertent magnet for Enoch traditions in and out of Mandaism. Thus, the examples of ancient affinities between Enoch (as depicted in the Book of Moses) and Enosh literature have been recognized by some scholars as deriving from fragments of Enoch (rather than Enosh) traditions.

In Mandaean religion, the rituals of water immersion are associated with Abel (compare SHFJST, OT1 p. 40, pp. 131–32). Indeed, Abel was said to have performed the first baptism—that of Adam, who prefigures every later Mandaean candidate for these repeated rituals. Following baptism, the Mandaeans perform rituals that include anointing and the pronouncing of the names of the gods upon the individual. The *kushta*, a ceremonial handclasp, is given three times in the immersion ritual, each one of which, according to Elizabeth Drower, "seems to mark the completion . . . of a stage in a ceremony." After death and ascent the "great veil of safety" is lifted for each of the faithful. At that moment Mandaean scripture records that a final *kushta* will also take place, albeit in the form of an embrace, called the "key of the *kushta* of both arms."

The idea of an atoning embrace can be compared with the symbolism in Jacob's wrestle (or embrace) with the angel (Genesis 32:24–32) and his subsequent embrace with Esau (Genesis 33:22–24); in the reconciliation of the father with his prodigal son in Jesus' parable (Luke 15:20); and in the eschatological embraces of Enoch's Zion and Latter-day Zion described in the Book of Moses story of the return of Enoch's city in the last days: "Then shalt thou and all thy city meet them there, and we will receive them into our bosom, and they shall see us; and we will fall upon their necks, and they shall fall upon our necks, and we will kiss each other" (Moses 7:63). See MOSESS 4; JMBBLOOD, 72; JMBWHAT, 21–24; JMBIGIL1, 863–82.

Enoch Tells of Adam's Baptism by Water and by Fire

⁶⁴ "And it came to pass, when the Lord had spoken with Adam, our father, that Adam cried unto the Lord, and he was caught away by the Spirit of the Lord, and was carried down into the water, and was laid under the water, and was brought forth out of the water. ⁶⁵ And thus he was baptized, and the Spirit of God descended upon him, and thus he was born of the Spirit, and became quickened in the inner man. ⁶⁶ And he heard a voice out of heaven, saying: 'Thou art baptized with fire, and with the Holy Ghost. This is the record of the Father, and the Son, from henceforth and forever.'"

Adam Receives the Fulness of the Priesthood; Is Made a Son of God

⁶⁷ "'And thou art after the order of him who was without beginning of days or end

6:63   and in earth, also serves as a witness of Him. Nibley observes: "There's a wonderful passage in Santillana on this. The ancients believed we live in the midst of a great manifold in which everything reflects everything else. This is a beautiful expression of it. . . . The earth is a reflection of heaven, and heaven a reflection of the earth. We use the language of one to describe what's going on in the other time and again. We regard the temple here, as the ancients always did, as reflecting the heavenly pattern" (HWNPGP, 280). See Moses 6:33. Compare Romans 1:19–20; Alma 30:41, 44; Helaman 8:24.

6:64   *caught away by the Spirit of the Lord, and . . . carried down into the water.* See Moses 5:9.

6:65   *baptized.* Logically, this baptism might have occurred soon after the angel's explanation of the meaning of the law of sacrifice (Moses 5:6–8). In addition to the explicit mention of the ordinance in Moses 6:65, Adam's baptism plausibly can be inferred from the mention of the Father, the Son, and the Holy Ghost in Moses 5:9.

6:66   *This is the record of the Father, and the Son.* See Moses 6:34, 61. Although the "Holy Ghost . . .[,] which beareth record of the Father and the Son" previously "fell upon Adam" for a moment (Moses 5:9), the "Comforter" that he is promised in Moses 6:61 will henceforth "abide" in him, recalling the promise in John 14:16 of "another Comforter" that would "abide" with the disciples "for ever."

In an 1839 discourse on the topic of the Second Comforter, the Prophet Joseph Smith taught that it is "our privilege to pray for and obtain" the knowledge that we are sealed up to eternal life. In order to prepare for this privilege, we are told in revelation to "give diligent heed to the words of eternal life" and to "live by every word that proceedeth forth from the mouth of God." The Prophet explained that initially it is the First Comforter, the Holy Ghost, which "shall teach you." Eventually, almost certainly in the next life, the joyous moment will come when, at last, as the Savior promised, "ye [shall] come to Me and My Father" (JSWORDS, Before 8 August 1839 (3), 14–15). See MOSESS 16.

6:67   *after the order of him who was without beginning of days or end of years.* There is a single highest order of the priesthood, but it is called by different names. For example, in Doctrine and Covenants we read about "they who are priests and kings, who have received of [God's] fulness, and of his glory." They are described in relation to variously named orders as being "after the order of Melchizedek, which was after the order of Enoch, which was after the order of the Only Begotten Son" (Doctrine and Covenants 76:56–57). Brigham Young explained:

Our calling is to preach the Gospel, initiate people into, and proceed with the organization of the kingdom of God as far as we can, preparatory to the coming of the Son of Man. We have commenced to organize . . . in the Holy Order that God has established for His people in all ages of the world when he has had a kingdom upon the earth. We may call it the Order of Enoch, the Order of Joseph, the Order of Peter, or Abraham, or Moses, and then go back to Noah (JD, 17:113).

of years, from all eternity to all eternity. [68] Behold, thou art one in me, a son of God; and thus may all become my sons. Amen.'"

6:67   *from all eternity to all eternity.* Compare Moses 7:29, 31. See also Moses 7:41, 53.

6:68   *son of God.* Compare Moses 6:15; 7:1; 8:13. Moses 6:67 makes it clear that to be made a son of God is to receive the fulness of the Holy Priesthood after the Order of the Son of God. Going further, Elder Bruce R. McConkie wrote:

> After baptism, and after celestial marriage, [Adam and Eve] . . . charted for themselves a course leading to eternal life, they pressed forward with a steadfastness in Christ (2 Nephi 31:20)—believing, obeying, conforming, consecrating, sacrificing—until their calling and election was made sure (2 Peter 1:10) and they were sealed up unto eternal life (Doctrine and Covenants 131:5).

Elder McConkie further taught: "We have power to become the sons of God, to be adopted into the family of the Lord Jesus Christ, to have Him as our Father, to be one with Him as He is one with His Father. . . . As the sons of God, we also have power to advance and progress until we become 'joint-heirs with Christ' (Romans 8:17), until we have 'conformed to the image' (Romans 8:29) of God's Son, as Paul expressed it" (JMBIGIL2, 84; MOSESS 21).

thus may all become my sons. The ordinances are the same for each and available to all. Compare Moses 7:1: "Many have believed and become the sons of God."

CHAPTER 7
ENOCH, THE PROPHET AND FOUNDER OF ZION

THOSE WHO BELIEVED ADAM'S TEACHINGS BECAME SONS OF GOD

7 [1] And it came to pass that Enoch continued his speech, saying: "Behold, our father Adam taught these things, and many have believed and become the sons of God, and many have believed not, and have perished in their sins,

7   Moses 7 builds on Enoch's previous credentials as a seer, preacher, and teacher to give us a sense of him as a prophet. The text is a witness of this transition, relating that after having concluded his *preaching* of the plan of salvation, "from that time forth Enoch began to *prophesy* . . . unto the people" (v. 2; emphasis added). In preparation for the visions that were the source of his prophecies, the Lord instructs Enoch to ascend Mt. Simeon, where he is "clothed upon with glory" as he speaks to the Lord "face to face" (vv. 3–4; MOSESS 22). He witnesses a vision of the tribes and is charged to call them to repentance (vv. 5–11; MOSESS 23). The enemies of the people of God come to battle but are defeated—not by military force, but rather by the "power of the language which God had given" to Enoch (vv. 12–17; MOSESS 6, 12, 24).

After a brief account of the founding of Zion, the City of Holiness (vv. 18–19), Enoch's "grand vision" opens. Most of part 1 of the grand vision is structured in the form of what scholars term a judgment speech (vv. 28–40), following the general model of Isaiah 1 and Deuteronomy 32 (MOSESS 25). The speech witnesses the sorrow of God and the heavens themselves for the wickedness and misery of the people (MOSESS 28). It also contains God's proposal for a merciful resolution of the people's troubles, "inasmuch as they will repent" and accept the suffering of His "Chosen" for their sins (v. 39; MOSESS 15). After hearing God's speech, Enoch is overcome and, in empathetic resonance, also bursts out in weeping. In a moving description of the depths of Enoch's sorrow, we are told that he "stretched forth his arms, and his heart swelled wide as eternity; and his bowels yearned; and all eternity shook" (v. 41; MOSESS 28).

In part 2 of the grand vision (vv. 44–67), the Lord informs and comforts Enoch with a vision of the "coming of the Son of Man" (v. 47; MOSESS 15) and of "all things, even unto the end of the world" (v. 67; MOSESS 29). Summarizing the happy culmination of Enoch's arduous mission, the chapter concludes with the report that Enoch and his righteous city of Zion were received up into God's own bosom (v. 69; MOSESS 30).

A count of the thematic resemblances between Moses 6–7 and ancient Enoch texts is discussed in figure 6–4. Of course, some are stronger and more specific than others. Using Loren T. Stuckenbruck's study as a model, motifs common to Moses 6–7 and ancient Enoch texts that are also found elsewhere in the Bible or other Second Temple texts were separated from those that appear exclusively or nearly exclusively in the sampled ancient literature on Enoch. The results were impressive. Of the thirty resemblances identified, twenty were to themes or terms/phrases that are rare or absent outside of the Enoch literature. Thus, it seems that the Book of Moses is not merely hitting on themes in the Enoch literature that are just as likely to be occur in biblical and Second Temple texts. Instead, Moses 6–7 seems to be especially well-tuned to Enoch-related themes.

7:1   ***Enoch continued his speech.*** This phrase signals the beginning of was called "Extracts from the Prophecy of Enoch" in the earliest publications of the Book of Moses (SHFJST, 103n2). Note that Enoch's discourse on "The Plan of Salvation" which ends here, began in Moses 6:43 with identical words: "Enoch continued his speech."

many have believed and become the sons of God. Importantly, the Hebrew term for "sons of God" is gender neutral. Thus, it would not be inappropriate to suggest that the term "children of God" be used in its place. However, it seems even more fitting to follow King Benjamin's example

Figure 7–1. *Detail of from the Manichaean Cosmology Painting depicting a solitary, repentant individual, possibly depicting Mahaway/Mahujah kneeling atop a high mountain.*

MAHIJAH/MAHUJAH/MAHAWAY'S SECOND, HEAVENLY JOURNEY TO ENOCH

In *BG*, Mahaway's role as a messenger and go-between for the *gibborim* results in his taking two separate journeys to meet Enoch. In contrast, readers of the Book of Moses usually assume that the similarly named Mahijah met Enoch only once (Moses 6:40). However, the OT1 Book of Moses manuscript seems to imply that Mahijah made a second journey to see Enoch alone at a sacred place, perhaps corresponding to Mahaway's second, heavenly journey in *BG* (see commentary on Moses 7:2).

In the detail from the Manichaean Cosmology Painting (MCP) shown above, a lone figure kneels repentantly on the top of the only other mountain shown in the scene. Significantly, the mountain on which the figure kneels is nearer to Mount Sumēru—in other words closer to the sacred center of the scene—than the other repentant *gibborim* who kneel more distantly to the north and east on the other side of the river.

So far as I am aware, no *BG* scholar has attempted to identify this uniquely prominent figure. However it is hard to imagine a better candidate than Mahijah/Mahujah/Mahaway. But why would a repentant Mahijah/Mahujah/Mahaway be perched alone on a mountain top? The OT1 version of Moses 7:2 provides a possible answer in its statement that "Mahujah and [Enoch] cried unto the Lord" (SHFJST, 103).

Moses 7:2 spells the similar name differently than Moses 6:40—"Mahujah" instead of "Mahijah." If the difference is taken as deliberate and meaningful—and if the name indeed refers to the same individual—the sacred setting of the change, in close association with the mention of Enoch's being "clothed upon with glory" (Moses 7:2) may be suggestive. The situation recalls the bestowal of "new" names upon biblical figures such as Abram/Abraham, Sarai/Sarah, Jacob/Israel, and others. In a description that seems to highlight both Enoch's personal investment in the spiritual progress of Mahujah/Mahaway as well as the sacred symbolism of names in initiatory rites, *BG* obliquely relates the brief remembrance of Mahaway that Enoch "very affectionately . . . called out my name." *BG* scholar Jens Wilkens comments, "One is tempted to postulate an emotional relationship between [Mahaway] and Enoch" (JWIREMARKS, 226).

Then, as Mahaway departed, Enoch spoke to him a last time: "I call you, o son of Virogdad, I know [this: you are like some of them." The sense of the warning seems to be "you are *too much* like some of them." Thus, the statement might be seen as anticipating that Mahujah/Mahaway, like the wicked faction of the *gibborim*, would ultimately reject the invitation to continue following Enoch. Later, *BG* records the following words as a lament for Mahaway's violent death: "Slain, slain was that angel who was great, [that messenger whom they had]. Dead were those who were joined with flesh" (Sundermann, *Mittelpersische*, M5900, l. 1574–77, as translated in JCRGIANTS, 123). See JMBGIANTS, 1108–14.

and are looking forth with fear, in torment, for the fiery indignation of the wrath of God to be poured out upon them."

THE HEAVENS OPEN AND ENOCH IS CLOTHED WITH GLORY

2 And from that time forth Enoch began to prophesy, saying unto the people, that: "As I was journeying, and stood upon the place Mahujah, and cried unto the Lord,

7:1   and speak of "sons and daughters of God" (Mosiah 5:7). Why so? Although the Church teaches that every mortal in the beginning was a child of heavenly parents, the scriptures frequently teach that only the most faithful of God's offspring will be given "power to become the sons [and daughters] of God" (John 1:12. Compare Psalms 2:7; 110:4; John 1:12–13; Romans 8:19; Ephesians 4:13; Hebrews 7:3; 1 John 3:1–3; Mosiah 5:7; 3 Nephi 9:17; Moroni 7:48; Doctrine and Covenants 128:23; Moses 6:22, 68; 7:1; 8:13). While the present verse is correct in describing "belief" as the first step, "becoming" is the natural result of *continued* belief and faithfulness. Compare SHFJST, NT2 p. 105, p. 442–43; Doctrine and Covenants 11:30.

looking forth with fear, in torment, for the fiery indignation of the wrath of God to be poured out upon them. This is a reference to the condition of those in spirit prison (Alma 40:14). Compare with the fate of the sons of the Watchers in *1 Enoch* 9:10 (GWN1ENOCH1, p. 202) and with the description in Jude 1:6 of the misery of "the angels which kept not their first estate" and who are "reserved in everlasting chains under darkness unto the judgment of the great day."

the wrath of God to be poured out upon them. Compare, for example Revelation 16:19: "the cup of the wine of the fierceness of [God's] wrath." In scripture, the symbol of the "cup" is sometimes linked to Jesus' sufferings (Mark 14:36; 3 Nephi 11:11). Other scripture paints God's wrath either as a liquid (Job 21:20; Hosea 5:10; Revelation 19:15) or as a fire kindled by God (Numbers 11:33; Psalm 106:40; Jeremiah 44:6). Perhaps there is a connection to the liquids poured out during some sacrificial ceremonies in sacred settings, often in connection with making covenants (Genesis 28:18; 35:14; Leviticus 14:10–18; 2 Kings 16:13; Hosea 9:4; Micah 6:7.

7:2   *stood.* In ancient world, standing before the Lord can symbolize the role of a king's attendant. It is a posture that demonstrates readiness to listen and promptly carry out divine instructions (JMBSTANDING, 75–76).

the place. Draper, Brown, and Rhodes observe that in a scriptural context the Hebrew term corresponding to "the place" often describes a sacred location (RDDPGP, 112; JMBGIANTS, 1112-13, 1236nn355–369).

Mahujah. Scholars agree that Mahujah is a variant on the name Mahijah (Moses 6:40; see figure 6–5), perhaps signaling that a new name had been given to him at this point in the account (JMBGIANTS, 1113–14).

Additional hints of the sacredness of the occasion are provided by differences in the OT1 manuscript of this verse. Based on these differences, Salvatore Cirillo argues for this reading: "As I was journeying and stood *in the place, Mahujah and I* cried unto the Lord. There came a voice out of heaven, saying—Turn ye, and get ye upon the mount Simeon" (SHFJST, 103). This reading turns the name Mahujah into a personal name instead of a place name—in other words, Enoch is seen as "standing *with*" Mahujah, rather than "*on* Mahujah" (JMBGIANTS, 1112). This interpretation also with *BG* text fragments that describe a second journey of Mahaway to visit Enoch and an illustration within the MCP that may be intended to show Mahaway praying on a high mountain (see figure 7–1). Non-Latter-day Saint scholar Salvatore Cirillo found such parallels impressive, concluding, "The emphasis that [Joseph] Smith places on Mahijah's travel to Enoch is eerily similar to the account of Mahaway to Enoch in [*BG*]" (JMBIGIL2, 45n96).

cried unto the Lord. As Draper, Brown, and Rhodes emphasize, it is the cry of the righteous that mobilizes the Lord to take action—whether it be in providing further knowledge and understanding (as we see in the story of Enoch), in taking action to correct injustices, or in delivering His people from their distress (RDDPGP, 113. See JMBIGIL2, 128).

"I Was Clothed Upon with Glory"

Figure 7–2. Frederick James Shields, 1833–1911: *Enoch*

The pseudepigraphal books of *2 Enoch* and *3 Enoch* claim to describe in detail the process by which Enoch was "clothed upon with glory" (Moses 7:3). As a prelude to Enoch's introduction to the secrets of creation, Andrei Orlov observes that both accounts describe a "two-step initiatory procedure" whereby "the patriarch was first initiated by angel(s) and after this by the Lord" Himself.

In *2 Enoch*, God commanded His angels to "extract Enoch from (his) earthly clothing. And anoint him with my delightful oil, and put him into the clothes of my glory" (FIA2ENOCH, 22:8 [J], p. 138). Philip Alexander speaks of Enoch's transfiguration as an "ontological transformation which blurred the distinction between human and divine," amounting to "deification." In the first chapter of the Book of Moses, Moses underwent a similar transformation. He explained that if he had seen God without such a change, he would have "withered and died in his presence; but his glory was upon me; and . . . I was transfigured before him" (Moses 1:11). After Enoch was changed, he resembled God so exactly that he was, in some Jewish accounts, mistaken for Him.

To summarize, in this event Enoch became a "son of God" through the sealing power, having been remade in God's "image" and "likeness" (Moses 6:68; 2:26). In this sense, sealing can be seen not only as the means of "linking" but also as the result of "identifying." Throughout history, seals have provided a unique stamp of identity on important documents—the image of the author being transferred, as it were, to the document itself. Similarly, Luke T. Johnson sees the scriptural concept of sealing as both an empowering and an "imprinting" process, echoing Alma's words about receiving God's "image" in our countenances (Alma 5:14).

After his glorification, Enoch declares "I know thee" and speaks of the "right" that God has given him to the divine throne (Moses 7:59). Note that Enoch did not then receive the divine throne itself, but rather was granted a promissory right to receive it at some future time. This theme is also very much at home in the pseudepigraphic Enoch literature. For example, in the *Book of Parables* we are told that God's Chosen One "will sit on the throne of glory" (GWN1ENOCH2, 45:3, p. 148). And in *3 Enoch*, Enoch declares, "He (God) made me a throne like the throne of glory" (PSA3ENOCH, 10:1, p. 263)). Hugh Nibley showed these resemblances to Enoch scholar Matthew Black and said that they "really knocked Professor Black over. . . . It really staggered him."

Agreeing with the Latter-day Saint view that every person is invited to follow in the footsteps of Enoch, Charles Mopsik concludes that Enoch's ascent should not be seen as a unique event. Rather, he writes that the "enthronement of Enoch is a prelude to the transfiguration of the righteous—and at their head the Messiah—in the world to come, a transfiguration that is the restoration of the figure of the perfect Man"—called in a Dead Sea Scrolls text "all the glory of Adam." Following this ideological trajectory to its full extent, Latter-day Saints see the perfect Man (with a capital *M*), into whose form the Messiah and Enoch and all the righteous are transfigured, as God the Father, of whom Adam, the first mortal man, is a type. Fittingly, as part of Joseph Smith's account of Enoch's vision, God proclaims His primary identity to be that of an "Endless and Eternal" Man, declaring, "Man of Holiness is my name" (Moses 7:35; see also Moses 6:57; MOSESS 22). See JMBGIANTS, 1115–18.

there came a voice out of heaven, saying—'Turn ye, and get ye upon the mount Simeon.' ³ And it came to pass that I turned and went up on the mount; and as I stood upon the mount, I beheld the heavens open, and I was clothed upon with glory; ⁴ and I saw the Lord; and he stood before my face, and he talked with me, even as a man talketh one with another, face to face; and he said unto me: 'Look, and I will show unto thee the world for the space of many generations.'"

ENOCH'S VISION AND PROPHECY TO THE TRIBES

⁵ "And it came to pass that I beheld in the valley of Shum, and lo, a great people which dwelt in tents, which were the people of Shum. ⁶ And again the Lord said unto me: 'Look'; and I looked towards the north, and I beheld the people of Canaan, which dwelt in tents. ⁷ And the Lord said unto me: 'Prophesy'; and I prophesied, saying: 'Behold the people of Canaan, which are numerous, shall go forth in battle

7:2   ***Turn ye.*** This command enjoins something more than physical movement. Though the Hebrew term *teshuvah* literally denotes "return," it also means "repentance" or "conversion" in its spiritual sense. The Lord turns to us when we turn to Him (see, e.g., Zechariah 1:3; Malachi 3:7). See figure 3–4.

    the mount Simeon. In an uncanonized revelation on Enoch found in Revelation Book 2, this place is called the "Mountain of God." The name Simeon (Hebrew *Shim'on*) is thought to come from the Hebrew *shama'* ("to hear"), as described in Genesis 29:33. Remembering that Enoch preached "upon the hills and the high places" (Moses 6:37), Nibley associates the term Simeon with the idea of "an audition, a hearing, attention, a place of preaching," or "conversation," and therefore with an "exchange of ideas" (HWNPGP, 281). Thus, Simeon is a fitting name for a meeting place between Enoch and the Lord. Incidentally, there is a Mt. Simeon (*Jabal Sem'an*) in Syria—also known as Mt. Nebo. There Moses received a vision of the promised land (JMBIGIL2, 129). See DCAEARLY, 555–56 for a discussion of a possible location for Mount Simeon.

7:3   ***I turned and went up on the mount.*** Enoch's response is immediate (RDDPGP, 113). The use of "I" rather than "we" implies that Mahujah/Mahaway declined to follow Enoch to higher ground.

    I was clothed upon with glory. This event anticipates v. 17, where not just Enoch but rather all his people will glorified. Nibley observes that putting on clothing in a temple context is in symbolic imitation of being transfigured to a glorious state (JMBIGIL2, 129; MOSESS 22).

7:4   ***face to face.*** Compare Moses 1:31 and Exodus 33:11.

    many generations. In vv. 4–11, Enoch is given a limited vision of the tribes that stops just short of the events of the Flood (MOSESS 23). Later, starting in v. 20, Enoch is given a grand vision that shows God's work on this earth from the beginning to the end. Why was such a vision necessary? Nibley observes, "Before the king can take over his throne, the king must go to heaven and see the field of his labors, which is shown him on a map, and receive his assignment" (HWNPGP, 281).

7:5   ***valley of Shum . . . people of Shum.*** Draper, Brown, and Rhodes point out that the joint reference to the "people of Shum" and the "valley of Shum" provides a precedent for naming places after a notable ancestor (RDDPGP, 115).

    Shum. "The name is likely a variant of Shem, itself meaning 'name'" (RDDPGP, 115).

7:6   ***people of Canaan.*** "This people is not the same as 'the seed of Cain' (v. 22). Although both groups were ostracized because of skin pigmentation (vv. 8, 22), their tribal names are of different origin" (RDDPGP, 115). Whether there is any connection between these antediluvian Canaanites and the later group of the same name that inhabited the area of Palestine is unknown. The first

array against the people of Shum, and shall slay them that they shall utterly be destroyed; and the people of Canaan shall divide themselves in the land, and the land shall be barren and unfruitful, and none other people shall dwell there but the people of Canaan; ⁸ for behold, the Lord shall curse the land with much heat, and the barrenness thereof shall go forth forever.' And there was a blackness came upon all the children of Canaan, that they were despised among all people. ⁹ And it came to pass that the Lord said unto me: 'Look'; and I looked, and I beheld the land of Sharon, and the land of Enoch, and the land of Omner, and the land of Heni, and

7:6	mention of "Canaan" in the Bible is as the name of the son of Ham, who was the son of Noah (Genesis 9:18). The "Canaanites" mentioned in Abraham 1:21–22 are said to have been Ham's descendants, but no explicit connection is made between them and the land of "Canaan" where Abraham was commanded to go when he left Ur of the Chaldees (Abraham 2:1–4).
7:7	***Prophesy.*** Having received his divine commission as a prophet, Enoch is now commanded to warn the people. The prophetic declaration he now utters now in heaven foreshadows the message he will later proclaim to the people themselves.

the land shall be barren and unfruitful. The punishment is "measure for measure." Because the Canaanites had wickedly conspired to exterminate the people of Shum and take their land, the land would be cursed for their sake. The curse and its murderous provocation parallel the experience of Cain on a larger scale (Moses 5:36). Note that this prophecy about the unfruitfulness of the land is in direct contrast with the Lord's promise given in Exodus 23:26 to the Israelites, who were to be given their own land of Canaan with the promise that: "There shall be none barren or unfruitful in your land." Note that my translation here deliberately parallels the wording of the verse in Moses by drawing on the synonymous adjectives of the Greek (rather than the Hebrew) text of Exodus (*ágonos* "childless" and *steira* "sterile"). These terms are "typically used for female infertility" but in Moses are applied poetically to the land itself (DMGEXODUS, 407).

barren. See v. 8: "The barrenness thereof shall go forth forever."

none other people shall dwell there but the people of Canaan. Here is a second contrast to the later Israelites in their land of Canaan. The Israelites were told that the other peoples inhabiting the land would be driven out little by little rather than all at once (Exodus 23:30). Unlike the Book of Moses people of Canaan, Israel was never alone in the promised land.

7:8	*curse the land.* The words are again reminiscent of the story of Cain (Moses 5:36; compare Moses 4:23). Contrast Moses 7:17, when the Lord "blessed the land" on behalf of the people of God.

the barrenness thereof shall go forth forever. See v. 7. In line with KPJMOSES, 164, the phrase ends with a period rather than a semicolon, indicating that what follows is Enoch's observation rather than the continuation of his prophecy.

a blackness. The fact that a blackness "came upon" the children of Canaan contradicts any notion that these people inherited dark skin because they were of the lineage of Cain (see related commentary in verses 6 and 22). Nibley's explanation of the Arab concept of *aswad* ("black") versus *abyad* ("white") is of interest here: those Arabs who live out in tents in the heat are called "black," while those who live in the shelter of stone houses in the city are seen as "white" (HWNPGP, 282). Also of interest is the fact that "black" and "white" in Arabic can be used to refer to levels of moral cleanliness and purity. Such a distinction is found in *3 Enoch* 44:6, where Rabbi Ishmael is shown the spirits suffering in Sheol and comments that "the faces of the wicked souls were as black as the bottom of a pot, because of the multitude of their wicked deeds" (PSA3ENOCH, p. 295). See further discussion in APSBOOK, 291–94.

they were despised among all people. Though the wicked who despised the Canaanites are not to be excused in the least for their hatred (see JMSBEHOLD), neither were the Canaanites exonerated by the Lord for their decimation of the people of Shum, as evidenced by the curse on their land in vv. 7–8. On this point, the otherwise insightful article on this topic by Adam Stokes

the land of Shem, and the land of Haner, and the land of Hanannihah, and all the inhabitants thereof; [10] and the Lord said unto me: 'Go to this people, and say unto them—"Repent," lest I come out and smite them with a curse, and they die.' [11] And he gave unto me a commandment that I should baptize in the name of the Father, and of the Son, which is full of grace and truth, and of the Holy Ghost, which beareth record of the Father and the Son."

THE POWER OF ENOCH'S WORD DEFEATS ENEMIES OF THE PEOPLE OF GOD

[12] And it came to pass that Enoch continued to call upon all the people, save it were the people of Canaan, to repent; [13] and so great was the faith of Enoch that he led

seems mistaken (ASPEOPLE). While Stokes rightfully notes that the seed of Cain are excluded from the Lord's cursing of the "residue of the people" in Moses 7:22, we unfortunately have no basis in the text nor any warrant for inferring indirectly that the Canaanites were also exempt from that penalty (contra ASPEOPLE, 163, 175–76). See commentary on v. 22 "the seed of Cain."

7:9   *Sharon.* "Sharon" appears as a place name in the Bible in 1 Chronicles 5:16; 27:29; Song of Solomon 2:1; Isaiah 33:9; 35:2; 65:10.

    Enoch. Presumably, this place was not named after the prophet but rather after Enoch, the son of Cain (Moses 5:42–43, 49).

    Omner. In the Book of Mormon, "Omner" is the name of a son of Mosiah (Mosiah 27:34).

    Heni. This name does not appear elsewhere in scripture.

    Shem. Besides being the name of Noah's son (see, for example, Moses 7:9; 8:12, 27), "Shem" is the name of a land in the Book of Mormon (Mormon 2:20–21). It is also used as a personal name in Mormon 6:14.

    Haner. This name does not appear elsewhere in scripture.

    Hanannihah. This name does not appear elsewhere in scripture.

7:10   *Go to this people.* Apparently, "this people" included the groups of people named in v. 9 but not the people of Canaan (see v. 12).

    Repent, lest I come out and smite them with a curse. The Lord's requirement that the people repent or be cursed is found throughout scripture. For example, the commandments given to Israel in Deuteronomy 28 include blessings and cursings conditioned on obedience. The result of continued rebellion is destruction or death.

7:11   *baptize in the name of the Father, and of the Son, which is full of grace and truth, and of the Holy Ghost.* Compare these instructions regarding baptism and the directive to preach repentance in the previous verse with the guidelines that the Lord gave to Adam regarding the teaching of his children (Moses 6:57–59). Although Moses 6:52 states that baptism should be performed in the name of the Son and vv. 57–59 show God referring to the Son and the Spirit in His explanation of spiritual rebirth, v. 11 marks the first example of using titles of all three members of the Godhead in the baptismal ordinance as is done today (Doctrine and Covenants 20:73).

    which beareth record of the Father and the Son. The same expression is used in Moses 5:9. The use of the term "record" recalls the titles of the Holy Ghost given in Moses 6:61, 66: "the record of heaven" and "the record of the Father, and the Son." See also Moses 6:63: "All things are created and made to bear record of me."

7:12   *all the people, save it were the people of Canaan.* The restricted scope of Enoch's ministry outlined here is in contrast to the universal extent of the teachings of the "preachers of righteousness" that preceded him (Moses 6:23). There is no explanation for why the people of Canaan are excluded from Enoch's preaching. Following the narrative, we may suppose that the reason relates to their violence against the people of Shum (Moses 7:7).

7:13   *so great was the faith of Enoch.* This is a fulfillment of Moses 6:32–34. When we read the text of

Figure 7–3. Left: *Detail from the Manichaean Cosmology Painting showing Enoch and four archangels who assisted him in the battle and the gathering*; Right: *Bas-relief showing Ashurbanipal, king of Assyria, stabbing a wounded lion. North Palace, Nineveh, Mesopotamia, Iraq, ca. 645–635 BCE.*

The "Roar of the Lions" and the Defeat of the *Gibborim*

Attributing the brevity of the witness of the battles between Enoch's people and the wicked *gibborim* in the Dead Sea Scrolls fragments of *BG* to "the sparsity of the preserved remains," John C. Reeves goes on to describe how "the Manichaean remnants of the *Book of Giants* preserve extensive testimony regarding this conflict" (JCRGIANTS, 122), including the role of angels who helped Enoch (see image above left). For example, here is an extract from a Manichaean *BG* fragment that gives a more detailed account of the final combat (WBHGIANTS, Text G, 69):

> the angels themselves descended from the heaven to the earth. And (when) the two hundred demons saw those angels, they were much afraid and worried. . . . they went to fight. And those two hundred demons fought a hard battle with the [four angels], until [the angels used] fire, naphtha, and brimstone.

As angels from heaven and the very elements of earth joined to defend the people of Enoch, the battles entered a new phase. Richard Draper, Kent Brown, and Michael Rhodes explain:

> Heretofore we have found reference to "enemies" who "came to battle" against the people of God." The account in Moses 7:15 [i.e., "the people that fought against God"] makes it clear that battling against God's people [had become] the same as battling against God Himself.

Moses 7:13 adds details to the story of the defeat of Enoch's enemies:

> And so great was the faith of Enoch that he led the people of God, and their enemies came to battle against them; and he spake the word of the Lord, and the earth trembled, . . . and *the roar of the lions* was heard out of the wilderness; and all nations feared greatly (emphasis added).

Relevant details about the victory of Enoch and the people of God are also found in the Dead Sea Scrolls fragments of *BG*, including a surprising direct parallel to the strange phrase about the "roaring" in Moses 7:13: "[I] waged war on them. . . . [But they] are more powerful than me. [. . .] The *roar of the wild beasts* has come" (emphasis added).

Brian R. Doak has persuasively described why accounts of military victories were often linked to a fight with a prestige animal (a lion) in the ancient Near East (see figure at right above). But, of course, the penchant for connecting these two motifs would have been just as unfamiliar to Joseph Smith as it is to nonspecialists today. Similar phrases about the roaring of lions/wild beasts does not seem to appear anywhere else in scripture or in Jewish tradition, but do occur in almost identical contexts in the Book of Moses and *BG*. Building our earlier discussion of the role reversal of Enoch and 'Ohya as "wild men" (see the commentary on Moses 6:38), we might see a similar turning of the tables when the wild beasts and lions are surprisingly made subject to the God of Enoch rather than (as would have been expected) to his wicked adversaries. Following the bread crumbs of scholars who see a connection between the *BG* and the biblical book of Daniel, we might go further to observe that the same God who "shut the lions' mouths" to save Daniel from harm (Daniel 6:22) opened the mouth of Enoch to destroy his enemies through the "power of [his] language" (Moses 4:19). See MOSESS 12 and 24; JMBGIANTS, 1118–23.

the people of God, and their enemies came to battle against them; and he spake the word of the Lord, and the earth trembled, and the mountains fled, even according to his command; and the rivers of water were turned out of their course; and the roar of the lions was heard out of the wilderness; and all nations feared greatly, so powerful was the word of Enoch, and so great was the power of the language which God had given him. ¹⁴ There also came up a land out of the depth of the sea, and so great was the fear of the enemies of the people of God, that they fled and stood afar off and went upon the land which came up out of the depth of the sea. ¹⁵ And the giants of the land, also, stood afar off; and there went forth a curse upon all people

7:13   JST Genesis 14:26–31 (SHFJST, OT1 pp. 33–34, p. 127), we see that performing such feats of great faith was an expected part of belonging to "the order of the covenant which God made with Enoch." Melchizedek, who was "ordained an high priest" after this order, demonstrated similar faith and worked similar miracles. Compare Jacob 4:6: "Wherefore, we search the prophets, and we have many revelations and the spirit of prophecy; and having all these witnesses we obtain a hope, and our faith becometh unshaken, insomuch that we truly can command in the name of Jesus and the very trees obey us, or the mountains, or the waves of the sea."

    their enemies came to battle against them . . . and the roar of the lions was heard out of the wilderness. Nibley summarizes this passage as follows: "The wicked move against Enoch and his people in force, but are themselves forced to acknowledge the superior power supporting the patriarch. . . . And then that striking passage, so surprisingly vindicated in other Enoch texts, of the roaring lions amidst scenes of general terror" (JMBIGIL2, 133). Remarkable parallels to the Book of Moses description of the battle can be found in *BG*. See figure 7–3; MOSESS 6, 12, 24; JMBGIANTS, 1118–23.

    he spake the word of the Lord. It is significant that our account does not speak of Enoch's military might in the midst of battle but rather of how "he spake the word of the Lord, and the earth trembled, and the mountains fled, even according to his command; . . . so powerful was the word of Enoch, and so great was the power of the language which God had given him," that "all nations feared greatly." Apparently, as with the Book of Mormon peoples, the "virtue of the word of God" spoken through those called of God "had more powerful effect upon the minds of the people than the sword, or anything else" (Alma 31:5). See MOSESS 6, 12, 24.

    rivers of water were turned out of their course. This event is a fulfillment of the promise in Moses 6:34. Remarkably, Enoch's experience in the book of Moses can be compared to an Enoch account from the Mandaean *Ginza*. See MOSESS 4 and the commentary on Moses 6:34.

7:14   ***a land out of the depth of the sea.*** Following the description of other geological changes that occurred when Enoch spoke the word of the Lord is the mention of a landmass that arose "out of the depth of the sea." Nibley describes Jewish traditions that tell of the perturbation of the waters of the earth both before and after Enoch's time: "The really spectacular show in the Enoch literature is the behavior of the seas. Like the alternating drought and flood from the skies, there is either too much sea or not enough. Before 'the floods came and swallowed them up,' the sea first drew back in places, leaving its coastal beds high and dry in anticipation of the great tsunami (sea wave) which came with the earthquake" (HWNENOCH, 202).

7:15   ***giants.*** This is one of two references to "giants" in the Book of Moses—the other is Moses 8:18. Note that a distinction is made between the giants and the "enemies of the people of God" (Moses 7:14)—though we are probably safe to assume that the giants were not friendly to the people of Enoch either. There are also reports of "giants" (Hebrew *nephilim*) in the Bible. Genesis 6:4 relates that "there were giants (*nephilim*) in the earth in those days." Also, when Israelite spies went into the land of Canaan, they returned and reported that there were men of great height that inhabited the land. Among these men were "the sons of Anak, which come of the giants" (Numbers 13:32–33). In *1 Enoch*, these giants are explicitly connected with fallen angels (known

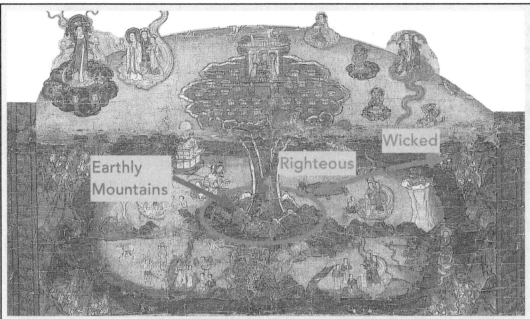

Figure 7–4. *Detail of the Manichaean Cosmology Painting with annotations showing the movement of the righteous and the wicked toward or away from Mount Sumēru respectively. Note the small mountains at the foot of Sumēru where the cities of the righteous were said to have been located.*

THE GATHERING OF ZION

The repentance of the the *gibborim* in response to Enoch's preaching was not universal. For example, a Manichaean fragment of *BG* tells us that a righteous faction were "glad at seeing the apostle" (that is, Enoch) and "assembled before him." But those who are called "tyrants and criminals" became "afraid."

Book of Moses readers will recall that the righteous followers of Enoch were eventually brought to a place of safety where "the Lord came and dwelt with his people. . . . And Enoch . . . built a city that was called the City of Holiness, even Zion" (Moses 7:16, 19). An interesting feature of one of the Manichaean *BG* fragments is that it not only tells us of such a gathering but also of the *direction* the people traveled:

> And [angels] led one half of them eastwards, and the other half westwards, on the skirts of four huge mountains, towards the foot of the Sumēru [= "good Mēru"] mountain, into thirty-two towns which the Living Spirit had prepared for them in the beginning.)

Although this *BG* passage highlights only the prominent role of the angels in leading the battles and gathering the righteous, we can safely presume that the role of Enoch was closely intertwined with that of the angels. For example, elsewhere in *BG* Enoch is said to have been protected by these angels (WBHGIANTS, text A, frg. 1, p. 61) and the angels and Enoch seem to be shown together visually in the Manichaean Cosmology Painting (see figure 7–3). Although no reason is given for why only one part of the *gibborim* were led westward to the cities, *BG* scholar Matthew Goff concluded that "the division of the [*gibborim*] along an east-west axis suggests two opposed fates for them—one half was killed and the other survived." Going further, we might infer that some of the [*gibborim*] repented and changed their ways while others did not. The angels ultimately led the wicked to their eventual destruction in the east—away from the "sacred center"—while the righteous went westward to inhabit cities near the foot of the holy mountain that had been prepared for them "in the beginning" (see the annotations on the figure above).

There is another important detail that should be signaled: *BG* describes the righteous dwelling "westwards, on the skirts of four huge mountains" (WBHGIANTS, txt A, frg. 1, p. 61). Significantly, this imagery recalls Moses 7:17, which relates that the righteous "were blessed upon the mountains, and upon the high places, and did flourish." Where in all the ancient Enoch tradition do we find the remarkably similar story of the gathering of Enoch's converts to a community of refuge in the mountains? Only in *BG* and the Book of Moses.

For more details, see MOSESS 10–13, 24.

that fought against God; [16] and from that time forth there were wars and bloodshed among them.

ENOCH'S PEOPLE GATHER TO ZION AND KEEP THE LAW OF CONSECRATION

But the Lord came and dwelt with his people, and they dwelt in righteousness. [17] The fear of the Lord was upon all nations, so great was the glory of the Lord, which was upon his people. And the Lord blessed the land, and they were blessed upon the mountains, and upon the high places, and did flourish.

[18] And the Lord called his people ZION, because

7:15   as the Watchers). In this tradition—which is inspired by Genesis 6:1–4 but rejected by the Book of Moses (see 8:13–14) (see figure **8-3**)—the giants are the offspring of the Watchers and mortal women. Jubilees 7:21–25 indicates that one of the reasons that the Lord sent the great Flood was to cleanse the earth of the wickedness and violence of the *nephilim*. For a discussion of the *nephilim* and the related term *gibborim*, see figure 6-4 and MOSESS 5.

     a curse. Not a curse on the land but on the people themselves who, "from that time forth," engaged in "wars and bloodshed" (v. 16).

     all people that fought against God. The "enemies of the people of God" (v. 14) are now described as the enemies of God Himself.

7:16   *the Lord came and dwelt with his people.* Compare Revelation 21:3. Joseph Smith taught that Enoch brought his people "into the presence of God" (JSWORDS, Before August 1839 (1), 9). Brigham Young further said that their calling and election was made sure and that they entered into the rest of the Lord (JD, 3:320). They became members of the church of the Firstborn, which also has been called the church of Enoch (Doctrine and Covenants 76:67).

7:17   *The fear of the Lord was upon all nations.* Compare 2 Chronicles 17:10. The language recalls the Lord's deliverance of Israel from Egypt and prophecies of the events of the last days. See Isaiah 2:10, 19, 21; 24:23; 29:8 (2 Nephi 27:3); 31:4; 60:1–22; Revelation 6:12–17; 16:17–21; 1 Nephi 22:14.

     the glory of the Lord, which was upon his people. Previously, it was Enoch who was "clothed upon with glory" (v. 3). Now all his people have been glorified.

     blessed the land. Contrast v. 8, when the Lord cursed the land of the people of Canaan.

     blessed upon the mountains, and upon the high places. Mountains and high places are the favored locations for sanctuaries (RDDPGP, 120). See figure 7-4 and MOSESS 24.

7:18   *the Lord called his people ZION.* The word "Zion," which probably predates the arrival of the Israelites, may be related to the Hebrew root ṣwn (Arabic ṣâna), which means "to protect, preserve," defend, " consistent with its description as a fortified hill in 2 Samuel 5:7 (see also APSBOOK, 297n50). This is consistent with Zion's depiction in Doctrine and Covenants 45:66 as "a land of peace, a city of refuge, a place of safety for the saints of the Most High God."

     In contrast to typical biblical usage that associates "Zion" with a place-name the environs of Jerusalem, in Doctrine and Covenants 97:21 the Lord applies the name to a group of *people*: "for this is Zion—the pure in heart." Draper, Brown, and Rhodes observe that in Moses 7:18 it is the Lord "who conferred the name on His people, itself a sacred act" (RDDPGP, 120). The Lord called His people Zion because they kept the crowning covenant of *the law of consecration*, identified in scripture as "the law of a celestial kingdom" (Doctrine and Covenants 88:22). In their faithfulness to this and all others of the Lord's covenants, "they were of one heart and one mind, and dwelt in righteousness; and there was no poor among them" (Moses 7:18).

     In Isaiah 51:16 there is a precedent for the Lord's definition of Zion as a people rather than a place. As part of a passage that evokes a new creation of heaven and earth, God reaffirms His unwavering love by declaring the covenant formula: "I . . . say unto Zion, Thou art my people" (compare Isaiah 49:2; Hosea 1:8–11; 2:23). President George Q. Cannon taught: "As a people

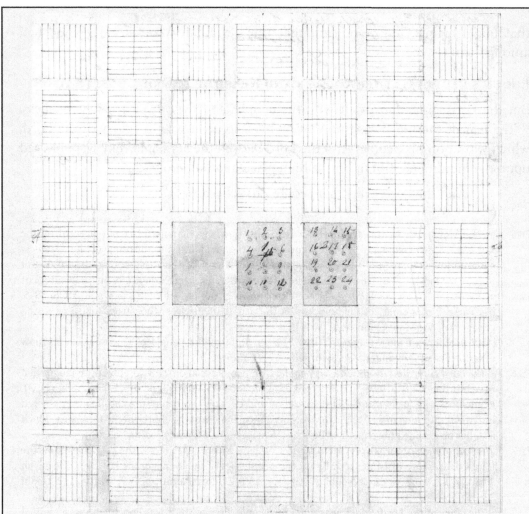

Figure 7–5. *Original City of Zion Plat Drawing (detail), with twenty-four numbered temple sites located in the center, June 1833.*

THE HIEROCENTRIC LAYOUT OF LATTER-DAY ZION

Whether or not by sheer coincidence, the symbolic geography shared by the Manichaean *BG* fragments and the Manichaean Cosmology Painting (MCP) are mirrored in a general way in the itinerary of the gathering and the layout for Joseph Smith's City of Zion in Missouri. Intriguingly, this latter-day city is described in modern scripture in close connection with descriptions of Enoch's ancient city (see for example, Doctrine and Covenants 45:11–14). As the righteous of Enoch's day were remembered by *BG* as having been divinely led westward, so the early Saints were told by the Lord: "gather ye out from the eastern lands" and "go ye forth into the western countries" (Doctrine and Covenants 45:64, 66).

Moreover, in both cases the destination of the western movement of each group is identified as a unique hierocentric location (see figure 4–3): for Enoch's people that location was Mount Sumēru in the middle of the world map, while for the early Saints that location was "Mount Zion, which shall be the city of New Jerusalem" (Doctrine and Covenants 84:2), a relatively central location on the North American continent. Significantly, the city of New Jerusalem envisioned by the Saints is expressly called in revelation, "the center place" (Doctrine and Covenants 57:3) or "center stake" (Brigham Young, JD, 18:242).

Finally, while the cosmology painting depicts Mount Sumēru with thirty-two or thirty-six palaces at its summit, the plat for the city of Zion featured twenty-four numbered temple sites at its center. Thus, in the MCP depiction of *BG*, in the Book of Moses, and in the envisioned latter-day City of Zion, "God . . . dwelt in the midst" (Moses 7:69), literally and symbolically in the sacred center of His gathered people.

they were of one heart and one mind,
and dwelt in righteousness;
and there was no poor among them.

 ^19 And Enoch continued his preaching in righteousness unto the people of God. And it came to pass in his days, that he built a city that was called the City of Holiness, even ZION.

ENOCH'S GRAND VISION: ZION BLESSED BUT ALL OTHERS CURSED

^20 And it came to pass that Enoch talked with the Lord; and he said unto the Lord: "Surely Zion shall dwell in safety forever." But the Lord said unto Enoch: "Zion have I blessed, but the residue of the people have I cursed." ^21 And it came to pass

7:18   we are expecting the day to come when Jesus will descend in the clouds of Heaven; but before this day comes . . . the organization of society that exists in the heavens must exist on the earth; the same condition of society, so far as it is applicable to mortal beings, must exist here" (JD, 13:99). The conditions for such a society have been achieved only rarely in human history, as part of projects requiring long, sustained effort. Terryl and Fiona Givens observe: "All who have attempted to reenact Enoch's enterprise have found the transition from worldly ways to celestial society a more taxing challenge than anticipated. The hard lesson has been, that 'Zion cannot be built up unless it is by the principles of the law of the celestial kingdom' (Doctrine and Covenants 105:5). Rome is not the only city that cannot be built in a day" (TLGGOD, 114). See MOSESS 30.

one heart and one mind. At a conference of the Church held soon after Moses 7 was dictated, the Lord emphasized one of the most important lessons of Moses 7: "I say unto you, be one; and if ye are not one ye are not mine" (Doctrine and Covenants 38:27). Speaking in Nauvoo to the Relief Society, the Prophet Joseph Smith likewise taught, "All must act in concert, or nothing can be done" (JSTPJS, 30 March 1842, 202).

no poor among them. Compare 4 Nephi 1:3. Enoch and his people were, in the words of William W. Phelps, "above the pow'r of mammon" (Hymn text for "Adam-ondi-Ahman"). Latter-day Saint pioneer and author George W. Crocheron asks: "What was the primal cause which brought about this happy condition of society, socially, religiously and industrially? It was due to the people having consecrated their time, talents, and all their earthly possessions, to one common end—the good of the whole community." "The people of Zion live together in love as equals," observes A. Don Sorensen. "As equals, all receive the things that are necessary for survival and well-being, according to their circumstances, wants, and needs." See JMBIGIL2, 136.

7:19   *Enoch continued his preaching . . . unto the people of God.* Though Enoch apparently had left off the teaching of other groups, he "continued his preaching . . . unto the people of God."

the City of Holiness, even Zion. Compare v. 62: "an Holy City." Here we see the name Zion applied to the City of Holiness that Enoch built. However, it should be remembered that the city merits its appellation only because the people themselves are holy as God is holy (cf. Moses 6:57 and 7:35)—this because they, individually and as a community, are worthy to be called Zion.

7:20   *Enoch talked with the Lord.* Enoch's grand vision of eternity came about because he "talked with the Lord." The Lord responded to his questions with this all-encompassing vision. As in *3 Enoch* 45 (PSA3ENOCH, pp. 296–99), the result of Enoch's willingness to ask questions of the Lord resulted in his being shown all generations of humankind from beginning to end.

Several additional details from Enoch's vision are provided in an uncanonized revelation on Enoch in Joseph Smith's *Revelation Book 2*. For example, we learn that Enoch's vision included important events from premortal life. We are told that Enoch saw "the beginning, the ending of men; he saw the time when Adam his father was made, and he saw that he was in eternity before a grain of dust in the balance was weighed. He saw that he emanated and came down from God." The revelation was versified and published as a song. See JMBIGIL2, 449–57.

Surely Zion shall dwell in safety forever. Rejoicing in the happy fate of his people, Enoch

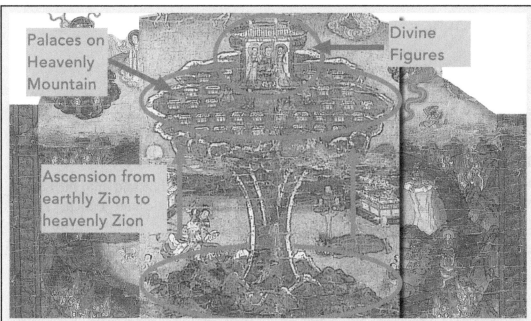

Figure 7–6. *Detail of Manichaean Cosmology Painting suggesting the ascent and transformation of thirty-two divinely prepared cities of earthly "Zion" to thirty-two palaces of heavenly "Zion" atop Mount Sumēru. The palaces surround a deity with two attendants within a thirty-third palace.*

"Zion Was Taken Up into Heaven"

BG scholar Gåbor Kósa sees the thirty-two palaces, shown "on the 'foliage' [at the top] of the tree-like Mount Sumēru" above, as implying "a divine association; this is reinforced by the presence of three divine figures in front of the [much bigger] thirty-third palace, with the central figure seated on a lotus throne and the two acolytes standing on either side. All in all, this seems to indicate the purely divine nature of this Manichaean Mount Sumēru" (GKGIANTS, 171–72). In addition, Kósa sees the description of the mountain with its tree-like iconography as resonating with the description of the mountain of God and the Tree of Life in *1 Enoch* 25:2–4 (GWN1ENOCH1, p. 312):

> Then I answered him—I, Enoch—and said, "concerning all things I wish to know, but especially concerning this tree." And he answered me and said, "this high mountain that you saw, whose peak is like the throne of God, is the seat where the Great Holy One, the Lord of glory, the King of eternity, will sit, when he descends to visit the earth in goodness. And (as for) this fragrant tree, no flesh has the right to touch it until the great judgment, in which there will be vengeance on all and a consummation forever.

The scene also evokes the imagery of Nephi's vision (1 Nephi 11:1, 3–4, 8, 25):

> I was caught away . . . into an exceedingly high mountain . . . And I said: I desire to behold the things which my father saw. And the Spirit said unto me: Believest thou that thy father saw the tree of which he hath spoken? . . . And I looked and beheld a tree; . . . and the beauty thereof was far beyond, yea, exceeding of all beauty. . . . And I . . . beheld that the tree of life was a representation of the love of God.

Going further, although Kósa recognizes an obvious correspondence of some kind between the visual depiction of thirty-two palaces at the top of Mount Sumēru and the report in a Manichaean *BG* fragment of "thirty-two towns" for the repentant *gibborim* at the base of Mount Sumēru he finds it difficult to reconcile the fact that the *palaces* shown at the top of the image above "are definitely not *towns*; [neither are they] at the *foot* of the mountains" as is described in the text of *BG* (GKGIANTS, 171–72, emphasis added).

In trying to answer the questions over which Kósa puzzled, we should recall that the Book of Moses chronicles a transformation of the *earthly* Zion, symbolically located in the *foothills* of the "mountain of the Lord," into a *heavenly* Zion, as shown in the annotated figure above. In this way, the redemptive *descensus* initiated by Jared and his brethren (see commentary on Moses 6:21) culminated in the glorious *ascensus* led by Enoch (Moses 7:69):

> And Enoch and all the people walked with God, and he dwelt in the midst of Zion; and it came to pass that Zion was not, for God received it up into his own bosom; and from thence went forth the saying, Zion is Fled.

that the Lord showed unto Enoch all the inhabitants of the earth; and he beheld, and lo, Zion, in process of time, was taken up into heaven. And the Lord said unto Enoch: "Behold mine abode forever."

7:20   exulted: "Surely Zion shall dwell in safety forever." God's reply was a gentle rebuke, affirming his love for Zion while reminding Enoch that His fatherly care extended beyond the righteous to those who have chosen the way of suffering: "Zion have I blessed, but the residue of the people have I cursed" (v. 20). God's love for those who have brought the curse of wickedness upon themselves is expressed not only by His weeping for them (Moses 7:28), but also by sending His Son, who will suffer for the sins of all who are willing to repent (Moses 7:39).

7:21   *in process of time.* Zion was received into heaven only after Enoch successfully completed his 365-year ministry (v. 68). As Elder Neal A. Maxwell observes, "Enoch—brilliant, submissive, and spiritual—knew what it meant to see a whole city-culture advance in 'process of time.' He could tell us much about so many things, including patience." Elder Maxwell also said, "The city of Enoch was not prefabricated and put up in a day. The city was built incrementally and spiritually as the individuals in that city were built incrementally and spiritually. That near-celestial culture was constructed only as individuals were improved." See JMBIGIL2, 137.

taken up into heaven. Though some early Church leaders taught that the physical city of Zion was taken up into heaven, it should also be remembered that the primary meaning of Zion is a Christlike people (see vv. 18–19). When v. 63 describes the return of the "city" of Zion, it speaks of the warm fellowship of affection between its heavenly and earthly inhabitants, not of a restoration of buildings, streets, and gardens, as is sometimes mistakenly imagined. See figure 7–6.

Behold mine abode forever. Elsewhere, the Lord uses the related term "dwell" instead of "abide," promising that the Son of Man would "dwell on the earth in righteousness for the space of a thousand years" (verse 65) and that "Zion shall dwell in safety forever" (verse 20). This raises a question. Though Moses 7:21 says that "Zion was taken up into heaven," it will later return to earth (Moses 7:62). So how can Zion be God's "abode forever"? Are we meant to understand that God will come to live on earth permanently? Yes and no. It should be remembered that when Zion returns to a renewed earth, the veil that separates heaven and earth will be rent (Moses 101:23; 67:10) and there will no longer be the same distinction between them—earth and heaven will be "gather[ed] together in one" (Doctrine and Covenants 27:13). Thus, even when God is not dwelling on earth, He will be "there" (compare Moses 7:30).

Further clarifying this idea, Elder James E. Talmage explained, "The actual person of any one member of the Godhead [cannot] be physically present in more than one place at one time." However, Blake T. Ostler explains that the Prophet Joseph Smith's revelations describe "God's immanence—the doctrine that God is present to but is not identical with all realities. Immanence is more than omnipresence or being present at all places. Immanence includes the notion that God is: (1) present in terms of power and awareness at all places; (2) able to effectuate His will at all places without intermediary; and (3) the experience or information of every reality is included within God's experience and knowledge" (JMBIGIL2, 138). It is through God's immanence that He will abide in Zion—and His Saints will abide in Him—even when He is not physically present.

abode. The use of the word "abide" (in the sense of an enduring relationship of intimate indwelling) or "abode" (in the sense of an enduring dwelling place) is a distinctive characteristic of the account of Enoch. The two terms appear nowhere else in the Pearl of Great Price. Their dense frequency of six appearances within two chapters (Moses 6:26, 34, 61; 7:21, 48, 64) can be contrasted with their significantly rarer frequency of eight appearances (only four with the same sense of meaning) in the entire Book of Mormon. The English terms "abide" and "abode" in the sense of divine indwelling also appear frequently in the Gospel of John (John 1:32; 14:16, 23; 15:4, 6, 7, 10). The Greek term *mone*, which is translated as "abode" in John 14:23 ("We [that is, the Father and the Son] will come unto him, and make our abode with him," speaking of the Second Comforter) and as "mansions" in John 14:2 ("In my Father's house are many mansions: . . . I go to prepare a place for you," speaking of the final reward of Jesus' disciples), suggests a permanent dwelling place. On the related term "bosom," see Moses 7:31.

Figure 7–7. *Angel of Revelation 14:6, Carrying a Scroll*

"ANGELS DESCENDING OUT OF HEAVEN"

Like the angel of Revelation 14:6 shown here (though certainly lacking the elegant robe, massive wings, and other Victorian trappings), the *BG* character Mahaway was envisioned as having "mounted up in the air like strong winds and [flying] with his hands like an eagle to the east of the earth and he passed above in the direction of the Paradise of Justice." Unlike the angels of Revelation 14:6 and Moses 7:25, Mahaway was not sent to proclaim the Gospel, but rather carried urgent questions to Enoch from a party of anxious *gibborim*.

Though in the symbolic geography of the ancient world a central, cosmic mountain typically represents the most sacred place on earth, the "east edge" of terrestrial geography, the dawn horizon, the location of the boundary where the round dome of heaven meets the square plane of earth, is not only where visions of God are often situated but also the "launching point" from which heavenly ascents took place.

Consistent with this view, in *1 Enoch* the prophet himself described his journey as taking him to "the ends of the earth, on which the heaven rests, and the gates of heaven open," and gave a brief account of its great beasts and birds with beautiful voices (GWN1ENOCH1, 33:1–2, p. 329). Likewise, the description of Methuselah's journey to the end of the earth in the *Genesis Apocryphon*, where Enoch's "dwelling is with the angels," "can be plausibly understood as [an allusion] to the [Garden of] Eden" (GWN1ENOCH1, 106:7, p. 536; Matthew Goff).

Couched within this symbolic geography, Mahaway's second journey to visit Enoch in *BG* "is clearly from the west to the east and back again" (JWIREMARKS, 222). Among his other qualifications to make this voyage to the eastern end of the earth, he seems to be "the only giant with wings" (JWIREMARKS, 225). Just as Enoch, who flew east with the angels, is said in ancient traditions to have used "this mode of transportation . . . to visit areas that normally humans cannot reach," so also, according to *BG* scholar Matthew Goff:

> the flight of Mahaway should be understood in a similar way. [He] is able to reach Eden because he can fly over a desolate desert that would be, following this logic, impossible to cross on foot. This underscores the extraordinary and difficult nature of [his] voyage. Asking Mahaway to undertake such an arduous journey highlights how seriously [the *gibborim*] wanted an interpretation to the two visions of 'Ohyah and Hahyah.

See JMBGIANTS, 110–11; MOSESS 24.

²² And Enoch also beheld the residue of the people which were the sons of Adam; and they were a mixture of all the seed of Adam save it was the seed of Cain, for the seed of Cain were black, and had not place among them. ²³ And after that Zion was taken up into heaven, Enoch beheld, and lo, all the nations of the earth were before him; ²⁴ and there came generation upon generation; and Enoch was high and lifted up, even in the bosom of the Father, and of the Son of Man; and behold, the power of Satan was upon all the face of the earth.

²⁵ And he saw angels descending out of heaven; and he heard a loud voice saying:

7:22   ***the residue of the people which were the sons of Adam.*** "The residue of the people" refers to all those who had not been taken up to heaven with the city of Enoch. Might this phrasing, which specifically distinguishes the people who were "the sons of Adam," allow for the possibility of the presence of non-Adamic lineages on the earth at that time? See figure 2–5 and the commentary on Moses 7:52.

   the seed of Cain were black. Other than a possible allusion in a JST addition to Genesis 9:26, there is no explicit connection in scripture made between the "seed of Cain" (who "were black") and the people of Canaan mentioned in Moses 7:8 ("There was a blackness came upon all the children of Canaan"). The two groups are mentioned in different visions and their tribal names are of different origins (RDDPGP, 115, 126n10). Moses 7:22 might be understood in connection with the "mark" of Cain (Moses 5:40). Of course, decoding the nature of that mark is not a straightforward matter (see figure 5–8). That said, Joseph Smith, the translator of this verse, and other early Church leaders seem to have understood that Black people were the descendants of Cain, as was the common belief in the nineteenth century (see JSJOURNALS2, 25 January 1842, 30; SRHNOAH, 12). Happily, verse 22 makes it clear that the seed of Cain is exempt from the curse the Lord pronounced in v. 20 because they (in contrast to the Canaanites) were not considered part of the "residue of the people." See commentary on "they were despised" in v. 8.

7:23   ***Zion was taken up into heaven.*** See v. 21.

   Enoch beheld. Now that the prologue has ended, its poignant message underscored with eloquent restraint, the grand vision opens. What did Enoch see? With "all the nations of the earth . . . before him," Enoch saw "the power of Satan . . . upon all the face of the earth" (vv. 23–24).

   all the nations of the earth. Is this referring to the same group that is referred to in v. 45 as "all the families of the earth"?

7:24   ***Enoch was high and lifted up.*** Because of Enoch's continued "faith" (v. 13) and "righteousness" (v. 19), he was "high and lifted up . . . in the bosom of the Father, and of the Son of Man." This is the first mention of the Son of Man in this chapter. The parallel between Enoch being lifted up in this verse and the Son of Man being "lifted up on the cross, after the manner of men," in v. 55 is noteworthy. In addition, there may be some connection between the idea of being "lifted up" and initiation into the heavenly mysteries. In the *Book of Parables*, Enoch recounts, "The angel Michael, one of the archangels, took me by my right hand, and raised me up, and brought me out to all the secrets; and he showed me all the secrets of mercy." A little later, Enoch was proclaimed to be "that Son of Man" (GWN1ENOCH2, 71:3, p. 320; 71:14, p. 321). In this instance the meaning is a "Son of the *Heavenly* Man" or a "Son of God," a concept that may be disconcerting to some readers but which poses no problem for Latter-day Saint theology.

   in the bosom of the Father, and of the Son of Man. See v. 31.

   the Son of Man. See Moses 6:57; 7:47.

   the power of Satan was upon all the face of the earth. Once Zion was taken up, Satan's power was unrestrained.

7:25   ***angels descending out of heaven.*** The Lord's response to Satan's derision is a merciful rescue mission for the residue of the people who have not been caught up to Zion. Note that the same phrase is repeated in v. 27. Compare Alma 10:19–22; 12:29; 13:22; 32:23; Revelation 8:13.

   a loud voice. Compare v. 56. In scripture, this phrase is most often associated with pain,

Figure 7–8. Rembrandt, 1606–69: *Jeremiah Lamenting the Destruction of Jerusalem*, 1630

A Chorus of Weeping

Within the Book of Moses, the stories of rescue and exaltation in the accounts of Noah and Enoch share a common motif of water. On one hand, Noah's waters are the waters of destruction, the floods of an all-consuming deluge that cleanses the earth as a prelude to a new creation. On the other hand, Enoch's waters are the waters of sorrow, the bitter tears that precede the terrible annihilating storm. Indeed, in Moses 7, not one but three distinct parties weep for the wickedness of humankind: God (v. 28), the heavens (vv. 28, 37), and Enoch himself (vv. 41, 49). In addition, a fourth party, the earth, complains and mourns—though does not specifically "weep"—for her children (vv. 48–49).

The complaining voice of the earth. With respect to the complaints of the earth described in Moses 7:48–49, valuable articles by Andrew Skinner and Daniel C. Peterson, following Hugh Nibley's lead, discuss interesting parallels in ancient sources. Peterson follows J. J. M. Roberts in citing examples of Sumerian laments of the mother goddess and showing how a similar motif appears in Jeremiah in the guise of "the personified city as the mother of her people" (MOSESS 26). He shows this by way of analogy to the role of the mourning earth as "the mother of men" in the Book of Moses (Moses 7:48). Significantly, although the motif of a complaining earth is not found anywhere in the Bible, it does turn up in *1 Enoch* (GWN1ENOCH1, 7:4–6, p. 182; 8:4, p. 188; 9:2, 10, p. 202; 87:1, p. 364) and *BG* (DWPDSS, 4Q203 frg. 8 l. 9–11, p. 945).

The weeping voice of the heavens. Jewish tradition links the weeping of the heavens with the separation of the "waters above" and the "waters beneath" by the firmament during the second day of Creation (MOSESS 27). Given the creation setting of this motif, it is not surprising that the Book of Moses associates the weeping of the heavens with the story of the Flood, which, in essence, recounts the alienation of the earth from the heavens and their reuniting in the "re-creation" of a new earth and a new covenant with the righteous "Noah" as its new "Adam."

The weeping voices of God and Enoch. The tradition of a weeping prophet is perhaps best exemplified by Jeremiah, who cried out in sorrow, "Oh that my head were waters, and mine eyes a fountain of tears, that I might weep day and night for the slain of the daughter of my people!" (Jeremiah 9:1). Less well known is the story of Enoch as a weeping prophet. For example, in *1 Enoch* 95:1, his words are near those of Jeremiah: "O that my eyes were a [fountain] of water, that I might weep over you; I would pour out my tears as a cloud of water, and I would rest from the grief of my heart" (GWN1ENOCH1, 460). In the *Midrash Rabbah* on Lamentations, Enoch is portrayed as weeping in likeness of God as a cop. nsequence of the destruction of the Israelite temple. I have found no similar scene in the ancient literature relating to any other prophet, but here in *Midrash Rabbah* and in the Book of Moses it is specifically connected with Enoch. Having seen God weep, Metatron (who is Enoch in his glorified state), said, "'Sovereign of the Universe, let me weep, but do Thou not weep.' He replied to him: 'If thou lettest Me not weep now, I will repair to a place which thou hast not permission to enter, and will weep there'" (JMBIGIL2, 106, 114–15).

See JMBREVISITING; MOSESS 25–29.

"Wo, wo be unto the inhabitants of the earth." [26] And he beheld Satan; and he had a great chain in his hand, and it veiled the whole face of the earth with darkness; and he looked up and laughed, and his angels rejoiced. [27] And Enoch beheld angels descending out of heaven, bearing testimony of the Father and Son; and the Holy Ghost fell on many, and they were caught up by the powers of heaven into Zion.

ENOCH'S GRAND VISION: GOD AND THE HEAVENS WEEP FOR THE WICKED

[28] And it came to pass that the God of heaven looked upon the residue of the people, and he wept; and Enoch bore record of it, saying: "How is it that the heavens weep,

7:25   disappointment, grief, anger, or warning (e.g., Moses 1:19, 22; 6:37; 7:25, 56). Less often it signals rejoicing, covenant making, or praising (JMBIGIL2, 140).

  Wo, wo be unto the inhabitants of the earth. The first burden of the angels is to proclaim faith and repentance, preparing the world to receive the ordinances of the gospel.

7:26   ***a great chain.*** Compare v. 57. Satan's chain is for imprisoning those who will perish in the Flood. Compare Alma 12:10–11; Doctrine and Covenants 123:7–8. *1 Enoch* 53:3–4 also mentions chains, but in this case they are for imprisoning Azazel and his angels (GWN1ENOCH2, p. 194).

  it veiled the whole face of the earth with darkness. Satan's chains are designed to block the light. God's curtains are designed to let in as much light as possible, to whatever degree the world is ready to receive it (v. 30).

  he looked up and laughed, and his angels rejoiced. Compare 3 Nephi 9:2 ("The devil laugheth, and his angels rejoice, because of the slain of the fair sons and daughters of my people; and it is because of their iniquity and abominations that they are fallen!"), and contrast 3 Nephi 27:30 ("The Father rejoiceth, and also all the holy angels, because of you and this generation; for none of them are lost"). In the last days, as in some earlier dispensations, the heavens will again rejoice while the devil will come down in "great wrath, because he knoweth that he hath but a short time" (Revelation 12:12).

7:27   ***angels descending out of heaven.*** An identical phrase is also found in v. 25.

  bearing testimony of the Father and Son. The second burden of the angels, having preached faith and repentance (v. 25), was to teach the ordinances of the gospel through bearing testimony of the Father and Son.

  many . . . were caught up by the powers of heaven into Zion. The mission was successful. "Many" were converted by the Holy Ghost and, after having received the appropriate ordinances, were translated to join those in Zion.

7:28–40   ***A comparison with Isaiah 1.*** While Charles Harrell has argued that "Moses 7 accentuates only [God's] wrath rather than his tender-heartedness," a useful corrective to this perspective may be found through comparing this chapter to suitable Old Testament analogues. While the fusion of justice and mercy in the character of God may seem like an irreconcilable contradiction in modern thinking, ancient scripture writers had no problem in putting these seemingly opposite ideas together—often in proximity within a single chapter of scripture. This general Old Testament model is best exemplified in two classic chapters of the Old Testament: Isaiah 1 and Deuteronomy 32. For example, Moses 7:28–41 resonates with selected themes mentioned by John Hobbins in his outline of Isaiah 1, including:

- God's call for heaven and earth to witness His grievance
- The relationship of privilege and obligation entailed by a Father and His children
- The actions God will take in response to the wayward and defiant state of His children, and
- God's proposal for a merciful resolution of His children's troubles.

For a detailed discussion of a response to Harrell's arguments and a presentation of the literary structure of this scriptural passage, see JMBTEXTUAL, 104–122; MOSESS 25. See also TLGGOD.

7:28   ***the God of heaven . . . wept.*** Compare Jacob 5:41; 3 Nephi 17:21–22. Elder Neal A. Maxwell

and shed forth their tears as the rain upon the mountains?" [29] And Enoch said unto the Lord: "How is it that thou canst weep, seeing thou art holy, and from all eternity to all eternity? [30] And were it possible that man could number the particles of the earth, yea, millions of earths like this, it would not be a beginning to the number of thy creations; and thy curtains are stretched out still; and yet thou art there, and thy bosom is there; and also thou art just; thou art merciful and kind forever;

7:28 comments, "Enoch saw the God of Heaven weep over needless human suffering" (JMBIGIL2, 176).

  Note that the OT2 manuscript was amended to read that Enoch wept instead of God (see SHFJST, 618, emphasis added): "And it came to pass, that *Enoch* looked upon the residue of the people and wept; *and he beheld and lo! the heavens wept also*, and shed forth *their* tears as the rain upon the mountains." For a discussion of this change and of the weeping of God and Enoch, see figure 7–8; JMBREVISITING; JMBTEXTUAL, 104–122, and MOSESS 25, 28.

  the residue of the people. In other words, those who had not been caught up into Zion. Compare v. 22.

  their tears. Compare Doctrine and Covenants 76:26, where the "heavens wept over" the fallen Lucifer.

7:29 *Enoch said unto the Lord.* OT1 and OT2 have "Enoch said unto the *heavens*" (SHFJST, 106, 618; emphasis added).

  How is it that thou canst weep . . . ? Terryl and Fiona Givens observe: "The question here is not about the reasons behind God's tears. Enoch does not ask, why do you weep, but rather, how are your tears even possible, 'seeing thou art holy, and from all eternity to all eternity?' Clearly, Enoch, who believed God to be 'merciful and kind forever,' did not expect such a being could be moved to the point of distress by the sins of His children" (JMBIGIL2, 142).

  thou art. "I am" and "thou art" statements describing the attributes of God and His prophets appear frequently in the visions of Moses (Moses 1:3, 4, 6, 7, 13, 16, 25, 26) and Enoch (Moses 6:31, 51, 67, 68; 7:29, 30, 35, 47–48, 53, 59).

7:30 *millions of earths like this.* Compare Moses 1:33: "Worlds without number have I created."

  thy curtains are stretched out still. Nibley explains:

> In the ongoing creation the establishment of new worlds is accompanied or represented by a stretching out of curtains. These would seem to keep each world in its proper relationships to the others. A commonplace of apocalyptic literature is that God Himself is necessarily screened from sight by a veil, as by the cloud on the Mount of Transfiguration (Matthew 17:5; Mark 9:7; Luke 9:34). . . . The purpose of numerous curtains or veils is to apportion to each world the light it is ready to receive. When Moses asked about the other worlds, the Lord informed him that he was not to know about them at the present and Moses agreed to be satisfied with learning "concerning this earth, and the inhabitants thereof, and also the heavens, and then thy servant will be content" (Moses 1:36) (HWNENOCH, 244, 245).

Draper, Brown, and Rhodes raise an additional matter with more general application: "It is possible that long as the curtains are stretched so that they in effect hide God, He is not moving decisively to intervene in a matter, such as the Flood. If this is the case, His parting of the curtains or the veil means that He is about to take action (see Luke 3:21; Acts 10:11; 1 Nephi 1:8; Helaman 5:48)" (RDDPGP, 129).

  yet thou art there, and thy bosom is there; and also thou art just; thou art merciful and kind forever. Elder Neal A. Maxwell asks, "Are not those the very same fundamental facts which you and I likewise find most crucial and most reassuring?" (JMBIGIL2, 143).

  thy bosom is there. An amendment to OT2 changes the word "bosom" to "presence" (SHFJST, 618). Compare Doctrine and Covenants 88:13: "the power of God who sitteth upon his throne, who is in the bosom of eternity, who is in the midst of all things."

  just . . . merciful and kind. See v. 31.

7:31 *thou hast taken Zion to thine own bosom.* In the Bible, the English word "bosom" corresponds

³¹ and thou hast taken Zion to thine own bosom, from all thy creations, from all eternity to all eternity; and naught but peace, justice, and truth is the habitation of thy throne; and mercy shall go before thy face and have no end; how is it thou canst weep?"

³² The Lord said unto Enoch: "Behold these thy brethren; they are the workmanship of mine own hands, and I gave unto them their knowledge, in the day I created them; and in the Garden of Eden, gave I unto man his agency; ³³ and unto thy brethren have I said, and also given commandment, that they should love one another, and

to the Hebrew terms *heq* and *hoq* and to the Greek *kolpos*. The Hebrew terms take one of three basic meanings: (1) "lower, outer front of the body where loved ones (infants and animals) are pressed closely; . . . [also] lap"; (2) "fold of the garment, above the belt where hands were placed and property kept"; and (3) the base of the temple altar. Craig Keener comments further:

> Holding an object to one's bosom declared the specialness of that object, and the image could be used to depict God's relation with *Torah*. . . . The image also represented a position of intimacy for people, thus Jesus elsewhere in the gospel tradition used being in Abraham's bosom as an image of intimacy and fellowship with Abraham. Because the phrase often appears in man-woman or parent-child relations, and because the text [of John 1:18] speaks of "the Father," the affectionate image may be that of a son on his father's lap (JMBIGIL2, 143).

Strikingly, in the Book of Moses, the term "bosom" is used six times in Moses 7 (vv. 24, 30, 31, 47, 63, 69)—and nowhere else in the rest of the Book of Moses. Each time it alludes to the "bosom of the Father" (v. 47), expressing the close intimacy between God and those who dwell in His presence. Of perhaps most relevance here is that the foundation stone of the temple, the place of greatest holiness, is said in rabbinic readings of Ezekiel 43:14 to be "set in the bosom of the earth" (JMBIGIL2, 144). Perhaps not unrelated to this temple imagery is the scriptural description of the bosom as an individual's receptacle of the Holy Ghost that may "burn" to indicate that something is "right" (Doctrine and Covenants 9:8).

Whether Enoch is directly in God's physical presence or experiencing God's intimate immanence at the far reaches of His stretched-out curtains (Moses 7:30), he can always truly say, "Thou art there, and thy bosom is there" (v. 30; JMBIGIL2, 144; MOSESS 30).

peace, justice, and truth. Compare Moses 6:61 ("mercy, truth, justice, and judgment") and 7:30 ("just . . . merciful and kind").

how is it thou canst weep? Enoch asked the question a third time, clearly perplexed by the concept of a suffering God. "The answer, it turns out, is that God is not exempt from emotional pain. Exempt? On the contrary, God's pain is as infinite as His love. He weeps because He feels compassion" (TLGGOD, 24–25). Elder Jeffrey R. Holland taught that this scene teaches more about the nature of God than could volumes of theology (JMBIGIL2, 144).

7:32t   **they are the workmanship of mine own hands.** See Moses 6:33. Compare *2 Enoch* 44:1: "The Lord with his own two hands created mankind" (FIA2ENOCH, p. 170). The Lord refers to His hands four times in Moses 7 and once in Moses 6. All creation (Moses 7:37, 40), including humankind (v. 32), are "the workmanship of [His] hands." He can stretch forth His hands and hold all the creations that He has made (v. 36).

knowledge. This verse was significantly modified in OT2 (SHFJST, 618). See Moses 4:3.

in the Garden of Eden, gave I unto man his agency. Compare *2 Enoch* 30:14–15: "I gave [Adam] free will; and I pointed out to him the two ways—light and darkness" (FIA2ENOCH, p. 152).

7:33   **that they should love one another.** Compare Leviticus 19:18; John 13:34–35; 15:12, 17. Elder Neal A. Maxwell observes, "Most strikingly, the Lord . . . focused on the fact that the human family should love one another and should choose God as their Father. The two great commandments!" (JMBIGIL2, 146).

that they should choose me, their Father; but behold, they are without affection, and they hate their own blood; ³⁴ and the fire of mine indignation is kindled against them; and in my hot displeasure will I send in the floods upon them, for my fierce anger is kindled against them.

³⁵ "Behold, I am God; Man of Holiness is my name; Man of Counsel is my name; and Endless and Eternal is my name, also. ³⁶ Wherefore, I can stretch forth mine hands and hold all the creations which I have made; and mine eye can pierce them also, and among all the workmanship of mine hands there has not been so great wickedness as among thy brethren. ³⁷ But behold, their sins shall be upon the heads

7:33 *choose me, their Father.* OT2 changes this phrase to read "serve me their God" (SHFJST, 618). Compare *2 Enoch* 30:14–15, where the Lord instructs Adam: "And I said to him, 'This is good for you, but that is bad,' so that I should come to know whether he has love toward me or abhorrence, and so that it might become plain who among his race loves me" (FIA2ENOCH, p. 152).

   In *3 Enoch* 4:3, the hard words of Job 21:7–15 are directly linked not to Job but to Enoch himself (PSA3ENOCH, 4:3, p. 258). In defiance of the Lord's entreaty to "love one another, and . . . choose me, their Father," the wicked are depicted as "say[ing] unto God, . . . Depart from us: for we desire not the knowledge of thy ways. What is the Almighty, that we should serve him? And what profit should we have, if we pray unto him?" (Job 21:14–15; compare Exodus 5:2; Malachi 3:13–15; Mosiah 11:27; Moses 5:16). John C. Reeves characterizes these words as "a blasphemous rejection of divine governance and guidance . . . wherein the wicked members of the Flood generation verbally reject God." Enoch is said to have prophesied a future judgment on such "ungodly sinners" who have uttered "hard speeches . . . against [the Lord]" (Jude 1:15, citing *1 Enoch* 1:9—see GWN1ENOCH1, p. 142; JMBIGIL2, 146).

   they are without affection, and they hate their own blood. See Moses 5:32, 47–50; 6:31; 7:7.

7:34 *hot displeasure . . . kindled.* See the commentary for Moses 6:27. The flames of humankind's violence are matched in kind by the fiery displeasure of God's anger. The Flood will quench them both.

7:35 *Man of Holiness is my name.* Note that in v. 19 Zion is called the City of Holiness. Frederick Borsch discusses precedents in many ancient traditions for the idea of God as "the Man" and for His relationship to mortals who can, after their ascension, become "Sons of Man," as Enoch did in Jewish tradition (SKBMAN; JMBIGIL2, 147).

   Man of Counsel. Compare the divine title of "Counsellor" given in Isaiah 9:6. The Septuagint translation of that verse calls the name of the child of prophecy "the Messenger of Great Counsel."

   Endless and Eternal. Compare Doctrine and Covenants 19:4–12.

7:36 *I have made.* See Moses 6:33.

   mine eye can pierce them also. Compare Doctrine and Covenants 121:4: "O Lord God Almighty, maker of heaven, earth, and seas, . . . let thine eye pierce"; and Moses 6:32: "No man shall pierce thee."

   there has not been so great wickedness as among thy brethren. Neither had there been so great righteousness among a whole society as among the people of Enoch. Nibley comments:

    The Lord said unto Enoch: "Zion have I blessed, but the residue of the people have I cursed" (Moses 7:20). The separation would have to continue until finally "Zion, *in the process of time,* was taken up into heaven" (Moses 7:20–21; italics added). We see the division of the people at every stage of the history: when "their enemies came up to battle against them," Enoch "led the people of God," while "all nations feared greatly" (Moses 7:13). . . . The result was two worlds, Zion, inhabited by people of "one heart and one mind" (Moses 7:18), the other wracked by continual "wars and bloodshed" (Moses 7:16) (HWNENOCH, 262–63).

7:37 *Satan shall be their father.* Compare 1 John 3:10; Alma 5:39–41; 30:60. Satan is the father of lies

of their fathers; Satan shall be their father, and misery shall be their doom; and the whole heavens shall weep over them, even all the workmanship of mine hands; wherefore should not the heavens weep, seeing these shall suffer?

³⁸ "But behold, these which thine eyes are upon shall perish in the floods; and behold, I will shut them up; a prison have I prepared for them. ³⁹ And that which I have chosen hath pled before my face. Wherefore, he suffereth for their sins; inasmuch as they will repent in the day that my Chosen shall return unto me, and until that day they shall be in torment;

and contention (John 8:44; 2 Nephi 2:18; 9:9; Ether 8:25; 3 Nephi 11:29; Moses 4:4).

father. OT2 gives this word as "master" (SHFJST, 619). Compare Mosiah 4:14.

misery shall be their doom. Compare Moses 7:41. Those who "perish from that which is good" become "miserable forever" (2 Nephi 2:5; compare 2 Nephi 2:18). Terryl and Fiona Givens write: "It is not [the people's] wickedness, but their 'misery,' not their disobedience, but their 'suffering,' that elicits the God of Heaven's tears. . . . In the vision of Enoch, we find ourselves drawn to a God who prevents all the pain He can, assumes all the suffering He can, and weeps over the misery He can neither prevent nor assume" (TLGGOD, 25).

should not the heavens weep, seeing these shall suffer? Elder Neal A. Maxwell observes, "When Enoch saw the heavens weep, they reflected the same drenching and wrenching feelings of the Father." Tragically, humankind was heedless and the suffering was needless (JMBIGIL2, 148).

There is a similar scene in *3 Enoch* 44:7–8, in which the righteous who have ascended to heaven pray to the Holy One (PSA3ENOCH, p. 295): "Lord of the Universe, how long will you sit upon your throne, as a mourner sits in the days of his mourning, with your right hand behind you, and not redeem your children . . . ?" They wonder when God will show His compassion and save His children, who are described in poetic terms as being "His right hand." God answers by explaining that He cannot save His people "in their sins" (Alma 11:36–37): "Since these wicked ones have sinned thus and thus, . . . how can I deliver my sons from among the nations of the world, reveal my kingdom in the world before the eyes of the gentiles and deliver my great right hand which has been brought low by them?" (JMBIGIL2, 148).

7:38   *a prison have I prepared for them.* Compare 1 Peter 3:19–20; Doctrine and Covenants 38:5; Moses 7:57. Correspondingly, in *BG* we read: "he has imprisoned us and overpowered yo[u" (DWPDSS, 4Q203, frg. 7b, col. i, l. 5, p. 945). Arguing on the basis of 1 Peter, Nibley gives hope of eventual deliverance for at least some of these souls who will perish in the Flood: "Those in prison, chains, and darkness are only being kept there until the Judgment, which will liberate many, not only because of their repentance, but through the power of the Atonement. . . . It was specifically the spirits who were disobedient in Enoch's day who were to enjoy the preaching of the Lord and the promise of deliverance in the meridian of times (1 Peter 3:19–20)" (HWNENOCH, 192). See MOSESS 13.

7:39   *until that day they shall be in torment.* Enoch's dialogue with the Lord continues to follow the general pattern of Isaiah 1, where, according to John F. Hobbins, "Yahweh's decision not to blot the people out entirely, despite the defection, is . . . recounted" (JMBTEXTUAL, 119). Here, the way is open not only for the living but also for the dead—those who refused to hear the Gospel while yet on earth. Deliverance to these souls will come after the working out of the Atonement of God's "Chosen" (v. 38), "inasmuch as they will repent" (v. 39).

Doctrine and Covenants 38:5 says the wicked will be "kept in chains of darkness until the judgment of the great day, which shall come at the end of the earth." Compare *3 Enoch* 44:1, 3, 5, where Enoch/Metatron shows "where the souls of the wicked stand, and where the souls of the intermediate stand." The angel Samki'el "is in charge of the souls of the intermediate, to support them and purify them from sin, through the abundant mercies of the Omnipresent One." Those in the "intermediate" place are "purified of their iniquity by fire" (PSA3ENOCH, pp. 294–95).

⁴⁰ Wherefore, for this shall the heavens weep, yea, and all the workmanship of mine hands."

Enoch's Grand Vision: Enoch Weeps over His Brethren

⁴¹ And it came to pass that the Lord spake unto Enoch, and told Enoch all the doings of the children of men; wherefore Enoch knew, and looked upon their wickedness, and their misery, and wept and stretched forth his arms, and his heart swelled wide as eternity; and his bowels yearned; and all eternity shook. ⁴² And Enoch also saw Noah, and his family; that the posterity of all the sons of Noah should be saved with a temporal salvation; ⁴³ wherefore Enoch saw that Noah built an ark; and that the Lord smiled upon it, and held it in his own hand; but upon the residue of the wicked the floods came and swallowed them up. ⁴⁴ And as Enoch saw this, he had bitterness of soul, and wept over his brethren, and said unto the heavens: "I will refuse to be comforted."

7:40   ***for this shall the heavens weep.*** Similarities with *3 Enoch* 44 continue in the account of the weeping of the patriarchs: "At once Abraham, Isaac, and Jacob [who were in heaven] began to weep. . . . Thereupon Michael, the Prince of Israel, cried and lamented with a loud voice" (PSA3ENOCH, 44:10, p. 296).

7:41   ***told Enoch all the doings of the children of men.*** Compare *2 Enoch* 53:2: "See how I have written down all the deeds of every person before the creation, and I am writing down what is done among all persons forever" (FIA2ENOCH, p. 180).

   looked upon their wickedness, and their misery, and wept. Enoch's question about the weeping of the heavens in Moses 7:29 formed the opening bookend of a powerful verbal envelope (or "inclusio") whose closing is finally found in verse 40. Having concluded His answer to Enoch, God now reiterates His solidarity with the sorrowing of the heavens ("wherefore, for *this* shall the heavens weep"). In eloquent brevity God acknowledges that the bitter cup of weeping now also extends to include the earth and its creatures ("yea, and *all* the workmanship of my hands").

   In verse 41 Enoch weeps at last. Only now does the realization of the depth of God's empathy draw out Enoch's full response, at the moment when "his heart swelled wide as eternity"—in other words, as wide as God's heart. Now Enoch unites his own voice with the weeping heavenly chorus in a grand finale. Terryl and Fiona Givens describe this event:

   > Witnessing God's weeping over His children is only half the journey Enoch makes. What transpires next to the prophet may be the only—it is surely the most vivid—example given in scripture of what the actual process of acquiring the divine nature requires. . . . As Enoch plumbs the mystery of the weeping God, he learns just what it means to be like Him. Seeking insight and understanding into eternal things, Enoch is raised to a perspective from which he sees the world through God's eyes. . . . Taught of highest things by the weeping God, Enoch becomes the weeping prophet. His experience of the love that is indiscriminate in its reach and vulnerable in its consequences takes him to the heart of the divine nature. (TLGGOD, 105)

7:41   See Moses 7:44 and MOSESS 25, 28. See also *1 Enoch* 95:1, where Enoch, seeing the wickedness of the people, exclaims, "O that my eyes were a fountain of water, that I might weep over you; I would pour out my tears as a cloud of water and I would rest [cf. Moses 7:54] from the grief of my heart" (GWN1ENOCH1, p. 460). See also *2 Enoch* 41:1, where Enoch recounts: "And I saw all those from the age of my ancestors, with Adam and Eve. And I sighed and burst into tears" (FIA2ENOCH, p. 166).

   his heart swelled wide as eternity. In OT2, this reads "he beheld eternity" (SHFJST, 619).

ENOCH'S GRAND VISION: ENOCH REJOICES IN THE SON OF MAN

But the Lord said unto Enoch: "Lift up your heart, and be glad; and look." ⁴⁵ And it came to pass that Enoch looked; and from Noah, he beheld all the families of the earth; and he cried unto the Lord, saying: "When shall the day of the Lord come?

his bowels yearned. These three words express the depth of Enoch's pity and compassion in poetic terms. Later, Enoch will hear his poignant feelings echoed in "a voice from the bowels" of the earth lamenting the wickedness of men (v. 48). In modern English, the word "heart" might be a better equivalent. However, in Joseph Smith's time, the figurative uses of the word "bowels" to represent the "interior part of any thing; as in the bowels of the earth" and the "seat of pity or kindness" would have been well understood (Noah Webster, JMBIGIL2, 151). These senses came from scripture, where the Hebrew term *meim* and the Greek term *splagchna* were both usually translated as "bowels" in the King James Bible, whether meant literally or figuratively. For example, Jeremiah expressed his grief for his people as follows: "My bowels, my bowels! I am pained at my very heart" (Jeremiah 4:19). Likewise, Paul admonished the Saints to "put on . . . bowels of mercies, kindness, humbleness of mind, meekness, longsuffering" (Colossians 3:12).

shook. In the scriptures, shaking and trembling are indicators of deep emotion, whether positive or negative. Sometimes such references are to individuals and nations; other times they describe a figurative shaking of heaven, earth, or of "all eternity" as is pictured here.

7:42   *Enoch also saw Noah, and his family.* Compare *1 Enoch* 106:16, where Enoch prophesies the destiny of Noah and his sons: "And this child that was born to you will be left upon the earth, and his three children will be saved with him, when all men on the earth die" (GWN1ENOCH1, 536).

the posterity of all the sons of Noah should be saved with a temporal salvation. The verse speaks only of a "temporal salvation," meaning that those who escape death will not necessarily evade the effects of unrepentant persistence in sin.

7:43   *held it in his own hand.* Although the Bible does not mention explicitly God's role during the Flood, *1 Enoch's Book of Parables* 67:2 contains a description similar to the Book of Moses: "I will put my hand upon [the ark] and protect it" (GWN1ENOCH2, p. 273).

swallowed them up. "Swallow" is tied to punishment in several other places in scripture (RDDPGP, 133). See Exodus 15:12; Numbers 16:32; Psalm 21:9; 2 Nephi 26:5; Alma 36:28; Helaman 8:11.

7:44   *wept.* See v. 41. Enoch first wept over humankind's wickedness. Then he wept over their destruction. Finally, he will weep over the complaints of the suffering earth (vv. 48–49).

I will refuse to be comforted. Nibley comments: "Enoch is the great advocate, the champion of the human race, pleading with God to spare the wicked and 'refusing to be comforted' until he is shown just how that is to be done. He feels for all and is concerned for all. He is the passionate and compassionate, the magnanimous one who cannot rest knowing that others are miserable. He is the wise and obedient servant, the friend and helper of all, hence the perfect leader and ruler" (HWNENOCH, 21).

Lift up your heart, and be glad; and look. Terryl and Fiona Givens write: "In the midst of Enoch's pain, God commands him to 'Lift up your heart, and be glad; and look.' Only then does he see 'the day of the coming of the Son of Man.' Recognizing in Christ's advent the great work of healing and redemption, 'his soul rejoiced'" (TLGGOD, 106).

7:45   *all the families of the earth.* Does this refer to the same group that was earlier called "all the nations of the earth"? (v. 23).

When shall the day of the Lord come? Enoch wants to know when the Messiah will come so the righteous may be "sanctified and have eternal life" (v. 45). Compare *3 Enoch* 45, where Enoch/Metatron sees the sad parade of generations, ending with the appearance of "the Messiah son of Joseph" and "the Messiah son of David," who will lead Israel to final victory (PSA3ENOCH, pp. 296–99).

the day of the Lord. Here "the day of the coming of the Son of Man" (v. 47) means the time

When shall the blood of the Righteous be shed, that all they that mourn may be sanctified and have eternal life?" ⁴⁶ And the Lord said: "It shall be in the meridian of time, in the days of wickedness and vengeance." ⁴⁷ And behold, Enoch saw the day of the coming of the Son of Man, even in the flesh; and his soul rejoiced, saying: "The Righteous is lifted up, and the Lamb is slain from the foundation of the world; and through faith I am in the bosom of the Father, and behold, Zion is with me."

ENOCH'S GRAND VISION: THE EARTH MOURNS AND THE LORD COVENANTS

⁴⁸ And it came to pass that Enoch looked upon the earth; and he heard a voice from the bowels thereof, saying: "Wo, wo is me, the mother of men; I am pained, I am weary, because of the wickedness of my children. When shall I rest, and be cleansed from the filthiness which is gone forth out of me? When will my Creator sanctify me, that I may rest, and righteousness for a season abide upon my face?"

⁴⁹ And when Enoch heard the earth mourn, he wept, and cried unto the Lord,

---

7:45   when Jesus Christ would live on the earth. Later, the same words are used to refer to His Second Coming (v. 65).

    all they that mourn. Compare Matthew 5:4. This group includes both the compassionate righteous and the wicked who are shut up in prison.

7:46   ***in the days of wickedness and vengeance.*** The "days of wickedness and vengeance" in the "meridian of time" parallel "the days of wickedness and vengeance" (v. 60) at the Second Coming.

7:47   ***the Son of Man.*** See Moses 6:57. The title "Son of Man," which is a notable feature of the *Book of Parables* in *1 Enoch*, also appears in marked density throughout the Book of Moses vision of Enoch (Moses 7:24, 47, 54, 56, 59, 65). Moreover, the related titles of "Chosen One" (v. 39), "Anointed One" (= Messiah, see v. 53), and "Righteous One" (Moses 6:57; 7:45, 47, 67) each appear prominently in both the *Book of Parables* and the Book of Moses Enoch story. The titles of "the Lamb" (Moses 7:47), "the King of Zion" (v. 53), "the Rock of Heaven" (v. 53), and "the Only Begotten" (Moses 6:52, 57, 59, 62; 7:50, 59, 62) appear only in the Book of Moses. The title "the Lord" is used whenever one of the more specific titles is not employed. See MOSESS 15.

    The Righteous is lifted up, and the Lamb is slain from the foundation of the world. Elder Neal A. Maxwell comments: "Enoch at first 'had bitterness of soul,' refusing to be comforted. Then the Lord showed him Jesus' great rescuing and redeeming Atonement, which was to be accomplished in the meridian of time" (JMBIGIL2, 154). Witnessing this focal point of divine love and mercy, Enoch's "soul rejoiced" (Moses 7:47).

7:48   ***a voice from the bowels thereof.*** See v. 41. See also figure 7–3 and MOSESS 25, 26.

    Wo, wo is me, the mother of men; I am pained, I am weary, because of the wickedness of my children. Compare Jeremiah 4:19. O. Glade Hunsaker notes: "The poetry of Moses is striking. For example, Enoch hears and describes the personified soul of the earth alliteratively as the 'mother of men' agonizing from the bowels of the earth that she is 'weary' of 'wickedness.' The tension of the drama resolves itself as the voice uses assonance in pleading for 'righteousness' to 'abide' for a season" (JMBIGIL2, 154). Although the complaining earth motif is not found anywhere in the Bible, it does turn up in other ancient Enoch sources including *1 Enoch* and *BG*. See figure 7–8.

7:49   ***when Enoch heard the earth mourn, he wept.*** See v. 44.

saying: "O Lord, wilt thou not have compassion upon the earth? Wilt thou not bless the children of Noah?" [50] And it came to pass that Enoch continued his cry unto the Lord, saying: "I ask thee, O Lord, in the name of thine Only Begotten, even Jesus Christ, that thou wilt have mercy upon Noah and his seed, that the earth might never more be covered by the floods." [51] And the Lord could not withhold; and he covenanted with Enoch, and sware unto him with an oath, that he would stay the floods; that he would call upon the children of Noah; [52] and he sent forth an unalterable decree, that a remnant of his seed should always be found among all nations, while the earth should stand; [53] and the Lord said: "Blessed is he through whose seed Messiah shall come; for he saith: 'I am Messiah, the King of Zion, the Rock of Heaven, which is broad as eternity; whoso cometh in at the gate and climbeth up by me shall never fall; wherefore, blessed are they of whom I have spoken, for they shall come forth with songs of everlasting joy.'" [54] And it came to

7:50   *thine Only Begotten.* Compare 6:52, 57, 59, 62; 7:50, 59, 62. See v. 47.

7:51   *he covenanted with Enoch.* OT1 reads, more plausibly, "Noah" instead of "Enoch" (SHFJST, 108). JST Genesis 9:21–25 connects the covenant God made with Noah and the similar covenant that He had made previously with Enoch: "I [will] remember the everlasting covenant, which I made unto thy father Enoch" (SHFJST, 117).

   sware unto him with an oath. Later, the account tells of how the oath was fulfilled. See v. 60.

7:52   *sent forth.* See Moses 6:30.

   an unalterable decree. See Moses 6:30.

   a remnant of his seed should always be found among all nations. See Moses 8:3. OT2 reads, "From a remnant of his seed should come all nations" (SHFJST, 621). From the preceding verses, we can infer that "his" means "Noah's." Compare *1 Enoch* 65:12, where Enoch tells Noah that the Lord has "established your righteous seed (to be) kings and for great honors, and from your seed there will flow a fountain of the righteous and the holy, and they will be without number forever" (GWN1ENOCH2, p. 273). Nibley sees this and related verses as raising the possibility of surviving non-Noachian lineages:

> God promised Enoch "that he [God] would call upon the children of Noah; and he sent forth an unalterable decree, that a remnant of his seed [Enoch's through Noah] should always be found among all nations, while the earth should stand; and the Lord said: Blessed is he through whose seed Messiah shall come" (Moses 7:51–53). Methuselah boasted about his line as something special (Moses 8:2–3). Why special if it included the whole human race? These blessings have no meaning if all the people of the earth and all the nations are the seed of Noah and Enoch. What other line could the Messiah come through? Well, there were humans who were not invited by Enoch's preaching—not included among the residue of the people not entering Enoch's city. They were "the residue of the people which were the sons of Adam; and they were a mixture of all the seed of Adam save it was the seed of Cain, for the seed of Cain . . . had not place among them" (Moses 7:22) (HWNBEFADAM, 79).

7:53   *Messiah, the King of Zion, the Rock of Heaven.* See v. 47.

   whoso cometh in at the gate and climbeth up by me shall never fall. Draper, Brown, and Rhodes comment: "The language is that of entry and ascent, of effort and struggle. Its first sense points metaphorically to temples, whose architecture carries the worshiper inward and upward toward the presence of God" (RDDPGP, 143).

pass that Enoch cried unto the Lord, saying: "When the Son of Man cometh in the flesh, shall the earth rest? I pray thee, show me these things."

ENOCH'S GRAND VISION: CRUCIFIXION AND RESURRECTION

[55] And the Lord said unto Enoch: "Look," and he looked and beheld the Son of Man lifted up on the cross, after the manner of men; [56] and he heard a loud voice; and the heavens were veiled; and all the creations of God mourned; and the earth groaned; and the rocks were rent; and the saints arose, and were crowned at the right hand of the Son of Man, with crowns of glory; [57] and as many of the spirits as were in prison

7:55   *the Son of Man lifted up on the cross.* Compare 1 Nephi 11:33; 19:10; Jacob 1:8; Moses 7:47. See also Moses 7:24.

7:56   *a loud voice.* See v. 25.

    the heavens were veiled. Compare v. 61. See also Matthew 27:51: "The veil of the temple was rent in twain from the top to the bottom."

    the earth groaned; and the rocks were rent. Compare Matthew 27:51: "And the earth did quake, and the rocks rent."

    the saints arose. Compare Matthew 27:52; Helaman 14:25.

7:57   *as many of the spirits as were in prison came forth, and stood on the right hand of God.* See v. 38.

    chains of darkness. See vv. 26, 38.

7:59   *the Son of Man ascend up unto the Father.* Compare John 20:17; Acts 1:9–11; Moses 7:47, 55. See Moses 7:24.

    I know thee. The kind of knowledge referred to here is the result of Enoch's personal encounter with the Lord (Moses 6:34). During that encounter, Enoch also received the blessing of "a right to [God's] throne" (Moses 7:59).

In His High Priestly Prayer, Jesus said, "And this is life eternal, that they might know thee the only true God, and Jesus Christ, whom thou hast sent" (John 17:3). Elder Bruce R. McConkie explained, "This doctrine is that mortal man, while in the flesh, has it in his power to see the Lord, to stand in His presence, to feel the nail marks in His hands and feet, and to receive from Him such blessings as are reserved for those only who keep all His commandments and who are qualified for that eternal life which includes being in His presence forever" (JMBIGIL2, 157).

    thou hast made me. See Moses 6:33.

    given unto me a right to thy throne. Note that Enoch is not given the divine throne but rather is granted a promissory right to receive it at some future time. Moreover, it is "not of [him]self" but "through the Lord's own grace" that he receives this right. Compare *1 Enoch* 45:3, which tells of how God's Chosen One "will sit on the throne of glory" (GWN1ENOCH2, p. 148). In *3 Enoch* 10:1, Enoch declares, "He (God) made me a throne like the throne of glory" (PSA3ENOCH, p. 263). See figure 7–2.

7:60   *to fulfil the oath.* Compare v. 51, where the Lord made His oath. Earlier in v. 60, the Lord's solemn answer to Enoch's question was confirmed by the use of a first person reference: "*As I live*, even so will I come" (emphasis added).

7:61   *the day shall come that the earth shall rest.* The earth will rest at last after the Second Coming.

    a veil of darkness shall cover the earth. Compare v. 56 ("the heavens were veiled") and Doctrine and Covenants 38:8 ("The veil of darkness shall soon be rent"), which suggest that this veil is a symbol of humankind's stubborn refusal to be guided by, or perhaps even to acknowledge the possibility of, direct communication from heaven. Sadly, as a result of that refusal, the world will be left in darkness and despair. Compare Doctrine and Covenants 110:1: "The veil was taken from our minds." See also a phrase added to the end of JST Genesis 9:26: "and a veil of darkness shall cover him."

came forth, and stood on the right hand of God; and the remainder were reserved in chains of darkness until the judgment of the great day. [58] And again Enoch wept and cried unto the Lord, saying: "When shall the earth rest?"

[59] And Enoch beheld the Son of Man ascend up unto the Father; and he called unto the Lord, saying: "Wilt thou not come again upon the earth? Forasmuch as thou art God, and I know thee, and thou hast sworn unto me, and commanded me that I should ask in the name of thine Only Begotten; thou hast made me, and given unto me a right to thy throne, and not of myself, but through thine own grace; wherefore, I ask thee if thou wilt not come again on the earth."

Enoch's Grand Vision: Zion, the Lord's Abode at His Return

[60] And the Lord said unto Enoch: "As I live, even so will I come in the last days, in the days of wickedness and vengeance, to fulfil the oath which I have made unto you concerning the children of Noah; [61] and the day shall come that the earth shall rest, but before that day the heavens shall be darkened, and a veil of darkness shall cover the earth; and the heavens shall shake, and also the earth; and great tribulations shall be among the children of men, but my people will I preserve; [62] and righteousness will I send down out of heaven; and truth will I send forth out of the earth, to bear testimony of mine Only Begotten; his resurrection from the dead; yea, and also the resurrection of all men; and righteousness and truth

my people will I preserve. Elder Neal A. Maxwell comments, "God preserved and prepared Enoch's people in the midst of awful and enveloping evil, and, reassuringly, he has promised his people in our own time that though 'great tribulations shall be among the children of men, . . . my people will I preserve'" (JMBIGIL2, 158).

7:62   *righteousness will I send down out of heaven; and truth will I send forth out of the earth.* The phrase "And righteousness will I send down out of heaven; and truth will I send forth out of earth" recalls a similar phrase in Psalm 85:11. However, the sequence of the terms "truth" (Hebrew *'emet*) and "righteousness" (Hebrew *tsedaqah*) is inverted, and, more importantly, different actions are indicated. In the psalm, the personification of the divine traits is used to create a metaphor of peace and prosperity in the land, whereas in Moses 7:62, it helps depict the coming forth of a united testimony from above and below of the Only Begotten—specifically of His resurrection and "the resurrection of all men."

Latter-day Saint readers understand the imagery of v. 62 as referring to the Restoration of the gospel. The united testimony of righteousness and truth rends the veil of darkness described in verse 61, enabling the restoration of the gospel with a fulness of ancient authority, powers, and ordinances. Heavenly messengers (perhaps meant to include the Savior, "the Righteous" Himself [vv. 45, 47]) are to be sent "down out of heaven," and "truth" (referring to the Book of Mormon and perhaps to other "hidden" books revealed or rediscovered in modern times) is to be sent "forth out of the earth." The personification of "righteousness" in the Book of Moses is apt in light of the use of divine virtues as the names of heavenly messengers in *1 Enoch* 40:8–9 (GWN1ENOCH1, p. 130). Moreover, as George Mitton observes, the Book of Mormon as a testimony of the risen Lord is equally fitting since "the symbol of its coming forth from the earth is reminiscent of the Lord's resurrection" (MOSESS 29).

7:62   *his resurrection from the dead . . . and . . . the resurrection of all men.* How well does the mention of resurrection of the "Only Begotten" and of "all men" fit into the ancient Enoch literature? With respect to views within the Dead Sea Scrolls on the role of the Messiah as an

will I cause to sweep the earth as with a flood, to gather out mine elect from the four quarters of the earth, unto a place which I shall prepare, an Holy City, that my people may gird up their loins, and be looking forth for the time of my coming; for there shall be my tabernacle, and it shall be called Zion, a New Jerusalem." [63] And the Lord said unto Enoch: "Then shalt thou and all thy city meet them there, and we will receive them into our bosom, and they shall see us; and we will fall upon

7:62   agent of the Resurrection, the *Messianic Apocalypse* closely parallels the Gospels' use of Isaiah 26 and 61 to describe what Christians understand to be the mission of Jesus. Among other things, this text declares that "his Messiah . . . will heal the badly wounded and will make the dead live" (MOSESS 29).

With this and a related passage in mind, Benjamin Wold argues that a personal, bodily resurrection in the last days is envisioned, not merely a temporary restoration to life for individuals or a symbolic restoration of Israel. Of course, evidence for an early Israelite belief in a personal resurrection is controversial. However, in light of the testimony of the Book of Moses Enoch account, it is significant that some of the earliest and most explicit descriptions of the resurrection in Jewish literature that do exist are found in the Enoch literature, specifically within the *Book of Parables*. The *Book of Parables* is also rich in descriptions of the Son of Man that, for Christians, seem to relate to other aspects of the mission of Jesus Christ—for example, *1 Enoch* 62:13–16 (GWN1ENOCH2, pp. 254–55. See MOSESS 29; SKBMAN.

righteousness and truth will I cause to sweep the earth as with a flood. The description of the flood of righteousness and truth that will effect the gathering of the elect in the last days seems to be fashioned as a deliberate counterpoint to the account of the flood of water that brought about the destruction of the wicked in Noah's day. Further explaining the gathering, the Prophet Joseph Smith declared, "Men and angels are to be co-workers in bringing to pass this great work, and Zion is to be prepared, even a new Jerusalem, for the elect that are to be gathered from the four quarters of the earth, and to be established an holy city, for the tabernacle of the Lord shall be with them" (JSTPJS, November 1835, 84).

as with a flood. Noah's flood brought destruction, whereas this flood will bring salvation. In contrast to the canonical text, OT1 uses a definite article "as with *the* flood," while OT2 reads "as *the* flood," making clear parallels with the flood of Noah (SHFJST, 109, 622, emphasis added).

unto a place which I shall prepare. Compare *4 Ezra* 13:35: "Zion will come and be made manifest to all people, *prepared* and built, as you saw the mountain carved out without hands." See also *2 Baruch* 4:2–3: "It is that [city] which will be revealed, with me, that was already *prepared* from the moment that I decided to create Paradise." Likewise, the *Book of Giants* speaks of the gathering place of Enoch's people as having been "*prepared* for them in the beginning" (WBHGIANTS, Text G, 69, emphasis added). See JMBIGIL2, 159.

an Holy City. See v. 19. Compare the emphasis in *1 Enoch Book of Parables* 45:5, which also emphasizes the holiness of the place to which the righteous will be gathered: "And my chosen ones I shall make to dwell on it, but those who commit sin and error will not set foot on it" (GWN1ENOCH2, p. 148). *Jubilees* 1:28 also declares that "Zion and Jerusalem will be holy" (JMBIGIL2, 162).

looking forth for the time of my coming. "Looking forth" is more than merely watching for the signs of the Lord's coming. It is also living in a manner that pays heed to His warning words (RDDPGP, 147).

7:62   ***there shall be my tabernacle.*** The Lord does not say that His tabernacle will be *in* the Holy City but rather that His tabernacle "*shall be called* Zion, a New Jerusalem" (v. 62; emphasis added). In other words, it seems that the entire city will be God's tabernacle. This is consistent with Revelation 21, where the entire celestial city is described in terms of temple architecture.

it shall be called Zion, a New Jerusalem. Jewish tradition describes a "New Jerusalem." According to *Testament of Levi* 10:5, "For the house which the Lord shall choose shall be called

their necks, and they shall fall upon our necks, and we will kiss each other; [64] and there shall be mine abode, and it shall be Zion, which shall come forth out of all the creations which I have made; and for the space of a thousand years the earth shall rest."

Jerusalem, as the book of Enoch the Righteous maintains" (MOSESS 29; emphasis added). This account may be alluding to *1 Enoch* 90:28–29, which tells of how the old house (that is, the old city of Jerusalem) is removed and replaced with a new house (that is, New Jerusalem) (GWN1ENOCH1, p. 402). Moreover, in *2 Enoch* 55:2 [J], Enoch calls the place of his ascent "the highest Jerusalem" (FIA2ENOCH, p. 182; MOSESS 29). See Hebrews 11:16; 12:22–24; Revelation 3:12; 21:2; 3 Nephi 20:22; 21:23–24; Ether 13:2–10; Doctrine and Covenants 42:67; 133:56.

7:63   ***thou and all thy city meet them there.*** The heavenly city of Zion will meet and unite with its earthly counterpart, Zion, the New Jerusalem. See figure 7–9. Compare Doctrine and Covenants 45:11–15, which was received on March 7, 1831, just a few months after Moses 7 was recorded. See also JST Genesis 9:21–25 (SHFJST, OT1 p. 24, pp. 116–17).

The descent of the heavenly Jerusalem is described in Revelation 21:2, as well as in pseudepigraphic and rabbinic sources. Howard Schwartz summarizes Jewish traditions:

> Some say that in the future God will cause the Jerusalem on high to descend from heaven fully built, and will set it on the tops of four mountains: Mount Sinai, Mount Tabor, Mount Carmel, and Mount Hermon (Isaiah 2:2; 52:7). Then the Temple will sing aloud, and the mountains will answer the song. So too will Jerusalem serve as a beacon to all of the nations, and they will walk in her light. Thus will God announce the Redemption.

In *4 Ezra* 7:26–28, we read: "For behold, the time will come, when the signs which I have foretold to you will come to pass; the city which now is not seen shall appear, and the land which now is hidden shall be disclosed. And everyone who has been delivered from the evils that I have foretold shall see my wonders. For my son the Messiah shall be revealed with those who are with him, and those who remain all rejoice four hundred years" (A variant of the verse reads "one thousand years.") See JMBIGIL2, 160.

    we will receive them into our bosom. See v. 31. Notice the "we" in this phrase, indicating that the gathered elect will be welcomed into both the bosom of the Lord and of Enoch and his people.

    they shall see us. See Moses 6:35. Draper, Brown, and Rhodes comment, "The verb 'to see' points to the quality of the Lord's sight, effectively permitting people to see as He sees (1 John 3:2)" (RDDPGP, 147). Doctrine and Covenants 76:94 explains, "They who dwell in his presence are the church of the Firstborn; and they see as they are seen, and know as they are known, having received of his fulness and of his grace."

    we will kiss each other. As in v. 62, the imagery is similar to Psalm 85, but significantly, in this instance, it also resembles *1 Enoch* 11:2 (GWN1ENOCH1, p. 216)—again with an important difference. In Psalm 85 and *1 Enoch*, divine attributes (mercy, truth, righteousness, and peace) meet and kiss, whereas in the Book of Moses it is Enoch's city and the Lord Himself that fall upon the necks of the righteous and kiss them, as they would kiss a returning prodigal. Robert Alter, writing about Psalm 85, captures the commonality of spirit with Moses 7:63: "This bold metaphor focuses the sense of an era of perfect loving harmony. Rashi imagines a landscape in which all Israelites will kiss one another" (RABIBLE, 3:206n11. See also MOSESS 29).

N. T. Wright, an Anglican bishop and New Testament scholar, described the uniting of heaven and earth as follows: "God made heaven and earth; at last, he will remake both and join them together forever. And when we come to the picture of the actual end in Revelation 21–22, we find not ransomed souls making their way to a disembodied heaven but rather the new Jerusalem coming down from heaven to earth, uniting the two in a lasting embrace" (JMBIGIL2, 160).

7:64   ***there shall be mine abode.*** See v. 21.

    I have made. See v. 33.

    for the space of a thousand years the earth shall rest. At last the fulfillment of God's promise.

Figure 7–9. Linda McCarthy, b. 1947: *The City of Enoch*, 2002

"Let Zion in Her Beauty Rise"

Linda McCarthy's elegant digital watercolor depicts the heavenly and earthly cities of Zion just as they are about to meet and merge, their glories mutually reflecting in serene splendor. This scene is captured poetically in Edward Partridge's hymn: "Let Zion in her beauty rise; / Her light begins to shine, / Ere long her King will rend the skies, / Majestic and divine. / The Gospel's spreading through the land, / A people to prepare, / To meet the Lord and Enoch's band, / Triumphant in the air" (*Hymns* [1985], no. 41). Describing this moment, the Lord told Enoch, "Then shalt thou and all thy city meet them there, and we will receive them into our bosom, and they shall see us; and we will fall upon their necks, and they shall fall upon our necks, and we will kiss each other" (Moses 7:63).

N. T. Wright, the well-known Anglican bishop and New Testament scholar, describes the uniting of heaven and earth as follows:

> God made heaven and earth; at last he will remake both and join them together forever. And when we come to the picture of the actual end in Revelation 21–22, we find not ransomed souls making their way to a disembodied heaven but rather the new Jerusalem coming down from heaven to earth, uniting the two in a lasting embrace (MOSESS 29).

Several passages in the ancient Enoch literature echo the themes of the Book of Moses. For instance, in the *Book of Parables* (*1 Enoch* 45:4–5) we read: "On that day, I shall make my Chosen One dwell among them, and I shall transform heaven and make it a blessing and a light forever; and I shall transform the earth and make it a blessing. And my chosen ones I shall make to dwell on it" (GWN1ENOCH2, p. 148).

Just as the first book of the Bible, Genesis, recounts the story of Adam and Eve being cast out from the Garden of Eden, so its last book, Revelation, fittingly prophesies a permanent return for the sanctified to paradise (Revelation 22:1–5). In that day, the veil that separates humankind and the rest of fallen creation from God will be swept away and all shall be "done in earth, as it is in heaven" (Matthew 6:10). In the original Garden of Eden, "there was no need for a temple—because Adam and Eve enjoyed the continual presence of God." Likewise, in John's vision "there was no temple in the Holy City, 'for its temple is the Lord God'" (William J. Hamblin and David Rolph Seely; see Revelation 21:22). To reenter the renewed "garden" at that happy day is to return to the original spiritual state of immortality and purity and to know the oneness that existed at the dawn of creation, before the creative processes of division and separation began. See JMBIGIL2, 102.

ENOCH'S GRAND VISION: ENOCH SEES ALL THINGS; HAS A FULNESS OF JOY

⁶⁵ And it came to pass that Enoch saw the day of the coming of the Son of Man, in the last days, to dwell on the earth in righteousness for the space of a thousand years; ⁶⁶ but before that day he saw great tribulations among the wicked; and he also saw the sea, that it was troubled, and men's hearts failing them, looking forth with fear for the judgments of the Almighty God, which should come upon the wicked. ⁶⁷ And the Lord showed Enoch all things, even unto the end of the world; and he saw the day of the righteous, the hour of their redemption, and received a fulness of joy.

7:64   See Revelation 20:2–7; Doctrine and Covenants 29:11; 77:12; 88:110; Moses 7:65; Articles of Faith 1:10. Draper, Brown, and Rhodes comment: "This news was what Enoch had been praying to learn since he had heard the groaning complaint of the earth (vv. 48–49). By postponing his response to Enoch's request for this information, the Lord had led Enoch in vision through the corridor of history to the Millennium" (RDDPGP, 148).

Again, the ancient Enoch literature echoes the themes of the Book of Moses. In the Enochian *Book of Parables* 45:4–5 we read, "On that day, I shall make my Chosen One dwell among them, and I shall transform heaven and make it a blessing and a light forever; and I shall transform the earth and make it a blessing. And my chosen ones I shall make to dwell on it" (GWN1ENOCH2, p. 148).

7:65   *the day of the coming of the Son of Man.* See v. 45. *Jubilees* 1:28 describes this event as follows: "And the Lord will appear in the sight of all. And everyone will know that I am the God of Israel and the father of all the children of Jacob and king upon Mount Zion forever and ever" (JMBIGIL2, 162).

7:66   *great tribulations among the wicked.* Passages in the *Book of Parables* describe similar troubles for the wicked at the time of the coming of the Son of Man (GWN1ENOCH2, 38:1–6, p. 95; 45:1–2, 6, p. 148; 46:4–8, p. 153).

7:67   *the Lord showed Enoch all things.* Compare *2 Enoch* 40:1: "Now therefore, my children, I know everything; some from the lips of the Lord, others my eyes have seen from the beginning even to the end" (FIA2ENOCH, p. 165). Though Enoch is said to have seen "all things" in this supernal vision, Brigham Young doubted that such a thing could have been possible in any ultimate sense of the expression (JD, 8:17):

Understand eternity? There is not and never was a man in finite flesh who understands it. Enoch has been referred to in this matter. How many of the Gods and kingdoms he saw when the vision of his mind was opened, it matters not. If he had seen more than he could have enumerated throughout his long life, and more than all the men on earth could multiply from the time his vision opened until now, he would not have attained to the comprehension of eternity. How much Enoch saw, how many worlds he saw, has nothing to do with the case. This is a matter that wise men know nothing about.

even unto the end of the world. In Joseph Smith—Matthew 1:4, the "end of the world" is equated to "the destruction of the wicked." Compare Matthew 13:49: "The harvest is the end of the world."

received a fulness of joy. Compare 3 Nephi 17:20: "my joy is full." See MOSESS 29.

Figure 7–10. *Enoch Ascends to Heaven*. British Library, MS Cotton Claudius B fol. 11v

ENOCH AS A TEACHER AND FORERUNNER

Enoch (Henoch or Hanoch, Heb. *ḥănôk*) sounds identical to the Hebrew passive participle of the verbal root *ḥnk*, "train up" "dedicate." Thus, for a Hebrew speaker, the name *ḥănôk*/Enoch would evoke "trained up" or "initiated" — bringing to mind not only the general role of a teacher, but also the idea of someone who was familiar with the temple and could train and initiate others as a hierophant. Before it became the name of the post-Mosaic Feast of Dedication, the Hebrew noun *ḥănukkâ* had reference to the "consecration" or "dedication" of the temple altar, including the sacred dedication of the altar for Solomon's temple.

Strengthening the connection of Enoch's name to the temple, we note that in Egyptian, the *ḥnk* verbal root denotes to "present s[ome]one" with something, to "offer s[ome]thing" or, without a direct object, to "make an offering." The Egyptian nouns *ḥnk* and *ḥnkt* denote "offerings." In other words, it is a cultic term with reference to cultic offerings.

Enoch initially describes himself as an uninitiated "lad" lacking power of speech. Likewise David, early in his career, is similarly described as an *'elem* ("young man," "youth," "lad," pausal *'ālem*) in 1 Samuel 17:56 and Jonathan's servant is described synonymously as both a *na'ar* ("young man," "lad") and an *'elem* in 1 Samuel 20:22. One of the etymological associations suggested for *'elem* is that it "is related to the root of [*'wlm*], "unknowing, uninitiated." In Arabic *'lm* is the primary verb for "to know." Alma the Elder, whose name probably derives from *'elem*, is introduced into the Book of Mormon as a "young man" who "believed the words of Abinadi" (Mosiah 17:2) and then taught those words on his way to becoming the founder of what became the Nephite church and a religious movement. The aforementioned biographical description of Alma harks back to Nephi's autobiography: "I, Nephi [*nfr* > *nfi* =good], having been born of goodly parents, therefore I was taught somewhat in all the learning of my father . . . yea, having had a great knowledge of the goodness and the mysteries of God." Thus, when we read Moses 6:21: "And Jared taught Enoch in all the ways of God," we should not take this as merely a general statement that Enoch knew something about religious matters, but specifically that he was familiar with temple rites and what we would today call "the doctrine of Christ," a key teaching of Moses 6–7.

The theme of the doctrine of Christ brings us to the essential role of the saving ordinances, including not only baptism and the gift of the Holy Ghost but also temple ordinances. Hugh Nibley cited the Enoch scholar André Caquot as saying that Enoch is (HWNENOCH, 19–20):

> "in the center of a study of matters dealing with initiation in the literature of Israel." Enoch is the great initiate who becomes the great initiator. . . . The Hebrew book of Enoch bore the title of Hekhalot, referring to the various chambers or stages of initiation in the temple. Enoch, having reached the final stage, becomes the Metatron to initiate and guide others. "I will not say but what Enoch had Temples and officiated therein," said Brigham Young, "but we have no account of it" (JD, 18:303). Today we do have such accounts.

See MOSESS 14, MLBYOUNG.

Epilogue: God Receives Zion up into His Own Bosom

⁶⁸ And all the days of Zion, in the days of Enoch, were three hundred and sixty-five years. ⁶⁹ And Enoch and all his people walked with God, and he dwelt in the midst of Zion; and it came to pass that Zion was not, for God received it up into his own bosom; and from thence went forth the saying,

"Zion is Fled."

7:68   *three hundred and sixty-five years.* The Book of Moses applies this duration to "all the days of Zion" (v. 68), whereas the Bible applies it to the age of Enoch when he was translated (Genesis 5:23–24). In contrast to the Bible, Moses 8:1 says that "all the days of Enoch were four hundred and thirty years."

7:69   *walked with God.* Compare Genesis 5:24; Doctrine and Covenants 107:48–49; Moses 6:34, 39; 8:27. See also Moses 6:34. Joseph Smith expected the Saints in our time to prepare to walk with God, saying, "The Lord was going to make of the Church of Jesus Christ a kingdom of Priests, a holy people, a chosen generation, as in Enoch's day" (JSTPJS, 30 March 1842, 266).

    he dwelt in the midst of Zion. See v. 21.

    Zion was not. The Prophet taught: "When the world in general would not obey the commands of God, after walking with God, he translated Enoch and his church, and the Priesthood or government of heaven was taken away" (JSTPJS, 15 July 1842, 251). An explicit analogue to the Book of Moses idea that others besides Enoch ascended bodily with him is found in a Mandaean Enoch fragment and in late midrash (JMBIGIL2, 163–64). However, even more striking is the implication in *BG* that after having been gathered to divinely prepared cities of refuge, the righteous who responded to Enoch's preaching were taken up to live in the presence of God. See figures 7–4 and 7–6 and JMBGIANTS, 1123–33, 1143–46.

    received it up. Compare Doctrine and Covenants 45:11–12: "Enoch, and his brethren, . . . were separated from the earth, and were received unto myself."

    bosom. See v. 31 and MOSESS 30.

    Zion Is Fled. See Hebrews 6:18, which speaks of those "who have fled for refuge to lay hold upon the hope set before us." Philip Alexander argues that Enoch's title of Metatron was meant to "express the idea that Enoch was a *metator* [Latin "forerunner"] for the other adepts, showing them how they could escape from the wilderness of this world into the promised land of heaven." In similar fashion, Hebrews 6:19–20 presents Jesus as a "forerunner" who entered "into that within the veil" ahead of us (JMBIGIL2, 164). See figure 7–10.

CHAPTER 8
THE DAYS OF NOAH

ENOCH AND METHUSELAH

8 ¹ And all the days of Enoch were four hundred and thirty years. ² And it came to pass that Methuselah, the son of Enoch, was not taken, that the covenants of the Lord might be fulfilled, which he made to Enoch; for he truly covenanted with Enoch that Noah should be of the fruit of his loins. ³ And it came to pass that Methuselah prophesied that from his loins should spring all the

8   Noah is given a place of prominence in modern revelation, standing second only to Adam in dispensational authority. The Prophet Joseph Smith taught (JSTPJS, Before 8 August 1839, 157):

> The Priesthood was first given to Adam; he obtained the First Presidency, and held the keys of it from generation to generation. He obtained it in the Creation, before the world was formed, as in Genesis 1:26–28. He had dominion given him over every living creature. He is Michael the Archangel, spoken of in the Scriptures. Then to Noah, who is Gabriel: called of God to this office, and was the father of all living in this day, and to him was given the dominion. These men held keys first on earth, and then in heaven.

Gabriel (Noah) and Michael (Adam) are the only angels mentioned by name in the Bible (Daniel 10:13, 21; 12:1; Jude 1:9; Revelation 12:7). Gabriel interprets Daniel's dreams (Daniel 8:16; 9:21) and announces the births of John the Baptist and Jesus (Luke 1:19, 26). In Muslim teachings, Gabriel (Jibra'il) not only reveals God's word to Muhammad but frequently appears with the devil (Iblis) as his adversary in the stories of the prophets. There is also a worldwide literature concerning variously named Flood heroes (for example, Nu'u, Nuh, Nu Gua, Atrahasis, Utnapishtim, Ziusudra, Deucalion, Yima, and Manu).

Modern revelation has amplified what we know about Noah from the Bible. His birth was a fulfillment of a covenant God made with Enoch (Moses 7:52). Noah was ordained to the priesthood at age ten (Doctrine and Covenants 107:42–51). He taught the first principles and ordinances of the gospel and announced the coming of Jesus Christ in the meridian of time (Moses 8:16, 19, 23–24). He conferred the priesthood on his posterity (Doctrine and Covenants 84:14–15). As part of the restoration of the gospel, he visited the Prophet Joseph Smith (Doctrine and Covenants 128:21). Finally, in connection with the Second Coming, Noah will return to the earth to attend the "marriage supper of the Lamb" (Revelation 19:9; Doctrine and Covenants 27:5–7). See JMBIGIL2, 199–201.

Like the earlier chapters of Genesis, the story of Noah maintains a steady focus on temple symbolism (Moses 8; Genesis 6–9). That it repeats, with some variation, the themes of the Creation, the Garden of Eden, and the Fall of Adam and Eve has long been recognized by Bible scholars. What deserves greater appreciation, however, is the nature and depth of the relationship between these chapters and the liturgy and layout of temples, not only in Israel but also throughout the ancient Near East. See JMBIGIL2, 10–12, 253–338, 655–656 and figures 8–2, 3, 4, and 6.

8:1   *four hundred and thirty years.* Genesis 5:23 says that Enoch lived for "three hundred sixty and five years." The difference can be accounted for by adding the age of 65 years referenced in Moses 6:25—when Methuselah was born to him and Enoch received his prophetic call (Moses 6:26)—to the 365 years representing the length of Enoch's ministry during the "days of Zion" (Moses 7:68).

8:2   *for he truly covenanted with Enoch.* God's covenant with Enoch that Noah should be his descendant is not mentioned in the Bible, nor is it mentioned in the Book of Moses except in this verse. However, the Book of Moses does inform us that Enoch knew Noah would be saved from the Flood (Moses 7:42–43) and that the Lord "covenanted with Enoch, and sware unto him with an oath" that "the earth might never more be covered by the floods" (Moses 7:50–51). Enoch was told that the Son of Man would come again "in the days of wickedness and vengeance" and that He would "call upon the children of Noah" (Moses 7:51, 60).

Figure 8–1. *Donald Duck Gathers the Animals to the Ark*, 1999. From Walt Disney's *Fantasia 2000*.

SHOULD WE TAKE THE FLOOD STORY SERIOUSLY?

Given their status as targets of humor and caricature, the well-worn stories of Adam, Eve, and Noah are sometimes difficult to take seriously. However, a thoughtful examination of the scriptural record of these characters will reveal not simply tales of "piety or … inspiring adventures" but rather carefully crafted narratives from a highly sophisticated culture that preserve "deep memories" of revealed understanding. We do an injustice both to these marvelous records and to ourselves when we fail to pursue an appreciation of scripture beyond the initial level of cartoon cut-outs inculcated upon the minds of young children. André LaCocque observes: "To consider [such stories as tales] for children is only possible when the story is vaguely known, when it is considered from a distance, and with a preconceived feeling that nothing can be learned from so 'naïve' a tale" (ALTRIAL, 10–11). Hugh Nibley characterized the problem this way (HWNBEFADAM, 63):

> The stories of the Garden of Eden and the Flood have always furnished unbelievers with their best ammunition against believers, because they are the easiest to visualize, popularize, and satirize of any Bible accounts. Everyone has seen a garden and been caught in a pouring rain. It requires no effort of imagination for a six-year-old to convert concise and straightforward Sunday-school recitals into the vivid images that will stay with him for the rest of his life. These stories retain the form of the nursery tales they assume in the imaginations of small children, to be defended by grown-ups who refuse to distinguish between childlike faith and thinking as a child when it is time to "put away childish things" (1 Corinthians 13:11). It is equally easy and deceptive to fall into adolescent disillusionment and with one's emancipated teachers to smile tolerantly at the simple gullibility of bygone days, while passing stern moral judgment on the savage old God who damns Adam for eating the fruit He put in his way and, overreacting with impetuous violence, wipes out Noah's neighbors simply for making fun of his boat-building on a fine summer's day.

The profound accounts of primeval history deserve better treatment. To understand them for what they are, we need to bring our best to the task: the powerful tools of modern scholarship, the additional light shed by modern revelation, and, of no less importance, the consecrated dedication of inquiring minds and honest hearts diligently seeking divine inspiration. The simple fantasies of a "fanciful and flowery and heated imagination" (JSTPJS, 25 March 1839, 137) will not suffice.

192

kingdoms of the earth (through Noah), and he took glory unto himself. [4] And there came forth a great famine into the land, and the Lord cursed the earth with a sore curse, and many of the inhabitants thereof died.

[5] And it came to pass that Methuselah lived one hundred and eighty-seven years, and begat Lamech; [6] and Methuselah lived, after he begat Lamech, seven hundred and eighty-two years, and begat sons and daughters; [7] and all the days of Methuselah were nine hundred and sixty-nine years, and he died.

Lamech

[8] And Lamech lived one hundred and eighty-two years, and begat a son, [9] and he called his name Noah, saying: "This son shall comfort us concerning our work

8:3   *he took glory unto himself.* Although it is tempting to conclude that Methuselah "was not taken" with those of the city of Enoch before the Flood because of his boasting, the reason given in scripture for his continued presence on earth is "that the covenants of the Lord might be fulfilled, . . . that Noah should be of the fruit of [Enoch's] loins" (Moses 8:2). Methuselah, the son of Enoch, will become the grandfather of Noah.

8:4   *a great famine into the land.* Mosiah 1:17 explains that one purpose of "famine and sore afflictions" is to "stir [the people] up in remembrance of their duty" (compare Mosiah 9:3). Prophets have sometimes been commanded to use their sealing power to "smite the earth with famine" or dearth of rain (see, for example, Helaman 10:6).

8:7   *nine hundred and sixty-nine years.* Methuselah, the oldest living man on record in the Bible, died the same year as the Flood. Adding Methuselah's age when Lamech was born (187 [Moses 8:5]) to Lamech's age when Noah was born (182 [Moses 8:8]) and Noah's age when the Flood began (600 [Genesis 7:6]), we arrive at the 969 years.

8:8   *And Lamech lived one hundred and eighty-two years, and begat a son.* This statement signals the formal beginning of the Flood story.

8:9   *Noah.* Noah's name is almost certainly related to a Hebrew root meaning "to rest." Previously, Noah's name had been revealed to Enoch (Moses 7:42–43). Consistent with the Book of Moses, Enoch reveals the name of Noah to Lamech in *1 Enoch* 106:18 (GWN1ENOCH1, 106:18, 536).

    This son shall comfort us concerning the work and toil of our hands, because of the ground which the Lord hath cursed. Regarding the cursing of the ground, see Moses 4:23. Of course, Lamech did not know that the most significant relief from work and toil eventually would come not from Noah's labors on the land but rather from the personal part Noah would play in God's provisional lifting of the curse itself. "Noah is saved in order to worship, to offer the sacrifice . . . that is a 'rest/comforting' (*hannichoach*), that turns cursing into a blessing (see Genesis 8:21). Noah's priestly mediation is the means by which relief from the toil of the cursed ground became a reality: 'For God as well as for humanity, Noah is consolation for the fall of Adam' [David Damrosch]" (L. Michael Morales).

    Although the meaning of Noah's name (that is, "rest") seems clear as it stands, Lamech's explanation in Genesis 5:29 ("comfort" or perhaps relief) is problematic. In brief, the derivation of his name from the Hebrew leads us to expect the verse to read either "he called his name Noah, saying: This son shall give us rest . . ." or "he called his name Nahman, saying: This son shall comfort us . . ." The names of Noah and Nahman (or Menahem) are both witnessed in late Jewish tradition, and commentators have often incorporated both interpretations. According to Elizabeth Harper, however, "the use of the imprecise word play . . . is well within the bounds of biblical naming conventions which are rarely precise. It provides

SHOULD WE UNDERSTAND SCRIPTURE LITERALLY?

The Prophet Joseph Smith held the view that scripture should be "understood precisely as it reads" (JSWORDS, 29 January 1843, 161). Consistent with this view, our objective in the first part of this book has been to render "literal" interpretations of the characters in the Book of Moses. It must be realized, however, that what ancient peoples understood to be "literal" interpretations of scripture are not the same as what most people understand them to be in our day. Whereas we modernists typically apply the term "literal" to accounts that provide clinical accuracy in the journalistic dimensions of who, what, when, and where, premoderns were more apt to understand "literal" in the sense of "what the letters, that is, the words say." These are two very different modes of interpretation. As BYU professor James E. Faulconer observed: "'What x says' [that is, the premodern idea of "literal"] and 'what x describes accurately' [that is, the modernist idea of "literal"] do not mean the same, even if the first is a description."

Elaborating more fully on the limitations of modernist descriptions of scriptural events, Faulconer observes that the interest of premoderns (JMBIGIL2, 8–9):

> was not in deciding what the scriptures portray, but in what they say. They do not take the scriptures to be picturing something for us, but to be telling us the truth of the world, of its things, its events, and its people, a truth that cannot be told apart from its situation in a divine, symbolic ordering.

> Of course, that is not to deny that the scriptures tell about events that actually happened. . . . However, premodern interpreters do not think it sufficient (or possible) to portray the real events of real history without letting us see them in the light of that which gives them their significance—their reality, the enactment of which they are a part—as history, namely the symbolic order that they incarnate. . . . "Person A raised his left hand, turning it clockwise so that .03 milliliters of a liquid poured from a vial in that hand into a receptacle situated midway between A and B" does not mean the same as "Henry poured poison into Richard's cup." Only the latter could be a historical claim (and even the former is no bare description).

Of course, none of this should be taken as implying that precise times, locations, and dimensions are unimportant to the stories of scripture. Indeed, details given in Genesis about, for example, the size of Noah's Ark, the place where it landed, and the date of its debarkation are crucial to its interpretation. However, when such details are present, we can usually be sure that they are not meant merely to add a touch of realism to the account, but rather to help the reader make mental associations with stories and religious concepts found elsewhere in scripture. In the case of Noah, for example, these associations might echo the story of Creation or might anticipate the Tabernacle of Moses. It is precisely such backward and forward reverberations of related themes in disparate passages of scripture, rather than a photorealistic rendering of the Flood, that is our focus in the present commentary.

The literal understanding we seek of Book of Moses will be found in an unraveling of the interconnections among what Genesis scholar Ronald Hendel calls "the tangled plots of Genesis," and in an interpretive approach that attempts to comprehend how the individual story plots fit within larger meta-plots throughout the Pentateuch—and sometimes further afield. The table at right, derived by Wyatt from the work of A. J. Wensinck, shows "a typological reiteration of the same literary nexus [of the temple themes of chaos/flood, creation/exodus, and covenant] throughout the tradition, canonical and non-canonical."

See JMBIGIL2, 8–12.

	Chaos (flood)	*Creation (exodus)*	*Covenant*
Genesis	Genesis 1:2	Genesis 1:3-25	Genesis 1:26-31
Genesis	Genesis 7:17-8:9	Genesis 8:10-19	Genesis 8:20-9:17
Exodus	Exodus 1:22, 2:3-5	Exodus 14-15	Exodus 19-24, 32-34
Deutero-Isaiah	Isaiah 43:2, 48:10, 54:7-9	Isaiah 40, 41:18, 43:19, 46:6-8, 50:2, 51:9-11, 51:15	Isaiah 51:3, 52:7-12, 54 *passim*, 55 *passim* (esp. v. 3)
Pseudepigrapha	*Jubilees* 5:20-6:3, *T. Naphtali* 6:10-10, *1 Enoch* 65-66, 83, 89:1-9	*4 Ezra* 13:1-13, *1 Enoch* 89:10-40, *2 Enoch* 24-30	*Jubilees* 6:4-16
Gospels	John 1:1-5, 14-16	*Baptism:* Matthew 3, Mark 1:3-8, Luke 3:2-17, John 1:6-8, 19-28 *Stilling Storm:* Matthew 8:18, 23-27; Mark 4:35-41, Luke 8:22-25 *Walking on Sea:* Matthew 14:22-33, Mark 6:47-52 John 6:15-21, (21:1-14) Revelation 12:7-9, 21:1-22:5	Matthew 5-7

Figure 8–2. *Typology in Biblical Tradition.* After Wensinck and Wyatt

and toil of our hands, because of the ground which the Lord hath cursed." ¹⁰ And Lamech lived, after he begat Noah, five hundred and ninety-five years, and begat sons and daughters; ¹¹ and all the days of Lamech were seven hundred and seventy-seven years, and he died.

NOAH AND HIS SONS—THE SONS OF GOD

¹² And Noah was four hundred and fifty years old, and begat Japheth; and forty-two years afterward he begat Shem of her who was the mother of Japheth, and when he was five hundred years old he begat Ham. ¹³ And Noah and his sons hearkened unto the Lord, and gave heed, and they were called the sons of God.

SONS OF MEN ENTER MISMATCHED MARRIAGES WITH NOAH'S POSTERITY

¹⁴ And when these men began to multiply on the face of the earth, and daughters were born unto them, the sons of men saw that those daughters were fair, and

8:9 an unusual juxtaposition of comfort with work to make a daring and provocative claim. Noah will be the one to relieve the world of the consequences of the curse on the [ground]." Other suggestions—for example, that the "comfort" referred to is an explanatino of the origins of grape-growing and wine-making or that it relates to Noah's invention of the plow and other farming implements—seem far-fetched (JMBIGIL2, 224).

8:10 *five hundred and ninety-five years.* From Genesis 7:6, we can infer that Lamech died five years before the Flood.

8:12 *And Noah . . . begat Japheth; . . . Shem . . . and . . . Ham.* Though it is not specifically said that Ham had the same mother as Shem and Japheth, other references to Noah's "wife" imply that the three sons shared a mother. That said, the birth order of the three sons is in question. In OT1 and OT2 the sense of this verse was left unchanged, consistent with the statement in the King James Version of the Bible (KJV) that Shem was the oldest son (Genesis 6:10; SHFJST, 111, 623). However, sometime afterward the OT2 wording was crossed out and a revision was pinned to the manuscript. This revision unambiguously describes Japheth as the oldest son and corresponds to the current version of Moses 8:12. It is not known whether Joseph Smith authorized this change. Inexplicably, Genesis 10:21, which reads "Japheth the elder," was changed in the Joseph Smith Translation (JST) to read "Shem . . . which was the elder" (SHFJST, 119, 633). Some Jewish sources specifically name Japheth as the oldest son. Japheth is listed first in the table of the nations in Genesis 10:2–5, though there is some ambiguity in the Hebrew. That Shem is listed first in Genesis 5:32; 6:10; 7:13; 9:18; 10:1; 1 Chronicles 1:4; and Moses 8:27 may reflect his importance to the Israelites as their ancestor (RDDPGP, 159).

8:13 *the sons of God.* See figure 8–3 and the commentary on Moses 8:21 below.

8:14 *these men.* This refers to the sons of Noah mentioned in verse 13.

the sons of men saw that those daughters were fair. Genesis 6:2 reads differently: "The sons of God saw the daughters of men that they were fair." See figure 8–3. OT2 reads, "The sons of men saw that their daughters were fair" (SHFJST, 624). The current text dates from the 1902 edition of the Pearl of Great Price (KPJMOSES, 45).

the sons of men. In other words, men who stand outside the oath and covenant of the priesthood.

those daughters. In other words, the daughters of the sons of God, or the granddaughters of Noah.

fair. This is translated from the Hebrew *tobhoth,* which means literally "good." It is often used in similar contexts to mean specifically "good in appearance, beautiful," as in Exodus 2:2.

Figure 8–3. *Noah Emerging from the Ark in a Pose of Resurrection*,
catacombs of Saints Peter and Marcellinus, early fourth century

WHO WERE THE SONS OF GOD?

Moses 6:5–23 describes the ideal family order established by Adam and Eve. This same order is implied in Moses 8:13, where Noah and his righteous sons are mentioned. The patriarchal order of the priesthood that "was in the beginning" and that "shall be in the end of the world also" (Moses 6:7) is depicted as presiding over a worthy succession of generations in the likeness and image of Adam (Moses 6:10), just as Adam and Eve were made in the image and likeness of God (Moses 6:9, 22).

Indeed, transcending his status as a king and priest, Noah is sometimes portrayed in the Bible as a type of God Himself. Consider, for example, the microcosmic ark that Noah forms and fills with living creatures and food in imitation of God the Creator and his role as captain of the ark as it moves "upon the face of the waters" (Genesis 7:18)—assuming the role of God in the original creation of the earth. Recall also Noah's planting of an Eden-like garden after the emergence of dry land (Genesis 9:20), his later locus "in the midst of" (Genesis 9:21; cf. Genesis 2:9) the most sacred place in that garden, and his pronouncement of a curse on Canaan, the "serpent" who was responsible for the transgression of its sacred boundary (Genesis 9:25. See figure 8:6). Finally, note that Noah's three children are explicitly called the "sons of God" (Moses 8:13). Depictions of Noah in the catacombs like the one above show him rising out of the ark in a pose of resurrection, prefiguring the emergence of the Savior from His tomb.

In the context of Moses 8:13, the term "sons of God" refers to individuals who have been ordained to the Melchizedek Priesthood—perhaps having received the fulness of the priesthood and had their calling and election made sure (Moses 6:68). As defined in Doctrine and Covenants 76:56–60, "they are they who are priests and kings, who have received of his fulness, and of his glory; . . . wherefore, as it is written, they are gods, even the sons of God." Unlike other priesthood ordinations, the ordinance that conveys this power is administered directly by God Himself: "And [the high priesthood after the order of the covenant that God made with Enoch] was delivered unto men by the calling of his own voice" (JST Genesis 14:29).

Going further, Genesis 6:2 reads, "The sons of God saw the daughters of men that they were fair," a phrase that has been the source of unending controversy among scholars. However, contradicting ancient Jewish traditions that depict the unrighteous husbands of Genesis 6:2 as fallen angels, Moses 8:14 portrays these husbands as mere mortals, unrighteous men who married daughters of the covenant, that is, descendants of Seth and Noah: "the sons of men saw that those daughters were fair."

Like the Book of Moses, Islamic and Christian traditions typically reject the idea that the "sons of God" in Genesis 6:2 are fallen angels. However, in a further wrinkle, whether due to other authentic traditions or merely additional confusion, these traditions record that some of the "sons of God" (that is, covenant descendants of Seth and Noah) also entered into mismatched marriages. So, if these traditions are to be believed, we have two forms of mismatched marriages: 1. some unrighteous "sons of men" who married daughters of the covenant, as depicted in the Book of Moses; and 2. some unrighteous "sons of God" who married women who were *outside* the covenant, as described in Islamic and Christian traditions.

Further adding to the general disorder and confusion, note that the "sons of men" who married Noah's granddaughters *falsely* proclaimed themselves as "sons of God" in mocking response to Noah's preaching—see the commentary for Moses 8:21 herein.

they took them wives, even as they chose. [15] And the Lord said unto Noah: "The daughters of thy sons have sold themselves; for behold mine anger is kindled against the sons of men, for they will not hearken to my voice."

NOAH PROPHESIES AND TEACHES THE THINGS OF GOD

[16] And it came to pass that Noah prophesied, and taught the things of God, even as it was in the beginning. [17] And the Lord said unto Noah: "My Spirit shall not always strive with man, for he shall know that all flesh shall die; yet his days shall be an hundred and twenty years; and if men do not repent, I will send in the floods upon

took them wives. The Hebrew expression is the normal one for legal marriage. Correcting mistaken ideas about the meaning of the phrase, Umberto Cassuto explained, "The passage contains not a single word . . . alluding to rape or adultery or to any act against the Lord's will" (UCCOMMENTARY, 294). What Moses 8:15 will condemn is marriage outside the covenant by the granddaughters of Noah and the refusal of the "sons of men" to hearken to the Lord.

even as they chose. Genesis 6:2 reads: "of all which they chose." Perhaps the clearest translation is given by Claus Westermann, "just as their fancy chose" (CWGENESIS, 364). Although these few words—appended to the routine mention that the sons of men took wives—may seem innocuous to modern readers, they would have been evidence to ancient Israelites of a deliberate subversion of the established marriage selection process (MZBEREISHIS, 182n2). According to Westermann, choosing a spouse is portrayed here as a process of eyeing the "many beauties who take [one's] fancy" rather than "discovery of a counterpart, which leads to living as one in marriage" (CWGENESIS, 371). Leon R. Kass observed, "It would be characteristic of heroes (like Cain's Lamech) to find and seize the beautiful daughters, almost as trophies" (LRKWISDOM, 157).

Robert Alter notes that the Hebrew expression underlying the phrase "the sons of men saw that those daughters were fair" (Moses 8:14) parallels the temptation in Eden (Moses 4:12): "The woman saw that the tree . . . became pleasant to the eyes." The words describe a strong intensity of desire fueled by appetite—which Alter renders in his translation as "lust to the eyes" (RABIBLE, 1:16n6). As in the temptation of Eden, Satan's strategy was persuade God's children to subordinate divine law to the appeal of the senses (NMSGENESIS, 25).

8:15　*The daughters of thy sons have sold themselves.* A similar phrase occurs in 2 Kings 17:17, when the Israelites are accused of having "sold themselves to do evil in the sight of the Lord." The Hebrew term *wayyitmakkeru* is used here in the sense of selling oneself into slavery. Compare a related passage in *BG* where the *gibborim* are condemned for their "prostitution in the land" (4Q203, frg. 8, l. 6–9, Martínez translation, JMBIGIL2, 227). Nibley explained that the "daughters who had been initiated into a spiritual order . . . departed from it and broke their vows, mingling with those who observed only a carnal law" (HWNENOCH, 180).

mine anger is kindled. See Moses 6:27.

they will not hearken to my voice. The refusal of these mismatched couples to hearken to God's own voice was the catalyst that set in motion the ministry of Noah (Moses 8:19).

8:16　*the things of God, even as it was in the beginning.* In other words, the principles and ordinances of the gospel as originally revealed to Adam.

8:17　*My Spirit shall not always strive with man, for he shall know that all flesh shall die; yet his days shall be an hundred and twenty years.* Genesis 6:3 reads a little differently: "for that he also is flesh" instead of "for he shall know that all flesh shall die." A clearer translation might be: "My breath shall not abide in man forever, since he too is flesh; let the days allowed him be one hundred and twenty years" (NMSGENESIS, 45–46). In this verse, the "breath" or "spirit" referred to is best explained as the "breath of life" (Moses 3:7), whose presence or absence determines life or death (RDDPGP, 165).

Was the Ark Designed as a Floating Temple?

Figure 8–4. Stephen T. Whitlock, b. 1951: *Noah Sees the Ark in Vision*

Apart from the tabernacle of Moses (Exodus 25:8–40) and the Temple of Solomon (1 Chronicles 28:11–12, 19), Noah's ark is the only man-made structure mentioned in the Bible whose design was directly revealed by God (Genesis 6:14–16). In this detail from a window of the Holy Trinity Church in Stratford-upon-Avon, England, God shows the plans for the ark to Noah just as He later revealed the plans for the tabernacle to Moses. The hands of Deity display the image of the Ark on the heavenly veil as Noah, compass in his left hand, watches intently.

C. H. T. Fletcher-Louis, among others, has concluded that, like the tabernacle, Noah's ark "was designed as a temple" (JMBIGIL2, 235). The ark's three decks suggest both the three divisions of the tabernacle and the threefold layout of the Garden of Eden. Indeed, each of the decks of Noah's ark was exactly "the same height as the Tabernacle and three times the area of the Tabernacle court" (James D. G. Dunn and John W. Rogerson, JMBIGIL2, 211). Additionally, the same Hebrew word (*mikseh*) was used for the animal-skin covering of Noah's ark and that of the tabernacle (see, for example, Genesis 8:13; Exodus 26:14).

Further strengthening the association between the ark and the tabernacle is that the Hebrew term for Noah's ark (*tevah*) later became the standard word for the ark of the covenant in Mishnaic Hebrew. In addition, the Septuagint used the same Greek term, *kibotos*, for both Noah's ark and the ark of the covenant. The ratio of the width to the height of both these arks is 3:5 (see Genesis 6:15; Exodus 25:10).

Marking the similarities between the shape of the ark of the covenant and the chest-like form of Noah's ark, Claus Westermann describes Noah's ark as "a huge, rectangular box, with a roof" (CWGENESIS, 418). Some describe the roof as flat along the whole length of the vessel, whereas others interpret the phrase "in a cubit shalt thou finish it above" to indicate a plan for sloping the roof slightly (Genesis 6:16). Meir Zlotowitz points out the unlikely shape of such a boxlike craft, noting that the biblical account makes it clear that the ark "was not shaped like a ship and it had no oars." This design accentuated "the fact that Noah's deliverance was not dependent on navigating skills, [but rather happened] entirely by God's will" (MZBEREISHIS, 230), the ark's movement being solely determined by "the thrust of the water and wind" (Umberto Cassuto, JMBIGIL2, 265). Similarly, whether the dimensions of the seven-storied ark (or "temple"—*ekallu*) in the Mesopotamian flood story of *Gilgamesh* was shaped as what Steven W. Holloway describes as "a sea-going ziggurat" or instead as a "floating microcosm" in the form of a gigantic cube (as suggested by Jean Bottéro); the nautical improbability of such a vessel affirms the miraculous nature of the rescue (JMBIGIL2, 213).

Consistent with the emphasis on deliverance through the power of God rather than human navigation, the Hebrew word used in Genesis for "ark" (*tevah*) appears only once more in the Bible: as part of the story of the infant Moses, whose deliverance from death was also made possible by a free-floating watercraft—specifically a reed basket (Exodus 2:3, 5). Recent scholarship supports the idea that reeds were also used in the construction of Noah's ark. Note that in the Mesopotamian stories of *Atrahasis* and *Gilgamesh*, the flood hero obtains the construction materials for the building of a boat by tearing down a reed hut temple. Reed mats would be stitched to the hull and covered with pitch to make them waterproof. As it turns out, reinterpreting the vowels in the corresponding Hebrew term in the Bible, which was originally unmarked, would lead to an alternate translation signifying an ark that required "reeds" rather than "rooms." Evidence from elsewhere in the Bible also argues in defense of the following translation of Genesis 6:14 in the New Jerusalem Bible:

> Make yourself an ark out of resinous wood. *Make it with reeds* and caulk it with pitch inside and out. (JMBIGIL2, 221; emphasis added)

Thus, a puzzling inconsistency with the Mesopotamian accounts is resolved, at the same time further connecting the ark with the symbolism of ancient Israelite and Mesopotamian temples (JMBIGIL2, 210–21).

them." ¹⁸ And in those days there were giants on the earth, and they sought Noah to take away his life; but the Lord was with Noah, and the power of the Lord was upon him. ¹⁹ And the Lord ordained Noah after his own order, and commanded him that he should go forth and declare his Gospel unto the children of men, even as it was given unto Enoch.

THE SONS OF MEN MOCK NOAH AND REFUSE HIS TEACHING

²⁰ And it came to pass that Noah called upon the children of men that they should repent; but they hearkened not unto his words; ²¹ and also, after that they had

8:17   While some scholars prefer to see the mention of 120 years as "a reference to the interval of time remaining before the Flood" (NMSGENESIS, 46), the Book of Moses, consistent with other readers, seems to describe instead a limitation in the length of human life span in succeeding generations. Gordon J. Wenham observes, "In the post-flood period the recorded ages steadily decline, and later figures very rarely exceed 120" (GJWGENESIS, 142). Nahum Sarna concurs, noting that the shortening of human life is an indication of "moral and spiritual degeneration" (NMSGENESIS, 46). Leon R. Kass suggests reasons why short lives might be a blessing: "Perhaps a shorter life span could limit the damage any beastly man might cause. . . . Perhaps if men learned from observing the deaths of others that they too had limited time, they would use it better. Perhaps if they could not pretend to immortality, they would be more open to the truly eternal" (LRKWISDOM, 160–61).

My Spirit shall not always strive with man. This phrase is often misunderstood to mean that God's patience in working with sinners will eventually come to an end and that, when this point has been reached, God will withdraw the influence of His Spirit from them. However, any truth to this idea has nothing to do with the meaning of this phrase in the present verse. The word "spirit" mentioned here should not be capitalized, since it refers to the animating spirit of each individual that gives life to the body, not to the Holy Spirit. In modern scripture, similar phrases do seem to refer to the Holy Spirit (2 Nephi 26:11; Mormon 5:16; Ether 2:15).

8:18   *giants . . . sought Noah to take away his life.* Compare Moses 7:15; 8:26 and related commentary. The term "giants" corresponds to the Hebrew term *nephilim* (see figure 6-4). Surprisingly, the account of Josephus in *Antiquities of the Jews* 1:3:1 confirms the Book of Moses account: "For the tradition is that these men did what resembled the acts of those whom the Grecians call giants. But Noah was very uneasy at what they did; and being displeased at their conduct, persuaded them to change their dispositions and their acts for the better: but seeing they did not yield to him, but were slaves to their wicked pleasures, he was afraid they would kill him, together with his wife and children" (JMBIGIL2, 228).

8:19   *the Lord ordained Noah after his own order.* In other words, the Lord ordained Noah to "the Holy Priesthood, after the Order of the Son of God" (Doctrine and Covenants 107:3. Compare Alma 13:1–2, 9; JST Genesis 14:28 [SHFJST, 127]).

Gospel. This same gospel, including its ordinances, was received and preached by Adam. Alma 13:6 confirms that it is the duty of those of the higher priesthood "to teach [God's] commandments unto the children of men, that they also might enter into his rest" (RDDPGP, 167). Joseph Smith said, "The Gospel has always been the same; the ordinances to fulfill its requirements, the same, and the officers to officiate, the same; therefore, as Noah was 'a preacher of righteousness' [2 Peter 2:5] he must have been baptized and ordained to the priesthood by the laying on of hands, etc." (JSTPJS, 1 September 1842, 264).

8:20   *Noah called upon the children of men that they should repent.* Calling people to repentance was required by ancient concepts of biblical law "in order to establish intentionality and the degree of criminal responsibility. Their refusal to heed the call defines the degree of the criminal responsibility of the antediluvian sinners, and, consequently, the justice of their punishment" (Devorah Dimant, JMBIGIL2, 229).

hearkened not. The repetition of this phrase later in v. 24 underscores humankind's deliberate refusal of the Lord's entreaties.

Figure 8–5. Thomas Cole (1801-1848): *The Subsiding Waters of the Deluge,* 1829

DID THE FLOOD COVER THE ENTIRE EARTH?

One important lesson from the Book of Moses is that scripture is a product of a particular point of view. Hugh Nibley illustrated this idea (HWNBEFADAM, 64–66):

> The Latter-day Saints, [like other Bible readers,] are constantly converting statements of limited application to universal or at least sweeping generalities. To illustrate, I was told as a child that the Rocky Mountains, the Appalachians, and the Andes all came into existence overnight during the great upheavals of nature that took place at the time of the Crucifixion—an absurdity that plays into the hands of critics of the Book of Mormon. But what we find in the [Third] Nephi account when we read it carefully is a few sober, factual, eyewitness reports describing an earthquake of 8-plus on the Richter scale in a very limited area. Things that appear unlikely, impossible, or paradoxical from one point of view often make perfectly good sense from another.
>
> The *Nautical Almanac* gives the exact time of sunrise and sunset for every time of the year, yet astronauts know that the sun neither rises nor sets except from a particular point of view, the time of the event being strictly dependent on the exact location. From that point of view and that only, it is strictly correct and scientific to say that the sun does rise and set. Just so, the apparently strange and extravagant phenomena described in the scriptures are often correct descriptions of what would have appeared to a person in a particular situation. . . .
>
> So with Noah in the Ark. From where he was, "the whole earth" was covered with water as far as he could see (Genesis 8:9). . . . But what were conditions in other parts of the world? If Noah knew that, he would not have sent forth messenger birds to explore.

But doesn't Genesis 7:19 say that "the waters prevailed exceedingly upon the earth; and all the high hills, that were under the whole heaven, were covered"? Explaining his understanding of this verse, Walter Bradley observed:

> The Hebrew word *eretz* used in Genesis 7:19 is usually translated "earth" or "world" but does not generally refer to the entire planet. Depending on the context, it is often translated "country" or "land" to make this clear. . . . [For example, i]n Genesis 12:1, Abram was told to leave his *eretz*. He was obviously not told to leave the planet but rather to leave his country. . . . [Another] comparison to obtain a proper interpretation of Genesis 7:19 involves Deuteronomy 2:25, which talks about all the nations "under the heavens" being fearful of the Israelites. Obviously, all nations "under the heavens" was not intended to mean all on planet Earth.

Elder John A. Widtsoe, writing in 1943, summed up the important idea of taking point of view into account when interpreting scripture:

> We should remember that when inspired writers deal with historical incidents they relate that which they have seen or that which may have been told them, unless indeed the past is opened to them by revelation.
>
> [For example, t]he details in the story of the Flood are undoubtedly drawn from the experiences of the writer. . . . The writer of Genesis made a faithful report of the facts known to him concerning the Flood. In other localities the depth of the water might have been more or less.

See JMBIGIL2, 267–70.

heard him, they came up before him, saying: "Behold, we are the sons of God; have we not taken unto ourselves the daughters of men? And are we not eating and drinking, and marrying and giving in marriage? And our wives bear unto us children, and the same are mighty men, which are like unto men of old, men of great renown." And they hearkened not unto the words of Noah. ²² And God saw that the wickedness of men had become great in the earth; and every man was

8:21   ***we are the sons of God; have we not taken unto ourselves the daughters of men?*** In sarcastically calling their wives as "daughters of men," these puffed-up sons of men are also deliberately deprecating the former status of these women as "daughters of thy sons" (v. 15)—in other words, daughters of the sons of Noah, who were said to be "sons of God" (see v. 13). In brief, the light-minded jesting of these men turn the real situation upside down: they, the sons of men, make themselves out to be the sons of God while dishonoring their wives—the daughters of the sons of God—by lightmindedly characterizing them as the daughters of men.

In further confirmation of the idea that these wicked men are *not* the sons of God but are only falsely claiming to be, note that v. 20 asserts that "Noah called upon the children of men," not the "sons of God." Tellingly, Satan made the same duplicitous self-assertion as these men in Moses 5:13, saying, "I am also a son of God."

eating and drinking, and marrying and giving in marriage. The words "eating and drinking, and marrying and giving in marriage" "convey a sense of both normalcy and prosperity" (RDDPGP, 168), conditions of the mindset of the worldly in Noah's time that Jesus said would recur in the last days (Matthew 24:37–39). Frederick Dale Bruner perceptively observes: "One of the most surprising facts in Jesus' end-time teaching now is that the last times will be normal. According to this passage, there will be parties, gourmet meals, courtships, and weddings right into the cataclysmic coming of the Son of Man. . . . That is instructive. The Great Tribulation occurs while superficially all seems well. To the unobservant, it's party time" (JMBIGIL2, 229).

eating and drinking. Bruner's apt translation reads, "wining and dining" (JMBIGIL2, 229).

marrying and giving in marriage. OT1 and OT2 read "marrying and given in marriage" (SHFJST, 111, 624), perhaps reflecting the cultural view that it was the man who married and the woman who gave herself in marriage. The change to "giving," which matches the term in Matthew 24:38, first appeared in the 1878 edition of the Pearl of Great Price (KPJMOSES, 140).

our wives bear unto us children. Having been told by Noah that all humankind would be destroyed by the Flood if they did not repent, these "sons of men" who styled themselves "sons of God" are said in rabbinic sources to have defiantly threatened, "If this is the case, we will stop human reproduction and multiplying, and thus put an end to the lineage of the sons of men ourselves" (JMBIGIL2, 230).

mighty men, which are like unto men of old, men of great renown. Parallel phrases in Genesis 6:4 read more literally in Hebrew as follows: "the *gibborim* that are of old, the men of the name (*ha-shem*)." It is possible that the description of the "mighty men . . . of old" referred back to the *gibborim* of Enoch's day. The description also anticipates the person of Nimrod and the group who will build the Tower of Babel in Genesis 11. See JMBIGIL2, 41, 230, 288, 390, 414.

8:22   ***God saw that the wickedness of men had become great in the earth.*** The construction of this phrase is a deliberate parallel with Moses 8:14. Whereas "the sons of men saw that those daughters were fair" and acted according to their corrupted judgment, "God saw that the wickedness of men had become great in the earth" and determined to "destroy man" (Moses 8:22, 26). Umberto Cassuto summarized the unhappy situation: "God blessed mankind that they should be fertile and fill [that is, *replenish*] the earth [Genesis 1:28; Moses 2:28], and He implemented His promise: men began to *multiply* on the face of the [*earth*] [Genesis 6:1; Moses 8:14]. Man, however, was an ingrate: he, too, *increased* [that is, *had become great*], but it was [*wickedness*] that he increased [Genesis 6:5; Moses 8:22]; truly, he filled *the earth*, but he did so with *violence* [Genesis 6:11, 13; Moses 8:28, 30]" (UCCOMMENTARY, 302).

lifted up in the imagination of the thoughts of his heart, being only evil continually.

²³ And it came to pass that Noah continued his preaching unto the people, saying: "Hearken, and give heed unto my words; ²⁴ believe and repent of your sins and be baptized in the name of Jesus Christ, the Son of God, even as our fathers, and ye shall receive the Holy Ghost, that ye may have all things made manifest; and if ye do not this, the floods will come in upon you"; nevertheless they hearkened not. ²⁵ And it repented Noah, and his heart was pained that the Lord had made man on the earth, and it grieved him at the heart.

every man was lifted up in the imagination of the thoughts of his heart, being only evil continually. Genesis 6:5 reads differently: "every imagination of the thoughts of his heart was only evil continually." Nahum M. Sarna translates this more plainly and comments as follows, "Every product of the thoughts of [man's] heart was nothing but evil all the time. . . . In biblical psychology, mental phenomena fall within the sphere of the heart, which is the organ of thought, understanding, and volition, not of feeling" (NMSGENESIS, 46–47).

8:23   **Noah continued his preaching.** Noah's persistence in calling his generation to repentance is highlighted by the repetition of the description of his preaching in vv. 16, 20, and 23. The threefold reiteration of his preaching is matched by the people's threefold refusal to hearken (vv. 20, 21, 24). Only after we are told for the third time that the people "hearkened not" to Noah does God announce His judgment (v. 26).

8:24   **be baptized.** Compare Moses 6:52–53, 65–66; 7:11.

even as our fathers. OT1 and OT2 read "even as our fathers did" (SHFJST, 111, 625). The change to "even as our fathers" first appeared in the 1902 edition of the Pearl of Great Price (KPJMOSES, 140).

receive the Holy Ghost. OT1 reads "receive the gift of the Holy Ghost" (SHFJST, 111).

that ye may have all things made manifest. It is through the Holy Ghost that we "may know the truth of all things" (Moroni 10:5). More specifically, however, through additional ordinances associated with the "power and authority of the higher, or Melchizedek Priesthood," individuals may "have the privilege of receiving the mysteries of the kingdom of heaven, to have the heavens opened unto them, to commune with the general assembly and church of the Firstborn, and to enjoy the communion and presence of God the Father, and Jesus the mediator of the new covenant" (Doctrine and Covenants 107:18–19; RDDPGP, 169–70).

Affirming that the right of access to the highest privileges of the priesthood is available to all willing to meet its qualifications, the Prophet Joseph Smith said, "Let us seek for the glory of Abraham, Noah, Adam, the Apostles, who have communion with [knowledge of] these things, and then we shall be among that number when Christ comes" (JSTPJS, 2 July 1839, 162).

hearkened not. See vv. 20–21. Only after we are told this third time that the people "hearkened not" to Noah does God announce His judgment (v. 26).

8:25   **it repented Noah.** Genesis reads differently, "It repented the Lord." Robert J. Matthews explains: Many passages in the King James Version state that the Lord, in Old Testament times, "repented" of some deed, or some action that He had thought to do. It should be noted that in some of these instances the meaning does not imply that the Lord repented of a moral evil, but only that He was sorrowful over some consequence. In fact, the meaning of the Hebrew word *nicham*, which is often translated "to repent" in the King James Version, is "to sigh," and by extension "to be sorry, moved to pity or compassion," and also "to rue, suffer, grieve, or repent." However[,] since the English word "repent" is connected in modern usage to wrongdoing, it is probably best that some other word be used in describing the doings of the God of Israel (JMBIGIL2, 231).

NOAH IS RIGHTEOUS, BUT THE EARTH IS CORRUPT AND WILL BE DESTROYED

²⁶ And the Lord said: "I will destroy man whom I have created, from the face of the earth, both man and beast, and the creeping things, and the fowls of the air; for it repenteth Noah that I have created them, and that I have made them; and he hath called upon me; for they have sought his life." ²⁷ And thus Noah found grace in the eyes of the Lord; for Noah was a just man, and perfect in his generation; and he walked with God, as did also his three sons, Shem, Ham, and Japheth.

Joseph Smith made changes consistent with Matthews' suggestion in Moses 8:25, 26; Exodus 32:14; 1 Samuel 15:11; 2 Samuel 24:16; Psalm 135:14; Jeremiah 18:8, 10; 26:3, 13, 19; 42:10; Amos 7:3, 6; and Jonah 3:10. The Prophet said:

I believe the Bible as it read when it came from the pen of the original writers. Ignorant translators, careless transcribers, or designing and corrupt priests have committed many errors. As it read, Genesis 6:6, "It repented the Lord that he had made man on the earth"; also, Numbers 23:19, "God is not a man, that he should lie; neither the Son of man, that he should repent"; which I do not believe. But it ought to read, "It repented Noah that God made man." This I believe, and then the other quotation stands fair (JSTPJS, 15 October 1843, 327).

his heart was pained . . . , and it grieved him at the heart. According to Gordon J. Wenham, the three Hebrew roots (*naham, asa, asabh*)—respectively corresponding to Noah's repentance or regret, the creation of humankind, and Noah's grief—repeat the verbs in the same order that Lamech used them earlier in his optimistic naming speech for Noah (Moses 8:9: "comfort," "work," and "toil"). Noah's bitter disappointment clashes with Lamech's hoped-for comfort point by point. Wenham comments that the Hebrew root at the core of the phrase "it grieved him at the heart" "is used to express the most intense form of human emotion, a mixture of rage and bitter anguish" (GJWGENESIS, 144).

8:26   **man and beast, and the creeping things, and the fowls of the air.** Sea creatures are not mentioned because they will continue to live during the Flood.

    he hath called upon me. In other words, Noah has called on God for divine protection.

    they have sought his life. See Moses 8:18.

8:27   **just man.** The Hebrew term *tsaddik*, translated as "just man" and used here for the first time in the Bible, "implies one who is adjudged to be 'in the right,' which is its meaning in such texts as Exodus 23:7, Deuteronomy 25:1, and Proverbs 17:15. Accordingly, the term *tsaddik* describes one whose conduct is found to be beyond reproach by the divine Judge" (NMSGENESIS, 50). Leon R. Kass notes that the description of Noah's virtues shows us "that it is these qualities, not heroic manliness (prized everywhere else), that are divinely favored" (LRKWISDOM, 163). For almost six hundred years, Noah had remained just in the midst of a corrupt world.

    perfect. The Hebrew term *tamim*, translated as "perfect" and also used here for the first time in the Bible, "is mostly found in ritual contexts." It "describes a sacrificial animal that is without blemish, as in Exodus 12:5 and Leviticus 1:3, 10. Only such an animal is acceptable to God, says Leviticus 22:17–25. As applied to human beings, *tamim* acquired a moral dimension connoting 'unblemished' by moral fault—hence a person of unimpeachable integrity. Such an individual enjoys God's fellowship, according to Psalms 15 and 101:6" (NMSGENESIS, 50). According to Umberto Cassuto, the juxtaposed words *tsaddik* and *tamim*, when used together as in Moses 8:27, signify that Noah is "wholly righteous" (JMBIGIL2, 233).

    he walked with God. Noah's high standing in the eyes of God can be compared with that of Enoch, who was the only other mortal in scripture said to have "walked with God" (Genesis 5:24)—meaning, according to some scholars, that these two patriarchs attained the promise of "eternal life" while still in mortality (JMBIGIL2, 202). Moses 6:68 and 7:1 affirm that Adam and "many" others in the early patriarchal lines also received this blessing.

Was Noah Drunk or in a Vision?

Figure 8–6. Tissot: *Noah in Vision*

In Genesis 9, we meet an industrious Noah diligently tending his vineyard, in striking contrast to a later depiction in the same chapter that describes him as being in an inebriated stupor. Scholars have noted the odd inconsistency between these two scenes. Can these two opposing pictures of Noah be reconciled?

It is difficult to know whether this contradiction is the result of different traditions, textual misunderstanding, or the abbreviated nature of the biblical account. But evidence gathered by Andrei Orlov (and others) indicates that there was in some periods of Jewish history a "systematic tendency" to defame or belittle Noah as a consequence of "debates about sacrificial practice and priestly succession." What seems certain is that Genesis, as we have it today, deliberately frames this sequel to Noah's Creation and Garden story as a replay of the scene of the Adam and Eve's Fall and judgment in Eden. Usually, the instigator of this "Fall" is seen to be Noah, who, it is said, succumbed to the intoxicating influence of wine from his vineyard. Here we take a different view—for more detail see MOSESS 77 and JMBARK.

What tent did Noah enter in Genesis 9:21? Remarking the feminine possessive that normally would mean "her tent," some Jewish traditions take these words as a reference to the tent of Noah's wife. Others see it as a reference to Shekhinah, the divine feminine symbol of the glory of God or to the *he* of the name Jehovah, hence reading the term as the "Tent of Yahweh," the holy sanctuary. In light of this and other evidence, verse 21 might be better read: "And he drank of the wine, and was drunken; and he was uncovered within [*the tent of Yahweh*]."

How are we to understand the mention that Noah "was drunken"? Most rabbinical sources make no attempt at explanation or justification Noah's drinking but instead roundly criticize his actions. However, according to a late, secondhand remembrance of a statement by Joseph Smith, Noah "was not drunk, but in a vision." Note that neither the Bible nor Joseph Smith offers any condemnation of Noah's supposed drunkenness. The Prophet's view agrees with the pseudepigraphal *Genesis Apocryphon* which, immediately after describing a ritual where Noah and his family drank wine, details a divine dream-vision. As further evidence that Noah's ritual resulted in revelation, Jewish scholar Yitzak Koler concurred that Noah was enwrapped in a vision while in the tent. He said "this explains why Shem and [Japheth] refrained from looking at Noah even after they had covered him, significantly '*ahorannît* [Hebrew "backward"] occurs elsewhere with regard to avoidance of looking directly at God in the course of revelation." Thus, we might read the verse: "And he drank of the wine, and was [*in a vision*]; and he was uncovered within [*the tent of Yahweh*]."

How does wine play into the picture? It should be remembered that priesthood ordinances often included sacramental drinks. For example, in Genesis 14, we read that Melchizedek brought "bread and wine" to Abraham before making him a king and a priest after Melchizedek's holy order. The blessing Noah gave after the wine in *Genesis Apocryphon* parallels the Melchizedek story. *Jubilees* provides further evidence that Noah's drinking of the wine should be seen in a ritual context. We are told that Noah "guarded" the wine until the fifth New Year festival, the "first day on the first of the first month," when he "made a feast with rejoicing. And he made a burnt offering to the Lord." In light of this evidence, verse 21 might be read: "And [*as part of the ordinance*] he drank of the wine, and was [*in a vision*]; and he was uncovered within [*the tent of Yahweh*]."

How do we make sense of Noah's being "uncovered" during his vision? When Saul, like the prophets who were with him, "stripped off his clothes . . . and prophesied before Samuel and . . . lay down naked all that day and . . . night," it means only that he was "divested of his armor and outer robes." In a similar sense, when we read in John 21:7 that Peter "was naked" as he was fishing, it means that "he had laid off his outer garment, and had on only his inner garment or tunic." Thus, we read: "And [*as part of the ordinance*] he drank of the wine, and was [*in a vision*]; and he was [*divested of his outer garment*] within [*the tent of Yahweh*]."

What was the sin of Ham and Canaan? Jewish traditions assert that the garment made by God for Adam was handed down to Noah, who wore it when he offered sacrifice. Could it be that just as it is specifically pointed out in scripture that Noah "removed the [skin] covering of the Ark" in Genesis 8:13, he subsequently removed his own ritual garment of skins? This "garment of repentance," which, by the way, was worn in those times as outer rather than inner clothing, might have been taken off by Noah in preparation for his being "clothed upon with glory." Of relevance is that some ancient readers state that Ham not only saw but also took the "skin garment" of his father, intending to usurp his priesthood authority. Coupling this idea with the understanding that Noah was in vision, we might read verse 22 as follows: And Ham, the father of Canaan, [*took*] the [*skin garment*] of his father [*while Noah was beholding the glory of God*].

²⁸ The earth was corrupt before God, and it was filled with violence. ²⁹ And God looked upon the earth, and, behold, it was corrupt, for all flesh had corrupted its way upon the earth. ³⁰ And God said unto Noah: "The end of all flesh is come before me, for the earth is filled with violence, and behold I will destroy all flesh from off the earth."

8:27   Enoch and Noah, whose names are mentioned together three times in the story of the Flood (Moses 8:2, 19; JST Genesis 9:21–24 [SHFJST, 127]), are the only two included in the genealogical list of the patriarchs whose deaths are not mentioned. John Sailhamer observes that both "found life amid the curse of death," both were rescued from death by the hand of God, and each in his turn was a rescuer to others (JHSGENESIS, 74–75).

8:28   *corrupt.* The "key Hebrew stem *sh-ḥ-t* occurs seven times" in the story of Noah (NMSGENESIS, 51). "In order to grasp the full significance of the verb *ṣaḥath* here, we must bear in mind the words of Jeremiah 28:3–4 concerning the potter: 'So I went down to the potter's house, and there he was working at his wheel. And the vessel he was making of clay was spoiled.' The material did not receive the form that the potter wished to give it; it assumed another shape and the vessel was spoiled in his hand. Then the potter changed the material back into a shapeless mass, and made of it another vessel in accordance with his desire" (Umberto Cassuto, JMBIGIL2, 233).

violence. The Hebrew term *ḥamas* corresponds to synonyms such as "'falsehood,' 'deceit,' or 'bloodshed.' It means, in general, the flagrant subversion of the ordered processes of law" (NMSGENESIS, 51). This description starkly contrasts with the just conduct of Noah (Moses 8:27). Leon R. Kass describes the deplorable state of of Noah's world, which is (according to the Gospels—Matthew 24:37) the same state we are in today (LRKWISDOM, 162):

> Self-conscious men . . . betake themselves to war and to beautiful (but not good) women, seeking recognition for their superhuman prowess. Whether from rage over mortality, from jealousy and resentment, or from a desire to gain favor from beautiful women, or to avenge the stealing of their wives and daughters, proud men are moved to the love of glory, won in bloody battle with one another. The world erupts into violence, the war of each against all. What ensues is what [English philosopher Thomas] Hobbes would later call 'the state of nature,' that is, the state characterized by absence of clear juridical power and authority, in which the life of man is nasty, brutish, and—through violence—short. Bloody destruction covers the earth.

8:30   *God said unto Noah.* In Mesopotamian accounts of the Flood, the supreme god consults only with his divine assembly about the Flood. However, the flood hero learns about the impending destruction when one of the lesser gods surreptitiously conveys the secret to him. By way of contrast, in the story of Noah, God makes the prophet aware of His intentions and speaks directly to him. Because the order to board the ark occurs forty days after the New Year, it is reasonable to suppose that this first communication occurred on the first day of the New Year (Umberto Cassuto, JMBIGIL2, 233; compare NMSGENESIS, 51).

destroy all flesh from off the earth. The Hebrew verb for "destroy" (*mashitam*) is "identical with the one used three times above in the sense of 'corrupt' and so inscribes a pattern of measure for measure" (RABIBLE, 1:27n13). What man has ruined, God will obliterate. The term is often translated "wipe out" or "blot out" because, according to Gordon J. Wenham, "it is used of erasing names from records (Exodus 17:14; 32:32–33) and wiping plates (2 Kings 21:13). Since water was sometimes used for achieving this result (Numbers 5:23), the very word chosen perhaps hints at how the complete annihilation of mankind will be secured" (GJWGENESIS, 145).

all flesh. Most scholars interpret the term "all flesh" to mean that the destruction will include both humankind and land animals.

from off the earth. Genesis Rabbah understands this phrase as "*with* the earth," saying, "Even the three handbreadths of earth which the plow can penetrate in the earth [i.e., the topsoil] were wiped away by the water" (JMBIGIL2, 234). "This reflects the biblical idea that moral corruption physically contaminates the earth, which must be purged of its pollution" (NMSGENESIS, 51).

HISTORY OF THE BOOK OF MOSES

THE placement of the Book of Moses as part of the Pearl of Great Price obscures the fact that it was actually produced in June 1830 as part of the "Joseph Smith Translation" of the Bible (JST). Below is a brief history of the JST and how its first chapters were excerpted to become the Book of Moses.

Background. During the translation of the Book of Mormon, Joseph Smith would have encountered passages that spoke of "plain and precious things" that had been removed from the Bible and of the coming forth of "other books" in the last days that would "make known the plain and precious things which [had] been taken away" (1 Nephi 13:40). In events that anticipated their involvement in restoring lost stories and teachings from the Bible, Joseph Smith and Oliver Cowdery had already produced what can be seen as a "new translation" of portions of John 21 in April 1829 (Doctrine and Covenants 7).

Significantly, there is support for the idea that Joseph Smith and Oliver Cowdery made specific preparations for the work of Bible translation. For example, in October 1829, they purchased a Bible that was eventually used in the preparation of the JST.[1] Though there is currently no independent evidence that this copy of the Bible was acquired with a new translation in mind, the time frame of the purchase is suggestive. The pioneering JST scholar Robert J. Matthews concluded, "It is possible that they were thinking of a new translation of the Bible even at that early date."[2]

If we assume for a moment that the Bible was purchased in October 1829 in anticipation of a new work of translation, how can the months of delay before it started be explained? Simply put, it was not until June 1830 that Joseph Smith was able to free himself to begin the new work of translation that was intended to restore "many important points, touching the salvation of men, [that] had been taken from the Bible, or lost before it was compiled."[3]

Translation history. JST scholar Kent P. Jackson summarizes the translation history:[4]

Not long after the Church was organized in the spring of 1830, Joseph Smith began a careful reading of the Bible to revise and make corrections in accordance with the

---

1   Kent P. Jackson. "Joseph Smith's Cooperstown Bible: The Historical Context of the Bible Used in the Joseph Smith Translation." *BYU Studies* 40, no. 1 (2001): 41–70. https://scholarsarchive.byu.edu/byusq/vol40/iss1/3/, 41.

2   Robert J. Matthews. *"A Plainer Translation": Joseph Smith's Translation of the Bible—a History and Commentary*. Provo, UT: Brigham Young University Press, 1975, 26.

3   Joseph Smith Jr. "History, 1838–1856, volume A-1 [23 December 1805–30 August 1834]," p. 183. https://www.josephsmithpapers.org/paper-summary/history-1838-1856-volume-a-1-23-december-1805-30-august-1834/189. Spelling and punctuation have been modernized.

4   K. P. Jackson, "Cooperstown Bible," 59–60.

inspiration he would receive. From that labor came the revelation of much truth and the restoration of many of the "precious things" that Nephi had foretold would be taken from the Bible (1 Nephi 13:23–29). In June 1830, the first revealed addition to the Bible was set to writing. Over the next three years, the Prophet made inspired changes, additions, and corrections while he filled his calling to provide a more correct translation for the Church. Collectively, these are called the "Joseph Smith Translation."

The first revelation of the Joseph Smith Translation is what we now have as Moses 1 in the Pearl of Great Price—the preface to the book of Genesis.[5] Beginning with Genesis 1:1, the Prophet apparently had the Bible before him and read aloud from it until he felt impressed to dictate a change in the wording. If no changes were required, he read the text as it stood. Thus dictating the text to his scribes, he progressed to Genesis 24, at which point he set aside the Old Testament as he was instructed in a revelation on March 7, 1831 (see Doctrine and Covenants 45:60–62). The following day, he began revising the New Testament. When he completed John 5 in February 1832, he ceased dictating the text in full to his scribes and began using an abbreviated notation system. From that time on, it appears that he read the verses from the Bible, marked in it the words or passages that needed to be corrected, and dictated only the changes to his scribes, who recorded them on the manuscript.

Following the completion of the New Testament in February 1833, Joseph Smith returned to his work on the Old Testament. He soon shifted to the abbreviated notation system for that manuscript also. . . . [During this last phase of Old Testament translation,] he dictated only the replacement words, as he had done earlier with the New Testament. At the end of the Old Testament manuscript, after the book of Malachi, the scribe wrote the following words: "Finished on the 2nd day of July 1833." That same day the Prophet and his counselors—Sidney Rigdon and Frederick G. Williams, both of whom had served as scribes for the new translation—wrote to Church members in Missouri and told them, "We this day finished the translating of the Scriptures, for which we returned gratitude to our Heavenly Father."

Did "finished" mean "final"? Despite the fact that the JST manuscript was marked as "finished," it would be a mistake to assume that the Book of Moses is currently in any sort of "final" form. As Robert J. Matthews aptly put it, "Any part of the translation might have been further touched upon and improved by additional revelation and emendation by the Prophet."[6]

In translating the Bible, Joseph Smith's criterion for the acceptability of a given reading was sometimes pragmatic rather than absolute. For example, after quoting a verse from Malachi in a letter to the Saints, he admitted that he "might have rendered a plainer translation." However, he said that his wording of the verse was satisfactory in this case because the words were "sufficiently plain to suit [the]

---

5 For arguments that the JST may have already been anticipated when Moses 1 was received, see Jeffrey M. Bradshaw, "Book of Moses Textual Criticism 3: Was the Book of Moses Simply an Unplanned Afterthought to Moses 1? A Response to Thomas A. Wayment. 'Intertextuality and the Purpose of Joseph Smith's New Translation of the Bible," 2020. In *Interpreter Blog.* https://www.interpreterfoundation.org/blog-book-of-moses-textual-criticism-3was-the-book-of-moses-simply-an-unplanned-afterthought-to-moses-1.

6 R. J. Matthews, *Plainer*, 215.

purpose as it stands" (Doctrine and Covenants 128:18).

There is another reason we should not think of the Book of Moses as being in its "final" form. Careful study of the translations, teachings, and revelations of Joseph Smith suggests that he sometimes knew more about certain matters—for example, sacred or sensitive topics—than he felt at liberty to teach publicly at a given time. [7]Even after Joseph Smith was well along in the translation process, he seems to have believed that God did not intend for him to publish the JST in his lifetime. For example, writing to W. W. Phelps in 1832, he said: "I would inform you that [the Bible translation] will not go from under my hand during my natural life for correction, revisal, or printing and the will of [the] Lord be done."[8]

Although in later years Joseph Smith reversed his position and made serious efforts to prepare the manuscript of the JST for publication, his own statement makes clear that at first he did not feel at liberty to share publicly all he had learned during translation. George Q. Cannon remembered Joseph Smith saying that he intended to go back and rework some portions of the Bible translation to add in truths he was previously "restrained . . . from giving in plainness and fulness."[9] In short, we should not be surprised if some important public or private teachings given later in Joseph Smith's life are missing from the JST.

Publication history. In August 1832, the first extract from JST Genesis, corresponding to Moses 7, was published in the Church's newspaper *The Evening and the Morning Star.* Publication continued with additional extracts from the new translation (Moses 6:43–68; 5:1–16; and 8:13–30) in March and April 1833.[10] Two years later, several verses from what is now Moses 2–5 were used in the publication of the *Lectures on Faith* within the 1835 Doctrine and Covenants. Finally, the Visions of Moses (Moses 1) appeared in the January 16, 1843 edition of the *Times and Seasons.* Although the JST had progressed to the point where the Prophet was planning publication of the entire manuscript in its current form, continual lack of time and means prevented it from appearing during his lifetime.[11]

---

7   Jeffrey M. Bradshaw, "Now That We Have the Words of Joseph Smith, How Shall We Begin To Understand Them? Illustrations of Selected Challenges Within the 21 May 1843 Discourse on 2 Peter 1." *Interpreter: A Journal of Mormon Scripture* 20 (2016): 47-150. https://journal. interpreterfoundation.org/now-that-we-have-the-words-of-joseph-smith-how-shall-we-begin-to-understand-them/, 50–51.

8   Joseph Smith Jr. "Letter to William W. Phelps, 31 July 1832," p. 5. https://www.josephsmithpapers. org/paper-summary/letter-to-william-w-phelps-31-july-1832/5. Spelling and punctuation have been modernized.

9   George Q. Cannon. 1888. *The Life of Joseph Smith, the Prophet.* 2nd ed. Salt Lake City: Deseret News, 1907, 129n. In a letter to her son Joseph on 10 February 1867, Emma Smith also mentioned the "unfinished condition of the work." (Cited in *Joseph Smith's "New Translation" of the Bible.* Independence, MO: Herald House, 1970, 11.)

10   For a detailed history of the text of the Book of Moses, see Kent P. Jackson. *The Book of Moses and the Joseph Smith Translation Manuscripts.* Provo, UT: Religious Studies Center, Brigham Young University, 2005. https://rsc.byu.edu/book/book-moses-joseph-smith-translation-manuscripts.

11   R. J. Matthews, *Plainer,* 391.

Drawing on the earlier newspaper publications, Elder Franklin D. Richards included portions of the Book of Moses in the first edition of the Pearl of Great Price, printed in England in 1851. The portions published by Elder Richards in the first version of the Pearl of Great Price were based on what had been published in Church periodicals (*The Evening and the Morning Star* [August 1832 to April 1833] and the *Times and Seasons* [January 1843]) as well as from a no-longer-extant personal handwritten copy of some additional unpublished portions of these revelations. Taken together, these represented about three-fourths of the current content of the Book of Moses. The abrupt ending of our current Book of Moses in the middle of the story of Noah is explained simply by the fact that this is where the *Times and Seasons* happened to have concluded their printing of excerpts from the JST, so it was all that was available to Elder Richards at the time.

The Prophet's wife Emma kept the original JST manuscripts until 1866, when they were given to the Reorganized Church of Jesus Christ of Latter Day Saints (RLDS, now known as the Community of Christ) and used to produce the original Inspired Version" (IV) of the Bible in 1867. When Elder Orson Pratt revised the Pearl of Great Price in 1878, he completely replaced the previously used Book of Moses text with a version based on the 1867 RLDS publication of the IV. A major revision of the Book of Moses was prepared by Elder James E. Talmage for a new edition of the Pearl of Great Price published by the Church in 1902. Small changes were made for a subsequent edition in 1921.

Based on new a review of available manuscripts, the RLDS Church published a "new corrected edition" of the IV in 1944. However, because Latter-day Saint scholars had not yet had an opportunity to compare the IV to the original manuscripts, its initial acceptance by Church members was limited.[12] An exhaustive study by Brigham Young University (BYU) religion professor Robert J. Matthews was published in 1975. He established that the 1944 and subsequent editions of the "Inspired Version," notwithstanding their shortcomings, constituted a faithful rendering of the work of the Prophet Joseph Smith and his scribes—insofar as the manuscripts were then understood.[13]

With painstaking effort over a period of eight years, and with the generous cooperation of the Community of Christ, a facsimile transcription of all the original manuscripts of the JST was at last published in 2004.[14] A detailed study of the text of the portions of the JST relating to the Book of Moses appeared in 2005.[15] Taken

---

12   Thomas E. Sherry. "Changing Attitudes toward Joseph Smith's Translation of the Bible." In *Plain and Precious Truths Restored: The Doctrinal and Historical Significance of the Joseph Smith Translation*, edited by Robert L. Millet and Robert J. Matthews, 187–226. Salt Lake City: Deseret Book, 1995.

13   R. J. Matthews, *Plainer*, 200–201. See also K. P. Jackson, *Book of Moses*, 20–33.

14   Scott H. Faulring, Kent P. Jackson, and Robert J. Matthews, eds. *Joseph Smith's New Translation of the Bible: Original Manuscripts*. Provo, UT: Religious Studies Center, Brigham Young University, 2004. These manuscripts can also be found at https://www.josephsmithpapers.org.

15   K. P. Jackson, *Book of Moses*.

together, these studies grant us greater clarity than ever before.

In 1979 and 1981, The Church of Jesus Christ of Latter-day Saints first published new editions of the scriptures that contained, along with various study aids, extracts of many (but not all) revisions from the JST.[16] In addtion to new footnotes and headings, four changes were made in the text of the Book of Moses.[17] A few minor changes to the Book of Moses were later included in a 2013 edition.

Although the JST is not the official Bible of the Church, it is seen as an invaluable aid in scripture study and a witness for the calling of the Prophet Joseph Smith.[18] The early chapters of JST Genesis (corresponding to Moses 1–8) and Matthew 24 (corresponding to Joseph Smith—Matthew) hold a place of special importance since they are included in the Pearl of Great Price.

Book of Moses manuscripts. The earliest extant dictation manuscript of the first 24 chapters of Genesis is called Old Testament 1 (OT1). This material was later copied to a second manuscript (OT2), which also contained a translation of additional Old Testament chapters. The bulk of Joseph Smith's additions and revisions to OT2 took place between March 1831 and July 1833, though the Prophet continued to make a few revisions and to prepare the manuscript for printing until his death in 1844. OT2 contains many minor revisions in wording over the earlier draft, though relatively little in the way of substantive prophetic additions. Besides OT1 and OT2, some individuals made personal copies of extracts from the translation.

When the RLDS publication committee prepared the "Inspired Version" they had inadvertently failed to incorporate many of the changes made in the latest version of the OT2 manuscript. For this reason, many passages in the current Latter-day Saint edition also follow the OT1.

Perhaps providentially, however, the portions of OT1 retained in the current canonical version of the Book of Moses (as well as portions not included) sometimes seem to have provided a superior reading.[19] Like the original manuscript of the Book of Mormon, OT1 seems to have included significant phrases and literary features that were later omitted or obscured by OT2 edits.[20]

---

16   For more about the selection process for included excerpts and a useful collection of significant changes not contained in the Latter-day Saint edition of the Bible, see Thomas E. Sherry and W. Jeffrey Marsh. "Precious Truths Restored: Joseph Smith Translation Changes Not Included in Our Bible." *Religious Educator* 5, no. 2 (2004): 57–74. https://rsc.byu.edu/vol-5-no-2-2004/precious-truths-restored-joseph-smith-translation-changes-not-included-our-bible.

17   See K. P. Jackson, *Book of Moses*, 1–52, for details of changes made in various editions.

18   Latter-day Saint Bible Dictionary, s.v. "Joseph Smith Translation."

19   Jeffrey M. Bradshaw, Matthew L. Bowen, and Ryan Dahle. "Textual Criticism and the Book of Moses: A Response to Colby Townsend's 'Returning to the Sources,' Part 1 of 2." *Interpreter: A Journal of Latter-day Saint Faith and Scholarship* 40 (2020): 99–162. https://journal.interpreterfoundation.org/textual-criticism-and-the-book-of-moses-a-response-to-colby-townsends-returning-to-the-sources-part-1-of-2/, 115–22.

20   Bradshaw, "Textual Criticism," 156–57nn131–133.

INTRODUCTION TO JOSEPH SMITH—MATTHEW

In the April 2020 conference, President Russell M. Nelson boldly characterized the "future of the Church" as "preparing the world for the Savior's Second Coming."[1] Among other things, he said:

> We are . . . building up to the climax of this last dispensation—when the Savior's Second Coming becomes a reality. . . . It is our charge—it is our privilege—to help prepare the world for that day. . . .

> Do whatever it takes to strengthen your faith in Jesus Christ by increasing your understanding of the doctrine taught in his restored Church and by relentlessly seeking truth. Anchored in pure doctrine, you will be able to step forward with faith and dogged persistence and "cheerfully do all that lies in [your] power" to fulfill the purposes of the Lord (see Doctrine and Covenants 123:17).

One way to strengthen our faith and increasing our understanding is to study what Jesus Christ Himself said about the events preceding His coming. Nowhere in scripture are these events described more completely and more plainly than in Joseph Smith's inspired translation of Matthew 24.

SIMILARITIES AND DIFFERENCES OF JS—MATTHEW TO RELATED ACCOUNTS

The most obvious difference between Joseph Smith—Matthew and Matthew 24 is that the new translation has added about 50 percent more words to the text. But as the table below indicates,[2] there is much more of interest than the *quantity* of new material in the structure of the translation and its relationship to various scripture texts:

- Joseph Smith—Matthew makes a clear division between the events contemporary with the early disciples (vv. 1–21a) and those of the last days (vv. 21b–55), thus addressing long-standing uncertainties among Matthew scholars.

- To make the time frames of the events described more clear, Joseph Smith—Matthew *reorders* some of the verses. In some cases, similar phrases are *repeated*, indicating parallels between earlier and later events. Repeated verses or portions of verses are shown in the table by parentheses surrounding verse numbers. The verse numbers appear without parentheses in their primary context (past versus future).

---

1   Russell M. Nelson, "The Future of the Church: Preparing the World for the Savior's Second Coming." *Ensign* 50, April 2020, 12–17. https://www.churchofjesuschrist.org/study/ensign/2020/04/the-future-of-the-church-preparing-the-world-for-the-saviors-second-coming?lang=eng, 13, 14, 17.

2   Adapted from David Rolph Seely. "The Olivet Discourse (Matthew 24–25; Mark 13; Luke 21:5–36)." In *The Gospels*, edited by Kent P. Jackson and Robert L. Millet. *Studies in Scripture*, 5:391–404. Salt Lake City: Deseret Book, 1986, 395, with a new column added for Doctrine and Covenants 45.

Joseph Smith—Matthew	Matthew 24	Doctrine and Covenants 45	Joseph Smith—Matthew	Matthew 24	Doctrine and Covenants 45
1	23:39		24–26	25–27	
		16a	27	28	24–25
2	1	16b	28	(6a)	(26)
		17–19	29	7	33
3	2	20	30	(12)	27
		21	31	14	28–30
4–6	3–5		32	(15)	31–32
7–9	9–11		33	29	42
10	12	(27)	34	34	(21)
11	13		35a	35	22
12	15	(32)	35b		23
13–18	16–21		36	30	39–41, 44, 47–55
19	8		37a	31a	45, 46a
20–21a	22		37b	31b	43, 46b
21b–22	23–24		38–39	32–33	36–38
23a	6a	26	40–54	36–51	
23b	6b	34–35	55		

(The left margin marks the upper portion of the table as "Past" and the lower portion as "Future.")

Table JS—Matthew–1. *Comparison of JS—Matthew, Matthew 24, and Doctrine and Covenants 45*

- Significant overlap exists between Doctrine and Covenants 45 and the two versions of Matthew 24, commending the idea that the three texts should be studied together. Note that much of what is contained in section 45 is either omitted or worded differently in the Matthew accounts. Other sections of the Doctrine and Covenants also contain significant overlaps in subject matter.[3]

- The Prophet changed the corresponding record in Mark to conform to the revised Matthew, "generally deleting verses in Mark that differed from Matthew and adding Matthew material not found in the King James text of Mark."[4]

- By way of contrast, Joseph Smith's translation of Luke "allows sharp differences to stand. Joseph Smith largely left Luke in the King James format, differing as it does in much wording from Matthew and Mark; Joseph Smith even added new verses to Luke's report of the Olivet discourse that increase Luke's individuality."[5]

Taken together, Richard L. Anderson concluded that the Prophet's

sweeping changes are only loosely tied to the written record that stimulated the new information. . . . One may label this as "translation" only in the broadest sense, for his

---

3   For example, Doctrine and Covenants 29, 43, 116, 133. See Kent P. Jackson. "The Signs of the Times: 'Be Not Troubled.'" In *The Doctrine and Covenants*, edited by Robert L. Millet and Kent P. Jackson. *Studies in Scripture*, 1:186–200. Salt Lake City: Deseret Book, 1989.

4   Richard Lloyd Anderson. "Joseph Smith's Insights into the Olivet Prophecy: Joseph Smith 1 and Matthew 24." In *Pearl of Great Price Symposium: A Centennial Presentation* (November 22, 1975), 48–61. Provo, UT: Department of Ancient Scripture, Religious Instruction, Brigham Young University, 1976, 49.

5   Anderson, "Joseph Smith's Insights," 50.

consistent amplifications imply that the Prophet felt that expansion of a document was the best way to get at meaning. If unconventional as history, the procedure may be a doctrinal gain if distinguished from normal translation procedure, for paraphrase and restatement are probably the best way to communicate without ambiguity. The result may be the paradox of having less literally the words of Bible personalities while possessing more clearly the meaning that their words sought to convey.[6]

SIGNIFICANCE FOR LATTER-DAY SAINTS

Although the prophecies of Joseph Smith—Matthew generated great interest among the early Saints, they have been relatively neglected since. In 1975, Richard L. Anderson commented that Joseph Smith—Matthew, "of all the Pearl of Great Price sections, . . . is probably least commented on."[7] His observation is likely still true today, but it is to be earnestly hoped that this trend of neglect will not continue forever.

At the end of the chapter on the fall of Jerusalem in Hugh Nibley's priesthood quorum study guide to the Book of Mormon, he posed an enigmatic question to his readers: "Explain the saying 'Wo to the generation that understands the Book of Mormon!'"[8] In response, he received inquiries asking whether he had written the question backward—in other words, that he meant instead to say "does *not* understand." Later he explained:

> It was a happy generation to which the abominations of the Nephites and Jaredites seemed utterly unreal.[9]

> For our generation the story [of the Book of Mormon] rings painfully familiar. . . . The generations that *understand* the Book of Mormon must needs be in the same situation that the ancient Americans were in, and people in such a predicament are to be pitied.[10]

So might it be said for those who see and understand the signs of the times reported in Joseph Smith—Matthew: "Wo be unto that generation!" But even more piteous is the state of Saints who have had the complete outline for the last days right in front of them since 1831, but because of indifference remain blind and ignorant to it.

> *Note*: In the commentary, references to Joseph Smith—Matthew will be abbreviated to JS—Matthew. "Matthew" will be used in mentions of the the King James translation. NT1 and NT2 refer to the original manuscripts of the Joseph Smith Translation of the New Testament. See the section entitled "History of Joseph Smith—Matthew" for more details.

---

6   Anderson, "Joseph Smith's Insights," 50.

7   Anderson, "Joseph Smith's Insights," 48.

8   Hugh W. Nibley. 1957. *An Approach to the Book of Mormon*. 3rd ed. Collected Works of Hugh Nibley 6. Salt Lake City: Deseret Book, 1988, 119.

9   Unidentified source, cited in Boyd J. Petersen. "Something to Move Mountains: The Book of Mormon in Hugh Nibley's Correspondence." *Journal of Book of Mormon Studies* 6, no. 2 (1997): 1–25. https://scholarsarchive.byu.edu/cgi/viewcontent.cgi?article=1164&context=jbms, 21.

10   Hugh Nibley to Parley H. Merrill, June 18, 1957, cited in Petersen, "Something," 22, emphasis added.

JOSEPH SMITH—MATTHEW

An extract from the Translation of the Bible as Revealed to Joseph Smith the Prophet in 1831: Matthew 23:39 and Chapter 24.

JESUS PROPHESIES OF HIS GLORIOUS RETURN

1 [1] "For I say unto you, that ye shall not see me henceforth and know that I am he of whom it is written by the prophets, until ye shall say: 'Blessed is he who cometh in the name of the Lord, in the clouds of heaven, and all the holy angels with him.'" Then understood his disciples that he should come again on the earth, after that he was glorified and crowned on the right hand of God.

1   The story opens on the heels of the narration of the seven woes that Jesus pronounced on the scribes and Pharisees. Anticipating His own demise, an event that would be spurred on by the hands of His own people, Jesus reminds His listeners that the shedding of the blood of the righteous has been the preoccupation of the wicked from the primeval times of Abel up to the more recent news of Zacharias—profanely slain in the very courtyard of the temple (Matthew 23:35). In closing, Jesus quotes Jeremiah's lament: "Behold, *your* house is left unto you desolate!" (Matthew 23:38, emphasis added; cf. Jeremiah 22:5). No longer is the temple His *Father's* house (Matthew 21:13)—as in the days of Jeremiah, the temple has been abandoned by God and left in the hands of its usurpers. The temple is now ripe for destruction.

     After saying this much as preface to our chapter, Jesus broadens His message to include warnings not only for the little group that stands before Him but also for Jerusalem—and ultimately for all people, both Jews and Gentiles. As the scope of His intended audience widens, so also His words begin to penetrate the depths of time, illuminating the "end of the world" (JS—M 1:4). Though Jesus has given pointed instructions for His first-century disciples about how to survive the calamities that will soon befall them in light of impending persecutions and the eventual destruction of Jerusalem a few decades later, He devotes most of His discourse to describing what latter-day disciples will need to know to recognize and navigate the unprecedented events of the end times. Jesus outlines the great work of the final gathering of covenant Israel. Then, in language that frequently echoes the more limited catastrophes of the first century, He describes the all-encompassing signs that will shake the heavens and the earth in anticipation of His glorious Second Coming.

1:1   *ye shall not see me henceforth and know that I am he of whom it is written by the prophets.* Matthew 23:39 reads more briefly, "Ye shall not see me henceforth." The added phrase underscores that had the people not ignored or scorned the words of the biblical prophets, they would have known that Jesus was the central figure of whom these prophets had spoken anciently.

     until ye shall say: 'Blessed is he who cometh in the name of the Lord, in the clouds of heaven, and all the holy angels with him.' Matthew 23:39 reads more briefly, "Blessed is he that cometh in the name of the Lord," quoting the greeting traditionally given by the priests to festival pilgrims on their way to the temple (Psalm 118:26). Pointedly, Jesus Himself had been greeted by these words at His triumphal entry into Jerusalem (Matthew 21:9). Again, the added phrase in JS—Matthew makes explicit what was left implicit in Matthew's text: there will be no opportunity to welcome the Redeemer to Jerusalem again until the day He returns in His glory.

     Then understood his disciples that he should come again on the earth. This addition to Matthew makes it clear that the Second Coming was a new idea to the disciples. Indeed, that is what will prompt the second part of their two-part question in JS—Matthew 1:4. In Doctrine and Covenants 45:16, the Savior declares that His coming will be "to fulfil the promises that I have made unto your fathers." Verses 17 and 19 of the same section also speak of the Resurrection and of the destruction, scattering, and restoration of Israel.

JESUS PROPHESIES THE DESTRUCTION OF HEROD'S TEMPLE

² And Jesus went out, and departed from the temple; and his disciples came to him, for to hear him, saying: "Master, show us concerning the buildings of the temple, as thou hast said—'They shall be thrown down, and left unto you desolate.'"
³ And Jesus said unto them: "See ye not all these things, and do ye not understand them? Verily I say unto you, there shall not be left here, upon this temple, one stone upon another that shall not be thrown down."

THE DISCIPLES ARE WARNED; THEY ARE TO STAND IN THE HOLY PLACE

⁴ And Jesus left them, and went upon the Mount of Olives. And as he sat upon the Mount of Olives, the disciples came unto him privately, saying: "Tell us when shall these things be which thou hast said concerning the destruction of the temple, and

1:2   *for to hear him.* Matthew 24:1 reads "for to shew him the buildings of the temple." While one might read Matthew 24:1 merely as an indicator of the "disciples' touristic enthusiasm" ("See what manner of stones and what buildings are here!" [Mark 13:1]), the JS—Matthew additions to the verse make it clear that the disciples were seeking to know whether Jesus really meant what He said about the temple: "Can He really mean that such a splendid complex is to be abandoned [and destroyed]? At any rate, their superficial admiration for the buildings forms a powerful foil to Jesus' negative verdict on them" (RTFMATTHEW, 887). Doctrine and Covenants 45:18 notes that the "enemies" of the disciples had falsely predicted "that this house shall never fall."

    one stone upon another. "The Greek term for stone, *lithos*, often has to do with a quarried and cut stone, one that is shaped to fit in a certain place. All of the fitted stones that make up the temple and its grounds will be pounded 'to powder'" (Luke 20:18; SKBLUKE, 937).

1:3   *and do ye not understand . . . ?* As earlier in v. 1, the added phrase highlights the fact that the disciples are slow to comprehend.

1:4   *Jesus left them, and went upon the Mount of Olives.* "While there is little direct verbal link with Ezekiel's vision of the glory of God leaving the temple (Ezekiel 10:18–19; 11:22–23), the reader might be expected to remember that powerful imagery, especially when Jesus immediately goes and sits on the Mount of Olives, the 'mountain east of the city' where the Lord's glory also stopped after going out over the east gate of the temple (Ezekiel 11:23)" (RTFMATTHEW, 887).

    the disciples came unto him privately. "According to Mark 13:3, only four disciples, 'Peter and James and John and Andrew,' the first-called pairs of brothers, are present at Jesus' sermon on the Mount of Olives. More generally, Matthew 24:3 mentions 'disciples' and, in a change to Mark 13, JST Mark 13:7 notes the presence of 'disciples,' implying more than the four men" (SKBLUKE, 938).

    what is the sign of thy coming. "The term translated 'sign' (Greek *sēmeion*) here points to an apocalyptic expectation or portent, not to a proof" (SKBLUKE, 939). Signs that are sought as proofs are usually condemned (for example, Matthew 12:39, 16:4; JSWORDS, 2 July 1839, 413).

    which thou hast said concerning the destruction of the temple, and the Jews. The disciples' question had two parts. This added phrase makes it clear that Jesus' answer to the first part of the question will refer to events in their lifetimes (vv. 5–21a). The answer to the second part of the question will address the events of the last days (vv. 21b–55).

    or the destruction of the wicked, which is the end of the world. Though the disciples had no way of knowing how far off the last days were to be, they did seem to understand that Jesus' Second Coming signaled the beginning of the Millennium, not the ultimate end of things (RDDPGP, 304).

    end of the world. "A familiar Jewish expression for the crisis which was expected to bring the

the Jews; and what is the sign of thy coming, and of the end of the world, or the destruction of the wicked, which is the end of the world?" ⁵ And Jesus answered, and said unto them: "Take heed that no man deceive you; ⁶ for many shall come in my name, saying—'I am Christ'—and shall deceive many; ⁷ then shall they deliver you up to be afflicted, and shall kill you, and ye shall be hated of all nations, for my name's sake; ⁸ and then shall many be offended, and shall betray one another,

present world order to a close and to inaugurate the 'age to come'" (RTFMATTHEW, 535). The idea is always closely associated with the Judgment. The wicked, being of a telestial nature, will be swept from the earth as part of a preliminary judgment at the beginning of the Millennium, while all those fit to abide at least a terrestrial glory will remain on the paradisiacal earth. See figure JS—Matthew-6.

1:5   **Take heed that no man deceive you.** Elder James E. Talmage observes that while the second part of the question addressed the *time* of Jesus' return, His reply, surprisingly, "dealt not with dates, but with events; and the spirit of the subsequent discourse was that of warning against misapprehension, and admonition to ceaseless vigilance" (JETJESUS, 528). The disciples thought they needed a timetable so they wouldn't "miss the boat"; Jesus knew the biggest danger was in their boarding the *wrong* boat.

1:6   **many shall come in my name.** "The plain sense of Jesus' words points to those who claim to represent him but do not, to those who claim his authority but do not possess it. . . . Uttering 'my name' raises a host of connections to Jehovah in the Old Testament, particularly in light of the divine name that follows" (SBKLUKE, 939–940).

    I am Christ. In other words, "I am the Messiah." Thus, we are not speaking of impostors who would claim to be the person of Jesus, but rather of those who would feign that they had "come in [His] name" (v. 6) and had been appointed to His calling as the Anointed One. For example, a Jewish figure with a large following in the early second century who claimed the title "Messiah" was Bar Kokhba. In addition, v. 9 speaks of "many false prophets." History records several examples of individuals who fit this mold (RTFMATTHEW, 902–3; HWNPGP, 318–19, 322; STLRABBINIC, 379, 381). The prophecy is directly confirmed in 1 John 2:18: "As ye have heard that antichrist shall come, even now are there many antichrists."

    Verses 6–7 of Matthew 24, which discuss wars and earthquakes, were removed from their original position following v. 5 and placed as vv. 23 and 29 in JS—Matthew. This makes it clear that these verses concern events of the last days. V. 8 of Matthew 24 is also moved later in JS—Matthew (v. 19). However, this change in position does not affect its application to the first-century time frame.

1:7   **deliver you up to be afflicted, and shall kill you.** The disciples would be afflicted by their countrymen, though sometimes family and fellow Christians became the persecutors (see SKBLUKE, 946). "A regional leader named Diotrephes opposed John, refusing to receive him or any other Church authorities, and excommunicating any who did (see 3 John). Paul came to death's door, it seems, because 'Alexander the coppersmith [a member] did [Paul] much evil' by turning away any who might help Paul at his trial before Nero Caesar (see 2 Timothy 4:14)." Government opposition was also the cause of many problems. "Peter and John were both arrested numerous times and even beaten by the authorities. Stephen and James were martyred" (RDDPGP, 306). See also SKBLUKE, 947–948 and compare JST Mark 13:11.

    for my name's sake. "At first glance, the phrase simply ties to afflictions suffered because of loyalty to Jesus. But more is at play here. The mention of 'name' lifts up links to the name of God. Specifically, a person's loyalty to God's name in the Old Testament rests on covenant agreements that are made and renewed at the temple and in worship settings during prayer and other sacred activities (see Genesis 4:26; 12:8; 1 Kings 18:36–37; Malachi 1:11; Moses 6:3–4). In addition, Jesus' name comes from heaven and thus bears special meaning to those who tie themselves to him and to his cause (see Luke 1:31; Matthew 1:21)" (SBKLUKE, 944).

Figure JS—Matthew–2. J. James Tissot, 1836–1902: *The Prophecy of the Destruction of the Temple*, 1886–94

JS—Matthew Reverses the Meaning of "Stand in the Holy Place"

Within Jesus' discourse to the Apostles on the Mount of Olives, He gave one of the most controversial prophecies of the New Testament:

> When ye therefore shall see the abomination of desolation, . . . stand in the holy place. (Matthew 24:15)

Comparing the verse in Matthew to its equivalent in JS—Matthew, we see that the Prophet has rendered this passage in a way that radically changes its meaning. Rather than describing how the "*abomination of desolation*" (= "the abomination that brings destruction") will "stand in the holy place," the JS—Matthew version enjoins the *disciples* to "stand in the holy place" when the "abomination of desolation" appears (JS—Matthew 1:12–13). In these and related verses in the Doctrine and Covenants, the sense of this phrase in the synoptic Gospels is turned upside down. In short, rather than describing how an *evil thing* would stand the holy place, thereby *profaning* it, modern scripture applies the phrase to ancient and modern disciples, admonishing *them* to stand in holy places and thereby be *saved*.

Though several Latter-day Saint scholars have offered interpretations and personal applications of the sense of these words as given in modern scripture, few have seriously explored how this change in meaning could be explained and defended. It is easy to see how, on the face of it, some readers might be (erroneously) led to conclude that Joseph Smith's rendering of the verse in question was an obvious and embarrassing mistake based on his admittedly rudimentary acquaintance with the Greek text of the New Testament. However, there is plentiful evidence to support an alternative claim: namely, that in the scriptural word picture of the righteous standing in holy places, Joseph Smith's interpretation—whether or not a consonant Greek reading is ever found—resonates with a potent metaphor from the heart of Judaism and early Christianity.

Examination of relevant passages in the Bible, in connection with the light shed by Jewish midrash and contemporary scholarship, shows that the idea behind Joseph Smith's application of the concept of standing in the holy place in JS—Matthew (as well as the associated idea of not being "moved" in verses such as Doctrine and Covenants 45:32), far from being a modern invention, reverberates throughout the religious thought of earlier times. Indeed, as Jewish scholar Avivah Zornberg has argued, the Hebrew Bible teaches that standing in the holy place—"hold[ing one's] ground," as it were, in sacred circumstances—is a powerful symbol of the central purpose of existence. This purpose can be expressed as follows: "being— *kiyyum*: to rise up (*la-koom*), to be tall (*koma zokufa*) in the presence of God" (AGZBEGIN, 21).

For additional discussion, see JMBSTANDING, 71–72, 74.

and shall hate one another; [9] and many false prophets shall arise, and shall deceive many; [10] and because iniquity shall abound, the love of many shall wax cold; [11] but he that remaineth steadfast and is not overcome, the same shall be saved.

[12] "When you, therefore, shall see the abomination of desolation, spoken of by Daniel the prophet, concerning the destruction of Jerusalem, then you shall stand

1:8   ***and shall hate one another.*** Present in NT1, this phrase was left out in NT2 and then restored in 1981.

1:10   ***the love of many shall wax cold.*** Iniquity is both the cause and result of a hardened heart. Thus, "the 'cooling' of love marks the end of effective discipleship" (**RTFMATTHEW**, 907. See also JMBFAITH, 77, 104–11). Such will also be the condition of many in the last days (v. 30).

1:11   ***he that remaineth steadfast.*** Matthew 24:13 reads "he that shall endure unto the end." In Latter-day Saint scripture, to "endure to the end" means to complete the path that leads to eternal life or, in other words, to come to the point of readiness where a sure promise of calling and election may, in God's time, be received (JMBFAITH, 71n54, 73–74, 82–90). However, Samuel T. Lachs bridges the King James and Joseph Smith translations by observing wordplay between a Hebrew term for "end" (*tāmam*) and a related term for "perfect, complete, wholehearted" (*tām*). Thus, we might read, "One who remains *tām* will be saved" (STLRABBINIC, 183; JMBFAITH, 71). Or, perhaps, "One who is 'able to endure all things' will be saved" (Articles of Faith 1:13; JMBFAITH, 111).

Draper, Brown, and Rhodes rightfully observe that the English term "*endurance* denotes holding firm, but it says nothing about the inward attitude of the person. Steadfastness adds this dimension, suggesting a firm, willful, and especially unwavering devotion" (RDDPGP, 307). Kenneth E. Bailey writes the following about the Greek term *hupomene*, meaning "patience," "endurance," and "steadfastness":

> *Hupo* has to do with "under" and *meno* means "to remain." As a compound, this word describes "The affliction under which one remains steadfast." If *makrothumia* [long-suffering] is the patience of the powerful, *hupomene* is the patience of the weak who unflinchingly endure suffering. . . . Jesus . . . is the supreme example of [this] virtue. (JMBFAITH, 71)

1:12   ***the abomination of desolation.*** The prophet Daniel (Daniel 8:13; 9:27; 11:31; 12:11) is the source for Matthew's description of the "abomination of desolation," better translated as the "abomination that brings desolation." In other words, the "abomination" (sacrilege) is the cause and "desolation" (devastation) is the effect. Thus, the battles that lead to the destruction of Jerusalem, as mentioned in Luke 21:20 and JS—Matthew 1:12, should be read as describing the prophesied "desolation" rather than the "abomination" that preceded it. As further evidence of the independence of the two terms, note S. Kent Brown's observation that the Greek term for "desolation" (*erēmōsis*) "without qualifiers, also appears in Doctrine and Covenants 29:8; 45:19, 21; and 112:24" (SKBLLUKE, 950).

While there is wide agreement about the "desolation," scholars disagree about the "abomination" Jesus described. See figure JS—Matthew-5 for one option. France argues that Matthew's failure to "produce a clearer and more convincing account" of the "abomination" is evidence that Matthew wrote his Gospel before "the climax of the war with Rome" (RTFMATTHEW, 913).

the destruction of Jerusalem. S. Kent Brown mentions that much of the city will be literally "flattened" in the destruction because "the supporting timbers will collapse, bringing the charred roofs and walls of home and buildings to the ground" (Luke 19:44; SKBLUKE, 883). Brown cites the Jewish historian Josephus (*Wars*, 7.1.1; also 6.9.4) to remark in support of the idea that the Romans will so deform Jerusalem after its capture "that future visitors will not believe that the city 'had ever been inhabited'" (SKBLUKE, 883).

you shall stand in the holy place. The Joseph Smith Translation (JST) reverses the meaning of this phrase. While Matthew describes how an *evil thing* (= "abomination") would stand in the holy place, thereby *profaning* it, JS—Matthew applies the phrase to ancient and modern disciples, admonishing *them* to stand in holy places and thereby be *saved*. For a discussion of this change in meaning, see figure JS—Matthew-2.

Figure JS—Matthew–3. J. James Tissot, 1836–1902: *The Guards Falling Backwards*, 1886–94

THE TEMPLE GUARDS' FAILURE TO STAND IN A HOLY PLACE

While Matthew, Mark, and Luke's accounts highlight the perfidy of Judas as the one who identified his Master to the temple guards, the Gospel of John instead emphasizes Christ's own mastery of the situation. Perhaps this is why the kiss of Judas does not appear in John's narrative. Herman N. Ridderbos explains, "Judas' task of identifying Jesus had been taken out of his hands" (JMBSTANDING, 85). Instead, when Judas enters the scene, Jesus is shown in full control of the arresting party by His startling self-identification:

> Jesus therefore, knowing all things that should come upon him, went forth, and said unto them, Whom seek ye?
>
> They answered him, Jesus of Nazareth. Jesus saith unto them, I am he. . . .
>
> As soon then as he had said unto them, I am he, they went backward, and fell to the ground. (John 18:4–6)

The King James translation of the Greek phrase *ego eimi* as "I am he" obscures an essential detail. In reality, Jesus has not said, "I am *he*," but rather "I AM," using a divine name that directly identifies Him as being Jehovah. Thus, asserts Raymond E. Brown, it is clear that the fall of the temple guards is no mere slapstick scene that might be "explained away or trivialized. To know or use the divine name, as Jesus does [in replying with 'I AM'], is an exercise of awesome power" (JMBSTANDING, 86).

In effect, in the Gospel of John the narrative takes the form of an eyewitness report of a solemn revelation to the band of arresting Jewish temple guards that they were standing, figuratively speaking, in a "Holy of Holies" made sacred by the presence of the embodied Jehovah, and that they, with full comprehension of the irony of their pernicious intent, were about to do harm to the very Master of the Lord's house, whose precincts they had been sworn to protect. As with the Israelites at Sinai who were unworthy and thus unable to stand in the holy place (see JMBSTANDING, 83–85), "those of the dark world fell back, repelled by the presence of the Light of the world" (WJHJOHN, 4–5).

To delve further into the symbolism of the scene, note that the Jews were generally prohibited from pronouncing the divine name Jehovah. As an exception, that name was solemnly pronounced by the high priest standing in the most holy place of the temple once a year, on the Day of Atonement. Upon hearing that name, according to the Mishnah, all the people were to fall on their faces. Was it any coincidence, then, that Jesus Christ, the great High Priest after the order of Melchizedek, boldly proclaimed His identity as the great "I AM" at the very place and on the very night He atoned for the sins of the world? Ironically, the temple guards who failed to fall on their faces at the sound of the divine name as prescribed in Jewish law were instead thrown on their backs in awestruck impotence.

For additional discussion, see JMBSTANDING, 85–87; MOSESS 69.

in the holy place; whoso readeth let him understand. [13] Then let them who are in Judea flee into the mountains; [14] let him who is on the housetop flee, and not return to take anything out of his house; [15] neither let him who is in the field return back to take his clothes; [16] and wo unto them that are with child, and unto them that give suck in those days; [17] therefore, pray ye the Lord that your flight be not in the winter, neither on the Sabbath day."

THE JEWS ARE WARNED OF GREAT TRIBULATION

[18] "For then, in those days, shall be great tribulation on the Jews, and upon the inhabitants of Jerusalem, such as was not before sent upon Israel, of God, since the beginning of their kingdom until this time; no, nor ever shall be sent again upon Israel. [19] All things which have befallen them are only the beginning of the sorrows which shall come upon them. [20] And except those days should be shortened,

1:12   *holy place; whoso readeth let him understand.* When Jesus told His disciples to "stand in the holy place," He was careful to qualify His instructions by saying, "Whoso readeth let him understand" (v. 12). This is because the "holy place" He had in mind was not the profaned temple of Jerusalem, but seemingly some place that was to be designated at the appointed time—perhaps in "the mountains" (v. 13; HWNPGP, 320–21; STLRABBINIC, 383), or maybe alternatively in the vicinity of Pella (in the lowlands of the Jordan River), as reported by Eusebius (*Ecclesiatical History*, III, 5.3) and Epiphanius (*Panarion*, XXIX, 7, 7–8; XXX, 2, 7), and as alluded to in the *Clementine Recognitions* (I, 37, 2; 39, 3 (Syriac); I, 39, 3 (Latin); see JBMOVE; SKBLUKE, 950). As another option, Julie M. Smith suggests the injunction for the disciples to seek the mountains may have been a symbolic reference to the temple as "the paradigmatic meeting place between humans and God" (JMSMARK, 687). In a contrast to Jesus' instructions, Josephus reports that false prophets had told Jerusalemites that they would be delivered if they stood firm (FJWARS 6:5:2 [285–86], p. 898). For readers in the last days (as opposed to first-century Christians), the idea of "holy places" should be understood differently. See figure JS—Matthew-6.

1:13   *let them who are in Judea flee.* "The reference to 'Judea' suggests that the period envisaged is before the final siege of Jerusalem, when the wider province was being brought under Roman control, but when escape was still possible. . . . The urgency of flight is underlined by the vivid images of the person who hears the news while resting on the roof of the house and dare not go inside (the roof was reached by an outside staircase) to pack a travel bag, and the field worker whose outer garment, removed for work, must be left behind" (RTFMATTHEW, 914).

1:16   *wo unto them that are with child.* "Terrible, indeed, would that day be for women hampered by the conditions incident to approaching maternity, or the responsibility of caring for their suckling babes. All would do well to pray that their flight be not be forced upon them in winter time; nor on the Sabbath, lest regard for the restrictions as to Sabbath-day travel, or the usual closing of the city gates on that day, should diminish the chances of escape" (JETJESUS, 530–31).

1:18   *great tribulation on the Jews.* JS—Matthew expands vv. 18–19 in order to assure that the unprecedented scale of suffering is adequately described through heavy layers of superlatives. All the sorrows that have befallen Israel in the past "are only the beginning of the sorrows which shall come upon them" (v. 19). This statement is made unconditionally; there is no further opportunity given for reprieve. For three years, from 67 to 70 CE, the Roman forces under Vespasian battled and then laid siege to Jerusalem. "During that time, the Jews suffered from brutal infighting, starvation, and plague. By the time the siege ended, thousands had died" (RDDPGP, 310).

there should none of their flesh be saved; but for the elect's sake, according to the covenant, those days shall be shortened."

GATHERING AND DESTRUCTION IN THE LAST DAYS

[21] "Behold, these things I have spoken unto you concerning the Jews; and again, after the tribulation of those days which shall come upon Jerusalem, if any man shall say unto you, 'Lo, here is Christ, or there,' believe him not; [22] for in those days there shall also rise false Christs, and false prophets, and shall show great signs and

---

1:20   *for the elect's sake, according to the covenant.* The "elect" are again referred to in vv. 23, 28. The presence of the "elect" in Jerusalem, like the "righteous" in Sodom (Genesis 18:22–32), "would alleviate the punishment the city deserves" (RTFMATTHEW, 916). The phrase "according to the covenant," mirrored in v. 22, is added in JS—Matthew, reminding the reader of God's promise to Abraham, Isaac, and Jacob that their posterity would be preserved as a people (RDDPGP, 311). Correcting the erroneous view that righteousness always prevents suffering, the Prophet Joseph Smith taught: "It is a false idea that the Saints will escape all the judgments while the wicked suffer, or all flesh is subject to suffer[ing] and 'the righteous shall hardly escape' [see Doctrine and Covenants 63:34]. Still many of the Saints will escape. . . . Yet many of the righteous shall fall prey to disease, to pestilence, etc., by reason of the flesh, and yet be saved in the Kingdom of God" (JSWORDS, 15).

        those days shall be shortened. "The horror was in fact 'cut short' by the Roman capture of the city after five months, bringing physical relief to those who had survived the famine in the city" (RTFMATTHEW, 915). The use of the passive voice, which omits the agent of the action ("shall be shortened"), is often used in scripture to indicate that the hand of God was at work.

        In S. Kent Brown's description of ensuing tribulation of Jerusalem, he emphasizes the Savior's pathos: "He desperately seeks to bring peace and salvation to his people but, painfully, through tears, knows that their representatives already conspire against him. . . . The verb "come near" (Luke 19:41) and the nouns "day" and "time" (Luke 19:42–44) all frame citizens' opportunities, at this critical and promising moment. . . . Painfully, and maliciously by week's end, the framework of promise will be bent and gnarled to show a wave-like landscape of missed opportunities and wrong decisions, of clear choices and bundgled judgments" (SKBLUKE, 884–85).

        According to the unique report of Luke (21:24), those who are left in Jerusalem "shall fall by the edge of the sword, and shall be led away captive into all nations; and Jerusalem shall be trodden down of the Gentiles, until the times of the Gentiles shall be fulfilled." Explaining the phrase, "the times of the Gentiles," S. Kent Brown writes: "In a word, most Jews of Jesus' era reject his message, thus propelling the Apostles toward the Gentiles. After the Gentiles receive the gospel, it will go to the Jews (see 1 Nephi 10:14; also Doctrine and Covenants 19:27; 20:9; 21:12; 45:25, 30). Importantly this situation will be true of 'the latter day' (3 Nephi 16:7; see 3 Nephi 16:4–15)" (SKBLUKE 953).

1:21   *after the tribulation . . . which shall come upon Jerusalem.* This phrase, added in JS—Matthew, serves as a hinge point in the chapter. The added words make it clear that the events related previously belong to the first century. Everything described from here on out will take place in the last days. Compare JST Luke 21:24.

1:22   *false Christs, and false prophets, and shall show great signs and wonders.* As in the time of the disciples (v. 6), false Messiahs and prophets will arise in the last days. The Israelites had already been warned about deceivers who would exhibit "great signs and wonders" as false proof of their calling from the time of Moses onward (Deuteronomy 13:2–3). Significantly, Draper, Brown, and Rhodes cite Elder Bruce R. McConkie for the teaching that a false prophet "need not be an individual but could instead be a form of worship, a false philosophy or ethical system, or a false church" (RDDPGP, 313–14).

wonders, insomuch, that, if possible, they shall deceive the very elect, who are the elect according to the covenant. ²³ Behold, I speak these things unto you for the elect's sake; and you also shall hear of wars, and rumors of wars; see that ye be not troubled, for all I have told you must come to pass; but the end is not yet.

²⁴ "Behold, I have told you before; ²⁵ wherefore, if they shall say unto you: 'Behold, he is in the desert'; go not forth: 'Behold, he is in the secret chambers'; believe it not; ²⁶ for as the light of the morning cometh out of the east, and shineth even unto the west, and covereth the whole earth, so shall also the coming of the Son of Man be.

²⁷ "And now I show unto you a parable. Behold, 'wheresoever the carcass is, there will the eagles be gathered together'; so likewise shall mine elect be gathered from the four quarters of the earth.

1:22   *deceive the very elect.* The term "very elect" refers to covenant Israel. Like the five wise virgins, those who "have taken the Holy Spirit for their guide" and who treasure God's word will be able to recognize deception (Doctrine and Covenants 45:57; JS—Matthew 1:37). This is one of many reasons why President Russell M. Nelson stated that "in coming days, it will not be possible to survive spiritually without the guiding, directing, comforting, and constant influence of the Holy Ghost" (RMNREV, 96).

1:23   *wars, rumors of wars.* These words predict a future of universal military conflict. The bloody consequences of war will be inescapable, signaled in every direction both by the frightening "noise of battle near at hand and the news of battles far away" (*New English Bible*).

1:25   *in the desert . . . in the secret chambers.* In other words, you will not find the Son of Man by looking for Him, whether you are looking outside or inside. In support of this clear contrast, Samuel T. Lachs conjectures that the Aramaic term for "in the open" was misread as "desert" (STLRABBINIC, 321).

1:26   *as the light of the morning.* JS—Matthew changes "lightning" to "light of the morning." In Jewish tradition, "the Messiah is often described as coming on a cloud together with flashing lightning which illumines the entire world" (STLRABBINIC, 121). However, Joseph Smith described the scene as follows: "As . . . the dawning of the morning makes its appearance in the east and moves along gradually, so also will the coming of the Son of Man be. It will be small at its first appearance and gradually become larger until every eye shall see it. Shall the Saints understand it? Oh, yes. Paul says so [1 Thessalonians 5:1–8]. Shall the wicked understand? Oh, no. They [will] attribute it to a natural cause" (JSWORDS, 181). In v. 36, this coming is called "the sign of the Son of Man." S. Kent Brown comments (SKBLUKE, 959, 960):

> On this occasion [the Savior] comes . . . descending from heaven. Concretely, He will arrive at several spots near one another, including the Mount of Olives (see Zechariah 1:4; Doctrine and Covenants 45:48; 133:20), Mount Zion (see Doctrine and Covenants 133:18), and Jeruslaem itself (see Doctrine and Covenants 133:21). . . .
>
> More concretely for His Apostles, Jesus affirms personally to them in his first-person account that, when He comes again, "if ye have slept in peace blessed are you; for as you now behold me and know that I am, even so shall ye come unto me" from their sleep in the grave. More than this, in that day "your redemption shall be perfected," bringing a glorious climax to their quest for eternal life (Doctrine and Covenants 45:46).

1:27   *wheresoever the carcass is, there will the eagles be gathered together.* The Greek word used can be understood as referring to "eagles," but the mention of a "carcass" and similar sayings in biblical sources (e.g., Job 39:29) and nonbiblical sources suggest that a vulture is meant (eagles eat live prey rather than carrion). See RTFMATTHEW, 897, 918; STLRABBINIC, 321.

so likewise shall mine elect be gathered. Since no application is given for the mini-parable in Matthew, a variety of proposals have been entertained. However, JS—Matthew straightforwardly

Figure JS—Matthew—4. William Blake, 1757–1827: *Sketch for "War Unchained by an Angel,"* ca. 1780–84

"Wars, and Rumors of Wars"

This sketch, a study for a lost work exhibited at the Royal Academy in 1784, was itself lost until recent times. Speaking as if he were standing before this scene, John Bright (1811–89), a Quaker, addressed the English House of Commons in fruitless opposition to the Crimean War. "As the war continued, Bright [had become] deeply distressed by the loss of life: 22,000 British soldiers died, but only 4,000 in action; the rest died from malnutrition, exposure, and disease" (Nicholas Elliott). In his famous speech delivered on February 23, 1855, Bright said, "The angel of death has been abroad throughout the land; you may almost hear the beating of his wings. There is no one as when the first-born were slain of old, to sprinkle with blood the lintel and the two side-posts of our doors, that he may spare and pass on; he takes his victims from the castle of the noble, the mansion of the wealthy, and the cottage of the poor and lowly." Bright's "oratory was so powerful that the House fell into complete silence. This, however, was not a view shared by his constituents in Manchester and he lost his seat at the ensuing election" (Bill Cash).

On Christmas Day, 1832, John Bright's contemporary, Joseph Smith, was troubled with night visions of war, "in which," according to Jedediah M. Grant,

> he saw the American continent drenched in blood, and he saw nation rising up against nation. He also saw the father shed the blood of the son, and the son the blood of the father; the mother put to death the daughter, and the daughter the mother; and natural affection forsook the hearts of the wicked; for he saw that the Spirit of God should be withdrawn from the inhabitants of the earth, in consequence of which there should be blood upon the face of the whole earth, except among the people of the Most High. The Prophet gazed upon the scene his vision presented, until his heart sickened, and he besought the Lord to close it up again.

The Prophet never recorded the vision in its fulness, though he did write a brief summary in section 87 of the Doctrine and Covenants (JMBIGIL2, 106).

²⁸ "And they shall hear of wars, and rumors of wars. ²⁹ Behold I speak for mine elect's sake; for nation shall rise against nation, and kingdom against kingdom; there shall be famines, and pestilences, and earthquakes, in divers places. ³⁰ And again, because iniquity shall abound, the love of men shall wax cold; but he that shall not be overcome, the same shall be saved. ³¹ And again, this Gospel of the Kingdom shall be preached in all the world, for a witness unto all nations, and then shall the end come, or the destruction of the wicked."

SECOND ABOMINATION OF DESOLATION; SIGNS OF THE SECOND COMING

³² "And again shall the abomination of desolation, spoken of by Daniel the prophet, be fulfilled. ³³ And immediately after the tribulation of those days,

> 'the sun shall be darkened,
> and the moon shall not give her light,
> and the stars shall fall from heaven,
> and the powers of heaven shall be shaken.'

1:27   interprets the enigmatic proverb as imagery for the worldwide gathering of Israel. Nibley explains: [The vulture imagery] puzzles so many people because it sounds so unpleasant to compare the elect gathering in the church to a carcass. . . . But the purpose of every image . . . is to emphasize one particular point. In verse 47 [it] says that the Lord will come as a thief in the night. Does that mean he is going to come to rob people, . . . that he is going to be dishonest? Of course not. It means he will . . . [take] you by surprise when you are not expecting it. . . .

     What happens where there is a carcass in the desert . . . ? The . . . vultures [come] . . . from all directions. All of a sudden they appear out of nowhere. It's quite miraculous to see. How do they know? . . . Their eyesight is absolutely fabulous. From miles away you see the specks coming, and where the carcass is they gather in a mysterious way from all directions (HWNPGP, 323).

     The themes of vv. 36–37 (= Matthew 24:30–31) parallel those of vv. 26–27, making it clear that the swift, sure assembly of the vultures is also a symbolic description of how the "angels . . . shall gather the remainder of [the] elect from the four winds, from one end of heaven to the other." In contrast to the Prophet's explanation of the parable of the mustard seed in which the birds in the branches of the mature mustard tree were said to represent angels sent to *assist with the gathering* (JSWORDS, 10), it seems that the "vultures" in this case represent those who are *being* gathered. In other words, like the "vultures," the "elect" will swiftly assemble "from the four winds, from one end of heaven to the other," to the "carcass," or "corpse" (Latin *corpus*), which is evidently meant to represent the body of the Church (Colossians 1:18; JETJESUS, 532), or the gathering places of the Saints. There they can be nourished by receiving the gospel and the fulness of the ordinances of the priesthood (JSWORDS, 212–13). The Prophet's interpretation connects the themes of vv. 26–27 and vv. 36–37 in a remarkably coherent manner. For more on the scattering and gathering in the context of Jesus' discourse, see Doctrine and Covenants 45:24–25.

1:29   ***nation shall rise against nation.*** "Throughout apocalyptic literature universal fighting is considered to be a sign that the end is approaching. 'When you see the kingdoms fighting against one another, look and expect the foot of the Messiah' (*Genesis Rabbah* 42:4)" (STLRABBINIC, 379; see figure JS—Matthew-4). More generally, in Matthew, the signs in JS—Matthew 1:28–29 are associated in Jewish tradition with "the beginning of the sorrows," understood as the "suffering pangs of the Messiah" that precede His coming. "The biblical material abounds with passages describing the troubles, woes, breakdown of family, and the general moral decline which

Figure JS—Matthew-5. J. James Tissot, 1836–1902: *The Raising of the Cross*, 1886–94

THE ABOMINATION OF DESOLATION IS TO BE REPEATED IN THE LAST DAYS

Because the "abomination" that Daniel referred to involved a disruption of temple sacrifices (Daniel 8:13; 9:27; 11:31; 12:11), most scholars accept that the "abomination" that Jesus prophesied would occur in the lifetime of the disciples had something to do with the desecration of Herod's temple. The problem is that, as Richard T. France admits, none of the possibilities adduced for a specific event of temple desecration in the first century CE "quite fits what [the verse in Matthew] says" (RTFMATTHEW, 913. See also STLRABBINIC, 382–83).

As a distinctly different possibility, Peter G. Bolt has argued that Jesus' reference to the "abomination" that would precede the destruction of Jerusalem was more likely a prophecy of the violent and ultimately fatal profanation of the temple of His own body—which He previously had said could be destroyed and raised up in three days (Matthew 26:61; Mark 14:58; John 2:19). Bolt asserts that in quoting the prophet Daniel, the Savior was using "apocalyptic language preparing the disciples for [His own] coming death. This fits with the rest of [the] story, for [there could be no] greater act of sacrilege than the destruction of God's Son in such a horrendous way" (PGBCROSS, 101). Had not Jesus referred to Himself earlier in Matthew 12:6 as "one *greater* than the temple"? (emphasis added). Note also Craig S. Keener's view that Daniel 9:26 "associates the ['abomination that maketh desolate'] with the cutting off of an anointed ruler, close to the time of Jesus" (CSKMATTHEW, 575; see also JBPIMMINENT, 147–49).

Going further, the Latter-day Saint view, based on an unambiguous statement in JS—Matthew 1:32, is that an "abomination of desolation" will similarly occur "*in the last days*." If one were to accept Bolt's argument that the first "abomination" had to do with the arrest and crucifixion of Jesus Christ, could one also identify a similar event corresponding to an end-time fulfillment of this prophecy? As it turns out, a scriptural analogue to the shedding of the innocent blood of Jesus Christ is found in the Jerusalem ministry of the two witnesses described in Revelation 11:2–12 (see also Doctrine and Covenants 77:15). Using temple language, the passage describes the witnesses as "the two olive trees, and the two candlesticks standing before the God of the earth" (Revelation 11:4). The length of their ministry, like that of the Savior, is described as corresponding to the prophet Daniel's apocalyptic period of 1,260 days. Underlining how these latter-day figures also replicate the death of Jesus Christ, John explicitly highlights the fact that they will be martyred in the place "where also our Lord was crucified" (Revelation 11:8). Having carefully scrutinized the evidence, Gregory Beale concludes that these "two witnesses are identified with *the* Witness" (GKBREVEL, 567):

> The pattern of the narrative of the witnesses' career in 11:2–12 is intended as a replica of Christ's career: proclamation and signs result in satanic opposition, persecution (John 15:20), and violent death in the city where Christ was crucified, the world looks on its victim and rejoices (John 16:20); then the witnesses are raised and vindicated by ascension in a cloud.

For additional discussion, see JMBSTANDING, 95–100; RDDREV, 394–416.

³⁴ "Verily, I say unto you, this generation, in which these things shall be shown forth, shall not pass away until all I have told you shall be fulfilled. ³⁵ Although, the days will come, that heaven and earth shall pass away; yet my words shall not pass away, but all shall be fulfilled.

1:29   will precede the coming great age and time of the redemption (Daniel 12:1; Hosea 13:13; Joel 2:10ff.; Micah 7:1–6; Zechariah 14:6ff.; 2 Timothy 3:1–7). These are augmented in the apocryphal literature as well as in rabbinic sources" (STLRABBINIC, 380; see also p. 381).

famines, and pestilences, and earthquakes. Throughout scripture, these signs are interpreted as evidence of divine displeasure. Doctrine and Covenants 45:33 adds that despite these signs, "men will harden their hearts against me, and they will take up the sword, one against another, and they will kill one another." This is more evidence that "again, because [of] iniquity . . . , the love of men shall wax cold" (JS—Matthew 1:30).

pestilences. In Luke 21:11,"the meaning of the term "pestilences" Greek *loimos* "has to do with diseases and plagues and is repeated in Doctrine and Covenants 45:25" (SKBLUKE, 941). See also Doctrine and Covenants 29:18–19 and the commentary below on v. 32.

1:31   *this Gospel of the Kingdom shall be preached in all the world.* Matthew 24:14 has been moved to this later position in JS—Matthew to make it clear that the complete fulfillment of this prophecy will be accomplished in the last days, not in the lifetime of the early disciples. Doctrine and Covenants 45:28–30 adds the following about the Restoration of the gospel that is here prophesied:

And when the times of the Gentiles is come in, a light shall break forth among them that sit in darkness, and it shall be the fulness of my gospel;

But they receive it not; for they perceive not the light, and they turn their hearts from me because of the precepts of men.

And in that generation shall the times of the Gentiles be fulfilled.

then shall the end come, or the destruction of the wicked. See v. 4.

1:32   *again shall the abomination of desolation.* On a second "abomination" that will occur in the last days, see figure JS—Matthew-5. With respect to latter-day "desolations," Doctrine and Covenants 45:31 mentions "an overflowing scourge" and "a desolating sickness [that] shall cover the land." "But," it continues in v. 32, "my disciples shall stand in holy places, and shall not be moved; but among the wicked, men shall lift up their voices and curse God and die."

1:33   *the sun shall be darkened . . . shall be shaken.* These lines are near quotations of the Septuagint version of Isaiah's judgments in Isaiah 13:10 and 34:4. See also Ezekiel 32:7–8; Amos 8:9; Joel 2:10, 30–31; 3:15; Luke 21:24–25; Revelation 6:12–13; Doctrine and Covenants 29:13–14; 34:7–9; 88:87; 133:49; and JSWORDS, Before 8 August 1839 (1), 11; 6 April 1843, 180. Doctrine and Covenants 45:42 reads "and the moon be turned into blood."

Further hints of "nature out of control . . . exist in Jesus' first person account: 'the whole earth shall be in commotion' and 'there shall be earthquakes also in divers places, and many desolations' and 'the earth shall tremble, and reel to and fro' and the earth's inhabitants 'shall see signs and wonders, for they shall be shown forth . . . in the earth beneath' (Doctrine and Covenants 45:26, 33, 48, 40; also 2 Nephi 6:15; 8:6). In related language, scripture pleads for people to repent in the aftermath or midst of alarming natural phenomena (see Revelation 9:20–21; 1 Nephi 19:11; Doctrine and Covenants 53:25; 88:87–91)" (SKBLUKE, 957).

1:35   *heaven and earth shall pass away.* "The use of 'heaven and earth' for permanence is common and often applied to the Law: e.g., . . . 'everything has its end, the heavens and earth have their end; only one thing is excepted which has no end, and that is the Law [= God's words]' (*Genesis Rabbah* 10:1)" (STLRABBINIC, 88).

all shall be fulfilled. JS—Matthew adds this phrase, underscoring the theme that every "jot" and "tittle" of what God has declared will stand (see Matthew 5:18; Alma 34:13; 3 Nephi 1:25; 12:18). Not one word, nor one letter, nor yet even one part of a letter of the prophecy will fail.

³⁶ "And, as I said before, after the tribulation of those days, and the powers of the heavens shall be shaken, then shall appear the sign of the Son of Man in heaven, and then shall all the tribes of the earth mourn; and they shall see the Son of Man coming in the clouds of heaven, with power and great glory."

The Lord's Warning to the Elect: the Parable of the Fig Tree

³⁷ "And whoso treasureth up my word, shall not be deceived, for the Son of Man shall come, and he shall send his angels before him with the great sound of a trumpet, and they shall gather together the remainder of his elect from the four winds, from one end of heaven to the other.

³⁸ "Now learn a parable of the fig tree—When its branches are yet tender, and it begins to put forth leaves, you know that summer is nigh at hand; ³⁹ so likewise, mine elect, when they shall see all these things, they shall know that he is near, even

1:36   *the sign of the Son of Man.* See v. 26. Doctrine and Covenants 45:39–41, 44, 47–55 greatly expands on the themes of this verse.

     then shall all the tribes of the earth mourn. France sees this phrase as being modeled on Zechariah 12:10: "They shall look on me whom they have pierced, and they shall mourn" (compare Zechariah 13:6; Doctrine and Covenants 45:52). He argues that in Zechariah the mourners are "the house of David and the inhabitants of Jerusalem" and that for this and other reasons the phrase should read, "All the tribes of the *land* mourn" (versus *"earth* mourn"), thus referring to Israel alone (RTFMATTHEW, 924–25).

1:37   *they shall gather . . . his elect.* See v. 27.

     with the great sound of a trumpet. "The instrument mentioned here (Greek *salpinx*) has three primary roles: to sound command during battle, to announce the arrival of dignitaries, and to signal the beginning and ending of periods of celebration. . . . In Joseph Smith—Matthew the trumpets seem to symbolize, first, missionary work—the Lord's telling His people, 'Declare my gospel as with the voice of a trump' (Doctrine and Covenants 24:12)—and, second, those events that finish His latter-day work and make preparation for the Second Coming (Doctrine and Covenants 77:12)" (RDDPGP, 318). See, e.g., Isaiah 27:13; 1 Corinthians 25:52; 1 Thessalonians 4:16; Revelation 1:10; 4:1; 8:13; 9:14; Mosiah 26:25; Alma 29:1; Mormon 9:13; and numerous verses in the Doctrine and Covenants.

1:38   *a parable of the fig tree.* Instead of declaring specific time frames, the Lord usually reveals signs to the Saints and expects them to learn through active watchfulness (RDDPGP, 318–19). "Importantly, the parable will become meaningful 'when the light shall begin to break forth,' likely a reference to the restoration of the gospel (Doctrine and Covenants 45:36)" (SKBLUKE, 961–62).

     The fig tree is an apt image for the parable for three reasons: (1) it enables wordplay on Hebrew terms for "end" (*qeẓ*) and "summer fruit" (*qayiẓ*; compare Amos 7:2); (2) the fig tree "puts out its leaves first, long before the vines"; and (3) the dry fig tree is a sign of desolation and judgment, "while the budding of the fig tree is a sign of God's blessing" (STLRABBINIC, 386–87). "The sprouting of fresh leaves on [the tree's] lifeless appearing branches . . . comes to symbolize the return of life to the earth and, even more, the coming of celestial life to the believer. Hence, by drawing attention to the fig tree, Jesus emphasizes the positive outcomes for His followers even though they will pass through daunting times" (SKBLUKE, 962).

at the doors; [40] but of that day, and hour, no one knoweth; no, not the angels of God in heaven, but my Father only. [41] But as it was in the days of Noah, so it shall be also at the coming of the Son of Man; [42] for it shall be with them, as it was in the days which were before the flood; for until the day that Noah entered into the ark they were eating and drinking, marrying and giving in marriage; [43] and knew not until the flood came, and took them all away; so shall also the coming of the Son of Man be. [44] Then shall be fulfilled that which is written, that in the last days, two shall be in the field, the one shall be taken, and the other left; [45] two shall be grinding at the mill, the one shall be taken, and the other left."

1:40   *But of that day, and hour, no one knoweth.* Nibley comments:

> How about the timing of this thing? He says there are no clocks. There are no stopwatches, but there are indicators. In economics you have market indicators. You can't be specific, . . . but there are indicators of which way the market will go. . . . But don't try to time it because that's dangerous, as he tells us later here. If you say "I know exactly when He is going to come," then we can enjoy ourselves until ten minutes before, and then we will be ready. If we know the General is coming to inspect, we can clean up the barracks and make everything perfect before he comes. It's the surprise inspection that catches you as you really are. That's what the Lord is going to do. It says here he is going to come as a thief in the night and catch you the way you really are (HWNPGP, 325).

1:43   *And knew not until the flood came.* Noah's preaching, like the Savior's teaching in the temple, was spoken "openly to the world . . . and in secret [he] said nothing" (John 18:20). The problem was not that their messages went unheard but rather that no one took them seriously. The situation is reminiscent of Søren Kierkegaard's parable of the "happy conflagration":

> It happened that a fire broke out backstage in a theater. The clown came out to inform the public. They thought it was just a jest and applauded. He repeated his warning, they shouted even louder. So I think the world will come to an end amid general applause from all the wits, who believe that it is all a joke (SKPARABLES, 3).

1:44   *two shall be in the field, the one shall be taken.* Scholars have debated the validity of the common Christian assumption that the one taken from each pair was caught up to meet the Lord in what some call the "Rapture." As it turns out, this interpretation is borne out by additional Latter-day Saint scripture such as Doctrine and Covenants 27:18: "Be faithful until I come, and ye shall be caught up, that where I am ye may be also" (RDDPGP, 321).

Samuel T. Lachs sees the "Roman practice of impressing people into governmental service (*angaria*)" as background for this unfamiliar imagery (STLRABBINIC, 321; see also p. 105). At any moment a Roman soldier might appear at your door and demand that you leave your own business to become a baggage carrier for him. Likewise, the Lord may, at the time you least expect it, require you to completely abandon your temporal pursuits and immerse yourself in whatever heavenly affairs need immediate attention as the Lord prepares His sudden descent in the clouds.

Of course, the important direction that readers are meant to understand is not that they should excitedly anticipate their future role in the new age—they do not know what that role will be, nor do they have the liberty to choose it—but rather that they must always live in view of the fact that they *cannot* know exactly when the current order of things will come to a halt and the day of preparation will be past. "For after this day of life, which is given us to prepare for eternity, behold, if we do not improve our time while in this life, then cometh the night of darkness wherein there can be no labor performed" (Alma 34:33). Nibley asks:

> How do you prepare for this? Do you hide in a cave? Do you build yourself a shelter? The Lord says it's not going to do you any good at all. That is not the way you [should] prepare this time. . . . As it is written, "Two shall be in the field, the one shall be taken, and the other left." There are no survival schemes. . . . They are side by side, the two women. [Sudden disappearances

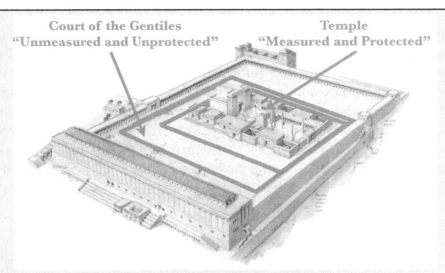

Figure JS—Matthew-6. *The Measurements of the Holy Place in Revelation 11*

THE SYMBOLISM OF "HOLY PLACES" IN THE LAST DAYS

When Jesus told His disciples to "stand in the holy place," He was careful to qualify His instructions by saying, "Whoso readeth let him understand" (JS—Matthew 1:12). This is because the "holy place" He had in mind was not the profaned temple of Jerusalem, but seemingly some place that was to be designated at the appointed time—perhaps in "the mountains" (v. 13) or, alternatively, in the vicinity of Pella (in the lowlands of the Jordan River), as reported by Eusebius and Epiphanius (see JBMOVE). As another option, Julie M. Smith suggests the injunction for the disciples to seek the mountains may have been a symbolic reference to the temple as "the paradigmatic meeting place between humans and God" (JMSMARK, 687).

With respect to "stand[ing] in holy places" in the *last* days (Doctrine and Covenants 45:32), the book of Revelation provides a symbolic description of a figurative place of safety that will be meaningful to Latter-day Saints. Revelation 11 opens with the angel's instruction to John to "measure the temple of God, and the altar, and them that worship therein" (v. 1). By way of contrast, John is told not to measure the areas lying outside the temple complex proper—in other words, the outer courtyard. In the context of the rest of the chapter, the meaning of the angel's instructions is clear: only those who are standing within the scope of John's measure—in other words, within the temple—will receive God's protection.

Of course, scripture is not speaking here of the measurements of a literal physical structure, but rather of the measurement or judgment of the community of disciples who have been called to form the living temple of God (1 Corinthians 3:16–17; 2 Corinthians 6:16; Ephesians 2:19–22; 1 Peter 2:5), each individual in his or her differing degree of righteousness (Doctrine and Covenants 88:28–31). Spiritually speaking, the worshippers standing in the holy place are those who have kept their covenants (Psalm 24:3–4). These are they who, according to Revelation 14:1, will stand with the Lamb "on . . . mount Sion." By way of contrast, all those standing in the outer courtyard, being unmeasured and unprotected, will be, in the words of the book of Revelation, "given unto the Gentiles" to be "tread under foot" (Revelation 11:2) with the rest of the wicked in Jerusalem. Ultimately, as we read in Doctrine and Covenants 101:24, "every corruptible thing . . . that dwells upon all the face of the earth . . . shall be consumed." By "every corruptible thing," the verse seems to mean every being that is of a *telestial* nature. Only those who can withstand at least a *terrestrial* (paradisiacal) glory will remain on the earth during the millennial reign of Christ (Articles of Faith 1:10). In that day, only those who remain in the holy place unmoved will be able to "*stand still*, with the utmost assurance, to see the salvation of God" (Doctrine and Covenants 123:17; emphasis added).

In summary, where are the "holy places" in which we are to stand? Of course, the frequently heard prophetic suggestions that such "holy places" include temples, stakes, chapels, and homes seem wholly appropriate. However, it should be remembered that what makes these places holy—and secure—are the covenants kept by those standing within. According to midrash, Sodom itself could have been a place of safety had there been a sacred circle of as few as ten righteous individuals in the city to "pray on behalf of all of them" (JMBSTANDING, 93).

For additional discussion of this symbolism, see JMBSTANDING, 90–93; RDDREV, 388–94.

THE LORD'S WARNING TO ALL: THE PARABLE OF THE SERVANTS

⁴⁶ "And what I say unto one, I say unto all men; watch, therefore, for you know not at what hour your Lord doth come. ⁴⁷ But know this, if the good man of the house had known in what watch the thief would come, he would have watched, and would not have suffered his house to have been broken up, but would have been ready. ⁴⁸ Therefore be ye also ready, for in such an hour as ye think not, the Son of Man cometh.

⁴⁹ "Who, then, is a faithful and wise servant, whom his lord hath made ruler over his household, to give them meat in due season? ⁵⁰ Blessed is that servant whom his lord, when he cometh, shall find so doing; and verily I say unto you, he shall make him ruler over all his goods. ⁵¹ But if that evil servant shall say in his

1:44   happen] that way in war time, too. . . . So what can you do about it? Don't prepare ahead of time and say, "I'm perfectly safe. I've got a plan that will make me perfectly safe." No, two can be together in the same situation. One is taken and the other is [not], and there is no way they can calculate which one it will be [or when it will happen]. (HWNPGP, 326)

The only safe solution is to be watchful and to live faithfully as if the Lord were coming at any moment. Those who heed prophetic counsel and take "the Holy Spirit for their guide" will prepare what few "needful thing[s]" must be "prepare[d]" to meet the exigencies of their particular situation, and then, with assurance, they will leave the rest to God (Doctrine and Covenants 45:57; 88:119). This is what it means to "stand in holy places" in the last days (see figure JS—Matthew–6).

1:46   *I say unto all men.* This addition made to JS—Matthew makes it clear that the final warnings of the chapter are directed not only to Jesus' disciples, nor merely to His countryfolk, but rather to all people. On the other hand, in Luke 12:41, Peter specifically asked Jesus in response to the parable of vv. 36–40, "Lord, speakest thou this parable unto us, or even to all?" Jesus gave a different answer in the JST: "I speak unto those whom the Lord shall make rulers over his household" (NT2, 77).

1:47   *if the good man of the house had known.* This brief parable reiterates the previous themes about the importance of perpetual readiness and watchfulness, especially for those who are stewards over the Lord's affairs, stressing particularly here that the Son of Man will come when He is least expected. In the Book of Mormon, on the eve of the day that unbelievers had vowed to put the believers to death, rejoicing in what seemed to be a sure knowledge that "the time [was already] past" for Christ's coming, the voice of the Lord came to Nephi, saying, "Lift up your head and be of good cheer; for behold, the time is at hand, and on this night the sign shall be given, and on the morrow come I into the world" (3 Nephi 1:6, 9, 12–13).

1:49   *a faithful and wise servant.* This second parable, whose protagonist is also the steward of the Lord's house, differs with the previous parable in its emphasis on the *consequences* of being negligent in the performance of duty.

to give them meat in due season. The description evokes the idea of the utter dependence of all members of the household on the steward for their survival. The phrasing parallels Psalm 145:15 ("The eyes of all wait upon thee; and thou givest them their meat in due season"), going so far as to suggest that the steward of the Lord's household occupies a position of responsibility comparable to God Himself. Because the servants assigned to the steward's care were given no money in payment for their toil, all they received for their needs came directly from him.

1:50   *he shall make him ruler over all his goods.* The reward of faithfulness in one's responsibilities to the Lord is evidently *more extensive* responsibilities (Matthew 25:14–30). As with Joseph in Egypt (Genesis 39:4–5; 41:37–46), the servant's wise stewardship over his household duties is

heart: 'My lord delayeth his coming,' [52] and shall begin to smite his fellow-servants, and to eat and drink with the drunken, [53] the lord of that servant shall come in a day when he looketh not for him, and in an hour that he is not aware of, [54] and shall cut him asunder, and shall appoint him his portion with the hypocrites; there shall be weeping and gnashing of teeth. [55] And thus cometh the end of the wicked, according to the prophecy of Moses, saying: 'They shall be cut off from among the people'; but the end of the earth is not yet, but by and by."

1:50   rewarded by making him overseer of everything the Lord owns. Draper, Brown, and Rhodes summarize the lesson of this illustration: "The Lord has promised, 'All thrones and dominions, principalities and powers, shall be revealed and set forth upon all who have endured valiantly for the gospel of Jesus Christ' (Doctrine and Covenants 121:29). There are no second-class citizens among the gods, but all become heirs of God and joint-heirs of Christ over all things (see Romans 8:17)" (RDDPGP, 321).

1:54   *cut him asunder.* Because the servant sinned knowingly, his consequences are severe. He is literally cut in two, in the manner of a sacrificial animal (RTFMATTHEW, 945).

1:55   *the end of the wicked, according to the prophecy of Moses.* On the "end" (= "destruction") of the wicked, see v. 4. On the prophecy of Moses, see Deuteronomy 18:16–19; Acts 3:22–23; JS—H 1:40.

HISTORY OF JOSEPH SMITH—MATTHEW

BY March 1831, Joseph Smith and his scribes had completed a translation of the Old Testament through Genesis 24:41. Recently, the Saints had been the subject of "many false reports, lies, and fo[o]lish stories" that were "circulated in every direction, to prevent people from investigating the work, or embracing the faith." "To the joy of the Saints,"[1] Joseph Smith received the revelation that is now known as Doctrine and Covenants 45.[2] The revelation not only provided needed encouragement and direction but also, unexpectedly, directed the Prophet to begin a new phase of his work of Bible translation. Following a long series of verses describing Jesus' instructions to His disciples on the Mount of Olives, the Lord said in Doctrine and Covenants 45:60–61:

> And now, behold, I say unto you, it shall not be given unto you to know any further concerning this chapter [i.e., Matthew 24], until the New Testament be translated, and in it all these things shall be made known;

> Wherefore I give unto you that ye may now translate it, that ye may be prepared for the things to come.

It would have been no surprise to anyone who knew Joseph Smith well that he immediately turned his attention from the translation of the Old Testament to the New as he had been instructed to do. As Richard L. Bushman has observed, the Prophet "spoke as if the revelations coming by his voice commanded him along with everyone else."[3] "Judging by his actions, Joseph believed in the revelations more than anyone. From the beginning, he was his own best follower. Having the word of God at his back gave him enormous confidence."[4] Joseph Smith began with chapter 1 of the Gospel of Matthew and reached chapter 24 a few months later.

Joseph Smith—Matthew manuscripts. There are two primary manuscripts for the Joseph Smith translation of Matthew: New Testament Manuscript 1 (NT1) and New Testament Manuscript 2 (NT2). Sidney Rigdon was the scribe for NT1, which began with Matthew 1:1 on March 8, 1831, and ended with Matthew 26:71 on an unknown date. Afterward, John Whitmer created NT2 by copying NT1. From that point on, NT2 was used for the work of translation and revision. The historical record indicates that Joseph Smith "edited the material three times before he was

---

1   "History, 1838–1856, volume A-1 [23 December 1805–30 August 1834]," p. 104. https://www. josephsmithpapers.org/paper-summary/history-1838-1856-volume-a-1-23-december-1805-30-august-1834/110.

2   "Revelation, circa 7 March 1831 [D&C 45]," p. 75. https://www.josephsmithpapers.org/paper-summary/revelation-circa-7-march-1831-dc-45/5.

3   Richard Lyman Bushman. "Joseph Smith and the Creation of the Sacred." In *Joseph Smith Jr: Reappraisals after Two Centuries*, edited by Reid L. Neilson and Terryl L. Givens, 93–106. Oxford: Oxford University Press, 2009, 98.

4   Richard Lyman Bushman. *Joseph Smith: Rough Stone Rolling; A Cultural Biography of Mormonism's Founder*. New York: Alfred A. Knopf, 2005, 173.

satisfied with it."[5]

Publication history. Widespread interest in this portion of the translation is indicated by reports from the 1830s and 1840s of stand-alone copies of JST Matthew 24 circulating among both members and nonmembers of the Church. In addition, the importance of the subject is evidenced by several revelations that describe the events of the last days, including Doctrine and Covenants 29 (1830); 1, 43, 45, and 133 (1831); and 116 (1838).[6]

An imperfectly edited single broadside sheet of about 8 by 12 inches containing the translation of Matthew 24 was printed and distributed sometime in the 1830s.[7] Franklin D. Richards used the broadside in the preparation of the first edition of the Pearl of Great Price in 1851. While Elder Richards' edition was primarily based on the NT1 manuscript, in his edition Orson Pratt relied almost entirely on the 1867 Reorganized Church of Jesus Christ of Latter Day Saints (RLDS) publication of the "Inspired Version," which primarily followed NT2 and introduced some other changes. Elder James E. Talmage changed the title of the translation to "Writings of Joseph Smith I," a name that remained until 1978, when it was renamed "Joseph Smith—Matthew." No changes to Joseph Smith—Matthew were made in the 2013 Latter-day Saint edition of the scriptures.

---

5   Richard D. Draper, S. Kent Brown, and Michael D. Rhodes. *The Pearl of Great Price: A Verse-by-Verse Commentary.* Salt Lake City: Deseret Book, 2005, 300.

6   David Rolph Seely. "The Olivet Discourse (Matthew 24–25; Mark 13; Luke 21:5–36)." In *The Gospels*, edited by Kent P. Jackson and Robert L. Millet. *Studies in Scripture*, 5:391–404. Salt Lake City: Deseret Book, 1986, 393.

7   Robert J. Matthews. *"A Plainer Translation": Joseph Smith's Translation of the Bible—a History and Commentary.* Provo, UT: Brigham Young University Press, 1975, 50. As of this writing, a facsimile of the broadside has not yet been made available on the Joseph Smith Papers website. However, John Corrill had the text of the broadside copied to the publication of his Church history ("John Corrill, *A Brief History of the Church of Christ of Latter Day Saints*, 1839," p. 48. https://www.josephsmithpapers.org/paper-summary/john-corrill-a-brief-history-of-the-church-of-christ-of-latter-day-saints-1839/46).

BIBLIOGRAPHY FOR THE BOOK OF MOSES COMMENTARY

Extensive alphabetical and topically organized bibliographies for the Book of Moses can be found on the websites of Pearl of Great Price Central (https://www.pearlofgreatpricecentral.org/bibliography-2/) and the Interpreter Foundation (https://interpreterfoundation.org/book-of-moses-essays/).

Below is an alphabetical list of primary references used within the footnotes of the commentary on the Book of Moses herein. Readers should consult these references for detailed discussions of topics. Wherever possible, links to online versions are given. To avoid unduly enlarging the length of the bibliography by including sources that appear only infrequently, the text will often refer readers to listed sources available in which the original quote appears along with detailed bibliographic information. Details about image permissions will also be found in these sources.

ACHBIBLE   Chouraqui, André, ed. *La Bible*. Paris, France: Desclée de Brouwer, 2003. https://nachouraqui.tripod.com/id91.htm.

ADAMGIRK   Stone, Michael E., ed. 1401-1403. *Adamgirkʻ: The Adam Book of Arakʻel of Siwnikʻ*. Translated by Michael E. Stone. Oxford, England: Oxford University Press, 2007. https://books.google.com/books?id=pCWQDwAAQBAJ.

AKRETRO   Kulik, Alexander. *Retroverting Slavonic Pseudepigrapha: Toward the Original of the Apocalypse of Abraham*. *Text-Critical Studies* 3, ed. James R. Adair, Jr. Atlanta, GA: Society of Biblical Literature, 2004.

ALONSLAUGHT   LaCocque, André. *Onslaught Against Innocence: Cain, Abel, and the Yahwist*. Eugene, OR: Cascade Books, 2008.

ALTRIAL   LaCocque, André. *The Trial of Innocence: Adam, Eve, and the Yahwist*. Eugene, OR: Cascade Books, 2006.

APSBOOK   Schade, Aaron P., and Matthew L. Bowen. *The Book of Moses: From the Ancient of Days to the Latter Days*. Salt Lake City and Provo, UT: Brigham Young University Religious Studies Center and Deseret Book, 2021.

ASPEOPLE   Stokes, Adam. "The People of Canaan: A New Reading of Moses 7." *Interpreter: A Journal of Latter-day Saint Faith and Scholarship* 47 (2021): 159–80. https://journal.interpreterfoundation.org/the-people-of-canaan-a-new-reading-of-moses-7/.

BCHBROKEN   Hafen, Bruce C. *The Broken Heart*. Salt Lake City, UT: Deseret Book, 1989.

BMM4EZRA   Metzger, Bruce M. "The Fourth Book of Ezra." In *The Old Testament Pseudepigrapha*, edited by James H. Charlesworth. 2 vols. Vol. 1, 517-59. Garden City, NY: Doubleday and Company, 1983. ttps://eclass.uoa.gr/modules/document/file.php/THEOL264/James%20H.%20Charlesworth%20The%20Old%20Testament%20Pseudepigrapha%2C%20Vol.%201%20Apocalyptic%20Literature%20and%20Testaments%201983.pdf.

MBHOW   Buber, Martin. "The How and Why of Our Bible Translation." In *Scripture and Translation*, edited by Martin Buber and Franz Rosenzweig, 205–19. Bloomington, IN: Indiana University Press, 1994.

CWGENESIS   Westermann, Claus, ed. 1974. *Genesis 1-11: A Continental Commentary*. 1st ed. Translated by John J. Scullion. Minneapolis, MN: Fortress Press, 1994.

DABPREPARE   Bednar, David A. "Prepared to Obtain Every Needful Thing." *Ensign* 49, May 2019, 101–04. https://www.ChurchofJesusChrist.org/general-conference/2019/04/54bednar?lang=eng.

DCAJSARCH   Calabro, David. "Joseph Smith and the Architecture of Genesis." In *The Temple: Ancient and Restored. Proceedings of the 2014 Temple on Mount Zion Symposium*, edited by Stephen D. Ricks and Donald W. Parry. *Temple on Mount Zion* 3, 165-81. Orem and Salt Lake City, UT: The Interpreter Foundation and Eborn Books, 2016. https://www.academia.edu/37488023/Joseph_Smith_and_the_Architecture_of_Genesis.

DCAEARLY   Calabro, David. "An Early Christian Context for the Book of Moses." In *Tracing Ancient Threads in the Book of Moses: Inspired Origins, Temple Contexts, and Literary Qualities*, edited by Jeffrey M. Bradshaw, David R. Seely, John W. Welch and Scott Gordon, 505–90. Orem, UT; Springville, UT; Redding, CA; Tooele, UT: The Interpreter Foundation, Book of Mormon Central, FAIR, and Eborn Books, 2021. https://journal.interpreterfoundation.org/an-early-christian-context-for-the-book-of-moses; https://www.youtube.com/watch?v=Bh6tyMm6sUA.

DCAMOSES   Calabro, David. "Of Moses, Mountains, and Models: Joseph Smith's Book of Moses in Dialogue with the Greek Life of Adam and Eve." Unpublished manuscript, 2022.

DCATHIS Calabro, David. "'This Thing Is a Similitude': A Typological Approach to Moses 5:1–15 and Ancient Apocryphal Literature." In *Tracing Ancient Threads in the Book of Moses: Inspired Origins, Temple Contexts, and Literary Qualities*, edited by Jeffrey M. Bradshaw, David R. Seely, John W. Welch and Scott Gordon, 468–504. Orem, UT; Springville, UT; Redding, CA; Tooele, UT: The Interpreter Foundation, Book of Mormon Central, FAIR, and Eborn Books, 2021. https://interpreterfoundation.org/conferences/2020-book-of-moses-conference/papers/ ; https://www.youtube.com/watch?v=Mvgn2fC4da8.

DCMZOHAR1 Matt, Daniel C., ed. *The Zohar*, Pritzker Edition. Vol. 1. Stanford, CA: Stanford University Press, 2004.

DHBCOSMOS Bailey, David H., Jeffrey M. Bradshaw, John S. Lewis, Gregory L. Smith, and Michael R. Stark, eds. *Science and Mormonism: Cosmos, Earth, and Man*. Interpreter Science and Mormonism Symposia 1. Orem and Salt Lake City, UT: Interpreter Foundation and Eborn Books, 2016. https://archive.org/details/CosmosEarthAndManscienceAndMormonism1.

DMGCURSE Goldenberg, David M. *The Curse of Ham: Race and Slavery in Early Judaism, Christianity, and Islam*. Princeton, NJ: Princeton University Press, 2003.

DMGEXODUS Gurtner, Daniel M. *Exodus: A Commentary on the Greek Text of Codex Vaticanus. Septuagint Commentary Series*, ed. Stanley E. Porter, Richard S. Hess and John Jarick. Leiden, The Netherlands: Brill, 2013.

DRSBOOK Seely, David Rolph. "The Book of Moses: Exploring the World OF the Text." In *Tracing Ancient Threads in the Book of Moses: Inspired Origins, Temple Contexts, and Literary Qualities*, edited by Jeffrey M. Bradshaw, David R. Seely, John W. Welch and Scott Gordon, 597–630. Orem, UT; Springville, UT; Redding, CA; Tooele, UT: The Interpreter Foundation, Book of Mormon Central, FAIR, and Eborn Books, 2021. https://www.youtube.com/watch?v=NgIOQdml24s.

DWPDSS Parry, Donald W., and Emanuel Tov, eds. *The Dead Sea Scrolls Reader*, 2nd ed., vol. 1. Leiden: Brill, 2013.

EDCPROLOGUE Clark, E. Douglas. "A Prologue to Genesis: Moses 1 in Light of Jewish Traditions." *BYU Studies Quarterly* 45, no. 1 (2006): 129–42. https://byustudies.byu.edu/content/prologue-genesis-moses-1-light-jewish-traditions.

FIA2ENOCH	Andersen, F. I. "2 (Slavonic Apocalypse of) Enoch." In *The Old Testament Pseudepigrapha*, edited by James H. Charlesworth. 2 vols. 1:91–221. Garden City, NY: Doubleday, 1983. https://eclass.uoa.gr/modules/document/file.php/THEOL264/James%20H.%20Charlesworth%20The%20Old%20Testament%20Pseudepigrapha%2C%20Vol.%201%20Apocalyptic%20Literature%20and%20Testaments%201983.pdf.
GAAGENESIS	Anderson, Gary A. *The Genesis of Perfection: Adam and Eve in Jewish and Christian Imagination*. Louisville, KY: Westminster John Knox Press, 2001.
GCTBLACK	Thomasson, Gordon C. "Matthew Black and Mircea Eliade meet Hugh Nibley." In *Hugh Nibley Observed*, edited by Jeffrey M. Bradshaw, Shirley S. Ricks and Stephen T. Whitlock, 423–32. Orem and Salt Lake City, UT: The Interpreter Foundation and Eborn Books, 2021.
GJWGENESIS	Wenham, Gordon J., ed. *Genesis 1-15. Word Biblical Commentary* 1: Nelson Reference and Electronic, 1987.
GKGIANTS	Kósa, Gábor. "The Book of Giants Tradition in the Chinese Manichaica." In *Ancient Tales of Giants from Qumran and Turfan: Contexts, Traditions, and Influences*, edited by Matthew Goff, Loren T. Stuckenbruck and Enrico Morano. *Wissenschlaftliche Untersuchungen zum Neuen Testament* 360, ed. Jörg Frey, 145-86. Tübingen, Germany: Mohr Siebeck, 2016.
GWN1ENOCH1	Nickelsburg, George W. E. *1 Enoch 1: A Commentary on the Book of 1 Enoch, Chapters 1–36, 81–108. Hermeneia—a Critical and Historical Commentary on the Bible*. Minneapolis, MN: Fortress Press, 2001. https://archive.org/details/1enochcommentary0001nick.
GWN1ENOCH2	Nickelsburg, George W. E., and James C. VanderKam. *1 Enoch 2: A Commentary on the Book of 1 Enoch, Chapters 37–82. Hermeneia—a Critical and Historical Commentary on the Bible*. Minneapolis, MN: Fortress Press, 2012. https://archive.org/details/1enochcommentary0002nick.
HWNBEFADAM	Nibley, Hugh W. "Before Adam." In *Old Testament and Related Studies. Collected Works of Hugh Nibley* 1, pp. 49–85. Salt Lake City: Deseret Book, 1986. https://archive.interpreterfoundation.org/nibley/pdf/Before-Adam.pdf.
HWNENOCH	Nibley, Hugh W. *Enoch the Prophet. Collected Works of Hugh Nibley* 2. Salt Lake City: Deseret Book, 1986.

HWNHIERO   Nibley, Hugh W. "The Hierocentric State." In *The Ancient State*, edited by Donald W. Parry and Stephen D. Ricks. *The Collected Works of Hugh Nibley* 10, 99-147. Salt Lake City, UT: Deseret Book, 1991.

HWNMESSAGE   Nibley, Hugh W. 1975. *The Message of the Joseph Smith Papyri: An Egyptian Endowment. Collected Works of Hugh Nibley* 16. 2nd ed. Salt Lake City: Deseret Book, 2005.

HWNMANS   Nibley, Hugh W. "Man's Dominion or Subduing the Earth." In *Brother Brigham Challenges the Saints*, edited by Don E. Norton and Shirley S. Ricks. The Collected Works of Hugh Nibley 13, 3-22. Salt Lake City, UT: Deseret Book, 1994. https://archive.bookofmormoncentral.org/sites/default/files/archive-files/pdf/nibley/2016-10-31/04_chapter_4.pdf.

HWNOPEN   Nibley, Hugh W. "To Open the Last Dispensation: Moses Chapter 1." In *Nibley on the Timely and the Timeless: Classic Essays of Hugh W. Nibley*, 1–20. Provo, UT: Religious Studies Center, Brigham Young University, 2004. https://archive.bookofmormoncentral.org/content/open-last-dispensation-moses-chapter-1.

HWNPATR   Nibley, Hugh W. 1980. "Patriarchy and Matriarchy." In *Old Testament and Related Studies. Collected Works of Hugh Nibley* 1, pp. 87–113. Salt Lake City: Deseret Book, 1986. https://archive.interpreterfoundation.org/nibley/pdf/Patriarchy-and-Matriarchy-1980-V2-B.pdf.

HWNPGP   Nibley, Hugh W. 1986. *Teachings of the Pearl of Great Price.* Provo, UT: Foundation for Ancient Research and Mormon Studies (FARMS), Brigham Young University, 2004.

JCRGIANTS   Reeves, John C. *Jewish Lore in Manichaean Cosmogony: Studies in the "Book of Giants" Traditions.* Monographs of the Hebrew Union College 14. Cincinnati, OH: Hebrew Union College Press, 1992. https://books.google.com/books?id=SvaKDwAAQBAJ.

JD   *Journal of Discourses.* 26 vols. Liverpool and London, England: Latter-day Saints Book Depot, 1853-1886. Reprint, Salt Lake City, UT: Bookcraft, 1966. https://contentdm.lib.byu.edu/digital/search/collection/JournalOfDiscourses3.

JHSGENESIS   Sailhamer, John H. "Genesis." In *The Expositor's Bible Commentary*, edited by Frank E. Gaebelein, 1-284. Grand Rapids, MI: Zondervan, 1990.

JHWGENESIS   Walton, John H. "Genesis." In *Genesis, Exodus, Leviticus, Numbers, Deuteronomy*, edited by John H. Walton. *Zondervan Illustrated Bible Backgrounds Commentary* 1, 2-159. Grand Rapids, MI: Zondervan, 2009.

JDLSTRONG   Lindsay, Jeffrey Dean, and Noel B. Reynolds. "'Strong Like unto Moses': The Case for Ancient Roots in the Book of Moses Based on Book of Mormon Usage of Related Content Apparently from the Brass Plates." In *Tracing Ancient Threads in the Book of Moses: Inspired Origins, Temple Contexts, and Literary Qualities*, edited by Jeffrey M. Bradshaw, David R. Seely, John W. Welch and Scott Gordon, 315–420. Orem, UT; Springville, UT; Redding, CA; Tooele, UT: The Interpreter Foundation, Book of Mormon Central, FAIR, and Eborn Books, 2021. https://journal.interpreterfoundation.org/strong-like-unto-moses-the-case-for-ancient-roots-in-the-book-of-moses-based-on-book-of-mormon-usage-of-related-content-apparently-from-the-brass-plates/ ; https://www.youtube.com/watch?v=kAwSKb7pTAI.

JMBARK   Bradshaw, Jeffrey M. "The Ark and the Tent: Temple Symbolism in the Story of Noah." In *Temple Insights: Proceedings of the Interpreter Matthew B. Brown Memorial Conference 'The Temple on Mount Zion,' 22 September 2012*, edited by William J. Hamblin and David Rolph Seely. Temple on Mount Zion Series 2, 25-66. Salt Lake City, UT: The Interpreter Foundation/Eborn Books, 2014. https://journal.interpreterfoundation.org/the-ark-and-the-tent-temple-symbolism-in-the-story-of-noah/.

JMBBLOOD   Bradshaw, Jeffrey M., and Matthew L. Bowen. "'By the Blood Ye Are Sanctified": The Symbolic, Salvific, Interrelated, Additive, Retrospective, and Anticipatory Nature of the Ordinances of Spiritual Rebirth in John 3 and Moses 6." In Stephen D. Ricks and Jeffrey M. Bradshaw, eds. *Sacred Time, Sacred Space, and Sacred Meaning. Proceedings of the Third Interpreter Foundation Matthew B. Brown Memorial Conference, 5 November 2016, Temple on Mount Zion Series*. Vol. 4. Orem and Salt Lake City, UT: The Interpreter Foundation and Eborn Books, 2020, pp. 43-237. http://templethemes.net/publications/Bradshaw%20and%20Bowen-By%20the%20Blood-from%20TMZ4%20(2016).pdf.

JMBBOOK   Bradshaw, Jeffrey M. "The Book of Moses as a Temple Text."

In *Tracing Ancient Threads in the Book of Moses: Inspired Origins, Temple Contexts, and Literary Qualities*, edited by Jeffrey M. Bradshaw, David R. Seely, John W. Welch and Scott Gordon, 421–68. Orem, UT; Springville, UT; Redding, CA; Tooele, UT: The Interpreter Foundation, Book of Mormon Central, FAIR, and Eborn Books, 2021. https://journal.interpreterfoundation.org/the-book-of-moses-as-a-temple-text ; http://templethemes.net/publications/210911-Bradshaw-Temple%20Text-s.pdf.

JMBENOCH   Bradshaw, Jeffrey M. "The LDS Book of Enoch as the Culminating Story of a Temple Text." *BYU Studies Quarterly* 53, no. 1 (2014): 39–73. https://byustudies.byu.edu/content/lds-story-enoch-culminating-episode-temple-text.

JMBEZEKIEL   Bradshaw, Jeffrey M. "The Ezekiel Mural at Dura Europos: A Witness of Ancient Jewish Mysteries?" *BYU Studies Quarterly* 49, no. 1 (2010): 4–49. https://scholarsarchive.byu.edu/byusq/vol49/iss1/2/.

JMBFAITH   Bradshaw, Jeffrey M. "Faith, Hope, and Charity: The 'Three Principal Rounds' of the Ladder of Heavenly Ascent." In *"To Seek the Law of the Lord": Essays in Honor of John W. Welch*, edited by Paul Y. Hoskisson and Daniel C. Peterson, 59-112. Orem, UT: The Interpreter Foundation, 2017. https://journal.interpreterfoundation.org/faith-hope-and-charity-the-three-principal-rounds-of-the-ladder-of-heavenly-ascent/.

JMBFREE   Bradshaw, Jeffrey M. "Freemasonry and the Origins of Latter-day Saint Temple Ordinances." In *Joseph Smith: A Life Lived in Crescendo*, edited by Jeffrey M. Bradshaw, in preparation. Orem and Tooele, UT: The Interpreter Foundation and Eborn Books, 2022. https://www.youtube.com/watch?v=H6VxyY2Y7ac.

JMBGATHERING   Bradshaw, Jeffrey M. *Enoch and the Gathering of Zion: The Witness of Ancient Texts for Modern Scripture*. Orem, Springville, and Salt Lake City, UT: The Interpreter Foundation, Book of Mormon Central, and Eborn Books, 2021. https://interpreterfoundation.org/books/enoch-and-the-gathering-of-zion/.

JMBGIANTS   Bradshaw, Jeffrey M. "Moses 6–7 and the *Book of Giants*: Remarkable Witnesses of Enoch's Ministry." In *Tracing Ancient Threads in the Book of Moses: Inspired Origins, Temple Contexts, and Literary Qualities*, edited by Jeffrey M.

Bradshaw, David R. Seely, John W. Welch and Scott Gordon, 1041–256. Orem, UT; Springville, UT; Redding, CA; Tooele, UT: The Interpreter Foundation, Book of Mormon Central, FAIR, and Eborn Books, 2021. https://www.youtube.com/watch?v=HP6GYxbieNQ; https://journal.interpreterfoundation.org/moses-6-7-and-the-book-of-giants; http://templethemes.net/publications/210911-Bradshaw-jmb-s.pdf.

JMBIGIL1   Bradshaw, Jeffrey M. *Creation, Fall, and the Story of Adam and Eve*. Updated ed. *In God's Image and Likeness* 1. Salt Lake City: Eborn Books, 2014. https://archive.org/details/140123IGIL12014ReadingS.

JMBIGIL2   Bradshaw, Jeffrey M., and David J. Larsen. *Enoch, Noah, and the Tower of Babel. In God's Image and Likeness* 2. Salt Lake City: Interpreter Foundation and Eborn Books, 2014. https://archive.org/details/131203ImageAndLikeness2ReadingS.

JMBMARI   Bradshaw, Jeffrey M., and Ronan James Head. "The Investiture Panel at Mari and Rituals of Divine Kingship in the Ancient Near East." *Studies in the Bible and Antiquity* 4 (2012): 1–42. https://scholarsarchive.byu.edu/cgi/viewcontent.cgi?article=1002&context=sba.

JMBMORM   Bradshaw, Jeffrey M., and Ronan J. Head. "Mormonism's Satan and the Tree of Life (Longer version of an invited presentation originally given at the 2009 Conference of the European Mormon Studies Association, Turin, Italy, 30-31 July 2009)." *Element: A Journal of Mormon Philosophy and Theology* 4, no. 2 (2010): 1-54. http://www.templethemes.net/publications/1%20-%20Bradshaw%20Head%20-%20Mormonisms%20Satan%20and%20the%20Tree%20of%20Life.pdf.

JMBMOSES   Bradshaw, Jeffrey M. *Temple Themes in the Book of Moses*. 2014 update ed. Salt Lake City, UT: Eborn Publishing, 2014. https://archive.org/download/150904TempleThemesInTheBookOfMoses2014UpdatedEditionSReading; Spanish: http://www.templethemes.net/books/171219-SPA-TempleTempleThemesInTheBookOfMoses.pdf.

JMBOATH   Bradshaw, Jeffrey M. *Temple Themes in the Oath and Covenant of the Priesthood*. 2014 update ed. Salt Lake City, UT: Eborn Books, 2014. https://archive.org/details/151128TempleThemesInTheOathAndCovenantOfThePriesthood2014Update; https://archive.org/details/140910TemasDelTe

mploEnElJuramentoYElConvenioDelSacerdocio2014Upda
teSReading.

JMBREVISITING Bradshaw, Jeffrey M., Jacob Rennaker, and David J. Larsen. "Revisiting the Forgotten Voices of Weeping in Moses 7: A Comparison with Ancient Texts." *Interpreter: A Journal of Mormon Scripture* 2 (2012): 41-71. https://journal.interpreterfoundation.org/revisiting-the-forgotten-voices-of-weeping-in-moses-7-a-comparison-with-ancient-texts/.

JMBSTANDING Bradshaw, Jeffrey M. "Standing in the Holy Place: Ancient and Modern Reverberations of an Enigmatic New Testament Prophecy." In *Ancient Temple Worship: Proceedings of the Expound Symposium, 14 May 2011*, edited by Matthew B. Brown, Jeffrey M. Bradshaw, Stephen D. Ricks and John S. Thompson. *Temple on Mount Zion* 1, 71-142. Orem and Salt Lake City, UT: The Interpreter Foundation and Eborn Books, 2014. Reprint, *Interpreter: A Journal of Latter-day Saint Faith and Scholarship* 37, 163–236, https://journal.interpreterfoundation.org/standing-in-the-holy-place-ancient-and-modern-reverberations-of-an-enigmatic-new-testament-prophecy/. https://journal.interpreterfoundation.org/standing-in-the-holy-place-ancient-and-modern-reverberations-of-an-enigmatic-new-testament-prophecy/.

JMBSTRONGER Bradshaw, Jeffrey, and Matthew L. Bowen. "'Made Stronger Than Many Waters': The Names of Moses as Keywords in the Heavenly Ascent of Moses." In *Tracing Ancient Threads in the Book of Moses: Inspired Origins, Temple Contexts, and Literary Qualities*, edited by Jeffrey M. Bradshaw, David R. Seely, John W. Welch and Scott Gordon, 943–1000. Orem, UT; Springville, UT; Redding, CA; Tooele, UT: The Interpreter Foundation, Book of Mormon Central, FAIR, and Eborn Books, 2021. Reprint, *The Temple: Past, Present, and Future. Proceedings of the Fifth Interpreter Foundation Matthew B. Brown Memorial Conference, 7 November 2020*, edited by Stephen D. Ricks and Jeffrey M. Bradshaw. Temple on Mount Zion 6, 239–96. Orem and Salt Lake City, UT: The Interpreter Foundation and Eborn Books, 2021. https://www.youtube.com/watch?v=hk6nB9_PC-A ; http://templethemes.net/publications/210911-Bradshaw-jb-s.pdf.

JMBTEXTUAL Bradshaw, Jeffrey M., and Ryan Dahle. "Textual Criticism and the Book of Moses: A Response to Colby Townsend's

'Returning to the Sources,' Part 1 of 2." *Interpreter: A Journal of Latter-day Saint Faith and Scholarship* 40 (2020): 99–161. https://journal.interpreterfoundation.org/textual-criticism-and-the-book-of-moses-a-response-to-colby-townsends-returning-to-the-sources-part-1-of-2/.

JMBTREE   Bradshaw, Jeffrey M. "The Tree of Knowledge as the Veil of the Sanctuary." In *Ascending the Mountain of the Lord: Temple, Praise, and Worship in the Old Testament*, edited by David Rolph Seely, Jeffrey R. Chadwick, and Matthew J. Grey, 49–65. Provo and Salt Lake City, UT: Religious Studies Center, Brigham Young University, and Deseret Book, 2013. http://www.templethemes.net/publications/4%20 Bradshaw.pdf.

JMBTWIN   Bradshaw, Jeffrey M., David J. Larsen, and Stephen T. Whitlock. "Moses 1 and the *Apocalypse of Abraham*: Twin Sons of Different Mothers?" In *Tracing Ancient Threads in the Book of Moses: Inspired Origins, Temple Contexts, and Literary Qualities*, edited by Jeffrey M. Bradshaw, David R. Seely, John W. Welch and Scott Gordon, 789–922. Orem, UT; Springville, UT; Redding, CA; Tooele, UT: The Interpreter Foundation, Book of Mormon Central, FAIR, and Eborn Books, 2021. https://journal.interpreterfoundation.org/moses-1-and-the-apocalypse-of-abraham-twin-sons-of-different-mothers/; https://www.youtube.com/watch?v=m-nyXh4JoAw.

JMBWHAT   Bradshaw, Jeffrey M. "What Did Joseph Smith Know bout Modern Temple Ordinances by 1836?" In *The Temple: Ancient and Restored. Proceedings of the 2014 Temple on Mount Zion Symposium*, edited by Stephen D. Ricks and Donald W. Parry. Temple on Mount Zion 3, 1-144. Orem and Salt Lake City, UT: The Interpreter Foundation and Eborn Books, 2016. http://www.jeffreymbradshaw.net/templethemes/publications/01-Bradshaw-TMZ%203.pdf.

JMBWHERE   Bradshaw, Jeffrey M., Matthew L. Bowen, and Ryan Dahle. "Where Did the Names 'Mahaway' and 'Mahujah' Come From?: A Response to Colby Townsend's 'Returning to the Sources,' Part 2 of 2," *Interpreter: A Journal of Latter-day Saint Faith and Scholarship* 40 (2020): 181–242. https://journal.interpreterfoundation.org/where-did-the-names-mahaway-and-mahujah-come-from-a-response-to-colby-townsends-returning-to-the-sources-part-2-of-2/.

JMSBEHOLD Sears, Joshua M. "'Behold These Thy Brethren!': Deeply Seeing All of Our Brothers and Sisters." In *Covenant of Compassion: Caring for the Marginalized and Disadvantaged in the Old Testament*, edited by Avram R. Shannon, Gaye Strathearn, George A. Pierce and Joshua M. Sears, 101–23. Provo, UT: Religious Studies Center, Brigham Young University; Salt Lake City, UT: Deseret Book, 2021. https://rsc.byu.edu/covenant-compassion/behold-these-thy-brethren.

JMSPARADOX Smith, Julie M. "Paradoxes in Paradise." In *Fleeing the Garden: Reading Genesis 2–3*, edited by Adam S. Miller. *Maxwell Institute Publications* 37, 6–26. Provo, UT: Brigham Young University Neal A. Maxwell Institute for Religious Scholarship, 2017. https://scholarsarchive.byu.edu/cgi/viewcontent.cgi?article=1036&conttext=mi.

JSDHC Smith, Joseph, Jr. *History of the Church of Jesus Christ of Latter-day Saints* (Documentary History). 7 vols. Salt Lake City, UT: Deseret Book, 1978. https://archive.org/details/HistoryOfTheChurchhcVolumes1-7original1902EditionPdf; https://catalog.churchofjesuschrist.org/record/50e98e37-2746-494a-adba-21cbeacc72ef/0.

JSJOURNALS2 Smith, Joseph, Jr., Andrew H. Hedges, Alex D. Smith, and Richard Lloyd Anderson. *Journals: December 1841-April 1843. The Joseph Smith Papers, Journals* 2, ed. Dean C. Jessee, Ronald K. Esplin and Richard Lyman Bushman. Salt Lake City, UT: The Church Historian's Press, 2011. https://www.josephsmithpapers.org/paper-summary/journal-december-1841-december-1842/1; https://www.josephsmithpapers.org/paper-summary/journal-december-1842-june-1844-book-1-21-december-1842-10-march-1843/1.

JSTPJS Smith, Joseph, Jr. 1938. *Teachings of the Prophet Joseph Smith*. Salt Lake City, UT: Deseret Book, 1969. https://scriptures.byu.edu/tpjs/STPJS.pdf.

JSWORDS Smith, Joseph, Jr., Andrew F. Ehat, and Lyndon W. Cook. *The Words of Joseph Smith: The Contemporary Accounts of the Nauvoo Discourses of the Prophet Joseph*. Provo, UT: Brigham Young University Religious Studies Center, 1980. https://rsc.byu.edu/book/words-joseph-smith.

JTMEDIATION   Taylor, John. *The Mediation and Atonement*. Salt Lake City, UT: The Deseret News, 1882. Reprint, Heber City, UT: Archive Publishers, 2000. https://archive.org/details/Media tionAndAtonementOfOurLordAndSaviorJesusChrist.

JWIREMARKS   Wilkens, Jens. "Remarks on the Manichaean *Book of Giants*: Once Again on Mahaway's Mission to Enoch." In *Ancient Tales of Giants from Qumran and Turfan: Contexts, Traditions, and Influences*, edited by Matthew Goff, Loren T. Stuckenbruck and Enrico Morano. *Wissenschlaftliche Untersuchungen zum Neuen Testament* 360, ed. Jörg Frey, 213-29. Tübingen, Germany: Mohr Siebeck, 2016.

JWWEXPERIENC   Welch, John W. "Experiencing the Presence of the Lord: The Temple Program of Leviticus." In *Sacred Time, Sacred Space, and Sacred Meaning. Proceedings of the Third Interpreter Foundation Matthew B. Brown Memorial Conference, 5 November 2016*, edited by Stephen D. Ricks and Jeffrey M. Bradshaw. Temple on Mount Zion 4, 265–300. Orem and Salt Lake City, UT: The Interpreter Foundation and Eborn Books, 2020, p. 280.

JWWPRIESTLY   Welch, John W., and Jackson Abhau. "The Priestly Interests of Moses the Levite." In *Tracing Ancient Threads in the Book of Moses: Inspired Origins, Temple Contexts, and Literary Qualities*, edited by Jeffrey M. Bradshaw, David R. Seely, John W. Welch and Scott Gordon, 163–256. Orem, UT; Springville, UT; Redding, CA; Tooele, UT: The Interpreter Foundation, Book of Mormon Central, FAIR, and Eborn Books, 2021. https://www.youtube.com/watch?v=rl2GrmG_DTQ ; https://interpreterfoundation.org/conferences/2020-book-of-moses-conference/papers/welch/.

KPJMOSES   Jackson, Kent P. *The Book of Moses and the Joseph Smith Translation Manuscripts*. Provo, UT: Religious Studies Center, Brigham Young University, 2005. https://rsc.byu.edu/book/book-moses-joseph-smith-translation-manuscripts.

LRKWISDOM   Kass, Leon R. *The Beginning of Wisdom: Reading Genesis*. New York City, NY: Free Press, Simon and Schuster, 2003.

LTSGIANTS   Stuckenbruck, Loren T. *The Book of Giants from Qumran: Texts, Translation, and Commentary*. Tübingen, Germany: Mohr Siebeck, 1997. https://www.scribd.com/document/364544071/222303395-Stuckenbruck-Loren-T-the-Book-of-Giants-From-Qumran-Tubingen-1997-pdf.

MBCHRISTMAS Barker, Margaret. *Christmas: The Original Story.* London, England: Society for Promoting Christian Knowledge, 2008.

MBOLDER Barker, Margaret. *The Older Testament: The Survival of Themes from the Ancient Royal Cult in Sectarian Judaism and Early Christianity.* London, England: Society for Promoting Christian Knowledge (SPCK), 1987.

MBWISDOM Barker, Margaret. "Where shall wisdom be found?" In Russian Orthodox Church: Representation to the European Institutions. http://orthodoxeurope.org/page/11/1/7.aspx.

MJJLOST Johnson, Mark J. "The lost prologue: Reading Moses Chapter One as an Ancient Text." *Interpreter: A Journal of Latter-day Saint Faith and Scholarship* 36 (2020): 145-86. https://journal.interpreterfoundation.org/the-lost-prologue-reading-moses-chapter-one-as-an-ancient-text/.

MZBEREISHIS Zlotowitz, Meir, and Nosson Scherman, eds. *Bereishis/Genesis: A New Translation with a Commentary Anthologized from Talmudic, Midrashic and Rabbinic Sources.* 2nd ed. Two vols. ArtScroll Tanach Series, ed. Rabbi Nosson Scherman and Rabbi Meir Zlotowitz. Brooklyn, NY: Mesorah Publications, 1986.

MLBBY Bowen, Matthew L. "'By the Word of My Power': The Divine Word in the Book of Moses." In T*racing Ancient Threads in the Book of Moses: Inspired Origins, Temple Contexts, and Literary Qualities*, edited by Jeffrey M. Bradshaw, David R. Seely, John W. Welch and Scott Gordon, 733–88. Orem, UT; Springville, UT; Redding, CA; Tooele, UT: The Interpreter Foundation, Book of Mormon Central, FAIR, and Eborn Books, 2021. https://www.youtube.com/watch?v=9aNM4SuYdlA ; https://interpreterfoundation.org/conferences/2020-book-of-moses-conference/papers/bowen/.

MLBGETTING Bowen, Matthew L. "Getting Cain and Gain." In *Name as Key-Word: Collected Essays on Onomastic Wordplay and the Temple in Mormon Scripture*, edited by Matthew L. Bowen, 209–36. Orem and Salt Lake City, UT: The Interpreter Foundation and Eborn Books, 2018. https://journal.interpreterfoundation.org/getting-cain-and-gain/.

MLBYOUNG	Bowen, Matthew L. "Young Man, Hidden Prophet: Alma." In *Name as Key-Word: Collected Essays on Onomastic Wordplay and the Temple in Mormon Scripture*, edited by Matthew L. Bowen, 91-100. Orem and Salt Lake City, UT: The Interpreter Foundation and Eborn Books, 2018. https://journal.interpreterfoundation.org/alma-young-man-hidden-prophet/.
MOSESS	"Book of Moses Essays," www.pearlofgreatprice.org/category/book-of-moses/, www.interpreterfoundation.org/book-of-moses-essays/. All references to these essays in the commentary use essay numbers instead of page numbers.
NMSGENESIS	Sarna, Nahum M., ed. *Genesis. JPS Torah Commentary*. Philadelphia, PA: Jewish Publication Society, 1989. https://www.scribd.com/document/413490930/Nahum-M-Sarna-the-JPS-Torah-Commentary.
OT1	Faulring, Scott H., Kent P. Jackson, and Robert J. Matthews, eds. "Old Testament Revision 1." *The Joseph Smith Papers*. https://www.josephsmithpapers.org/paper-summary/old-testament-revision-1/64.
OT2	Faulring, Scott H., Kent P. Jackson, and Robert J. Matthews, eds. "Old Testament Revision 2." *The Joseph Smith Papers*. http://www.josephsmithpapers.org/paper-summary/old-testament-revision-2/.
PSA3ENOCH	Alexander, Philip S. "3 (Hebrew Apocalypse of) Enoch." In *The Old Testament Pseudepigrapha*, edited by James H. Charlesworth. 2 vols. 1:223–315. Garden City, NY: Doubleday, 1983. https://eclass.uoa.gr/modules/document/file.php/THEOL264/James%20H.%20Charlesworth%20The%20Old%20Testament%20Pseudepigrapha%2C%20Vol.%201%20Apocalyptic%20Literature%20and%20Testaments%201983.pdf.
RABIBLE	Alter, Robert, ed. *The Hebrew Bible: A Translation with Commentary*. New York City, NY: W. W. Norton, 2019.
RDDPGP	Draper, Richard D., S. Kent Brown, and Michael D. Rhodes. *The Pearl of Great Price: A Verse-by-Verse Commentary*. Salt Lake City: Deseret Book, 2005, 12–236.
RDEENOCH	Eames, Rulon D. "Enoch: LDS Sources." In *Encyclopedia of Mormonism*, edited by Daniel H. Ludlow. 4 vols. 2:457–59. New York: Macmillan, 1992. http://www.lib.byu.edu/Macmillan/.

SHFJST   Faulring, Scott H., Kent P. Jackson, and Robert J. Matthews, eds. *Joseph Smith's New Translation of the Bible: Original Manuscripts*. Provo, UT: Religious Studies Center, Brigham Young University, 2004.

SKBENOCH   Brown, S. Kent. "Enoch, the Book of Moses, and the *Book of Giants*: More Light on the 1977 Visit of Professor Matthew Black to BYU." In *Interpreter Foundation Blog*. https://interpreterfoundation.org/enoch-the-book-of-moses-and-the-book-of-giants/.

SKBMAN   Brown, S. Kent, and Jeffrey M. Bradshaw. "Man and Son of Man: Probing Theology and Christology in the Book of Moses and in Jewish and Christian Tradition." In *Tracing Ancient Threads in the Book of Moses: Inspired Origins, Temple Contexts, and Literary Qualities*, edited by Jeffrey M. Bradshaw, David R. Seely, John W. Welch and Scott Gordon, 1257–332. Orem, UT; Springville, UT; Redding, CA; Tooele, UT: The Interpreter Foundation, Book of Mormon Central, FAIR, and Eborn Books, 2021. http://templethemes.net/publications/210911-Brown%20Bradshaw%202021-s.pdf; https://www.youtube.com/watch?v=axRLPR8T5Ck.

SOSIAM   Smoot, Stephen O. "'I Am a Son of God': Moses' Prophetic Call and Ascent into the Divine Council." In *Tracing Ancient Threads in the Book of Moses: Inspired Origins, Temple Contexts, and Literary Qualities*, edited by Jeffrey M. Bradshaw, David R. Seely, John W. Welch and Scott Gordon, 923–42. Orem, UT; Springville, UT; Redding, CA; Tooele, UT: The Interpreter Foundation, Book of Mormon Central, FAIR, and Eborn Books, 2021. https://www.youtube.com/watch?v=ZOs3-3MqSOE.

SRHNOAH   Haynes, Stephen R. *Noah's Curse: The Biblical Justification of American Slavery*. Oxford, England: Oxford University Press, 2002.

TLGGOD   Givens, Terryl L., and Fiona Givens. *The God Who Weeps: How Mormonism Makes Sense of Life*. Salt Lake City, UT: Ensign Peak, 2012.

UCCOMMENTARY   Cassuto, Umberto. *A Commentary on the Book of Genesis. Vol. 1: From Adam to Noah*. Translated by Israel Abrahams. 1st English ed. Jerusalem: The Magnes Press, The Hebrew University, 1998.

BIBLIOGRAPHY FOR THE BOOK OF MOSES

VPHGENESIS   Hamilton, Victor P. The Book of Genesis: Chapters 1-17. Grand Rapids, MI: William B. Eerdmans Publishing, 1990.

WBHGIANTS   Henning, W. B. "The Book of the Giants." *Bulletin of the School of Oriental and African Studies*, University of London 11, no. 1 (1943): 52-74. https://www.cambridge.org/core/journals/bulletin-of-the-school-of-oriental-and-african-studies/article/book-of-the-giants/F09AF3F19C427A250B9D562F82640944.

BIBLIOGRAPHY FOR THE JOSEPH SMITH—MATTHEW COMMENTARY

Below is an alphabetical list of primary references used within the footnotes of the commentary on Joseph Smith—Matthew. Readers should consult these references for detailed discussions of topics and complete references to quoted sources. Wherever possible, links to online versions are given. To avoid unduly enlarging the length of the bibliography by including sources that appear only infrequently, the text will often refer readers to listed sources available in which the original quote appears along with detailed bibliographic information. Details about image permissions will also be found in these sources.

AGZBEGIN   Zornberg, Avivah Gottlieb. *Genesis: The Beginning of Desire*. Philadelphia, PA: Jewish Publication Society, 1995.

BRMMORTAL   McConkie, Bruce R. *The Mortal Messiah: From Bethlehem to Calvary*. 4 vols. 2:3. Salt Lake City: Deseret Book, 1979–81, 421–63.

CSKMATTHEW   Keener, Craig S. *The Gospel of Matthew: A Socio-rhetorical Commentary*. Grand Rapids, MI: William B. Eerdmans, 2009.

DRSOLIVET   Seely, David Rolph. "The Olivet Discourse (Matthew 24–25; Mark 13; Luke 21:5–36)." In *The Gospels*, edited by Kent P. Jackson and Robert L. Millet. *Studies in Scripture*, 5:391–404. Salt Lake City: Deseret Book, 1986.

FJWARS   Josephus, Flavius. "The Wars of the Jews." In *The New Complete Works of Josephus*. Translated by Paul L. Maier and William Whiston, 667–936. Grand Rapids, MI: Kregel Publications, 1999.

GKBREVEL   Beale, Gregory K. *The Book of Revelation: A Commentary on the Greek Text*. Grand Rapids, MI: William B. Eerdmans, 1999.

HWNPGP   Nibley, Hugh W. 1986. *Teachings of the Pearl of Great Price*. Provo, UT: Foundation for Ancient Research and Mormon Studies (FARMS), Brigham Young University, 2004.

JBMOVE   Bourgel, Jonathan. "The Jewish-Christians' Move from Jerusalem as a Pragmatic Choice." In *Studies in Rabbinic Judaism and Early Christianity: Text and Context*, edited by Dan Jaffé. Ancient Judaism and Early Christianity 74, pp. 107–38. Leiden: Brill, 2010. https://www.academia.edu/4909339/The_Jewish_Christians_Move_from_Jerusalem_as_a_Pragmatic_Choice.

JBPIMMINENT   Payne, J. Barton. *The Imminent Appearing of Christ*. Grand Rapids, MI: William B. Eerdmans, 1962.

JETJESUS   Talmage, James E. 1915. *Jesus the Christ*. Classics in Mormon Literature. Salt Lake City: Deseret Book, 1983.

JMBFAITH   Bradshaw, Jeffrey M. "Faith, Hope, and Charity: The 'Three Principal Rounds' of the Ladder of Heavenly Ascent." In *"To Seek the Law of the Lord": Essays in Honor of John W. Welch*, edited by Paul Y. Hoskisson and Daniel C. Peterson, 59–112. Orem, UT: Interpreter Foundation, 2017. http://www.jeffreymbradshaw.net/templethemes/publications/Pages%20from%20Welch%2020170705.pdf. Reprinted in *Interpreter: A Journal of Latter-day Saint Faith and Scholarship* 39 (2020): 207–60. https://journal.interpreterfoundation.org/faith-hope-and-charity-the-three-principal-rounds-of-the-ladder-of-heavenly-ascent/.

JMBIGIL2   Bradshaw, Jeffrey M., and David J. Larsen. *Enoch, Noah, and the Tower of Babel*. In God's Image and Likeness 2. Salt Lake City: Interpreter Foundation and Eborn Books, 2014. https://archive.org/details/131203ImageAndLikeness2ReadingS.

JMBSTANDING   Bradshaw, Jeffrey M. "Standing in the Holy Place: Ancient and Modern Reverberations of an Enigmatic New Testament Prophecy." In *Ancient Temple Worship: Proceedings of the Expound Symposium* (May 14, 2011), edited by Matthew B. Brown, Jeffrey M. Bradshaw, Stephen D. Ricks, and John S. Thompson. Temple on Mount Zion 1, pp. 71–142. Orem and Salt Lake City, UT: Interpreter Foundation and Eborn Books, 2014. http://www.templethemes.net/publications/04-Ancient%20Temple-Bradshaw.pdf. Reprinted in *Interpreter: A Journal of Latter-day Saint Faith and Scholarship* 37 (2020): 163–236. https://journal.interpreterfoundation.org/standing-in-the-holy-place-ancient-and-modern-reverberations-of-an-enigmatic-new-testament-prophecy/.

JMSMARK   Smith, Julie M. *The Gospel according to Mark. Brigham Young University New Testament Commentary*. Provo, UT: BYU Studies, 2018.

JSWORDS   Smith, Joseph, Jr. *The Words of Joseph Smith: The Contemporary Accounts of the Nauvoo Discourses of the Prophet Joseph*. Edited by Andrew F. Ehat and Lyndon W. Cook. Salt Lake City: Bookcraft, 1980. https://rsc.byu.edu/book/words-joseph-smith. Spelling and style are modernized in all quotations from this work.

KWPJSTSEC   Perkins, Keith W. "The JST on the Second Coming of Christ." In *The Joseph Smith Translation: The Restoration of Plain and Precious Things*, edited by Monte S. Nyman and Robert L. Millet. Religious Studies Center Monograph Series 12, 237–49. Provo, UT: Religious Studies Center, Brigham Young University, 1985. https://rsc.byu.edu/joseph-smith-translation/jst-second-coming-christ.

NT1   Faulring, Scott H., Kent P. Jackson, and Robert J. Matthews, eds. "New Testament Revision 1." *The Joseph Smith Papers.* http://www.josephsmithpapers.org/paper-summary/new-testament-revision-1/.

NT2   Faulring, Scott H., Kent P. Jackson, and Robert J. Matthews, eds. "New Testament Revision 2." *The Joseph Smith Papers.* https://www.josephsmithpapers.org/paper-summary/new-testament-revision-2/1.

PGBCROSS   Bolt, Peter G. *The Cross from a Distance: Atonement in Mark's Gospel.* New Studies in Biblical Theology 18. Downers Grove, IL: InterVarsity Press, 2004.

RDDJSMSIGNS   Draper, Richard D. "Joseph Smith—Matthew and the Signs of the Times." In *The Pearl of Great Price*, edited by Robert L. Millet and Kent P. Jackson. *Studies in Scripture*, 2:287–302. Salt Lake City: Randall, 1985.

RDDPGP   Draper, Richard D., S. Kent Brown, and Michael D. Rhodes. *The Pearl of Great Price: A Verse-by-Verse Commentary.* Salt Lake City: Deseret Book, 2005, 299–324.

RDDREV   Draper, Richard D., and Michael D. Rhodes. *The Revelation of John the Apostle. BYU New Testament Commentary.* Provo, UT: BYU Studies, 2016.

REV7MAR1831   "Revelation, circa 7 March 1831 [D&C 45]," p. 75. *The Joseph Smith Papers.* https://www.josephsmithpapers.org/paper-summary/revelation-circa-7-march-1831-dc-45/5.

RLAJSINSIGHTS   Anderson, Richard Lloyd. "Joseph Smith's Insights into the Olivet Prophecy: Joseph Smith 1 and Matthew 24." In *Pearl of Great Price Symposium: A Centennial Presentation* (November 22, 1975), 48–61. Provo, UT: Department of Ancient Scripture, Religious Instruction, Brigham Young University, 1975.

RTFMATTHEW   France, Richard Thomas. *The Gospel of Matthew.* New International Commentary on the New Testament. Grand Rapids, MI: William B. Eerdmans, 2007.

RMNREV   Nelson, Russell M. "Revelation for the Church, Revelation For Our Lives." *Ensign* 48, May 2018, 93-96. https://www.churchofjesuschrist.org/study/general-conference/2018/04/revelation-for-the-church-revelation-for-our-lives?lang=eng.

SHFJST   Faulring, Scott H., Kent P. Jackson, and Robert J. Matthews, eds. *Joseph Smith's New Translation of the Bible: Original Manuscripts.* Provo, UT: Religious Studies Center, Brigham Young University, 2004.

SKBLUKE   Brown, S. Kent. *The Testimony of Luke. Brigham Young University New Testament Commentary.* Provo, UT: BYU Studies, 2015.

SKPARABLES   Kierkegaard, Søren. *Parables of Kierkegaard.* Edited by Thomas C. Oden. Princeton, NJ: Princeton University Press, 1978.

STLRABBINIC   Lachs, Samuel Tobias. *A Rabbinic Commentary on the New Testament: The Gospels of Matthew, Mark, and Luke.* Hoboken, NJ: KTAV, 1987.

WJHJOHN   Hamblin, William J. "John 17:6, Name." Unpublished manuscript in the possession of the author. December 11, 2010.